The International
Business Environment

The International Business Environment

Leslie Hamilton and

Philip Webster

OXFORD
UNIVERSITY PRESS

OXFORD
UNIVERSITY PRESS

Great Clarendon Street, Oxford OX2 6DP

Oxford University Press is a department of the University of Oxford.
It furthers the University's objective of excellence in research, scholarship,
and education by publishing worldwide in

Oxford New York

Auckland Cape Town Dar es Salaam Hong Kong Karachi
Kuala Lumpur Madrid Melbourne Mexico City Nairobi
New Delhi Shanghai Taipei Toronto

With offices in

Argentina Austria Brazil Chile Czech Republic France Greece
Guatemala Hungary Italy Japan Poland Portugal Singapore
South Korea Switzerland Thailand Turkey Ukraine Vietnam

Oxford is a registered trade mark of Oxford University Press
in the UK and in certain other countries

Published in the United States
by Oxford University Press Inc., New York

British Library Cataloguing in Publication Data
Data available

Library of Congress Cataloging in Publication Data
Data available

Typeset by Graphicraft Limited, Hong Kong
Printed in Great Britain by Ashford Colour Press Ltd, Gosport, Hampshire

ISBN 978–0–19–921399–3

1 3 5 7 9 10 8 6 4 2

Editor acknowledgements

We are indebted to all of the Oxford editorial team for their terrific support throughout, especially Angela Adams (Commissioning Editor) for encouraging us to develop the idea for the book, and Helen Adams and Gina Policelli (Development Editors) for their constant support and guidance.

Over the years spent teaching at Leeds Met we have been grateful for the comments and reflections of our domestic and foreign students who have taken the International Business Environment module and we hope that we have learned from these to produce a book which meets the needs of the intended wider audience of future students.

Oxford University Press acknowledgements

In listing those whom OUP would like to thank, we include the many reviewers who made a direct contribution to the way this book was put together. We express our gratitude to all who helped us, but especially:

Steve Rodgers, University of Gloucestershire
Fragkiskos Filippaios, Kent Business School
Rob Haywood, University of Brighton Business School
Colin Turner, Heriot-Watt University
Nuran Fraser, Manchester Metropolitan University
Sharon Loane, University of Ulster
Ron Thomas, Portsmouth Business School
John Hart, London Metropolitan University
Chengang Wang, University of Bradford
David Edelshain, City University London
Eleanor Davies, University of Huddersfield
Deli Yang, Bradford University School of Management
Kurt Pedersen, Aarhus University
Jends Graff, Umea University
Mo Yamin, University of Manchester
Bill McCormick, University of Sunderland
Peter Chadwick, University of Gloucestershire

Steve Millard, Bucks New University
Kirsten Foss, Copenhagen Business School
Sonny Nwankwo, University of East London

The authors and publisher are grateful to those who granted permission to reproduce copyright material.

Crown copyright is reproduced under Class License Number C2006010631 with the permission of OPSI and the Queen's Printer for Scotland.

Every effort has been made to trace and contact copyright holders but this has not been possible in every case. If notified, the publisher will undertake to rectify any errors or omissions at the earliest opportunity.

Brief contents

PART ONE Global Context   1

PART TWO Global Issues   147

Detailed contents

PART ONE Global Context   1

List of figures

List of tables

Guide to the book

This book is aimed at level 1 and 2 undergraduate students and Masters level students taking an introductory module on either the Business Environment or International Business Environment on business or related courses. It will provide a thorough underpinning for those modules, at level 2 or 3, or masters level, which deal with International Business Management or Strategy.

The International Business Environment takes, as its starting point, a global perspective with a focus on understanding the global economy, the globalization process, and its impact on international business organizations. It examines the institutions and processes of the global economy and the economic, political, technological, and socio-cultural environment within which business organizations operate.

The International Business Environment is based on a module which the authors have successfully taught for a number of years. The authors have combined experience in academia of module development, and delivery at undergraduate and postgraduate level and this has provided the foundation for this text. Les and Phil have vast experience of teaching International Business Environment and Business Strategy and the text benefits from this experience and the feedback from students, including many international students, on these modules.

Why use this book?

This book is aimed at undergraduate students studying the International Business Environment as part of a Business or International Business degree. It also offers an essential knowledge base for postgraduate students in Business, especially those specializing in the International Business Environment.

The text provides comprehensive coverage of the core topics that are central to the International Business Environment. Each topic is presented with a balance of theory, case studies, and exercises aimed to develop the reader's ability to understand and analyse the internal and external environmental factors affecting the business environment.

The case studies and examples used throughout the text identify the opportunities and threats to business organizations arising from changes in the global business environment. Detailed case studies, highlighting key concepts and issues from the chapter, are provided at the start and the end of each chapter.

Structure of the book

The book is divided into two parts. The first section, The Global Context, includes Chapters One to Four and sets the context for the international business environment, while in the second section, Global Issues, Chapters Five to Twelve deal with a range of global issues.

The first chapter of the book describes the process of the globalization of markets and production, and examines the key drivers and barriers to that process. It emphasizes the increasing complexity and interdependence of the world economy, concluding that the opportunities and threats arising from the global business environment can have consequences for all business organizations. Chapter Two examines in more detail some of the more important features of the world economy. It identifies the pattern of global wealth and poverty, the pattern of international trade, and flows of foreign direct investment. Chapters Three and Four include detailed analytical frameworks which provide the tools to enable students to undertake an analysis of external environmental issues and how these impact on business organizations. Chapter Three looks at the analysis of industries while Chapter Four places this analysis within an examination of the global macroenvironment using the familiar PESTLE framework. This framework is then used to assess country attractiveness as markets or locations for production. Chapters Five to Ten analyse in more detail the issues in the socio-cultural, technological, political, legal, financial, and ecological environments respectively. Chapter Eleven provides an analysis of global aspects of Corporate Social Responsibility, and Chapter Twelve considers the challenges firms are likely to face in the future.

How to use this book

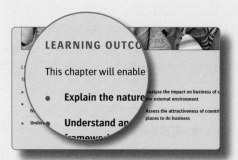

Learning outcomes

A bulleted outline of the main concepts and ideas starts every chapter. These serve as helpful signposts to what you can expect to learn from each chapter.

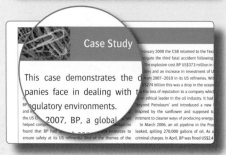

Case study

Each chapter begins with a case study that provides you with an introduction to the topic area and helps to set the scene.

Mini case

The book is packed with examples that link the topics to real-life organizations and help you gain an understanding of the international business environment.

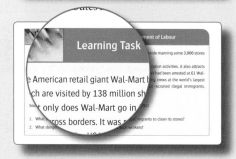

Learning tasks

Short questions and examples put the topic into context and give you the opportunity for discussion.

End-of-chapter case study

A longer case study with questions at the end of each chapter provides an opportunity to apply what you have learnt and analyse a real-life example.

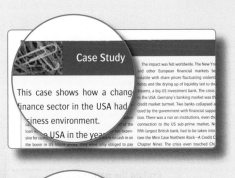

Chapter summary

Each chapter ends with a brief summary of the most important arguments developed within that chapter to help you recap on what has been covered.

Review questions

These are designed to test what you have learnt in the chapter and extend your understanding. These questions may also be used as the basis for seminar discussion and coursework.

Further reading

An annotated list of recommended reading will help guide you through the literature in each subject area.

Glossary

Key terms are highlighted in blue where they first appear. They are also defined in the glossary at the end of the book.

How to use the Online Resource Centre

www.oxfordtextbooks.co.uk/orc/hamilton_webster/

For students

Multiple choice questions

Ten multiple choice questions for each chapter provide a quick and easy way to test your understanding during revision. These self-marking questions give you instant feedback, and provide page references to the textbook to help you strengthen your knowledge and focus on areas which may need further study.

Web exercises

A set of exercises to help further your knowledge of the international business environment. You will be asked to find out information and answer questions based on web links to relevant articles and websites.

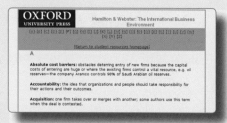

Glossary

A list of all key terms from the text.

Web links

A set of links to organizations which feature in the text is listed to help you with research.

For lecturers

PowerPoint lecture slides

A suite of PowerPoint slides has been designed by the authors for use in your lecture presentations which highlight the main points from each chapter. These can easily be customized to match your own lecture style.

Answers to review questions

Suggested answers to the end-of-chapter review questions in the book succinctly highlight the main points students should be covering in their answers.

Answers to case study questions

Guidance on answering the questions in the end of chapter case studies is provided to emphasize the key points students should be including in their responses.

Figures and tables

All figures and tables from the text are provided for downloading into presentation software or for use in assignments and exam material.

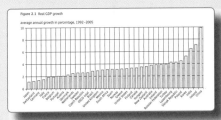

Exam and assignment questions

Additional questions are provided for use in your group tutorial work, exams, and assignments.

About the authors

Leslie Hamilton is currently an associate member of staff at Leeds Metropolitan University and holds an MSc in Economics from the University of Hull. He has more than 30 years' experience of teaching at both undergraduate and postgraduate levels, mostly in the areas of the International Business Environment, and the European Union. In the Business School at Leeds Metropolitan Les was responsible for developing and leading a large module on the Global Business Context. He has taught in France, Germany, Hong Kong, Russia, and Spain. Les worked for two years in the Netherlands researching the economic and social implications of EU policies towards the regions, and examining issues around migration. His other publications cover a variety of topics including the EU, international business, and the business environment.

Philip Webster is a Programme Director for Undergraduate Studies at Leeds Business School and Principal Lecturer in Business Strategy and International Business. He graduated from the University of Leeds with an MA in Economic Development and worked in financial services and the computing industry before moving into education. Phil has over 30 years' experience of teaching International Business Environment, Business Strategy and Business Ethics, and Corporate Social Responsibility. He has taught mainly in the UK but also in India, Sabah, and Hong Kong. Phil has also worked and lived in Malaysia.

Contributor

Dorron Otter is Head of the School of Applied Global Ethics at Leeds Metropolitan University. Dorron has extensive experience of developing new approaches to learning and teaching in introductory economics and business modules, and has led wider curriculum developments in these and other areas. While he has wider research interests, in the political economy of global development and responsibilities as an academic manager, Dorron retains his passion and commitment to teaching issues relating to the business environment.

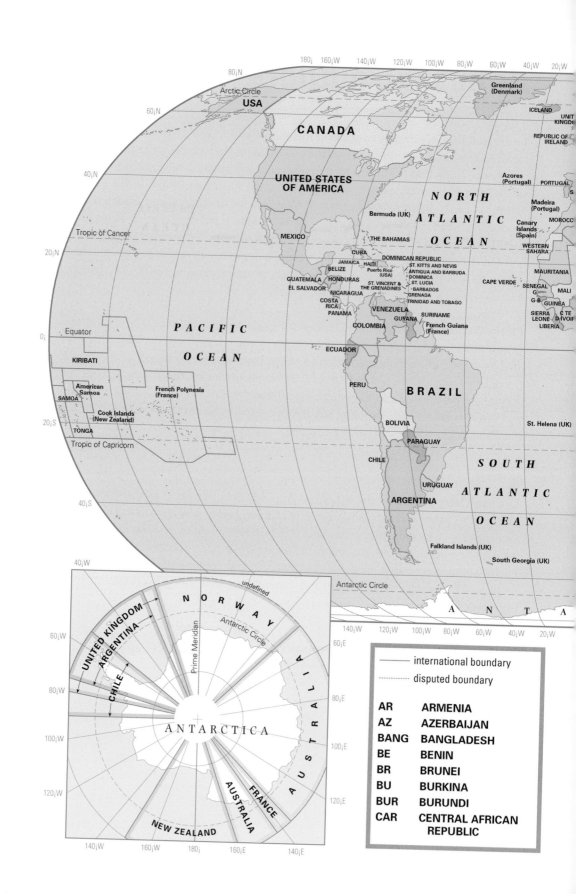

180¡ 160¡W 140¡W 120¡W 100¡W 80¡W 60¡W 40¡W 20¡W

80¡N

Arctic Circle

USA

Greenland
(Denmark)

ICELAND

UNIT
KINGDO

60¡N

CANADA

REPUBLIC OF
IRELAND

40¡N

UNITED STATES
OF AMERICA

N O R T H

Azores
(Portugal)

PORTUGAL

S

A T L A N T I C

Madeira
(Portugal)

MOROCC

Bermuda (UK)

Canary
Islands
(Spain)

Tropic of Cancer

MEXICO

THE BAHAMAS

O C E A N

WESTERN
SAHARA

20¡N

CUBA

DOMINICAN REPUBLIC

JAMAICA HAITI
Puerto Rico
(USA)

ST. KITTS AND NEVIS
ANTIGUA AND BARBUDA
DOMINICA

MAURITANIA

BELIZE

GUATEMALA HONDURAS
EL SALVADOR
NICARAGUA

ST. VINCENT &
THE GRENADINES

ST. LUCIA
BARBADOS
GRENADA

CAPE VERDE

SENEGAL
G

MALI

G-B GUINEA

COSTA
RICA
PANAMA

TRINIDAD AND TOBAGO

SIERRA
LEONE

C TE
D IVOIR

VENEZUELA

SURINAME

LIBERIA

COLOMBIA

GUYANA

French Guiana
(France)

0¡

Equator

P A C I F I C

ECUADOR

KIRIBATI

O C E A N

PERU

B R A Z I L

American
Samoa

French Polynesia
(France)

SAMOA

Cook Islands
(New Zealand)

20¡S

TONGA

BOLIVIA

St. Helena (UK)

Tropic of Capricorn

PARAGUAY

CHILE

S O U T H

URUGUAY

A T L A N T I C

40¡S

ARGENTINA

O C E A N

Falkland Islands (UK)

South Georgia (UK)

Antarctic Circle

A N T A

40¡W

140¡W 120¡W 100¡W 80¡W 60¡W 40¡W 20¡W

60¡W

N O R W A Y

undefined

60¡E

UNITED KINGDOM

Antarctic Circle

ARGENTINA

Prime Meridian

80¡W

CHILE

80¡E

100¡W

A N T A R C T I C A

100¡E

A U S T R A L I A

120¡W

AUSTRALIA

FRANCE

120¡E

NEW ZEALAND

140¡W 160¡W 180¡ 160¡E 140¡E

———— international boundary

------- disputed boundary

AR	ARMENIA
AZ	AZERBAIJAN
BANG	BANGLADESH
BE	BENIN
BR	BRUNEI
BU	BURKINA
BUR	BURUNDI
CAR	CENTRAL AFRICAN REPUBLIC

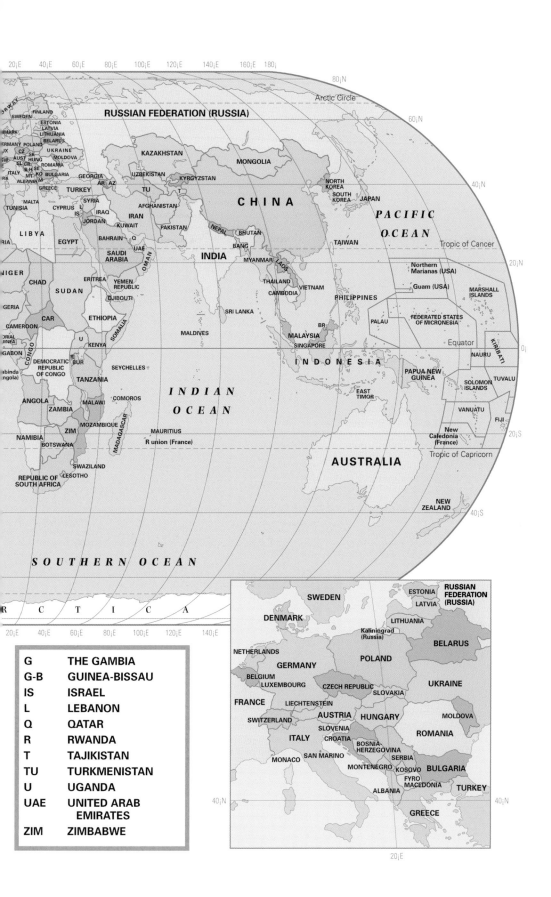

20¡E 40¡E 60¡E 80¡E 100¡E 120¡E 140¡E 160¡E 180¡

80¡N
Arctic Circle

60¡N

RUSSIAN FEDERATION (RUSSIA)

NORWAY
SWEDEN   FINLAND
ESTONIA
DENMARK   LATVIA
LITHUANIA
GERMANY POLAND   BELARUS
LUX   CZ   UKRAINE   KAZAKHSTAN   MONGOLIA
AUST HUNG   SK   MOLDOVA
SL CR ROMANIA   UZBEKISTAN   KYRGYZSTAN
ITALY B-H SE BULGARIA   GEORGIA
FRA   MT KO ALBANIA GREECE   TURKEY   AR AZ   NORTH   40¡N
MALTA   CYPRUS L SYRIA   TU   T   CHINA   KOREA   JAPAN
TUNISIA   IS IRAQ IRAN AFGHANISTAN   SOUTH
JORDAN KUWAIT   KOREA
LIBYA   EGYPT   SAUDI BAHRAIN Q PAKISTAN NEPAL BHUTAN   TAIWAN   Tropic of Cancer
ALGERIA   ARABIA   UAE   INDIA   BANG   20¡N
OMAN   MYANMAR LAOS   Northern
NIGER   CHAD   ERITREA YEMEN   THAILAND   Marianas (USA)
SUDAN   REPUBLIC   SRI LANKA   CAMBODIA VIETNAM   Guam (USA)   MARSHALL
DJIBOUTI   PHILIPPINES   ISLANDS
NIGERIA   BR   FEDERATED STATES
CAMEROON   CAR ETHIOPIA   MALDIVES   MALAYSIA   PALAU   OF MICRONESIA
EQUATORIAL   U KENYA   SOMALIA   SINGAPORE   Equator   0¡
GUINEA   NAURU
GABON CONGO R BUR   I N D O N E S I A   KIRIBATI
DEMOCRATIC   SEYCHELLES   PAPUA NEW
Cabinda REPUBLIC   GUINEA   SOLOMON TUVALU
(Angola) OF CONGO TANZANIA   EAST   ISLANDS
TIMOR   VANUATU
ANGOLA   COMOROS   FIJI
ZAMBIA MALAWI   INDIAN   New   20¡S
MOZAMBIQUE MADAGASCAR   OCEAN   AUSTRALIA   Caledonia
NAMIBIA ZIM   MAURITIUS   (France)
BOTSWANA   R union (France)   Tropic of Capricorn
SWAZILAND LESOTHO
REPUBLIC OF   NEW   40¡S
SOUTH AFRICA   ZEALAND

S O U T H E R N   O C E A N

A R C T I C A

20¡E   40¡E   60¡E   80¡E   100¡E   120¡E   140¡E

G	THE GAMBIA
G-B	GUINEA-BISSAU
IS	ISRAEL
L	LEBANON
Q	QATAR
R	RWANDA
T	TAJIKISTAN
TU	TURKMENISTAN
U	UGANDA
UAE	UNITED ARAB EMIRATES
ZIM	ZIMBABWE

RUSSIAN
FEDERATION
(RUSSIA)
SWEDEN   ESTONIA
LATVIA
DENMARK   LITHUANIA
Kaliningrad
(Russia)   BELARUS
NETHERLANDS
POLAND
GERMANY
BELGIUM   UKRAINE
LUXEMBOURG   CZECH REPUBLIC
SLOVAKIA
FRANCE   LIECHTENSTEIN
AUSTRIA HUNGARY   MOLDOVA
SWITZERLAND   SLOVENIA
ITALY   CROATIA   ROMANIA
BOSNIA-
SAN MARINO HERZEGOVINA SERBIA
MONACO   MONTENEGRO KOSOVO BULGARIA
FYRO
MACEDONIA   TURKEY
40¡N   ALBANIA   40¡N
GREECE

20¡E

PART ONE

Global Context

CHAPTER ONE

Globalization

LEARNING OUTCOMES

This chapter will enable you to:

- Explain the nature of globalization

- Assess the pace and extent of globalization

- Analyse the factors driving and facilitating globalization

- Explain the importance of globalization for organizations and countries

- Analyse the factors inhibiting globalization

Case Study Globalization and Dell

The globalization process involves the establishment of economic, political, social, and technological links among countries. This case illustrates how one company, Dell, got involved in, and profited from, the process of globalization. It shows: how Dell took advantage of the freeing up of cross-border trade and investment to set up a global supply chain across five continents and to penetrate foreign markets; how it had to adjust its products to different country contexts and how its production methods have been influenced by foreign firms.

The Company

Dell, based in Texas, is the world's second largest manufacturer of personal computers and has grown very fast. In the ten years up to 2007, sales increased from US$5 billion to US$57 billion. Profits are around the £3 billion mark. The company sells over 100,000 computers every day, most of them direct to the final customer via the internet.

The Global Supply Chain

To manufacture its products, Dell coordinates a global production network that spans the five continents of North and South America, Europe, Asia, and Australasia. Dell assembles most of

Source: www.dell.com

its machines in its own plants but outsources the supply of many components such as motherboards and CD/DVD drives to other companies and, as a result, is heavily reliant on foreign suppliers like Samsung of South Korea, Infineon of Germany, Foxconn in China, the Dutch firm Phillips, Nokia in Finland, and Sony of Japan. The whole production operation from the design to assembly stage can involve a dozen countries. The Dell Notebook illustrates the complex global nature of Dell's supply chain. The machine was designed by Dell engineers in Texas and Taiwan and assembled in Malaysia from parts made in China, the Philippines, Germany, Singapore, Costa Rica, Israel, India, Thailand, and Mexico.

Dell's production system aims to minimize the number of components held in stock. It does this by applying principles of lean manufacturing and just-in-time production first employed by Japanese manufacturers such as Toyota.

Selecting Locations

Dell's decisions about where to locate are driven by the desire to minimize costs and to extend the build-to-order, direct sales model around the world. Dell has taken advantage of the reduction and removal of barriers to trade and investment to locate in regions and sites that best meet its needs. Given the necessity to have production and support capabilities in the major markets, the company selects specific locations based on a combination of factors including the quality of labour and its cost—the company located in Ireland where labour cost were less than in most other members of the EU—now it is considering locating to one of the new EU member states in Eastern Europe, such as the Czech Republic, where workers are well-educated but much cheaper and less strongly unionized than in other EU countries; the quality of transport and telecommunications infrastructure—its sites in Tennessee are located close to major roads and to a Federal Express distribution centre—the availability, quality, and cost of telecommunications bandwidth are also factors, especially for call centres and data centres; access and proximity to markets—Malaysia is centrally located for markets in the Asia-Pacific region; government incentives—Ireland offered a low corporate tax rate, support in finding land, building facilities, and training employees and per capita ➔

→ grants for each employee; avoiding barriers such as tariffs that would make Dell's products uncompetitive—locating in Brazil and China not only gave good access to the South American and Chinese markets but also got around tariffs that would make Dell imported products too expensive.

As Dell moved beyond its home market in the USA, it had to adapt its business activities and organizational structure to the different markets in which it operates. While product develop-

ment is largely centralized in the USA and the same base products are sold worldwide, Dell has to customize its products for different regional and country markets with appropriate power supplies, keyboards, software, and documentation.

Sources: Thomas Friedman (2005), *The World is Flat: Brief History of the Globalized World in the 21st Century*, London: Allen Lane; www.dell.com; *Thomson 1 Banker Analytics*

Introduction

How is it that a teenager in the UK can press a key on his computer and immediately bring chaos to Houston, the biggest US seaport? Why do bar owners in Southern Spain rub their hands with glee when another low cost airline is set up in the UK? Why is it that a plane crashing into a building in New York can cause hotels in London to drop their prices or a Belgian airline to go bankrupt? Why should an outbreak of peace in the Middle East be good news for European gas consumers, in the form of lower gas bills, but bad news for BP and Shell shareholders? Why should a fall in the value of the US dollar lead to higher unemployment in Germany, or the collapse of Communism cause a rise in unemployment among steel workers in South Wales? How is it that a decision by an obscure bureaucrat in Brussels causes the giant US multinational, General Electric to abandon its US$40 billion takeover of the electronics firm, Honeywell or that an industrial dispute in Belgium results in British workers getting more training?

These are all examples of globalization—a major theme of the book. They show that events in one corner of the globe can have a major impact on others, sometimes good, sometimes bad. Business operates in a world where globalization is going on at an accelerating rate. As globalization progresses, it confronts business with significant new threats and opportunities in the external environment to which it has to respond. So globalization is important for business, but what is it and why is it so important?

The Process of Globalization

Globalization involves the creation of linkages or interconnections between nations. It is usually understood as a process in which barriers (physical, political, economic, cultural) separating different regions of the world are reduced or removed, thereby stimulating exchanges in goods, services, money, and people. Removal of these barriers is called liberalization.

As these exchanges grow, nations, and the businesses involved, become increasingly integrated and interdependent. Globalization promotes mutual reliance between countries. Globalization can have many advantages for business such as new markets, a wider choice of suppliers for goods and services, lower prices, cheaper locations for investment, and less costly labour. It can also carry dangers because dependence on foreign suppliers and markets leaves businesses vulnerable to events in foreign economies and markets outside their control.

Take the examples of Spain and Italy and their dependence on foreign countries for their energy supplies: they illustrate how important the interlinkages brought about by globalization can be, and what can happen when things go wrong. Since the 1980s, natural gas has become increasingly important in Spain as a source of energy. Spain itself produces an insignificant amount of oil and coal. As a result it depends on foreign suppliers for 99% of its natural gas requirements which is growing by 15% per annum. Three quarters of its gas supply comes from three African countries, Algeria, Nigeria, and Libya. These countries are potentially unstable both politically and economically. This leaves Spain's power stations and four million Spanish consumers very vulnerable to any instability with their African suppliers (see the International Atomic Energy Authority web site www.iaea.org; and Isbel).

Italy is dependent on cross-border supplies of electricity from Switzerland. In 2003 major sections of the Italian economy were brought to a standstill. What happened? A

Mini Case The Global Environment and Business

This case illustrates the importance of external factors for organizations. It shows how a company's performance can depend on a whole range of forces in the global environment. Factors such as the state of the global economy, events in foreign currency markets, changes in the price of oil, and the activities of foreign competitors can have important effects on competitiveness, sales, costs, and profits.

Evonik is a multinational company based in Germany. It has activities in the chemicals, energy, and real estate sectors, operates in more than 100 countries, and is one of the world's largest producers of specialist chemicals. It employs around 40,000 workers and has a turnover of just over €14 billion.

In 2007 the company reported that the global economy was growing, but more slowly than in the previous year. The strongest market growth was registered in China, India, and Russia, while growth in the USA, Japan and the Eurozone had faltered. The high oil price, the strength of the euro, and the weakness of the US dollar and the yen were having adverse effects on company earnings. The company had managed to

pass on to customers some of the higher raw material costs in the form of higher prices but was facing aggressive price competition from rivals in low-wage countries. The global demand for energy was increasing but the company was apprehensive that growing concerns about global warming would lead to tougher regulations on carbon dioxide emissions which could make their power stations uncompetitive.

Sales rose by 2% compared with the previous year. However, the hike in raw material costs caused by the increased price of oil, combined with the weakness of the US dollar and competitive price pressures, left the profit margin unchanged.

Source: Evonik Annual Report 2007

Now go to the Evonik web site (www.evonik.com), find the latest annual report and read the section entitled 'Management Report'. Make a list of the external forces cited there and identify how they have affected the company's recent performance.

tree in the Swiss Alps, uprooted by a strong gust of wind, had fallen on to a power line causing massive economic disruption. It left 57 million people in Italy without electricity. The entire country, with the exception of the island of Sardinia, was affected. Transport ground to a halt with tens of thousands of people left stranded on trains. Planes were unable to take off and traffic lights ceased operating. Hospitals were forced to use emergency generators, telephones and televisions went dead, and cars were unable to get out of electronically controlled garages. Shops were reduced to accepting nothing but cash and giving hand-written receipts because their electronic tills were not working.

Globalization also poses a threat insofar as it removes protection from domestic producers by opening up their markets to foreign competitors. In 2005, under pressure from domestic textile producers, the authorities in both the EU and the USA imposed restrictions on imports of cheap textiles from China.

Nations may also find that globalization causes them to specialize in producing those goods and services in which they are relatively more efficient. While this could generate benefits from economies of scale in production, it could also create dependence on a smaller range of products, and leave their economies more vulnerable to external events.

Globalization is not Global (yet)

Globalization is something of a misnomer because most foreign trade and investment takes place within and between the three great economic blocs:

- Western Europe dominated by EU member states;
- NAFTA comprising the USA, Canada, and Mexico; and
- Japan.

They are called the triad. Other parts of the world tend to play only a minor role. The majority of world trade takes place either within each triad member or between the blocs. However, most of this trade is internal i.e. NAFTA is not heavily dependent on trade with either the EU or with Japan.

This situation is reflected in the strategies pursued by big multinational companies. These organizations focus their strategies on the bloc where they produce. More than 90% of cars produced in Europe are sold there and a similar situation exists in North America (more than 85%) and Japan (more than 93%). This is also the case for steel, heavy electrical equipment, speciality chemicals, energy, transportation, and services (Rugman 2002). This concentration of trade in their own bloc is largely due to the size of their markets. Globally, rich countries make up less than a fifth of the world population but consume more than four fifths of the goods produced (World Bank 2005).

The number of countries making up the triad has changed over time. For example, membership of the EU increased to 27 in 2007 with the entry of ten Eastern European countries, Cyprus, and Malta. The USA is also pushing hard for the incorporation of Latin American countries with its proposal to set up the Free Trade Area of the Americas (FTAA).

Although the triad still accounts for over 50% of world exports and imports, its predominance is under threat from China whose share of world trade in manufacturing has grown very rapidly. China has become the second largest trader after Germany and ahead of the USA (World Trade Organization 2007).

The triad is also dominant in investment, but even here its position is under challenge from emerging countries such as China and India. This aspect is dealt with in the next section.

The Indicators of Globalization

There are three main economic and financial indicators of globalization, these are:

- international trade in goods and services
- the transfer of money capital from one country to another
- the movement of people across national borders.

Of the three, international trade and foreign investment are the most important. Each of the three indicators will be examined in turn.

International Trade

International trade means that countries become more interconnected through the exchange of goods and services, that is, through imports and exports. Between 1950 and 2006, world trade grew 27-fold in volume terms, three times faster than world output growth (WTO 2007). We can conclude from this that importing and exporting is becoming an ever more crucial component of global and national economic activity.

As can be seen in Figure 1.1, merchandise trade grew very quickly in the second half of the 20th century, particularly in manufactures which increased tenfold between 1950 and 1975. While the rate of growth subsequently fell, it was still very rapid. In the 1990s, world exports grew on average by almost 7% per annum with services exports growing even faster than those of goods. In the six years up to 2006, trade in both goods and services grew by about 10% on an annual basis but then growth started to tail off, slowing to between 4 and 5% by 2008 (www.wto.org). Over the same period, developing countries increased their share of merchandise trade to around one quarter (World Trade Organization 2007).

Multinational companies (MNCs) are major traders and account for a large proportion of international trade, with significant proportions accounted for by trade between subsidiaries within the same company. So for example, Ford makes gearboxes in its factory in Bordeaux and exports them to its assembly plants in other European countries. Around one half of US manufactured exports and more than 60% of its imports flow within MNCs. International trade has increased more rapidly than global output which has been increasing by around 3% per annum.

Figure 1.1 International trade by product group

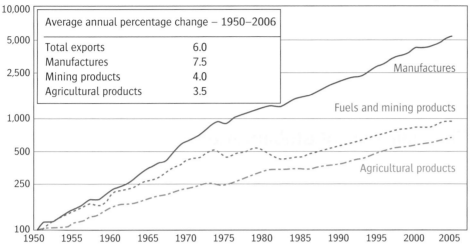

(Volume indices 1950–100)   Log scale

Average annual percentage change – 1950–2006	
Total exports	6.0
Manufactures	7.5
Mining products	4.0
Agricultural products	3.5

Source: WTO

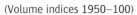

Learning Task

Examine Figure 1.1.

1. Compare and contrast the rates of growth of world exports of manufactures in the period between 1950 and 1975 with the period up to 2006. Try to come up with some explanations for the different rates of growth.

2. Since the mid 1980s the growth of exports of fuels and mining materials has accelerated. What link could there be between this growth and the rapidly expanding Chinese and Indian economies?

Some economies are particularly dependent on international trade. According to the World Trade Organization (WTO), exports and imports together amount to more than two thirds of China's Gross Domestic Product (the total value of a country's output of goods and services), more than half for the UK, but only around one quarter for the USA (http://stat.wto.org). Furthermore, the UK depends on customers in only two countries, the USA and Germany, for almost a third of its exports of goods. Events in those economies are outside the control of UK business but could have a major impact on it. For example, a rapid and simultaneous expansion of both economies would be very good news for sales of British manufactures but a recession, on the other hand, would mean a significant fall in turnover and profits. Dependence is also reflected in particular industries. For example, 65% of domestic demand for chemicals in the UK is satisfied by foreign suppliers. At the same time, the UK chemical industry is very dependent on foreign customers because their orders account for more than two thirds of sales (Annual Abstract of Statistics 2004).

Financial Flows

Foreign Indirect Investment

The second main driver is the transfer of money capital across borders.

This can take two forms. The first, Foreign Indirect Investment (FII, or Portfolio Investment), occurs where money is used to purchase financial assets in another country. These assets could comprise foreign stocks, bonds issued by governments or companies, or even currency. Thus, UK financial institutions such as HBOS and Barclays often purchase bonds or company shares quoted on foreign stock exchanges such as New York or Tokyo. Purchasers buy them for the financial return they generate. This activity has been increasing very rapidly—in the 1990s such trading was expanding at more than 20% per annum, helping to bring about an increased integration of financial markets. Growth faltered after the East Asian financial crisis of the late 1990s but picked up again in the new century. The interlinkages created by FII were demonstrated in 2006 when it was estimated that foreign financial institutions held more than 10% of the US$8 trillion in outstanding US residential mortgages in the form of mortgage-related securities. This left them vulnerable to the downturn in the US housing market which started in 2007 and led to a world-wide credit crunch (International Monetary Fund 2006) (see the section on financial crises in Chapter Nine and the end of chapter case study in Chapter Four).

Activity on the foreign exchange market is enormous. The average daily turnover worldwide in 2001 was US$1.4 trillion with most business taking place in the main financial centres of the triad: New York, London, and Tokyo. By 2007, turnover had more than doubled to US$3.2 trillion. Only a very small proportion of currency trading is associated with the financing of trade in goods and services—most goes on the buying and selling of financial assets (Bank of International Settlements 2007).

Foreign Direct Investment

The second form of capital movement is Foreign Direct Investment (FDI). FDI occurs when a firm establishes, acquires, or increases production facilities in a foreign country. MNCs are responsible for foreign direct investment and the massive increase that has occurred in FDI in the last 50 years.

The distinguishing feature between FII and FDI is that MNCs not only own the physical assets but also wish to exercise managerial control over them.

Countries can receive inflows of investment but they can also be sources of investment. The major recipients of FDI are the developed countries, mainly because of their large and affluent markets. In 2006, rich countries received around 60% of FDI inflows whilst

Figure 1.2 Inward FDI Flows US$m

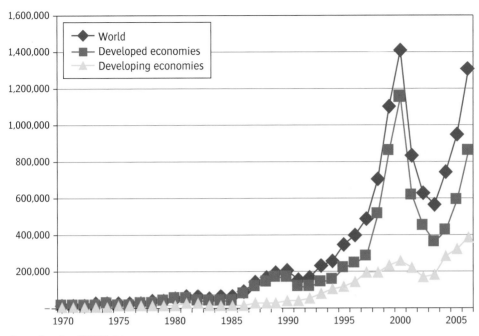

Source: based on UNCTAD data

they accounted for the vast majority—between 80 and 90% of the outflows (UNCTAD 2007; World Bank 2008a; Figure 1.2).

FDI grew spectacularly in the 1990s but declined steeply after 2000 due to weak growth of the world economy. The decline was halted in 2003/04. By 2006 it was once again approaching the peak of US$1.4 trillion reached in 2000.

In 2006 rich countries received just over 60% of FDI inflows with the USA being the most favoured location, particularly for firms from Western Europe and Asia. Developing economies accounted for the remaining 40%—with China, Hong Kong, and Singapore being the largest recipients (UNCTAD 2007).

FDI thus largely involves MNCs in rich countries investing in production facilities in other rich countries. The developing countries and Eastern Europe, having smaller and less lucrative markets, play only a minor part. Where FDI does take place in poor countries it is often to exploit natural resources such as oil or other minerals, to take advantage of cheap labour or, sometimes, to penetrate a market. China is favoured by foreign multinationals because labour is cheap and there is great market potential. Firms like Volkswagen, Toyota, Caterpillar, and Tesco have invested there to take advantage of cheap resources or to exploit the market.

According to UNCTAD (2007) there are some 78,000 multinational companies, with around three quarters of a million foreign affiliates. While the vast majority are based in

Figure 1.3 The world's top 25 non-financial TNCs, ranked by foreign assets, 2005[a] (Millions of dollars and number of employees)

Ranking by: Foreign assets	TNI	II	Corporation	Home economy	Industry	Assets Foreign	Assets Total	Sales Foreign	Sales Total	Employment Foreign	Employment Total	TNI (Per cent)	No. of affiliates Foreign	No. of affiliates Total
1	70	42	General Electric	United States	Electrical & electronic equipment	412.692	673.342	59.815	149.702	155.000	316.000	50.1	1184	1527
2	8	94	Vodafone Group PLC	United Kingdom	Telecommunications	196.396	220.499	39.497	62.428	51.052	61.672	82.4	77	210
3	85	72	General Motors	United States	Motor vehicles	175.254	476.078	65.288	192.604	194.000	335.000	42.9	91	158
4	16	61	British Petroleum Company PLC	United Kingdom	Petroleum expl./ref./distr.	161.174	206.914	200.293	253.621	78.100	96.200	79.4	417	602
5	29	80	Royal Dutch/Shell Group	United Kingdom, Netherlands	Petroleum expl./ref./distr.	151.324	219.516	184.047	306.731	92.000	109.000	71.1	507	964
6	38	43	ExxonMobil	United States	Petroleum expl./ref./distr.	143.860	208.335	248.402	358.955	52.920	84.000	67.1	258	331
7	64	95	Toyota Motor Corporation	Japan	Motor vehicles	131.676	244.391	117.721	186.177	107.763	285.977	51.8	141	391
8	79	56	Ford Motor	United States	Motor vehicles	119.131	269.476	80.325	177.089	160.000[b]	300.000	47.6	201	285
9	27	55	Total	France	Petroleum expl./ref./distr.	108.098	125.717	132.960	178.300	64.126	112.877	72.5	401	567
10	94	36	Electricite de France	France	Electricity, gas and water	91.478	202.431	26.060	63.578	17.801	161.50	32.4	218	276
11	73	51	France Télécom	France	Telecommunications	87.186	129.514	25.634	61.071	82.034	203.008	49.9	175	243
12	51	54	Volkswagen	Germany	Motor vehicles	82.579	157.621	85.896	118.646	165.849	345.214	57.6	199	279
13	63	74	RWE Group	Germany	Electricity, gas and water	82.569	128.060	23.390	52.081	42.349	85.928	52.9	248	432
14	53	88	Chevron Corp.	United States	Petroleum expl./ref./distr.	81.225	125.633	99.970	193.641	32.000	59.000	56.8	106	234
15	77	73	E.ON	Germany	Electricity, gas and water	80.941	149.900	29.148	83.177	45.820	79.947	48.8	367	639
16	24	52	Suez	France	Electricity, gas and water	78.400	95.085	39.565	51.670	96.741	157.639	73.5	440	613
17	87	59	Deutsche Telekom AG	Germany	Telecommunications	78.378	151.461	31.659	74.230	75.820	243.695	41.8	266	382
18	40	47	Siemens AG	Germany	Electrical & electronic equipment	66.854	103.754	64.447	96.002	296.000	461.000	65.3	877	1177
19	12	70	Honda Motor Company Limited	Japan	Motor vehicles	66.682	89.923	69.791	87.686	126.122	144.785	80.3	141	243
20	11	17	Hutchison Whampoa	Hong Kong, China	Diversified	61.607	77.018	24.721	31.101	165.590	200.000	80.8	75	83
21	67	38	Procter & Gamble	United States	Diversified	60.251	135.695	38.760	68.222	69.835	138.000	50.6	269	345
22	47	37	Sanofi-Aventis	France	Pharmaceuticals	58.999	102.638	18.901	34.013	69.186	97.181	61.4	142	181
23	89	77	ConocoPhillips	United States	Petroleum expl./ref./distr.	55.906	106.999	48.568	179.442	15.931	35.591	41.4	68	125
24	60	32	BMW AG	Germany	Motor vehicles	55.308	88.316	44.404	58.105	25.924	105.798	54.5	142	175
25	49	96	Nissan Motor Company Limited	Japan	Motor vehicles	53.747	97.661	59.771	83.440	89.336	183.356	58.5	54	172

Source: UNCTAD. World Investment Report 2007

rich countries, there are an increasing number of MNCs to be found in poor economies, two examples are: Tata of India and Hong Kong's Hutchison Whampoa.

Big MNCs are the most important foreign direct investors. Figure 1.3 shows the 25 biggest global companies ranked by the value of their foreign assets. The list is dominated by companies based in the advanced economies. Seven are US companies, 14 are Western European (6 German, 5 French, 2 British and 1 Anglo/Dutch), and three are based in Japan. Many of the largest companies are extremely international in their operations. Oil companies like ExxonMobil, BP, Shell, and Total, and others such as Vodafone, and Procter and Gamble, all generate more than 50% of turnover from foreign sales. Wal-Mart, the world's biggest retailer has expanded its foreign activities very rapidly. In the late 1990s Wal-Mart's sales from its foreign subsidiaries grew six fold. By 2007, it was employing more than half a million workers in over 3,000 stores in 14 countries, and across four continents (www.walmartstores.com).

However, the reality is that only a few of the 500 MNCs that dominate international business have a genuinely global presence. Most focus primarily on sales within their part of the triad. So American MNCs focus their strategy on North America, European companies on Western Europe, and Japanese MNCs on Asia. Rugman (2002) has found that many MNCs find it difficult to maintain profitable foreign operations.

Greenfield and Brownfield Investment

MNC investment overseas can be broken down into greenfield and brownfield investment. Greenfield investment involves the establishment of completely new production facilities, such as Ford setting up its new car factory near St Petersburg in Russia. Brownfield investment entails the purchase of already existing production facilities—the acquisition of Asda, the British supermarket chain, by Wal-Mart, is an example of brownfield investment. MNCs have undertaken massive brownfield investment. In 2000 they were involved in around 11,000 cross-border mergers to a value of more than US$1.1 trillion, two to three times greater than the figures for 1995. However, after 2000 there was a significant drop in merger activity to around US$380 billion by 2004 (see Figure 1.4). Merger activity then started to pick up so that by 2006 the total had reached some US$880 billion. The main purchasers were rich country MNCs, but companies from China, India, and Russia also played a prominent role. Consumer goods, services including financial services, energy, and basic materials were all major areas of activity. The biggest acquisition was the US$32 billion takeover of Arcelor, the European steel firm, by Mittal, originally Indian but now based in the Netherlands (UNCTAD 2007).

Another example of cross-border flows of money are migrant remittances. Migrants often send money to their home countries and the total amount has grown over time. They totalled some US$318 billion in 2007 with India, China, and Mexico as the three largest recipients, each receiving more than US$20 billion. The USA was the biggest source, sending some US$42 billion in 2006 (www.worldbank.org). Remittances are a vital source of foreign currency for some poor countries—Albania, Morocco, Jordan, and El Salvador are countries whose remittances from abroad equate to 10% or more of their GDP (Ratha *et al.* 2008).

Mini Case Cross-Border Mergers & Acquisitions—A Minefield

This case looks at the issues confronted by firms going in for cross-border mergers.

As we can see from Figure 1.4 there have been huge waves of cross-border mergers and acquisitions (M&As) indicating their popularity with business as a way of gaining competitive advantage. Such mergers have become a fundamental tool of business strategy. However, a number of studies have shown that the majority of these M&As are not successful. For example, a 2006 survey of business in North America, Europe, and Asia by the consultancy firm, Accenture, found most firms had not achieved the expected cost and revenue gains from cross-border M&As.

One notable example of the problems encountered in cross-border M&As was the acquisition of the American firm Columbia Pictures by Sony. Five years after paying a handsome premium for the company, Sony had to write down the value of its assets in Columbia by a massive US$3.2 billion. Many of the problems encountered by Sony reflect the issues to be confronted by firms involved in cross-border mergers. These include coming to terms with a very different business culture. Business is conducted very differently in Japan than in the USA. Such differences relate to the rules around corporate governance*, the power of shop floor workers, job security, differences in the legal and regulatory environment, and customer expectations. It is hardly surprising, says Finkelstein, that cross-border mergers are a potential minefield.

However, despite the evidence, cross-border M&As continue to be popular amongst businesses. The respondents in the Accenture survey, whilst recognizing the problems of integrating different cultures, still saw cross-border M&As as an essential part of their competitive strategy.

* corporate governance refers to the systems by which companies are directed and controlled particularly at the highest level of the organization.

Sources: Accenture, *Globalization and the Rise of Cross-Border Mergers and Acquisitions*; Sydney Finkelstein, *Cross Border Mergers and Acquisitions* available at www.tuck.dartmouth.edu

Figure 1.4 Cross-border M&As US$m

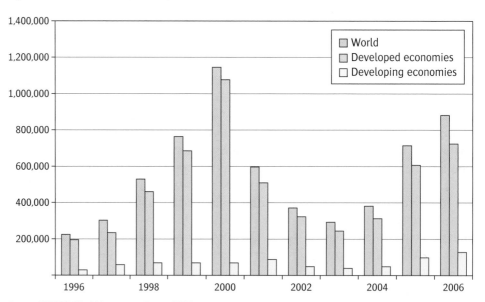

Source: UNCTAD, World Investment Report 2007

Migration

The globalization of markets has not been paralleled by the liberalization of labour flows. While globalization has led to the dismantling of barriers to trade in goods, services, and capital, barriers to cross-border labour movements are not falling as fast. Nevertheless, migration between developing and developed countries has continued. Flows of migrants are greatest to two triad members, North America and Europe—while Asia, Latin America, and Africa are major sources. The US population includes 38 million people born abroad (World Bank 2008b). That is the official figure, however the US authorities estimate that some 5 million people are living in the USA without permission, and the number is growing by more than quarter of a million each year.

According to the UN, the number of migrants (people currently residing for more than a year in a country other than where they were born) lies between 185 and 192 million—which is around 3% of the world's population. This meant that the migrant population had more than doubled in 25 years. Europe had most migrants with 56 million, Asia had 50 million, and Northern America 41 million. Almost one of every 10 persons living in the more developed regions is a migrant. In contrast, only one of every 70 persons in developing countries is a migrant. This increase in numbers has occurred despite the fact that during the last 30 years of the 20th century migration had become steadily more difficult—particularly for people in developing countries wanting to enter Europe. OECD (2007) figures show that migrants constitute a significant proportion of the population in some countries. In Australia, Canada, New Zealand, Luxembourg, and Switzerland the percentage is close to or exceeding 20%. The USA, along with certain European countries such as Austria, Germany, the Netherlands, and Sweden, has a percentage of immigrants at around 12%. It also found that the percentage exceeded 10% of the total population in Greece and Ireland, while it was about 10% in the UK. None of these compares with the Middle Eastern State of Qatar where more than three quarters of the population are migrants. Care needs to be taken regarding the accuracy of migration statistics because countries differ in their definition of 'migrant' and clandestine migrants are unlikely to be picked up by official statistics.

People move for a variety of economic, social, and political reasons. They may move voluntarily to find work, to earn higher wages, to study, or to reunite with their families. Widening inequalities in income and job opportunities increase the pressures to move. Movement may also be stimulated by employers in developed countries actively recruiting labour from abroad. The economic boom of the late 1950s and the 1960s caused countries like Germany, France, and the UK to run short of labour. Initially, they looked to other European countries that had been slower to industrialize—including Italy, Portugal, and Spain. In addition, some countries drew on their colonial ties. France turned to North Africa, and the UK to the Caribbean, and the Indian sub-continent. Germany, on the other hand, recruited short-term contract workers from countries adjacent to Western Europe, notably Yugoslavia and Turkey. Over this period net immigration for Western Europe reached around 10 million. European economies started to falter in the late 1960s and governments effectively closed the doors to migrants with the oil shock of 1973 when OPEC increased recessionary pressures by quadrupling the price of oil. At the start of the new century, the attitudes of certain governments towards migration have changed, as shortages of skilled workers have emerged. For example, the USA, UK, and Germany are starting to look much more favourably on the entry of workers with high levels of education and skills in areas such as IT.

Migration may also be involuntary where people, often in large numbers, are forced to migrate by political instability and violations of human rights—as we have seen for example in Zimbabwe and the Balkans. Natural disasters, such as hurricanes, earthquakes, and floods can also force people to move. Global warming is expected to cause extensive flooding in coastal areas of South East Asia which will cause large waves of migration.

Large short term movements of people also occur as a result of executives going on foreign business trips, students involved in study abroad, and tourism. In 2004, France, the most popular tourist destination, received more than 79 million tourists, the USA around 51 million, and China 50 million. Some small countries are heavily dependent on tourism for their income. In the Caribbean countries of St Lucia, Antigua, and the Bahamas, tourism contributes more than 30% to their GDP (UNWTO 2007).

Learning Task Wal-Mart and the Movement of Labour

The American retail giant Wal-Mart has half a million employees worldwide manning some 3,000 stores which are visited by 138 million shoppers each week.

Not only does Wal-Mart go in for large amounts of FDI in its globalization activities, it also attracts labour across borders. It was reported that more than 300 illegal workers had been arrested at 61 Wal-Mart stores in the USA as part of an investigation into contract cleaning crews at the world's largest retailer. The investigation involved allegations that a contractor had recruited illegal immigrants, mainly from Eastern Europe.

Source: *The Observer,* 26 October 2003; *Financial Times,* 24 October 2003

1. What are the advantages to Wal-Mart of employing illegal migrants to clean its stores?

2. What dangers might Wal-Mart face by taking on such workers?

Globalization is All-Pervasive

Although globalization is often seen as an economic phenomenon involving trade and investment, it also has many other cultural and social dimensions. Held (1999) argues that globalization is all-pervasive. He defines globalization as:

> the widening, deepening and speeding up of worldwide interconnectedness in all aspects of contemporary social life, from the cultural to the criminal, the financial to the spiritual (p 2).

As Held observes, globalization is not confined to economic life but also influences many other areas of society. And he contends that each of these areas is becoming more deeply affected by the phenomenon. Cultural life involving the attitudes, behaviour, and values that are characteristic of a society, can be influenced by the process. Globalization can influence culture through the transfer of knowledge, ideas, and beliefs across national borders.

Mass media, such as television and film, illustrate how culture has been influenced by globalization. American programmes such as *The Simpsons, Heroes* and *Friends* are watched worldwide. In Germany, in 2002, around one in four TV programmes was made in the USA while in Italy it was 15%. Similarly, US films like *The Matrix* and *Charlie's Angels* are widely shown around the world. In Mexico roughly four out of every five films shown are produced in US studios. The collapse of communism in Eastern Europe and the arrival of cable and satellite system opened up more markets to US media companies. However, commentators such as Tunstall (2008) see a challenge to the American TV and film industry from the growing capacity of China and India to become global media players, and the increasing competition from Latin America.

Learning Task

One of the authors, while on holiday in Spain, looked at the films showing in cinemas in Catalonia. This is what he found:

Country of Origin of Films on Show in Catalonia

Total on show:	59
Number made in:	
USA	28
Spain	10
Spain with other countries	3
Other countries	18

Source: *La Vanguardia*, 4 August 2003

Examine the table and answer the following questions:

1. What conclusions can be drawn regarding the cultural interconnectedness of Spain with other countries?

2. How do you explain the position of the USA?

Now look at the film listings for your town or local area and work out to what extent it is connected with foreign countries. You could, if you wish, carry out a similar exercise on television programmes to see how many are of foreign origin.

Diet is another area influenced by globalization. In France, the consumption of fast food such as hamburgers, and soft drinks like Coca Cola has increased and this is attributed by some commentators to the globalization of fast food chains like McDonalds and Burger King. The movement of people can also have an impact on diet. In the second half of the 20th century, many migrants came to the UK from India and Pakistan. With over 8,000 Indian restaurants in the UK, now almost all British towns and cities have an 'Indian' and it is claimed that the favourite meal, when eating out, is curry.

Another obvious route for transfer of culture across borders is through education. Universities in the USA, Western Europe, and Australia have enthusiastically embarked on campaigns to recruit students from abroad. Some have also gone in for FDI by setting up education facilities in other countries or have established partnerships with foreign colleges. The EU, through its Erasmus and Socrates programmes, has created large numbers of students studying in other member states. In a further move to facilitate the movement of students and workers across borders, more than 40 European countries have initiated a programme of reform of their university systems. The idea is to standardize the structure of university studies with degrees taking from three to four years and the introduction of a common system of assessment, the European Credit and Transfer System.

Another conduit for such transfers is through the world of work. For example, the UK and the USA have been favoured locations for Japanese car companies, in other words, capital has been moved to these countries from Japan. The movement of capital across national borders brings with it different ways of working such as Just-in-Time where suppliers deliver raw materials and components immediately before they are needed in the manufacturing process, or quality circles where small groups of employees meet together to identify how production could be improved. Domestic firms have, in turn, been influenced by this, e.g. Nissan has persuaded suppliers to alter their production methods. And Nissan's rivals such as General Motors, Ford, and Chrysler, finding their market shares slipping because of their inability to compete with the Japanese, have responded to the threat by introducing some of their working methods. As a result, in the UK and USA, car industry working methods have become similar to those in Japan. Another example concerns McDonalds setting up in Moscow in partnership with the City Council. It had to devise a strategy for dealing with a Russian workforce that had a reputation for being surly and slovenly. McDonalds introduced expatriate managers and training programmes to show the Russian staff how things should be done. Moscow City Council officials could not believe that the employees in the fast food outlet were Russian because they were so friendly.

The globalization process can also be seen in sport, where football players like David Beckham and Cristiano Ronaldo cross borders to play abroad. There has also been a rush of foreign direct investment into the English premier football league. Chelsea is owned by a Russian businessman, while Liverpool and Manchester United were acquired by US tycoons. Manchester United is promoted and known worldwide—it is marketed as an international brand and there is a lucrative trade in Manchester United team kits and other products outside the UK (for an interesting analysis of how cricket became globalized see Kaufman 2005). Furthermore, many of the top teams in England are now managed by foreigners.

A further impact of globalization is on health. A new treatment for disease, discovered in one country, can be quickly transferred to others, helping to limit the spread of disease and improve the quality of health care. On the other hand, diseases may also spread more quickly as people move across borders, e.g. the outbreak and spread of Severe Acute Respiratory Syndrome (SARS) in 2003.

SARS originated in Southern China. It then spread very quickly to other Asian countries, as well as Europe, North America, and Canada, which had over 300 cases. Illness can also be spread through trade. In 2004 it was found that poultry farmers in Vietnam and Thailand had contracted the virus associated with avian flu. The infection spread to other countries through cross-border trade in poultry and the movement of migratory birds.

With regard to crime: globalization, by removing barriers to movement, can make it easier for criminals to operate in other countries. Criminals can move more easily across borders, as can pornography, prostitution, and illegal substances such as drugs. Large amounts of cocaine are produced in Colombia and gangs there ensure that the drug finds its way to users in the USA. The Russian mafia is involved in trafficking women for the vice trade in Amsterdam. Communications technology facilitates the electronic movement across borders of money generated by these illegal activities into countries where the criminals can portray it as being derived from a legitimate source. Or they may move the money to countries where the laws regulating such money laundering activities are deficient.

Religion, or the spiritual dimension as Held calls it, is another area that is globalized. Major churches, for example the Catholic, Anglican, Muslim, and Jewish churches all operate multinationally and have been spreading their values over large parts of the world for the last 2,000 years. In the UK the established churches, such as the Church of England, are in decline in contrast to evangelical churches which have their roots in the USA and, ironically, have their roots in English Puritanism.

The Drivers of Globalization

In 1983 Theodore Levitt claimed:

> Gone are accustomed differences in national or regional preferences. Gone are the days when a company could sell last year's model—or lesser versions of advanced products —in the less developed world. Gone are the days when prices, margins and profits were generally higher than at home.

Although he was overstating the case he was making the point that technology, through communication, transport, and travel was driving the world towards convergence. In the business world the process of competition would drive firms to seek out these markets and force down prices by standardizing what was sold and how it was made in an effort to cut costs and to maintain profit. International competition is not a new business phenomenon, nor is FDI or international trade but, as we have seen in the first section, the process of globalization appears to be accelerating. The organization of trade is also different, with much of it taking place between and within large multinational organizations across borders which are increasingly irrelevant. It is supported by international organizations and agreements which did not exist a century ago.

The process is also embracing an increasing number of countries, as the free market ideology is accepted as the dominant economic philosophy. The countries of South East Asia, Latin America, India, Central and Eastern Europe, and even China have one by one bowed to the power of market forces.

The big MNCs have not been passive participants in this process. They are usually to be found at the forefront, pushing governments to open up their economies by removing barriers to trade and investment. Indeed, Rugman (2002) argues that their managers are the real drivers of globalization. MNCs encourage governments through pressure groups such as The European Round Table (ERT) which was set up by MNCs from 17 countries. It brings together leaders of around 45 of the biggest MNCs with a combined turnover of around US$1400 billion, employing about 4 million people worldwide. It was instrumental in promoting the idea of a single market for the EU and is very keen to integrate the former communist countries and the developing nations into a globalized system (see the ERT web site at www.ert.be). Similarly, the National Association of Manufacturers in the USA has pressed for markets to be opened up from Cape Horn, the southernmost tip in South America, to Alaska.

Competition then, is one of the dominant drivers in the process of globalization of the world economy. If your competitors are globalizing and capturing new growth opportunities, scale efficiencies, and gaining invaluable knowledge of global operations then you are likely to cease to exist or be forced into small domestic market niches unless you follow suit.

There are other drivers, although some might be more correctly labelled as 'facilitators'. In the next sections we look at the forces driving the globalization of business, the facilitating factors, and those forces which act as barriers, helping to keep business 'local'.

Political/Regulatory

Governments have taken steps to remove barriers to trade and the movement of finance through international organizations such as the General Agreement on Tariffs and Trade (GATT) and its successor organization the World Trade Organization (WTO) and they have also set up free trade areas, customs unions, or common markets.

- Free trade area—member states agree to remove tariffs and quotas on goods from other members of the area. Members have the freedom to set the level of tariff imposed on imports of goods from non-members of the area.

- Customs union— this is a free trade area but with the addition that members agree to levy a common tariff on imports of goods from non-members.

- Common market—this is a customs union but with the addition that member states agree to allow free movement of goods, services, capital, and labour.

There have been major reductions in the barriers to movement, particularly for goods and capital brought about by liberalization. These have been brought about multilaterally through negotiations in international institutions such as the General Agreement on Tariffs and Trade (GATT) and its successor organization, the WTO, or bilaterally between individual governments. Governments help bring about increased economic and political interlinkage by signing treaties setting up regional trade areas (RTAs) such as the

North Atlantic Free Trade Area (NAFTA) with the involvement of the USA, Canada, and Mexico where barriers to movement such as tariffs and quotas are abolished among the members. Other examples are, The Association of Southeast Asian Nations (ASEAN) incorporating 10 countries in South East Asia, and Mercosur comprising four countries in South America. The number of RTAs rose dramatically from about 30 in 1990 to 380 in 2007 (www.wto.org). The WTO expected that more than half of all trade would be conducted inside RTAs by 2005. While such bodies do promote integration among the members they often limit integration with non-members by maintaining barriers against imports from them.

Sometimes governments push integration further by agreeing to the establishment of customs unions which comprise a free trade area plus a common import tariff against non-members. Or they may set up a common market where there is complete freedom of movement for goods, services, capital, and people. One result of this removal of barriers to the movement of people in the EU is that someone in southern Spain could drive to Lapland without necessarily having to stop at a single border. Some members of the EU have taken the integration process even further by removing currency as a barrier by agreeing on the introduction of a common currency, the euro. Economic integration often then leads on to political integration. So EU member states are subject not only to EU laws but also to common policies in areas such as agriculture, the regions, and social policy.

Changes in political regimes have also helped reduce barriers, e.g. the collapse of communism in the late 1980s and early 1990s led to Eastern European countries becoming more interconnected economically, politically, and militarily particularly with Western Europe and the USA. Many of the former communist countries have joined NATO and the EU. China has opened up its economy to foreign investors and has joined the WTO.

Governments, particularly in poorer countries in Asia, Africa, and Latin America, anxious to promote economic development, facilitate the movement of capital into their countries by setting up export processing zones (epz) where MNCs can invest, produce, and trade under favourable conditions. China has 15 zones employing 40 million people. Kenya has 45 zones, while Honduras has 24. MNCs are usually given financial incentives to invest and often they are allowed to import goods and produce output free of tax. The International Labour Organization (Boyenge 2007) estimated that, in 2006, there were nearly 4,000 epz employing around 66 million people. There are also many free trade zones or freeports which are supposed to act as entrepots and be used for storage purposes.

Technological

Improvements in communications and reductions in transport costs have facilitated the movement of goods, services, capital, and people. Modern communications technology makes it easier for businesses to control far-flung empires. It further allows people to connect and interact over long distances, and with transport becoming easier and cheaper, goods and people are able to travel long distances quickly and at a relatively low cost. According to BA, the cost of flying has halved in 25 years and the cost of flying the Atlantic has fallen even faster, by half in 10 years (The Observer, 9 November 2003).

The internet and cheaper telephony not only make it easier for MNCs to control their foreign operations but also for migrants to maintain links with their countries of origin. Furthermore, it has been a major force in integrating the world's financial markets. A trader in a bank in New York can use the computer to monitor movements in share prices, interest rates, and currency rates in all the major financial markets and can respond by buying and selling almost simultaneously. Vast amounts of money can be transferred across borders at the press of a button.

In 1930, it cost more than a week's average wage in the UK for a three minute telephone call from London to New York. Now it costs a fraction of the average hourly wage and some commentators believe that technology and competition will halve the cost of calls almost every year over the first years of the 21st century. Demand for telecommunications has increased very rapidly. In the UK there were 45 lines per 100 inhabitants in 1990 but more than 58 a decade later, while in Latin America the number tripled. It took over a century to 1997 to reach one billion telephone subscribers but only another nine years to add a further three billion subscribers (Gray 2008).

The growth in demand for telecommunications services has recently been driven by the development of the cellular technology associated with mobile phones. Another factor, the internet, has revolutionized telecommunications. It has become a very cheap and reliable method of communicating text, data, and images and it is also being increasingly used for voice communication. The number of people in the world with internet access grew more than tenfold from less than 100 million in the mid 1990s to over 1 billion in 2006 with China having around 131 million users and India 68 million. However, although their numbers are huge, the proportion of people with internet access is lower in these countries compared with the rich countries of North America and North Western Europe (Computer Industry Almanac at www.c-i-a.com).

India is a good example of a country that has benefited from the impact of advances in communications technology. It has a ready supply of relatively cheap educated labour and has become an increasingly popular location for call centre jobs. This has come about as a result of the advances in communication technology which have significantly reduced the costs and improved the quality and reliability of telephony. The cost of a one minute phone call from India to the USA is just over 20 cents and around 15 cents to the UK. Consequently, there has been a movement of jobs from the UK and the USA to South East Asia. More than half of the world's top 500 companies outsource either IT or other business processes to India.

Technology can also have the effect of reducing movements of people. Improvements in the costs and quality of video links may mean that business executives do not need to attend meetings abroad. They can be virtual travellers interacting electronically through teleconferencing with fellow managers in other countries.

Economic

In many modern industries the scale of investment needed for research and development (R&D) and production facilities can mean that the size of a single domestic market is insufficient to support that industry. The production of electronic components requires high levels of investment in both R&D and the manufacturing process, and this drives firms to go global. This is especially so when product life cycles are shortening, increasing the pressure to recover investment quickly. Competitive pressures on costs also push firms to reduce product lines and to expand globally to seek every possible saving from economies of scale in R&D, manufacturing, and marketing.

The desire to cut costs can be seen in the aluminium industry. Aluminium is a relatively expensive metal to produce as it takes a lot of electricity to turn ore into metal. This is why aluminium firms locate their smelters in locations with access to cheap energy. Other industries will seek out cheap sources of labour. In the footwear industry, which uses relatively simple technology and is therefore labour intensive, labour costs represent about 40% of total costs. Hourly wages in some countries are very low. For example, in manufacturing, those in China are just 3% of those in the USA. As a result manufacturing has been relocating to countries with low labour costs such as China and India (Bureau of Labour Statistics at www.bls.gov).

Firms may globalize because they have outgrown their domestic market and in any case, the pace of growth in mature, developed economies for many industries is relatively modest. To maintain a rate of growth required by capital markets will mean for most of the world's leading companies that they must seek opportunities beyond their domestic borders.

The case of Wal-Mart is a very good example of this. Up to 1991 Wal-Mart was a purely American based company. Then it embarked on a joint venture with another retailer, Cifra, in Mexico. In just 11 years it developed 1,170 (27% of the total) stores outside the USA. Some commentators argued that it needed to do this in order to survive, to meet capital market requirements and the expectations of its own employees whose wealth was tied to a share purchase plan, the value of which depended on the growth prospects of the company (Gupta and Govindarajan 2004).

The rapid improvements in technology and the consequent reduction in communication and transport costs have enabled people to experience other societies' lifestyles first hand or through the medium of TV and film or the internet. This has led to a convergence in tastes which MNCs have been quick to exploit by creating global brands such as Coca Cola, Levi, Sony, Nike, and McDonalds. This has been called the 'Californiazation' or 'McDonaldization' of society (Ohmae 1985; Ritzer 2004, respectively).

Global companies mean global customers. Global customers require basic supplies of input materials, global financial and accounting services, and global hotel chains to house travelling executives. Dealing with one supplier of a standard product or service has many advantages for the global buyer; lower purchase costs, a standard product of consistent quality, lower administration costs, and more opportunities for cooperation with suppliers.

For example, Japanese banks became more global following the globalization of Japanese car manufacturers (an important customer).

Barriers to Globalization

Despite the fast pace of globalization, it remains the case that goods, services, capital, and people move more easily within nations than across borders. Trade between regions within nations is generally much higher than trade across borders even when adjusted for income and distance levels. This occurs even when trading restrictions appear to be low, for example, between Canada and the USA. This suggests that there remain important barriers to globalization. Rugman (2002) argues that government regulations and cultural differences divide the world into the three blocs of the triad.

Government Regulation

Legal and regulatory barriers can hinder the flow of goods and services and the movement of capital and people.

Tariffs and Subsidies

There remain numerous tariffs on imports of goods. Rich countries impose particularly high tariffs on goods coming from poor countries. As can be seen from Figure 1.2, the EU and the USA levy high tariffs on imports of agricultural products and textiles while tariffs imposed on goods from other rich countries are lower. On average the tariffs on poor countries' exports are four or five times higher. Such differences in tariffs help to explain why trade tends to take place within and between the rich countries of the triad.

It is not only rich countries who apply tariffs to imports. Poor countries impose tariffs as well and usually they are higher than rich country tariffs. India applies an average tariff of over 30% on imports of industrial products while the figure for Brazil is 14%.

Subsidies can take the form of financial grants or tax concessions and are often given to protect domestic firms from foreign competition. In the 27 individual member states of the EU, state assistance in 2006 amounted to about €50 billion, or just above 0.4% of EU GDP. Much of this assistance goes to firms operating in agriculture, fisheries, and transport but substantial amounts have also been given to firms in manufacturing and finance (EU Commission 2008).

Protectionist devices such as tariffs and subsidies are particularly prevalent in agriculture. They are often used by rich countries to protect their farmers. In 2004, OECD countries subsidised their farmers to the tune of US$380 billion. The USA, the EU, and Japan are amongst the biggest subsidisers. Taking the EU as an example, it protects its farmers in a variety of ways. It guarantees them high prices. It ensures that the guaranteed price is maintained by imposing tariffs on imports of agricultural produce. Surplus production, which would put downward pressure on prices, is either bought up by the EU authorities and put into storage, or is exported at a subsidised price. In the EU, each farmer receives around US$1,000 for each cow and a total of around US$133 billion a year is spent supporting farmers. American cotton farmers receive more in subsidies than the value of the cotton they produce (OECD).

These tariffs and subsidies make it difficult for poorer countries to sell their agricultural produce in rich country markets. However, subsidies can also be used to promote globalization. In export processing zones they are often used to attract foreign investors.

Governments in the rich countries usually give financial assistance to poor countries. Frequently, such aid is used to promote the interests of domestic firms. This is done by requiring the recipients to buy goods and services produced by firms in the donor country irrespective of whether they give best value for money. The US Agency for International Development requires that recipient countries must purchase goods and services from US companies. While that integrates the recipient economies with that of the USA it does freeze out non-US companies.

Controls on Capital

Controls on capital can take the form of either controls on inflows or outflows of foreign direct and indirect investment.

Big steps have been made in liberalizing the movements of capital. However, some countries have been more amenable to this than others. Thus India and South Korea have been reluctant to remove restrictions on capital inflows, and Japan has one of the most closed financial systems of all the advanced countries. Sometimes countries impose capital controls in times of economic crises. For example, when the South East Asian economy went into crisis in the second half of the 1990s, Malaysia responded by introducing controls on movements of short-term capital out of the country. It may be that countries are also reluctant to accept inflows of foreign direct investment where it involves sectors they regard as strategically important such as the basic utilities of gas, electricity, and water that are essential to everyone. France, for example, has shown itself very reluctant to open up certain sectors such as energy to foreign control and the USA and the EU are not prepared to cede control of their airline companies to foreign organizations. US law prevents foreign firms from buying more than 24.9% of an American airline (the corresponding figure for the EU is 49%).

Public Procurement

Government departments, nationalized industries, public utilities in telecommunications, gas, and water often spend large amounts of public money purchasing goods and services. Public procurement in the EU equates to 16% of GDP or €1,500 billion, in countries such as Sweden and Greece it accounts for more than 4% of their GDP. In the UK the government spends around £18 billion annually on the purchase of goods and services. Consequently, governments are very important customers for firms, particularly those producing goods and services for the defence, health, and education sectors. When issuing contracts, governments will often favour domestic producers over their foreign rivals even when domestic firms are more expensive.

An unusual illustration of discriminatory public procurement occurred after the invasion of Iraq by the coalition forces in 2003. The USA declared its intention only to give contracts for the rebuilding of Iraq to US companies and to firms based in countries that had supported the war.

Border and Immigration Controls

Border controls affect trade in goods. They can require the filling in of export/import forms and customs officers stopping vehicles and checking goods at the frontier. This can take time, add to traders' transport costs and make goods less competitive in the foreign market.

Many barriers remain to the movement of people. These include stringent visa requirements, quotas, requiring employers to search for a national employee before employing a foreign one, and refusal by the authorities to accredit foreign educational and vocational qualifications.

Most countries in the triad have laws controlling the entry of foreigners. US immigration laws make it difficult for people to enter the USA to find work or to study and the policy got stricter after September 11, particularly for people from Muslim countries in the Middle East. The USA permits around 675,000 immigrants each year. The law is aimed at keeping down the entry of unskilled workers, and attracting skilled workers and professionals.

The EU and Japan both control immigration, although these controls are under review given concerns that low birth rates and the aging of the population will cause shortages of workers. Migrants are seen as one part of the answer to this because they tend to be young and have a higher fertility rate than the indigenous population.

Technological

Technical standards and regulations can be formidable barriers. There are thousands upon thousands of different technical specifications relating to goods and services which can effectively protect domestic markets from foreign competition and consequently restrict trade. The EU has tried to deal with this through its Single Market programme. It uses the principle of mutual recognition whereby countries accept products from other member states so long as they do not constitute a danger to the consumer. But some products such as electric plugs, light bulbs, and televisions do not lend themselves to this approach. Even if member states were to recognize each other's standards, the Continental two-prong plug could not be sold in the UK where the three-pin plug is the norm. Companies in the service sector can also be hampered by the myriad of technical standards and requirements. Financial institutions such as banks may find it difficult to use the internet to sell their services in foreign markets because countries may lay down different solvency requirements, or different levels of liquidity for financial institutions operating in their territory. Regarding rail transport, countries have different electrification and signalling systems making it difficult for foreign train companies to enter and compete with domestic rail firms.

Different national policies towards what are called intellectual property rights (IPRs) could constitute barriers as well. IPRs relate to ideas and knowledge that are an increasingly important part of trade. They can take a number of forms, for example, the invention of new products and production processes, brand names, logos as well as books and films. Firms who own these argue that they should have the legal right to prevent others from commercially exploiting them. However the extent of protection and enforcement of these rights vary widely around the world. Some countries such as China and Malaysia do not offer the firms creating the ideas and knowledge much protection against counterfeiting. By all accounts it is very easy in Malaysia to obtain counterfeit versions of western music CDs, DVDs of popular firms made in the USA, and designer goods branded with the names of Versace, Louis Vuitton, and Rolex. Firms owning these IPRs argue that the lack of protection stunts their trade and FDI in those countries.

Cultural and Geographical Distance

Culture

Cultural distance can constitute an important barrier. This can take the form of differences in language, religious beliefs, race, national and regional tastes, and social norms and values which regulate what is regarded as acceptable behaviour and attitudes—these differences can constitute major impediments to globalization. Culture can be an important influence on consumer behaviour, work culture, and business practices. Thus, McDonalds cannot sell Big Macs in India because to Hindus the cow is sacred, nor can it assume that staff in Eastern Europe will have the same attitudes to work as its workers in the USA. Moreover, business practices may vary widely between countries. In China, for example, business culture is based on personal connections, as opposed to the Anglo-Saxon approach which places more value on getting the contract rather than on developing relationships. This means that companies have to take important cultural differences into account and to decide how to respond.

A classic example of a company failing to grasp the importance of culture was News International when it tried to enter the Asian market through its purchase of StarTV. The plan was to transmit US, English-language film and television programmes to the 5% of the population that was wealthy, educated, and had English as a second language. The neglect of cultural differences was costly for the company because it ended up making big losses. It only became successful when it recognized the cultural differences and started to make locally produced programmes in languages from Hindi to Mandarin.

Some goods and services are more sensitive than others to cultural differences. Ghemawat (2001) did some research on the impact of culture and found that products such as meat, cereals, tobacco, and office machines had to be adapted to local cultures, whereas firms producing cameras, road vehicles, cork and wood, and electricity did not need to adapt their products—or were under less compulsion to do so.

Corruption

Another area where cultural distance can cause problems for firms, concerns the issue of corruption. In some countries, in Africa and the Middle East for example, it is the norm for firms to reward individuals who help it to get business. However, in other countries such behaviour would be seen as corrupt and as such, would be deemed illegal. The prospect of prosecution in their home countries might deter firms from trading with, and investing in, countries where such behaviour is the norm.

Transparency International surveys show the degree of corruption as perceived in different countries by business people, academics, and risk analysts. The ratings range between 10 (highly clean) and 0 (highly corrupt). Rich countries, although not free of corruption, tend to get high scores. The ranks of the most corrupt are dominated by poor countries such as Bangladesh, Nigeria, Haiti, and Azerbaijan.

Firms generally find it much easier to operate in countries where the culture is similar to that of their home base. Cultural differences can be a significant barrier to globalization and ignoring them can be very costly (see Ghemawat 2001).

Mini Case Cultural Distance—Domino's Pizza

This case illustrates how companies wishing to profit from globalization have to take into account cultural differences in taste and eating habits.

The US firm Domino's Pizza is the world's second largest pizza chain with over 8,000 outlets in 55 countries across five continents. As it expanded around the world, the company found that it had to adapt both the product and the service to appeal to local consumers.

Icelanders prefer their pizza topped with fish while the French go for goat's cheese and lardons. In Taiwan, the favourite toppings are squid, crab, shrimp, and pineapple, whereas in Brazil pizza lovers go for mashed bananas and cinnamon. In Japan, mayonnaise, potato, maize, and bacon are the preferred options. Mexicans favour chorizo sausage and jalapeno peppers.

Domino's has found, simply by changing the toppings, that pizza is acceptable to consumers all round the world. But there can still be cultural complications. In India, the fact that Hindus cannot eat meat from cows meant Domino's had to replace pepperoni with a spicy chicken sausage. Most pizzas sold there are vegetarian. In Japan, where no word for pepperoni existed, they introduced it.

Domino's was able to export the idea of home delivery almost everywhere but not to China. In the capital, Beijing, Domino's had to fit tables in its restaurants. People in China, paying for a prepared meal, want to have somewhere to sit and eat it. Delivery can also be challenging in some markets. In Tokyo, where buildings are numbered not in sequence along streets but according to the date they were constructed, Domino's outlets each have a full-time employee whose job is to find locations on the map and tell drivers where to go.

Source: www.dominos.co.uk

Source: *Financial Times*, 26 November 2003; www.franchise-international.net; http://money.cnn.com

Learning Task

Some goods and services are more sensitive than others to cultural differences. Ghemawat did some research on the impact of culture and found the following:

More Sensitive Products	Less Sensitive Products
Meat	Cameras
Cereals	Road vehicles
Tobacco	Cork and wood
Office machines	Electricity

Discuss and advance explanations for Ghemawat's findings.

Geography

Geographical distance can also be a barrier. It has been shown that the more distance there is between countries, the less will be the trade between them (Ghemawat 2001). Geographical distance can make trade difficult particularly for firms producing goods that are low in value but high in bulk, such as cement or beer. The cost of transporting cement or beer over long distances would be prohibitive. Fragile or highly perishable products like glass and fruit may suffer similar problems. Firms can respond to the barrier posed by geographical distance in various ways. Brewers have responded either by taking over a foreign brewer or by granting a licence to firms in foreign markets to brew their beer. Thus barriers to one aspect of globalization, trade, result in globalization in another form, investment or licensing. Historically, geographical distance is likely to have declined in importance as transport has become cheaper and techniques for carrying fragile or perishable products more effective.

It would be unwise to assume that globalization is an unstoppable process and that barriers are continually being removed. Important barriers remain, and old barriers can be reintroduced. Early in the new century, for example, the US Government, under pressure from steel producers who were concerned about cheap imports, reintroduced tariffs of up to 30% on steel imports. This, in turn, provoked threats of retaliation, sometimes called tit-for-tat protectionism, from the EU, Japan, and several other countries, against US exports. In addition, new barriers can appear: where several companies are competing to develop a new product, the first to do so may establish its technical specifications as a standard for the new product which then acts as a barrier to trade.

The Benefits and Costs of Globalization for Business

Globalization can comprise major changes in the external environment of business. On the one hand, it creates opportunities for business, particularly for the big MNCs who are in the best position to take advantage. On the other hand, it can pose threats for business as well. We examine the benefits and costs in turn.

The Benefits for Business

The removal of barriers to trade or investment can open up markets to businesses that were previously excluded giving them the possibility of higher revenues and growth. The activities of car producers and tobacco firms in South East Asia illustrate this. As their traditional markets in North America and Western Europe have matured, General Motors, Ford, Volkswagen, Toyota, and others have all looked to the fast-expanding markets of South East Asia as a source of growth. China, with its rapidly growing car market, has been a particularly favoured location for car industry investment. Similarly, big tobacco firms such as Imperial Tobacco and Gallaher have formed partnerships with Chinese firms to produce and market their products to the 350 million smokers in China. Similarly, the fall of communism gave banks from the USA and Western Europe the opportunity to move into the former Communist bloc countries and, in many countries such as the Czech Republic, Bulgaria, and Croatia, have ended up controlling a majority of banking assets.

Globalization may give business access to cheaper supplies of final products, components, raw materials, or to other factors of production such as labour which lowers their costs and makes them more competitive. It is hardly surprising that firms such as HSBC, Tesco, ebookers, and BT have been relocating activities to India where graduates can be employed for around 14% of the corresponding salaries in the USA or the UK. The relatively low cost of IT professionals has also resulted in the biggest computer firms establishing operations in India. Similarly, China is not seen by Western MNCs simply in terms of its market potential but also as a very cheap source of supply. B&Q, the large chain of DIY stores, not only has stores in China but also sources US$1 billion/£600 million worth of products from China for its outlets in Europe. And UK firms such as pottery producer, Waterford-Wedgwood, domestic appliance maker, Kenwood, and pram manufacturer, Silver Cross have relocated production to China where there is an abundant supply of labour whose wages are less than one tenth of those of corresponding British workers (*The Guardian*, 19 November 2003).

Barrier removal may also allow firms to obtain previously denied natural resources. For many years Saudi Arabia was unwilling to give foreign firms access to its energy deposits. The Saudi authorities had a change of heart and Shell has signed a deal allowing it to explore for gas. With the collapse of communism Western firms have been vying to get a stake in the vast natural resource deposits of former republics in the Soviet Union such as Kazakhstan and Azerbaijan.

The Costs for Business

When firms globalize it means that they are opening themselves up to an environment that is more complex and risky. They are confronted by new sets of factors in the form of different political regimes, laws and regulations, tax systems, competition policies, and cultures. In extreme cases, they may find that the host government seizes their investment or takes discriminatory action against them. For example, the Egyptian Government confiscated a hotel property, claiming that it was on holy ground. In Ecuador, the Government cancelled an American logging firm's concession and gave it to the nephew of the president.

Fraport, the international airport operator based in Frankfurt, had significant difficulties in the Philippines when it built an airport terminal in Manila. Fraport poured US$384 million into completing the terminal and had to write off US$345 million in debts incurred through the project. Fraport's problems arose when a new government came into power in the Philippines and promptly cancelled the contract without negotiation. According to the company, the government repeatedly broke its contractual obligations and ignored normal legal procedures. In the company's view the investment had been expropriated. Fraport admitted that it failed fully to understand how politics work and how Philippine people think.

Thus we can see that globalization not only generates benefits but also costs. It is likely to pose problems for inefficient firms previously protected by barriers from foreign competition. National airlines such as Lufthansa, or telecommunications companies like France Telecom found it difficult to face up to the more intense competition engendered

Mini Case Globalization and Football

This case shows the impact of globalization on the supply of scarce resources, in this case, talented footballers, to Brazilian football clubs.

Brazilian football fans have long lamented the loss of their football stars as their best players leave for big contracts abroad.

While Brazil's diplomats complain about unfair farm trade at the World Trade Organization, at home the country's sports fans complain about the impact of globalization on their favourite pastime—football.

Arguably one of the largest sources of football talent in the world, Brazil itself has hardly any stars left. Fans and officials blame global capitalism. Brazil is a developing economy and is poor relative to its European counterparts. Its football clubs are in dire financial straits, so the best Brazilian players have been seeking greener grass in Europe.

The process is not new. Brazilian football icons went abroad long before Pele was lured to the New York Cosmos in the 1970s.

However, the exodus reached new proportions in the 21st century. In 2004 alone, 850 players left the country for hard currency contracts making Brazil the world's biggest exporter of footballers. It is hardly surprising that the national team comprises many foreign-based players. Kaka plays for AC Milan, Gilberto Silva for Arsenal, and Robinho for Real Madrid (more recently, Manchester City). The attraction for foreign clubs is that Brazilian players cost less than local footballers of equivalent talent.

The trend is taking its toll on attendances at football matches in Brazil where an average match attracts fewer than 8,000 supporters compared with 35,000 in Britain's Premier League.

As the head of a Brazilian fan club put it, 'Brazil has the best football in the world but we are losing all our top players, we feel betrayed.'

Sources: *The Economist*, 20 January 2005; *Financial Times*, 15 September 2003

Source: www.istockphoto.com

by the liberalization of civil aviation and telecommunications in the EU. Often the endangered businesses will pressurize governments to leave the protective barriers in place or to reintroduce the barriers previously removed—the US steelmakers being a good example of the latter. It may also be a particular threat for the less competitive small and medium-sized enterprises. Removal of the barriers may allow the entry of new competitors from abroad or it may permit existing customers to switch their custom to foreign suppliers who are cheaper or who can offer better product quality. British apple growers have suffered in this way—the big supermarket chains in the UK have transferred a large proportion of their custom away from domestic suppliers to foreign apple growers in places like Chile, Australia, New Zealand, and South Africa. Weaker domestic firms may find that their access to factors of production is threatened (see mini case on Brazilian Football for an example of this).

Globalization can also cause problems insofar as it raises the dependence of plants and firms on foreign markets and suppliers. As a result of NAFTA, more than 3,000 plants (called maquiladoras) were set up along the Mexico/USA border employing some 1,300,000 workers, producing goods for the North American market. They accounted for half of Mexico's exports. The dependence of so much output and so many jobs on the USA left those plants vulnerable to events in the US economy. When US consumers stopped buying, as the recession hit in 2001, the maquiladoras also began shedding workers. The Mexican Government estimates that over 400,000 jobs disappeared in the process. In the Mexican border towns they now say that when the US economy catches cold, Mexico gets pneumonia (Rosen 2003).

Globalization raises another issue for firms trading in goods and services and investing in productive activities abroad. Such firms prefer to operate in an environment where the financial and macroeconomic systems are stable and predictable. However, there is evidence that the economies of developing economies, whose financial systems have integrated with the rest of the world, are more subject to greater instability than other developing countries (Prasad et al. 2003). So it seems that the increasing integration of financial markets allows enormous sums of money to be moved effortlessly across borders leaving financial markets more vulnerable to instability, and the world financial system more prone to violent fluctuations in exchange rates and interest rates. Such fluctuations can pose a major risk to business costs, revenues, and profits. This was seen in 1992 when sterling, after it was forced to leave the ERM, fell by over 40% against the Japanese yen. Another example occurred during the financial crisis in the late 1990s when vast sums of money were moved out of South East Asia causing the exchange rates of countries like Thailand and Indonesia to collapse (see end Case Study Chapter Nine).

● CHAPTER SUMMARY

In this chapter we have explained the nature of globalization as a process through which barriers between nations are reduced. Nations thereby become increasingly interdependent, although we point out that most of this interdependence is between members of the triad, with the rest of the world playing a minor role. The dominance of the triad is being challenged by the emergence of China, India, and Russia as world economic powers. Increased interdependence is indicated by increases in exchanges across borders of goods and services, financial capital, and people.

We also make the point that globalization is not just about economic exchanges but has a cultural and social dimension. The media, our diet, education, work practices, sport, health, crime, and religion all demonstrate the impact of globalization.

The main drivers of globalization are identified as competition, reduction in regulatory barriers, improvements in technology, saturated domestic markets, the desire to cut costs, and the growth of global customers. There still remain important barriers to the process including regulation, technology, and cultural and geographic distance.

Globalization presents both opportunities and threats to business. On the one hand it presents access to new and bigger markets and to different and cheaper sources of raw materials, components, and labour. On the other the environment is more complex and less stable.

It is this environment and the implications for business that this book will explore. In the next chapter we will look at the global economy and explain in more depth some of the topics discussed in this chapter.

● REVIEW QUESTIONS

1. What is globalization?

2. How fast is globalization occurring?

3. Where is globalization mainly taking place? Why should that be the case?

4. Identify the main:

    • indicators of globalization

    • drivers of globalization

    • facilitators of globalization

5. What are the important barriers to globalization?

6. Outline the main advantages and disadvantages for business of globalization.

 Case Study **Globalization—Losers and Winners**

The EU Sugar Regime

For almost 40 years the EU protected its sugar farmers from foreign competition. It did this by guaranteeing its farmers a price which was three times higher than the price on the world market. The price level was maintained by setting quotas and tariffs on sugar imports. Any surpluses produced were sold to markets outside the EU at the world price. Firms processing the sugar beet were also guaranteed a minimum price for sugar.

In addition, the regime gave preferential treatment to 18 former European colonies in Africa, the Caribbean, and the Pacific. They were allowed to export, each year to the EU, 1.3m tons of raw sugar at fixed prices.

Brazil, Thailand, and Australia complained to the WTO claiming that the regime broke the WTO rules by subsidising exports. The WTO investigated and found in favour of the complainants.

When the decision was announced shares in EU sugar refiners such as Tate & Lyle, and Associated British Foods, which ➜

→ owns British Sugar in the UK, and the Spanish company Ebro Puleva fell sharply.

Then the EU Commission announced its intention to reform fundamentally the sugar regime to bring it into line with global trade rules. The EU Commission proposed that guaranteed prices for growers and processors would be cut by up to 42% over a three-year period. Farmers and firms unable to make money from sugar production would be offered compensation to leave the industry.

The reform came under immediate attack from French and Irish farmers and left processors fearful for their livelihoods. Sudzucker, the biggest sugar refiner in the EU, also criticized the proposed cuts in the guaranteed price. Ten countries, including Greece, Spain, Ireland, Hungary, and Italy, requested a slower and smaller price cut.

The Commission estimated that the reforms could force 7,500 beet farmers and 29,000 industrial workers out of the industry and around 40 processing plants could be closed. It said that sugar production was likely to be drastically reduced in Ireland, Greece, Italy, and Portugal and to fall significantly in Denmark, Finland, and Spain. In the more efficient producers such as the UK, France, and Germany production was unlikely to change.

The Africa, Caribbean, and Pacific group of countries said that the reduction in price would have a devastating effect upon their economies. In Guyana, for example, sugar production accounted for nearly one fifth of the whole economy and employed around 35,000 people.

On the other hand, the proposals were welcomed by countries such as Australia, Brazil, and Thailand and by producers of biscuits, cakes, chocolate, and confectionery.

Sources: http://europa.eu; www.bbc.co.uk; *Financial Times*, 29 April 2005; *The Guardian*, 1 July 2005

Questions

1. Explain how the sugar regime acted as a barrier to trade in sugar.

2. Give reasons why share prices of processing firms fell as a result of the WTO ruling.

3. Why is the EU proposing to reform the regime?

4. Explain why 10 EU countries asked for slower and smaller price cuts.

5. Why did countries like Brazil welcome the EU proposals?

6. Give reasons why sweet producers were happy with the reform proposals.

Online Resource Centre
www.oxfordtextbooks.co.uk/orc/hamilton_webster/

Visit the supporting online resource centre for additional material which will help you with your assignments, essays and research, or you may find these extra resources helpful when revising for exams.

● FURTHER READING

For a discussion of the debates and controversies around globalization see:

● Held, D. and McGrew, A. (2007) *Globalization/Anti-Globalization: Beyond the Great Divide,* 2nd edn. Cambridge: Polity

For an examination of the various theories around globalization and how the world economy has been transformed by MNCs, states, and interest groups see:

● Dicken, P. (2007) *Mapping the Changing Contours of the World Economy,* 5th edn. London: Sage

The next book discusses the relationship between globalization and climate change, terrorism, energy supply, population, and business:

● Moynagh, M. and Worsley, R. (2008) *Going Global: Key Questions for the 21st Century*. London: A&C Black

The following article looks at the globalization of a particular sport, cricket:

● Kaufman, J. and Patterson, O. (2005) 'Cross-National Cultural Diffusion: The Global Spread of Cricket'. *American Sociological Review*, Vol 70, No 1, February

● REFERENCES

Bank of International Settlements (2007) Triennial Central Bank Survey of Foreign Exchange and Derivatives Market Activity, April

Boyenge, J.-P. S. (2007) ILO database on export processing zones, International Labour Office, April

EU Commission (2008) State Aid Scoreboard, Spring

Ghemawat, P. (2001) 'Distance Still Matters: The Hard Reality of Global Expansion'. *Harvard Business Review*, September, 137–47

Gray, V. (2008) ICT Market Trends, Symposium organized by the International Telecommunications Union, February

Gupta Anil K. G. (2004) *Global Strategy and Organisation*. New York: John Wiley & Sons

Held, D., *et al.* (1999) *Global Transformations*. Stanford: Stanford University Press

International Monetary Fund (2006) *World Economic Outlook*, September

Isbel, P. (2006) *Energy Dependency and Spanish Interests*, ARI 32/2006, available at www.realinstitutoelcano.org

Levitt, T. (1983) 'The Globalization of Markets'. *Harvard Business Review*, May–June, 91–102

OECD (2007) International Migration Outlook

Office of National Statistics (2004) Annual Abstract of Statistics

Ohmae, K. (1985) *Triad Power: The Coming Shape of Global Competition*. New York: Free Press

Prasad, E., Rogoff, K., Wei, S.-J. and Kose, M. A. (2003) 'Effects on Financial Globalization on developing Countries: Some Empirical Evidence'. IMF Occasional paper No 220, September 3

Ratha, D., Mohapatra, S., Vijayalakshmi, K. M. and Xu, Z. (2008) Revisions to Remittance Trends 2007, *Migration and Development Brief 5, World Bank*, 10 July

Ritzer, G. (2004) *The McDonaldization of Society*. London: Pine Forge Press

Rosen, D. H. (2003) 'How China Is Eating Mexico's Lunch'. *The International Economy*, Spring, 78

Rugman, A. and Hodgetts, R. M. (2002) *International Business*. London: Prentice Hall

Tunstall, J. (2008) *The media were American: US media in decline*. Oxford: Oxford University Press

UNCTAD (2007) World Investment Report

UNWTO (2007) World Tourism Barometer, Vol 5, No 2, June

World Bank (2008a) MIGA Perspectives, January

World Bank (2008b) The Migration and Remittances Factbook

World Trade Organization (2007) World Trade Report

CHAPTER TWO

The Global Economy

LEARNING OUTCOMES

This chapter will enable you to:

- **Identify the global pattern of wealth**

- **Analyse the pattern of international trade**

- **Explain why countries trade with each other**

- **Identify the controls on trade**

- **Explain the pattern of FDI**

- **Identify the risks associated with FDI**

Case Study **China and the World Economy**

Globalization is a process whereby nations become increasingly interdependent largely through the exchange of goods and services, financial capital, and people. This case illustrates the case of China and its entry into the world economy. It shows how China transformed itself from a centralized, closed economy into a very open one and in the process became a leading world player: how growth has raised the living standards of some sectors of the economy but not all, and that rapid growth can also have its costs.

China joined the World Trade Organization (WTO) on 11 December 2001 submitting itself to a universal set of rules giving up some of the independence it had for so long defended. The process of moving the centrally planned economy of China to a more market oriented economy actually started in 1978 with the phasing out of collectivized agriculture. Other liberalization measures in relation to State Owned Enterprises, prices, domestic labour mobility, external trade, and FDI followed and by 2006 it had become the world's second largest economy with an estimated Gross Domestic Product (GDP) of over US$9 trillion (PPP) (Purchasing Power Parity—a measure which takes into account the relative cost of living). The USA was the biggest at over US$12 trillion.

The Chinese economy grew rapidly after 1978 averaging around 10% per year although with some wide fluctuation with growth as low as 4% and as high as 14% per annum. This resulted in a six-fold increase in GDP from 1984 to 2004.

Growth has been much more stable since 2000 with 2006 being the fourth year in a row with growth above 10% per annum. This has been very much an export led growth with exports growing at over 30% per year for the last five years. In 2007 China had the largest trade surplus in the world. It was also a very open economy with trade (imports plus exports) as a percentage of GDP measuring 72% in 2006, up from 44% in 2001. The USA by comparison is only 21%.

The Chinese economy is now a major world player and changes in that market have a significant knock-on effect on the rest of the world economy. In 2004 China accounted for a third of the growth in world demand for oil and was a major reason for the dramatic rise in oil prices in that year.

The sectors of the economy to benefit have been industry and services with agriculture now in decline. The main cities to benefit alongside Beijing have been those along the coastal region, and the well-to-do residents of those cities can now afford to buy imported luxury goods, such as the Mercedes, and can choose from a greater variety of goods available in the retail stores.

But it is not good news for all. The reduced tariffs on agricultural products have threatened the livelihoods of hundreds of millions of farmers. More than 100,000 people have lost jobs in State-owned banks as they adjust to a more competitive climate. While the economy may be the fastest growing, according to the World Bank, the poorest 10% of the population have seen their incomes fall in absolute terms. In 1998 the share of wages and household income was over 53% but by 2005 this had fallen to 41.4%.

China may well be the world's second largest economy but with a population of 1.3 billion the average income is still only US$1,290 (2005) up from US$285 in 1985; 150 million Chinese people still live on less than US$1 dollar per day. Income inequality has risen.

Twenty of the world's 30 most polluted cities are in China. Coal is the major energy source and there are plans to build more than 500 coal fired power stations to add to the 2,000 that already exist. Most of these are unmodernized and spew out clouds of carbon dioxide and sulphur dioxide. China's mines have the world's worst casualty rate. According to the Chinese media there were 2,456 accidents underground in 2005 leading to 3,818 deaths.

Source: www.istockphoto.com

Introduction

What is going to happen to the world economy next year? Which economies will grow the fastest? Which are the richest? Which are the poorest? Where are the new markets of the world? What sort of goods and services do they require? Who trades with whom? What trade restrictions are there in place? Where is most investment taking place and who is investing? In short how is globalization shaping the international economy of the future?

These are just a few of the many questions international businesses will be asking as globalization spurs their search for new markets and new locations to site their increasingly global activities. This chapter seeks to answer some of these questions. It looks at the incidence of global wealth and poverty and how this is likely to change in the future. It examines the pattern of international trade, why countries trade with each other and the international regulation of trade. The final section deals with flows of foreign direct investment and the associated risks.

Measuring the Size of the Global Economy

The most common method of measuring the size of an economy is by calculating Gross Domestic Product. This is the market value of total output of goods and services produced within a nation, by both residents and non-residents, over a period of time, usually a year.

In comparing the relative size of different economies one obvious problem is that the calculation of GDP is in a country's national currency. A common currency is required and this is normally the US$ using foreign exchange rates. This is not without its problems as foreign exchange rates reflect only internationally traded goods and services and are subject to short-term speculation and government intervention. For example, in the 1940s £1 sterling bought US$4. This rate was fixed as part of an international regime which considered that it was best for business if there was certainty about future exchange rates. In 1949 the UK Government, for domestic reasons, decided to devalue the £ to be worth only US$2.80. It remained at this rate until 1967 when it was further devalued to US$2.41. In 1971 the US moved to a floating exchange rate and other currencies followed suit. In the 1970s the £ floated and has varied from US$2.5 in the early 1970s to almost parity (US$1=£1) in 1984 and back to about US$2 in 2007. So measuring and comparing the wealth of the UK with the USA using foreign exchange rates would have indicated sudden changes in wealth which is clearly not the case, as the wealth of a mature economy such as the UK tends to change slowly, and fairly smoothly, over time.

This way of measuring GDP may indicate a country's international purchasing power but doesn't adequately reflect living standards. Most things, especially the basics of food, transport, and housing tend to be much cheaper in low income countries than in high income countries. A Western European travelling in much of Asia or Africa will find hotels, food, and drinks on average a lot cheaper than at home. The opposite of course is also true that people from those countries will find that their money does not go very far in Western Europe. A better indicator of living standards can be achieved by calculating

GDP by what is known as the purchasing power parity (PPP) method. This calculates GDP on the basis of purchasing power within the respective domestic market, i.e. what you can buy with a unit of a country's currency. The International Comparison Program, housed in the World Bank, collects information from 107 countries to establish PPP estimates. When these rates are used the relative size of developed economies is very much reduced and that of lower income countries much increased as indicated in Table 2.1. This table compares GDP and GDP per capita, both at current prices and PPP, of some of the richest and the poorest countries of the world. The data is derived from the International Monetary Fund's World Economic Outlook database.

The World Bank using a slightly different measure (Gross National Income which is GDP plus net income flows from abroad) classifies 209 countries into four different per capita income groups: low income, US$905 or less; lower middle income, US$906–US$3,595; upper middle income, US$3,596–US$11,115; and high income, US$11,116 or more.

Learning Task

From the information in the table complete the following tasks:

1. Explain why if the countries were ranked according to their nominal GDP or their PPP GDP the rankings vary depending on which measure of income is used.

2. Use your answer to Q1 to explain why the USA is more than 20 times richer than China according to GDP per capita but less than 10 times richer using the PPP figures.

3. Group the countries according to the World Bank classification of different income groups. Comment on their geographical spread.

GDP as an Indicator of the Standard of Living

Gross national income tells us the absolute size of an economy and will indicate that in nominal terms, according to the table overleaf, India is slightly larger than Australia and China and the UK are roughly the same size. However if we look at their respective GDPs using PPP we can see that India's GDP is more than 3 times that of Australia and China's is more than 3 times that of the UK. What does this tell us? Not a lot really because both India and China have big populations. When we take this into account to calculate on average how much of that GDP accrues to each person then, using PPP, we can see that Australia has a per capita income of $34,375, over 14 times that of India's $2,405 and the UK has a per capita income of $33,351 compared with China's $4,650.

Does this mean that UK citizens are seven times as well off as Chinese citizens?

It might but GDP only measures activity that takes place in the formal, officially recorded, economy. If an electrician does jobs for cash and doesn't declare the income to the tax inspector then there is additional output in the economy but it is not recorded.

Table 2.1 Gross National Income 2006

	GDP current prices $US mills	GDP PPP $US mills	population (,000)	GDP per capita current prices $US	GDP per capita $US (PPP)
Angola	45,167	73,401	15,864	2,847	4,626
Argentina	212,710	469,457	38,971	5,458	12,046
Australia	755,946	713,069	20,744	36,442	34,375
Azerbaijan	20,946	51,681	8,483	2,469	6,092
Bangladesh	64,854	190,643	156,117	415	1,221
Benin	4,749	11,307	7,612	624	1,485
Bolivia	11,235	36,864	9,627	1,167	3,829
Botswana	11,048	23,718	1,574	7.021	15,073
Brazil	1,072,360	1,696,000	186,771	5,742	9,081
Bulgaria	31,690	79,187	7,693	4,120	10,294
Cambodia	7,264	23,017	14,163	513	1,625
China	2,644,640	6,112,290	1,314,480	2,012	4,650
Egypt	107,375	367,406	72,131	1,489	5,094
France	2,252,110	1,956,780	61,355	36,706	31,893
Germany	2,915,870	2,668,950	82,293	35,433	32,432
Ghana	12,715	28,684	21,423	594	1,339
Haiti	4,661	10,514	8,478	550	1,240
India	877,224	2,665.500	1,108,000	791	2,405
Indonesia	364,379	767,508	222,051	1,641	3,456
Italy	1,858,340	1,714,950	58,435	31,802	29,348
Japan	4,377,050	4,091,950	127,746	34,264	32,032
Malaysia	156,091	327,376	26,392	5,914	12,404
Oman	35,729	56,405	2,546	14,032	22,152
Poland	341,724	567,696	38,141	8,959	14,884
South Africa	257,279	432,691	47,482	5,418	9,113
Sri Lanka	26,963	74,485	19,773	1,364	3,767
Sweden	393,606	317,737	9,113	43,190	34,865
UK	2,402,000	2,018,810	60,533	39,681	33,351
USA	13,194,700	13,194,700	299,077	44,118	44,118
Vietnam	60,995	198,742	84,401	723	2,355
World	48,435,985	60,295,212			

Source: International Monetary Fund, World Economic Outlook Database, April 2008

This is an example of activity in the so called 'shadow economy'. Others would be the non-declaration of income from self employment and all do-it-yourself and voluntary activities. If people were employed to do the latter then GDP would rise. According to Schneider and Enste (2002) the 'shadow economy' also encompasses illegal activities, trade in stolen goods, drug dealing, fraud, prostitution, gambling, and smuggling and they claim it is growing.

In the developing economies, Nigeria was estimated to have a shadow economy in 1998–99 of 77% of GDP, Thailand 70%, and Bolivia 67%. On the other hand the shadow economy in Hong Kong and Singapore was estimated at 14%, South Africa 11%, and Chile 19%.

In the OECD countries (Organization for Economic Co-operation and Development—mostly developed economies) Greece and Italy had the highest estimates at 27% and 30% respectively. The USA and Austria were 10%, and Switzerland 9%. In OECD countries the size of the shadow economy is reckoned to be growing, from 13% of GDP in 1990–93 to 17% in 1999–2000.

Learning Task

How would the shadow economies change the picture, were they to be included in official GDP figures?

Another problem with these measures is that they do not take into account environmental degradation and the depletion of natural resources. When oil is taken from the ground it is irreplaceable. The value of that oil is added to GDP but the depletion of reserves is not accounted for, even though it will affect the welfare of future generations. When the oil is turned into petrol that again adds to GDP but the damage done to the atmosphere when we use it in our cars is not deducted. GDP simply measures the additions to output without taking into account the negative effects of pollution, congestion, and resource depletion.

Welfare

GDP per person is often used as an indicator of welfare with the assumption that those nations with a high level of per capita income have a better quality of life. This may be true in most cases but GDP data tells us only about the average level of income. In all countries income is unevenly distributed and in some very unevenly. It also doesn't tell us if GDP is spent on health and education projects or on armaments or space projects. The United Nations Development Programme (UNDP) has developed a measure which captures some other elements of development, the Human Development Index (HDI). This is an aggregate measure of three features of development, life expectancy, education (adult literacy and average years of schooling), and standard of living (PPP per capita income). While the HDI is a much broader concept of development than is GDP it still does not measure all aspects of development. It does not for example say anything about gender inequalities or political participation which could be seen as important elements in any

Table 2.2 Human Development Index 2004

Rank	Country	HDI	Life expectancy at birth	Adult literacy rate % age 15 and older	Combined gross enrolment of primary and secondary schools	GDP per capita (PPP $US)	GDP per capita rank minus HDI rank
High	**Development**						
1	Norway	.965	79.6	99	100	38,454	3
3	Australia	.957	80.5	99	113	30,331	11
5	Sweden	.951	80.3	99	96	29,541	11
7	Japan	.949	82.2	99	85	2,951	11
8	USA	.948	77.5	99	93	39,676	−6
16	France	.942	79.6	99	93	29,300	1
17	Italy	.940	80.2	98.4	89	28,180	3
18	UK	.940	78.5	99	93	30,821	−5
21	Germany	.932	78.9	99	89	28,303	−2
36	Argentina	.863	74.6	97.2	89	13,298	10
37	Poland	.862	74.6	99	86	12,974	11
54	Bulgaria	.816	72.4	98.2	81	8,078	12
56	Oman	.810	74.3	81.4	68	15,259	−14
61	Malaysia	.805	73.4	88.7	73	10,276	−4
Medium	**Development**						
69	Brazil	.792	70.8	88.6	86	8,195	−5
81	China	.768	71.9	90.9	70	5,896	9
93	Sri Lanka	.755	74.3	90.7	63	4,390	13
99	Azerbaijan	.736	67	98.8	68	4,153	12
108	Indonesia	.711	67.2	90.4	68	3,609	8
109	Vietnam	.709	70.8	90.3	63	2,745	12
111	Egypt	.702	70.2	71.4	76	4,211	−2
115	Bolivia	.692	64.4	86.7	87	2,720	7
121	South Africa	.653	47	82.4	77	11,192	−66
126	India	.611	63.6	61.0	62	3,139	−9
129	Cambodia	.583	56.5	73.6	60	2,423	−4
131	Botswana	.570	34.9	81.2	71	9,945	−73
136	Ghana	.532	57	57.9	47	2,240	−9
137	Bangladesh	.530	63.3	41	57	1,870	7
Low	**Development**						
154	Haiti	.482	52	52	48	1,892	−11
161	Angola	.439	41	67.4	26	2,180	−32
163	Benin	0.428	54.3	34.7	49	1,091	−2

NB Many of the figures are UNESCO estimates because of a lack of reliable data.

Source: UNDP Human Development Report 2006

assessment of the quality of life. Table 2.2 gives HDI figures for the same countries as listed in Table 2.1 (plus Norway), but ranked according to the UNDP measurement of development which puts Norway at the top. Countries are classified into high, medium, or low development.

Income Inequality

The data in Table 2.1 gives us information about the total national income and average per capita income. It says nothing about how that income is distributed. There is a wide gap between rich and poor countries but within both rich and poor countries there is income inequality. According to the United Nations Development Programme Annual Report (2006) the gap in both rich and poor nations is growing. It goes on to say that the richest 2% of the world's adult population now owns more than half of global household wealth and the bottom half of adults own barely 1%. The gains from global growth are being highly unequally distributed. The data in Table 2.3 show the share of income of the poorest 10% and 20% compared with the richest 10% and 20% as well as the ratio of the richest 10% to the poorest 10%. Again this information is for the same countries as in Tables 2.1 and 2.2; the higher the figure in the last column then the greater the income inequality.

Learning Task

Looking at all of the information in the first three tables, select a high income country, a middle income country, and a low income country: what conclusions can you draw about life in each of these countries?

Economic Growth

Growth in national output (economic growth) is a key objective for all national governments as it is fundamental to raising standards of living. It is measured by the annual percentage change in a nation's gross domestic product. Quite modest rates of growth can have a significant effect on living standards if they are maintained. A growth rate of 2% would double real incomes every 36 years. We saw in the opening case study that China's GDP had increased six fold in just 20 years from 1984.

According to the International Monetary Fund (IMF), world GDP between 1992 and 2005 grew on average by 3.37% per year but in Figure 2.1 we can see that average growth rates for individual countries can vary quite markedly, from just over 1% in Japan to 10% in China. Growth in the most advanced and mature economies of the developed world, which account for 77% of world GDP, tends to be much lower than in the developing economies of the world. We can see in Table 2.4 that world growth rates since 2000 have varied from 2.2% to 5.0% but for the G7 (the most advanced economies of the world) the corresponding figures are 1.0% and 3.6% and for developing economies 3.8% and 7.8%. This is especially so in latter years, as some of the developing economies, especially

Table 2.3 Income inequality—share of income or consumption

HDI Rank	Country	Poorest 10%	Poorest 20%	Richest 10%	Richest 20%	Ratio of richest 10% to poorest 10%
3	Australia	2.0	5.9	25.4	41.3	12.5
5	Sweden	3.6	9.1	22.2	36.6	6.2
7	Japan	4.8	10.6	21.7	35.7	4.5
8	USA	1.9	5.4	29.9	45.8	15.9
16	France	2.8	7.2	25.1	40.2	9.1
18	UK	2.1	6.1	28.5	44.0	13.8
21	Germany	3.2	8.5	22.1	36.9	6.9
36	Argentina	1.1	3.2	39.6	56.8	34.5
37	Poland	3.1	7.5	27.0	42.2	8.8
54	Bulgaria	3.4	8.7	23.9	38.3	7.0
56	Oman	Na	Na	Na	Na	Na
61	Malaysia	1.7	4.4	38.4	54.3	22.1
81	China	1.8	4.7	33.1	50.0	18.4
93	Sri Lanka	3.4	8.3	27.8	42.2	8.1
99	Azerbaijan	5.4	12.2	18.0	31.1	3.3
108	Indonesia	3.6	8.4	28.5	43.3	7.8
109	Viet Nam	3.2	7.5	29.9	45.4	9.4
111	Egypt	3.7	8.6	29.5	43.6	8.0
115	Bolivia	0.3	1.5	47.2	63.0	168.1
121	South Africa	1.4	3.5	44.7	62.2	33.1
126	India	3.9	8.9	28.5	43.3	7.3
129	Cambodia	2.9	6.9	33.8	47.6	11.6
131	Botswana	0.7	2.2	56.6	70.3	77.6
136	Ghana	2.1	5.6	30.0	46.6	14.1
137	Bangladesh	3.9	9.0	26.7	41.3	6.8
154	Haiti	0.7	2.4	47.7	63.4	71.7
161	Angola	Na	Na	Na	Na	Na
163	Benin	3.1	7.4	29.0	44.5	9.4

Source: UNDP, Human Development Report 2006

China and India, have grown more quickly and taken a slightly larger share of world GDP. The IMF predicts that this trend is set to continue with the world economy growing at 4.57% per year between 2007 and 2013—the G7 economies growing at an average rate of 2.13% and the developing economies at 7.04%. The World Bank predicts that developing

Figure 2.1 Real GDP growth

average annual growth in percentage, 1992–2005

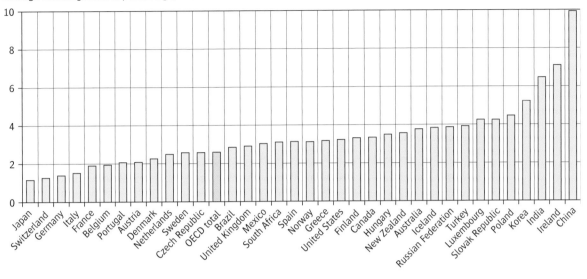

Source: OECD Factbook 2007

Table 2.4 Economic growth (annual % change in GDP)

	2000	2001	2002	2003	2004	2005	2006
World	4.7	2.2	2.8	3.6	5.0	4.4	5.0
G7	3.6	1.0	1.2	1.8	3.0	2.3	2.7
EU	3.9	2.1	1.4	1.5	2.7	2.1	3.3
Developing Economies	5.9	3.8	4.7	6.2	7.5	7.1	7.8
Sub-Saharan Africa	3.8	5.0	6.8	5.0	6.8	6.2	6.4
Brazil	4.3	1.3	2.7	1.1	5.7	3.2	3.8
China	8.4	8.3	9.1	10.0	10.1	10.4	11.1
India	5.45	3.9	4.6	6.9	7.9	9.1	9.7
Indonesia	5.4	3.6	4.5	4.8	5.0	5.7	5.5
Japan	2.9	0.2	0.3	1.4	2.7	1.9	2.4
Russia	10.0	5.1	4.7	7.3	7.2	6.4	7.4
United Kingdom	3.8	2.4	2.1	2.8	3.3	1.8	2.9
United States of America	3.7	0.8	1.6	2.5	3.6	3.1	2.9

Source: International Monetary Fund, World Economic Outlook Database, April 2008

countries will continue to grow more quickly than high-income ones in the next 25 years and that their share of world GDP will rise from 23% to 31% in 2030.

Implications for Business

As the developed economies of the world mature and their growth rates slow emerging market economies become attractive to international business both as markets and as locations for investment. Together they account for more than half the world population, have a young workforce, rising incomes and as such make excellent prospects for trade. They tend to have higher growth rates than mature economies indicating faster growing markets which businesses seek out. Growing economies need capital equipment, construction materials, power transmission equipment, and transport. According to the World Bank's Global Economic Prospects 2007 the 'global middle class' in developing countries will grow from about 400 million in 2006 to 1.2 billion in 2030. This 'middle class' will demand the type of consumer products enjoyed by the populations of the developed economies: cars, electronic goods, household appliances, and international travel. They will be more influential in shaping the economic and political policies of their own countries and the world economy.

Firms need to gather information to assess market opportunities. What we have looked at here is some of the information that would be useful in that assessment. They are not the only indicators and many others are considered in other chapters.

The Economist Intelligence Unit, for its indicators of market size, uses not only figures on population, GDP, imports, exports, and investment, but also figures on telephone subscribers, computer users, energy consumption, transport, and ownership of cars, TVs, and personal computers.

Mini Case Scotch Whisky

Scotch whisky drinks have fallen out of fashion, leading to a decline in European sales, but new markets in South America and Asia have saved the day. Many emerging market consumers can now afford to drink imported whiskies for the first time and distillers are seizing the opportunity to create a new image for their brands. Last year (2006) was a record year for Scotch Whisky exports with revenues rising 4% to nearly £2.5bn. Market growth of Scotch for 2005 in China was 115%, in Eastern Europe 30%, India 25%, Asia Pacific 18% and 11% in Latin America.

Source: *Financial Times*, 17 May 2007

Istock

Learning Task

What indicators of market size would be useful to firms selling the following products in emerging markets; whisky, cars, industrial machinery, personal computers, power transmission equipment?

In the next two sections we go on to look at two other aspects of international business: trade flows, and flows of investment.

International Trade

As we saw in the first chapter one of the key drivers of globalization is international trade, the exchange of goods and services between nations. In this section we will look in more detail at the pattern of global trade and put forward several theories to answer the question 'why do countries trade'? We will also look at the regulation of trade through the WTO.

The Pattern of Trade

Figure 1.1 in Chapter One showed international trade growing very quickly in the second half of the 20th century and more quickly than global output which had been rising at 3% per annum. In 1950 world exports were approximately US$0.5 trillion rising to US$12.5 trillion dollars in 2005. Of this US$12.5 trillion, most (US$10.1 trillion) was in merchandise trade, and the rest—US$2.4 trillion—was in services. Service trade grew more quickly than merchandise trade in the 1990s, but since 2003 the opposite has been the case (see Table 2.5). Exports as a percentage of world output were about 13% in 1970, 25% in 2005, and are predicted to be 34% in 2030 (World Bank 2007).

Merchandise trade comprises three categories, manufactured goods, mining, and agricultural products. The share of primary commodities in total world exports of merchandise trade has fallen dramatically. In 1960 primary commodities (excluding fuels)

Table 2.5 World exports of merchandise and commercial services 2005
billion dollars and percentage

	Value 2005	Annual percentage change			
		2000–05	2003	2004	2005
Merchandise	10,120	10	17	21	13
Commercial Services	2,415	10	15	19	11

Source: WTO

Table 2.6 Leading exporters and importers in world merchandise trade 2005
billion dollars and percentage

Exports				Imports			
Rank		Value	Share	Rank		Value	Share
1	Germany	969.9	9.3	1	USA	1,732.4	16.1
2	USA	904.4	8.7	2	Germany	773.8	7.2
3	China	762.0	7.3	3	China	660.0	6.1
4	Japan	594.9	5.7	4	Japan	514.9	4.8
5	France	460.2	4.4	5	UK	510.2	4.7
6	Netherlands	402.4	3.9	6	France	497.9	4.6
7	UK	382.8	3.7	7	Italy	379.8	3.5
8	Italy	367.2	3.5	8	Netherlands	359.1	3.3
9	Canada	359.4	3.4	9	Canada	319.7	3.0
10	Belgium	334.3	3.2	10	Belgium	318.7	3.0

Source: WTO

Table 2.7 Leading exporters and importers in world service trade 2005
billion dollars and percentage

Exports				Imports			
Rank		Value	Share	Rank		Value	Share
1	USA	354.0	14.7	1	USA	281.2	12.0
2	UK	188.7	7.8	2	Germany	201.4	8.6
3	Germany	148.5	6.2	3	UK	154.1	6.6
4	France	115.0	4.8	4	Japan	132.6	5.6
5	Japan	107.9	4.5	5	France	104.9	4.5
6	Italy	93.5	3.9	6	Italy	92.4	3.9
7	Spain	92.7	3.8	7	China	83.2	3.5
8	Netherlands	76.7	3.2	8	Netherlands	70.9	3.0
9	China	73.9	3.1	9	Ireland	66.1	2.8
10	Hong Kong	62.2	2.6	10	Spain	65.2	2.8

Source: WTO

Table 2.8 Intra- and inter-regional merchandise trade 2005
billion dollars

Origin	Destination							
	NA	S & C America	Europe	CIS	Africa	Middle east	Asia	World
North America	824	87	238	7	18	34	270	1,478
S and Central America	118	86	68	6	10	6	48	355
Europe	398	58	3,201	109	112	122	332	4,372
CIS	19	7	178	62	5	11	40	340
Africa	60	8	128	1	26	5	49	298
Middle east	66	3	87	3	5	54	281	538
Asia	608	51	498	37	54	89	1,424	2,779
World	2,093	301	4,398	224	240	321	2,443	10,159

Source: WTO

accounted for 38% of world exports, but by 2001 had fallen to only 12%. Over the same period the share of manufactured goods has increased from 51.3% to 74.1%. Developing countries have increased their share of world trade in manufactured goods from less than 25% in 1960 to less than 33% in 2002 with South East Asian countries being the main contributors to this growth. Other developing regions' exports did not see the same growth. African States' exports have averaged only 2% growth since 1980, while world exports have grown at 6% per annum. Developed economies still account for the majority of traffic—see Tables 2.6, 2.7, and 2.8.

Learning Task

1. For each region calculate the proportion of world merchandise trade.
2. What proportion of world trade is accounted for by North America and Europe?
3. For each region calculate the proportion of intra-regional trade, e.g. what proportion of Europe's trade is within Europe?
4. What conclusions can you draw form these and any other calculations?

Why do Countries Trade?

The earliest theory (17th and 18th century) in relation to international trade was that of mercantilism, which held that countries should maximize exports and try to limit imports as much as possible. Mercantilists viewed the accumulation of precious metals (gold and silver being the medium for settling international debts) as the only way to increase the wealth of the nation. Generating a trade surplus (when the value of exports exceeds the value of imports) was the aim of governments as this would result in an inflow of gold and silver. The governments of mercantilist nations such as Britain, The Netherlands, France, Spain, and Portugal restricted or banned imports with tariffs and quotas and subsidized domestic industries to encourage exports. At the same time they developed large colonies which provided cheap raw materials to a growing manufacturing base. This in turn exported finished goods to the colonies at much higher prices.

Mercantilists viewed exports as a good thing, as they stimulated industry and increased the number of jobs at home, and imports as bad, as this was a loss of demand and jobs. Although the mercantilist era ended in the 18th century neo-mercantilism or, as it is also known, economic nationalism continues. The USA and Germany in the late 19th century were able to erode Britain's dominance through protectionist policies. More recently post-war Japan has subsidized its domestic industries and protected them from foreign imports. It also had very tight controls on foreign exchange and foreign investment within Japan. These policies resulted in large trade surpluses.

Whereas mercantilists viewed trade as a zero sum game (i.e. one country could only gain if another lost) Adam Smith (1776) set out to prove that all could gain by engaging in free trade. Smith demonstrated that if countries specialized in producing the goods in which they were most efficient (i.e. in which they had an absolute advantage) then world output would be increased and the surpluses could be exchanged.

David Ricardo (1817) extended this theory to show that even when a country had an absolute advantage in the production of all goods total output could still be increased if countries specialized in the production of a good in which they had a comparative advantage. A country has a comparative advantage over another country if it can produce at a lower opportunity cost. In other words it has to forgo less than the other in order to produce it.

These theories help to explain the pattern of trade but don't tell us why one country should be more efficient than another and therefore what that country should specialize in. The factor proportions theory (or factor endowment theory), developed by Eli Heckser and Bertil Ohlin, explains that countries will produce and export products that utilize resources which they have in abundance, and import products which utilize resources that are relatively scarce. So Australia, with lots of land and a small population, exports mainly minerals (about 40%), beef, cereals, and dairy products. Its main imports are petrol, road vehicles, telecoms equipment, and industrial machinery (in total about 35%). China and India export goods and services which take advantage of cheap labour, whereas in Western Europe (where labour is expensive) there tends to be a concentration on relatively high value capital intensive industries.

Trade patterns seem to correspond quite well with this theory but there are weaknesses which Wassily Leontieff (1953) discovered in a study of US exports—some of which he found to be highly labour intensive and imports which were capital intensive. This became to be known as the Leontieff paradox. A weakness of the Heckser–Ohlin theory is that it treats all factors as homogeneous, when in fact they are not. Labour, for example, varies enormously in skill levels depending on the training and development undertaken.

When this was taken into account and skill intensity was measured then the results were more as predicted. The theory is further complicated when technology is considered. It had been assumed that technology is universally available, but there are in fact major lags in the diffusion of technology. However, one of the features of globalization is that this diffusion is becoming more rapid, especially the reduction in cost of collecting, analysing, and communicating information.

For much of the less developed world the pattern of trade predicted by these theories holds true, but this pattern has tended to favour the richer nations at the expense of the poor. This is especially the case for sub-saharan Africa. These countries produce and export primary products (other than oil) for which they have a comparative advantage and import manufactured goods for which they are at a comparative disadvantage. The problem is that the theories predict that total output is increased but say nothing about how that increase will be shared between countries. History shows that the demand for primary produce does not rise as quickly as the total rise in demand for all goods and services so there tends to be a long run deterioration in the terms at which primary produce exchanges for manufactured goods. In other words the price of manufactured goods tends to rise more quickly than the price of primary products. This, together with a very narrow range of products, probably goes a long way to explaining the low levels of income in those countries. Uganda, for example, relies heavily on agriculture which forms 30% of GDP but 80% of the population rely on it for their livelihood. It also forms 90% of export earnings, with coffee being the major export crop (20% of earnings in 2005)—consequently the economy is very susceptible to variations in the price of coffee. The main imports are oil and manufactured goods.

Another model to explain the pattern of trade in manufactured goods was developed in 1966 by Raymond Vernon (the International Product Life Cycle model). The different locations for production, and subsequent exports and imports was explained according to stages in the International Product Life Cycle. According to this theory products move through three phases: new product growth, maturing product, and standardized product.

The new product stage requires high levels of investment in research and design and a market with high purchasing power. Initial production volumes tend to be low with consumers paying a premium price for the new product. The market conditions for this scenario are found in the developed economies and this is where production is first located. During this stage firms monitor demand and make modifications to the product. Towards the end of this stage production increases and some exporting begins.

In the maturing product stage overseas markets become more aware of the product and exports increase. As they begin to account for an increasing proportion of sales then production facilities are set up in major markets either in subsidiaries or through licensing local manufacturers.

In the standardized stage new competitors selling similar products appear, the technology is widely available, and in order to maintain sales prices are reduced. Companies seek low cost production centres, often in developing economies. Products which were once exports now become imports.

Vernon was using this theory to explain the evolution of US firms and the associated pattern of US exports and imports, and at the time it fitted quite well. Since then the pattern of international investment has become much more complex as we saw with the case of Dell (Chapter One). Competition is much more international, product life cycles much shorter, and innovation may come from anywhere in the company's global production and marketing network. In an electronic age some firms are said to be 'born global', in that they start international activities right from the outset and move into distant, and sometimes multiple, markets right away.

What none of this explained was, as noted earlier, that most trade takes place, not between nations which are very different but, between similar, developed nations and that it is trade in similar goods—so called intra-industry trade. New trade theory in the 1980s explained that there were gains to be made from specialization and economies of scale and that those who were first to enter the market could erect entry barriers to other firms. As output increases the unit costs of production fall and new entrants are forced to produce at similar levels. The end result can be a global market supporting very few competitors.

A feature of intra-industry trade is product differentiation. Much international trade theory regards products as homogeneous but modern manufacturing firms produce a range of similar products appealing to different consumer preferences. For example a few car producers each manufacture a range of models and import and export to each other.

According to the country similarity theory (Linder 1961) this trade is determined not so much by cost difference but by similarity in the markets. As identified in Chapter One there are many barriers to globalization: such as geography, cultural difference, and corruption. It follows that firms will tend to do business with countries which are geographically close, culturally similar, have similar economic and political interests, have similar demand patterns, and are at similar levels of development.

The Competitive Advantage of Nations

In the 1980s Michael Porter undertook a study to find what made the major advanced nations competitive. He studied 10 of the most successful exporting nations and found that constant innovation and upgrading, in its broadest sense, was the key to competitive advantage. Constant, and often incremental, improvement is the key as almost any advantage could be replicated by others. According to Porter this advantage comes from four related attributes which he called 'the diamond of national advantage'. They were factor conditions, demand conditions, related and supporting industries, and firm strategy, structure, and rivalry.

Factor conditions: traditional theory said that nations would export those goods which made most use of the factors in which they were relatively well endowed. Porter distinguished between basic and inherited factors (such as raw materials and a pool of labour) and the created factors (a skilled workforce and scientific base) essential in modern, knowledge based industries. Where countries can create these advantages then they will be successful. He gave Denmark as an example where two specialist hospitals existed for the study and treatment of diabetes and was a world leader in the export of insulin.

Demand conditions: what is important is the nature of demand rather than the size of the market. Sophisticated and demanding buyers keep sellers informed of buyers' wants and give them early warning signs of shifts in market demand. It helps companies also if consumer tastes and national values are being exported to other countries, as the USA has done so successfully.

Related and supporting industries: the third determinant is the existence of internationally competitive firms within the local supply chain. They provide cost effective inputs and information on what is happening in the industry. Clusters of mutually reinforcing organizations tend to grow within the same geographical area. Porter used the example of the Italian shoe industry which benefits from the close proximity of world class leather-tanning and fashion-design industries.

Firm strategy, structure, and rivalry: the final determinant of national competitiveness refers to the ways in which companies are created, organized, and managed as well as the nature of domestic rivalry. Intense local competition leads firms to be innovative in seeking ways to outdo their domestic competitors. This in turn makes them more internationally competitive. The way in which firms are organized, managed, and the goals they set themselves as well as the structure of capital markets are all key to this rivalry.

Porter emphasizes the systemic nature of this diamond in that the points are dependent on each other. A nation may have sophisticated buyers but if the other conditions are not present then this is likely to lead to imports rather than domestic production. Low cost supplies may be available but if a firm easily dominates the market then this is not likely to lead to greater competitiveness. Domestic rivalry is probably the most important point of the diamond because of the improvement effect it has on all the others but clustering is also important because it magnifies the effect of the other elements (Porter 1990).

Porter also included two other variables as being important for the success of a nation, chance and government. Chance events are those outside the control of firms and even governments which can change very quickly the conditions in the 'diamond'. They include such things as wars, inventions, political decisions by foreign governments, shifts in the world financial markets or exchange rates (the case at the end of this chapter examines the worldwide repercussions of the credit crunch in the USA), discontinuities in input costs such as oil price shocks, major technological breakthroughs, and surges in world or regional demand.

Governments can influence the four broad attributes either positively or negatively through various policies such as subsidies, incentives, capital market controls, education policy, environmental controls, tax laws, and competition laws.

The complete model then becomes: see Fig 2.2.

Trade Intervention

All of the theories and models make the assumption that trade takes place freely between nations but, as noted in Chapter One, this is far from the case. Every nation imposes trade restrictions of some description. Generally their purpose is to limit imports by imposing tariff or non-tariff barriers, or to encourage exports by subsidizing exporting firms.

A tariff is a tax or duty placed on an imported good by a domestic government. Tariffs are usually levied as a percentage of the declared value of the good, similar to a sales tax.

Figure 2.2 Determinants of national competitive advantage

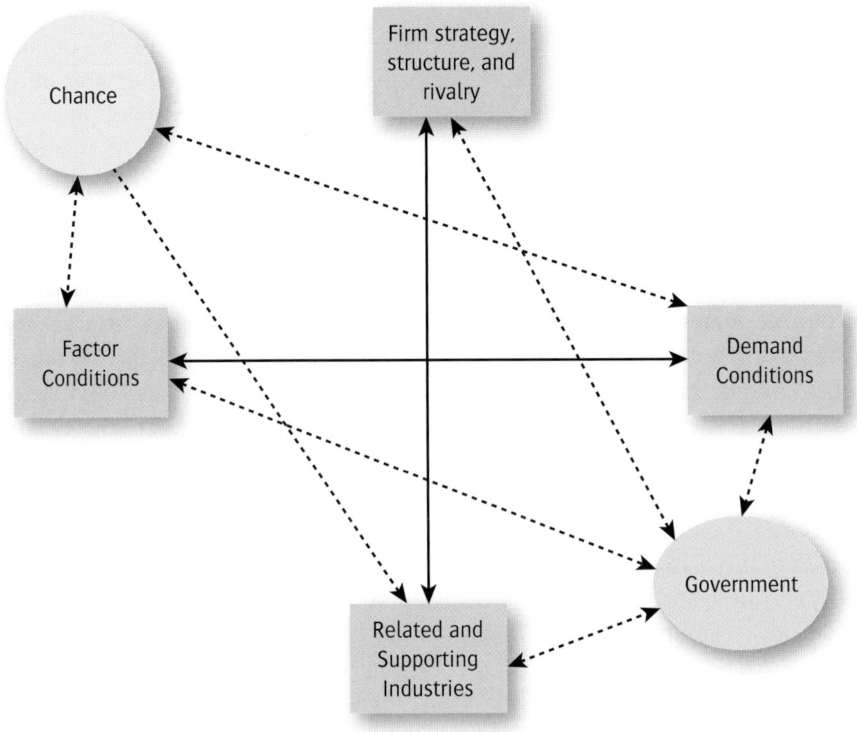

Source: Porter 1990

Unlike a sales tax, tariff rates are often different for every good and tariffs do not apply to domestically produced goods.

Non-tariff barriers can take a number of forms; quotas, licences, rules of origin, product requirements (standards, packaging, labelling and markings, product specifications) customs procedures and documentation requirements, local content rules, and exchange rate manipulation.

Subsidies can take many forms and can be difficult to identify and calculate. Financial assistance of any sort including cash payments, low interest loans, tax breaks, export credits and guarantees, export promotion agencies, free trade and export processing zones all distort trade in favour of domestic producers. According to the OECD (2006) support to agricultural producers amounted to US$280 billion or €225 billion in 2005.

Yet another way of affecting both imports and exports is by exchange rate manipulation. When two firms in different countries do business the prices they quote will be determined by a combination of their domestic price converted to the other's currency using foreign exchange rates. If £1 exchanges for US$2 then a UK exporter with a domestic

Mini Case China–USA trade wars

American senators in 2006 proposed a bill to impose an additional duty of 27.5% on all imports from China. They accused the Chinese of keeping the Yuan artificially undervalued against the US dollar. In 2005 the US trade deficit with China was US$200 billion or 27.5% of the total trade deficit. Others in the US accuse China of stealing US jobs, of selling abroad at unfair prices, and of violating workers' rights. On the other hand it is not at all clear that the Yuan is undervalued. China did allow the Yuan to appreciate against the dollar by about 3% in 2006 but if it had floated against a basket of currencies including the dollar, euro, and yen it would have actually depreciated against the dollar.

Opponents point out that those who stand to lose from a revaluation are poor US citizens who would find the prices, of many of the cheap goods from China they enjoy, rising: that many of the exporting firms are foreign owned, many American, having moved there to take advantage of lower production costs and that the very workers whose rights are allegedly being violated will be the first to suffer.

Whatever the truth of the matter, the danger is that this could lead to a trade war. In July, 2007 the *Guardian* reported a simmering trade war in which the USA had banned Chinese shrimp and four types of fish after finding traces of chemicals. China had retaliated by suspending some US pork and poultry imports and seizing and killing a shipment of 41 US homing pigeons because health certification was said to be incorrect.

---

price of £100 will quote US$200 to an American buyer. Any change in the exchange rate will affect the foreign exchange price. If the £ strengthens to £1 = US$2.5 then the US price will be US$250. In a competitive market a price rise might not be possible which would then mean that if the UK firm could only charge US$200 then it would only receive £80 of revenue. One way of maintaining the competitiveness of a country's exports would be to keep the value of its currency low in relation to others.

Rising trade tensions between the US and China have been fuelled by America's large trade gap with China which reached US$200 billion in 2005 as shoppers snapped up cheap consumer goods from the fast growing economy. The yawning trade deficit has stoked protectionist sentiment in Congress where lawmakers accused China of holding its currency at artificially low rates to boost its exports. They wanted to impose hefty import duties or other penalties on Chinese goods to narrow the US trade deficit with China.

Why Intervene?

National defence—it is argued that certain industries need defending from imports because they are vital in times of war. Weapons, transport, utilities, and food would probably fall into this category but where would the line be drawn? Similar arguments have been put forward to ban exports of technically advanced, especially military, products. The USA banned exports of satellites to China because this would have given the Chinese access to US military technology. It resulted in a fall in the American share of world satellite sales.

When US firms sell high-tech products and military equipment to allies the US Government tries to prevent the selling-on of such technology to countries such as China and Venezuela. In July, 2007 Saab withdrew from an international trade deal with Venezuela because of an arms ban imposed by the US on Venezuela. Bofors, a subsidiary of Saab, had for 20 years supplied Venezuela with weapons but the ban meant they could not sell any weapons with US-made parts.

To protect fledgling domestic industries from foreign competition—it is argued that industries in their infancy may need protection until they can compete internationally. This gives them time to grow to a size where they can gain economies of scale, learn from doing, and develop the supporting infrastructure discussed above. Some of the Asian economies, Japan, South Korea, and Taiwan have successfully protected infant industries until they have grown to compete internationally and the barriers have been removed. On the other hand some Japanese industries such as banking, construction, and retailing have remained protected and inefficient.

To protect domestic industries from foreign competition and thereby save jobs—governments often come under pressure to support industries in decline because the human cost involved in the event of sudden closure can be very high. Protection may be justified to delay the closure and allow time for adjustment.

To protect against over dependence on a narrow base of products—the law of comparative advantage tells us that countries should specialize in the production of goods in which they have a comparative advantage. For some countries this will result in a range of primary products for which demand is income inelastic. This could condemn these countries to persistent poverty so protection to expand the industrial base may be the only way to escape from poverty.

Political motives—the USA has an embargo on trade with Cuba because it disagrees with Cuba's politics.

To pursue strategic trade policy—by being the first in the market and establishing a dominant position—see above.

To protect domestic producers from dumping by foreign companies or governments—dumping occurs when a foreign company charges a price in the domestic market which is 'too low'. In most instances 'too low' is generally understood to be a price which is lower in a foreign market than the price in the domestic market. In other instances 'too low' means a price which is below cost, so the producer is losing money.

Retaliation—to respond to another country's imposition of tariffs or some other restriction or against 'dumping'.

To prevent the import of undesirable products—drugs, live or endangered animals, and certain foodstuffs may be deemed undesirable.

To resist cultural imperialism and/or maintain a particular lifestyle.

Learning Task

1. Which of the above do you think is justified and which is not?
2. For each identify the costs and the benefits of the policy.

Control of Trade

On 7 November 2006 the General Council of the World Trade Organization (WTO) approved Vietnam's accession to membership making it the 150th member. The WTO was the successor organization to the General Agreement on Tariffs and Trade established in 1947 with just 23 members. In the depression of the 1930s many countries had suffered from falling exports and had tried to solve their problems by restricting imports. Of course others retaliated and the net effect was a reduction, by a third, of world trade in manufactured goods. These beggar-my-neighbour trade policies were in part responsible for the war so there was a determination to devise a system in which there was much more economic cooperation. A much more ambitious scheme, the International Trade Organization, was proposed—covering not only trading relations but also financial arrangements, but this was blocked by the USA. This left the GATT as the only mechanism for regulating trade until the establishment of the WTO. The aim of the GATT was the reduction of tariffs and liberalizing trade giving countries access to each other's markets.

GATT's, and now the WTO's principles are:

- **Non-discrimination**. A country should not discriminate between trading parties. Under the 'most favoured nation' rule a member has to grant to all members the most favourable conditions it allows trade in a particular product. Once goods have entered a country then the 'national treatment rule applies' in that they should be treated exactly the same as domestic goods.

- **Reciprocity**. If a member benefits from access and tariff reductions made by another member then it must reciprocate by making similar access and tariff reductions to that member.

- **Transparency**. Member's trade regulations have to be published so all restrictions can be identified.

- **Predictability and stability**. Members cannot raise existing tariffs without negotiation so everyone can be confident there will be no sudden changes.

- **Freeing of trade**. General reduction of all barriers.

- **Special assistance and trade concessions for developing countries**.

Under the GATT these principles were applied only to merchandise trade and then some sectors such as agriculture and textiles were ignored. These have now begun to be addressed under the WTO. Another weakness with the GATT was the lack of any effective process for settling disagreements and a deterrent against offenders. The WTO now has a dispute resolution process and is able to take sanctions against offenders as it did against the USA in 2002. Under pressure from domestic steel producers the American administration imposed tariffs on steel imports. WTO members reported this and the WTO allowed other members to impose retaliatory tariffs. The US tariffs were removed.

Trade negotiations have taken place in a series of 'rounds'. There have been nine of these rounds if we include the current and incomplete Doha round. These are summarized in the table on page 58.

Table 2.9 GATT/WTO rounds

Period	Round	Countries	Subjects
1947	Geneva	23	Tariffs
1949	Annecy	13	Tariffs
1950–51	Torquay	38	Tariffs
1955–56	Geneva	26	Tariffs
1960–61	Dillon	26	Tariffs
1964–67	Kennedy	62	Tariffs, anti-dumping measures
1973–79	Tokyo	102	Tariffs, non-tariff measures and framework agreements
1986–94	Uruquay	123	Tariffs, agriculture, textiles and clothing brought into GATT. Agreement on services (GATS). Intellectual property (TRIPS). Trade related Investment (TRIMS). Creation of WTO and dispute settlement
2001–	Doha	141	Not yet resolved

Source: WTO

The GATT was a fairly loose arrangement, but the WTO is a permanent organization dealing with a much wider range of issues. About three quarters of its members are less developed countries. Its top level decision-making body is the Ministerial Conference which meets at least every two years, but below this are other committees which meet on a regular basis. It has permanent offices in Geneva.

The GATT/WTO has been successful in reducing tariffs on industrial products from an average of about 40% in 1947 to something like 4% today, but whether it increases trade is the subject of debate. Trade has increased and, as we have seen, faster than world GDP— but is this because of the measures taken by the GATT/WTO? Not according to Andrew Rose (2004) who found that trade had increased, but for members and non-members alike. On the other hand Subramanian and Wei (2005) found that GATT/WTO had served to increase trade substantially (possibly by US$8 trillion in 2000 alone), but that the increase had been uneven. Industrial countries witnessed a larger increase in trade than did developing countries, bilateral trade was greater when both partners undertook liberalization, and those sectors that did not liberalize did not see an increase in trade.

The WTO is not without its critics, as we have witnessed with the demonstrations by anti-globalist protestors at the Ministerial Council meetings from Seattle in 1999 to Hong Kong in 2005. The major criticism is that it is a club which favours the developed countries, at the expense of the less developed countries. Decision-making is by consensus, often following many rounds of meetings which favour those countries with the resources to have representatives present at these meetings. Many of the less developed countries are excluded from this process. Other arguments against are that market access in industry is still a problem for less developed countries; anti dumping measures have increased; that there are still enormous agricultural subsidies in the developed world (see Chapter One), and labour standards and the environment are ignored.

Mini Case Vietnam's Entry to the WTO

On 7 November 2006, after 12 years of talks, WTO members voted for Vietnam to become a member. What does it mean for Vietnam? On the positive side it will mean that Vietnam's exports will face fewer restrictions in the form of quotas and tariffs. In particular, US and EU quotas on textile and garment exports will end, and Vietnam will compete on a level playing field with other exporters who, since the beginning of 2005, have enjoyed quota free trade. It will mean more investment from developed economies, keen to take advantage of Vietnam's abundance of young, highly motivated, low waged workers. WTO accession means that Vietnam has had to open its markets and implement a lot of regulatory reform, thereby making it safer and more attractive to overseas investment.

On the negative side it has had to remove agricultural export subsidies, reduce substantially or eliminate some industrial subsidies, and reduce import tariffs. All of this will make it much more difficult for domestic industry to compete. Foreign ownership ceilings in the services sector have also been raised. It will retain protection in some sectors while the economy adjusts to the new situation.

Source: Photodisc

Some of these problems have led to the suspension of the latest round of talks which began in Doha, Qatar, in 2001. The previous round of talks in Seattle had ended in failure, and a major disagreement between developed and developing countries—the latter accused the WTO of being for free trade whatever the cost, a charge which the WTO contests (see 10 common misunderstandings about the WTO at www.wto.org). Whatever their protestations, the package for discussion at the Doha round has been called the Doha Development Agenda.

Foreign Direct Investment

At the start of the 21st century, FDI inflows dipped. Subsequently however, the long term upward trend reasserted itself with companies increasing their expenditure significantly on investment abroad—inflows of FDI grew by almost 30% between 2004 and 2005 (UNCTAD 2006). The main recipients were developed countries, such as the UK, followed by the USA and China, and then France. While the amount of FDI received by poorer countries rose, particularly in the oil and natural resources sectors in Africa and West Asia, their share in the total dropped (Figure 2.3). Firms in the primary sector were particularly active in cross-border M&As. Nevertheless, the service sector remains the dominant player in cross-border M&As. Within services, finance firms (comprising investment and commodity firms, private equity firms, and hedge funds) accounted for almost one third of the value of M&A deals. Oil and gas firms were next in the league table, followed by the telecommunications sector. Manufacturing FDI appeared to be on a downward trend (see Figure 2.4) (UNCTAD 2006).

The surge in FDI was mainly driven by an 88% increase in the value of cross border mergers and acquisitions (M&As) to US$796 billion. Worthy of note is the increasing role played by developing countries as sources of FDI, especially from Brazil, India, Russia, and China—this group of countries is often called BRIC. In 2005, developing countries

Figure 2.3 Share of the top 5 FDI recipient countries, 1980–2005

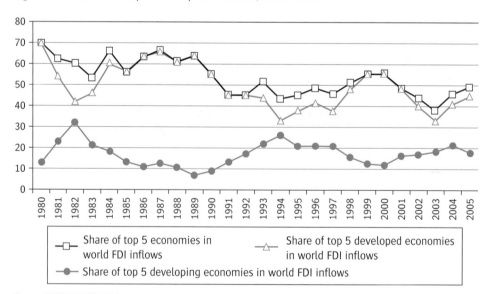

Source: UNCTAD, WIR 2006

invested US$117 billion abroad with China seeing a six fold increase in outward invest-
ments amounting to US$11 billion (UNCTAD 2006). Chinese, Indian, Brazilian, and
Middle Eastern companies have launched a string of ambitious takeover bids for Western
companies. For example, Dubai Ports World took over P&O Ferries; the Chinese electronics giant, TCL, acquired the television and DVD player operations of Thomson of
France; while its compatriot, Lenovo, agreed to buy IBM's personal computer business.
Some of these companies have grown fast enough to join the big global players. The China
National Petroleum Company (CNPC), for instance, is now 24 in the league table of the top
500 global companies. With regard to Indian companies, Ranbaxy is the ninth largest
pharmaceutical generics company in the world with more than three quarters of its revenues coming from overseas. Asian Paints is one of the 10 largest decorative paints makers in the world and has manufacturing facilities across 24 countries (Fortune Global 500,
2007 http://money.cnn.com; IBEF Research www.ibef.org).

Investment from poorer countries has been welcomed in the West. For instance, countries such as Italy, Germany, and US States like Illinois and South Carolina, with high rates
of unemployment, have made strenuous efforts to persuade Chinese companies to build
factories within their borders (*Financial Times,* 7 October 2005).

 Learning Task

Examine Figure 2.4, showing the breakdown of cross-border mergers by sector.

1. Comment on the changes in the relative importance of the primary, manufacturing, and service sectors in cross-border M&As.

2. How would you explain the increasing importance of the service sector in cross-border M&As?

3. What explanations could be advanced for the upturn in M&As in the primary sector after 2004?

Figure 2.4 Sectoral breakdown of cross-border M&A sales, 1987–2005

per cent

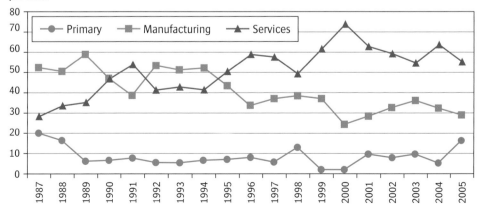

Source: UNCTAD

Divestment

Much attention is devoted to firms making the decision to invest abroad. However, business also goes in for divestment. Divestment occurs when a business reduces or disposes of its investment. This may be done because the firm wants to concentrate on more profitable activities. For example, BP divested its 270 petrol stations retail operations in Malaysia and Singapore in a move to cut poorly performing activities. Similarly, Wal-Mart withdrew from Germany and South Korea when it found that it could not compete with domestic rivals. The decision to divest could also be the result of an adverse change in the external environment. For example, as happened with the big oil majors, Exxon and Conoco Phillips when the Venezuelan Government wanted to exercise more control over its oil fields (*Financial Times*, 7 January 2004; *Business Week*, 28 July 2006; *USA Today*, 22 May 2006).

The Reasons for FDI

Businesses invest abroad for various reasons. The main motives can be summarized as:

- a quest for natural resources, particularly minerals and energy;
- the search for lower production costs;
- the need to get market access.

We look at each of these in turn.

Natural Resources

Businesses in the primary sector are the principal seekers of deposits of natural resources such as oil, gas, and other minerals. But deposits of natural resources are not spread evenly across the globe so resource-seeking firms such as mining groups like Rio Tinto and BHP Billiton and oil companies like Shell and Exxon must locate near deposits of natural resources.

With increasing demand for raw materials, from the fast growing economies of China and India, pulling up prices, combined with a lack of new deposits, mining companies are also looking to expand their deposits of mineral ores and their capacity to refine them (see Figure 2.5 for the fast-rising demand for minerals). To increase production capacity, Rio Tinto (one of the world's largest mining companies, mines for coal, copper, iron, bauxite, gold, titanium, lead, zinc, cobalt, nickel, and uranium) put in a bid in 2007 for the Canadian aluminium company Alcan (www.riotinto.com).

Oil companies face similar problems. Given the depletion of reserves in their current oil fields, and the rising price of oil, energy companies like BP, Exxon, and Shell are constantly on the look-out for new reserves. By 2005, firms in the oil and natural gas sector had become the most active acquirers of foreign firms—accounting for 14% of all cross-border M&As (UNCTAD 2006).

Competition from Developing Country MNCs

Western and Japanese MNCs not only compete with each other for access to natural resources, but also face increasing competition from companies based in poorer countries.

Figure 2.5 Growth in annual demand 2000–2006

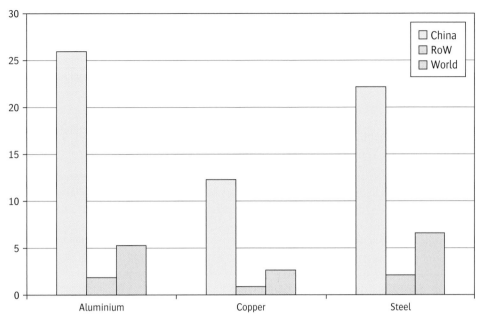

Source: Rio Tinto

In 2005, the Brazilian company CVRD bought Inco of Canada to become the second biggest mining group in the world. The following year, Mittal Steel, whose founder Lakshmi Mittal is of Indian origin, bought Luxembourg rival Arcelor for US$34 billion—thereby creating the world's biggest steel maker. Rusal, the Russian minerals company, became the largest aluminium company in the world when it took over another Russian company, SUAL, and the aluminium assets of the Swiss firm, Glencore. In the same year, Tata, one of India's biggest conglomerate firms, took over Corus, the European steel firm (Yahoo Finance; *Financial Times*, 22 November 2006 and 6 July 2007).

There is also fierce competition from China for resources. With just over 1.3 billion people, China is the world's most populous country and the second largest consumer of global oil supplies after the USA.

China's oil reserves are limited and its oil consumption, growing at 7% per annum, is almost double that of its output. By 2020, it is forecast that China will need to import 60% of its energy requirements. Ten years later, it is expected to have more cars than the USA, and to be one of the world's largest importers of oil. The Chinese authorities, well aware of their increasing dependence on imported oil, especially from the Middle East, have made aggressive efforts to secure oil and gas supplies all over the globe, in Africa, Latin America, and Central Asia. China National Offshore Oil Corp (CNOOC), a State-owned company, signed a deal to extract a million barrels of oil a day in Indonesia and a major contract to produce gas in Australia. China has also acquired interests in exploration and production in places like Kazakhstan, Russia, Venezuela, Sudan, West Africa, Iran, Saudi Arabia, and Canada. Latin America is also being targeted. China, in 2004, embarked on a

Mini Case China's Quest for Natural Resources

China is scouring the world for natural resources. It has been reported that Chinese officials visited every resource-heavy country in Africa in a bid to conclude long-term supply agreements with either governments or large corporations. In its attempt to clinch deals in Africa, China offered money to finance the development of infrastructure and trade. China has shown its willingness to take big risks by braving Africa's most volatile regions in its hunt for natural resources. CNOOC, the State-owned giant, won permission to search for oil in a violent and politically unstable Somalia—from which US oil companies had fled when the dictatorial regime was overthrown in the early 1990s. It also constructed oil pipelines in southern Sudan in the late 1990s when civil war raged between separatist rebels and the Islamist regime in Khartoum. Africa, with its enormous reserves of natural gas and oil has become the subject of fierce competition between energy companies. The oil is lower in sulphur than Middle Eastern crude which makes it cheaper to refine, and the geographic location allows easier delivery to Western markets. In 2005, the USA imported more oil from the Gulf of Guinea than it did from Saudi Arabia and Kuwait combined, and this is forecast to increase substantially. Western oil giants such as ExxonMobil, Chevron, France's Total, and Britain's BP and Shell plan to invest tens of billions of dollars in sub-Saharan Africa. Africa's oilfields have become an important battleground of influence between China, the USA, and India as they struggle to ensure they have sufficient energy to fuel future economic growth. It is forecast that Africa, which already contributes 12% of the world's liquid hydrocarbon production, will supply 30% of the world's growth by 2010.

Sources: *Financial Times*, 1 March 2006, 18 May and 14 July 2007; *New Statesman*, 18 June 2007; see also Ghazvinian 2007 and Taylor 2005)

US$100 billion investment programme in Latin America. It extended US$700 million in credit to Venezuela, and invested US$20 billion in Argentina (*The Times*, 20 July 2007). Chalco, China's largest metals and mining company, bought a Canadian company, Peru Copper, with interests in South America (*The Times*, 20 July 2007; *Financial Times*, 12 June 2007; see the Institute for the Analysis of Global Security web site at www.iags.org).

Lower Production Costs

Firms are often driven abroad by the need to find cheaper factors of production so as to cut costs. When jobs are transferred abroad, it is referred to as offshoring. This has gone on to such an extent that it is estimated that around 40% of US imports are produced by US companies, many of them in China (*Financial Times*, 10 July 2007).

With the increasing cost of labour in rich countries, industries, particularly labour intensive industries including textiles, clothing, and footwear, and firms assembling electronic components have looked abroad for cheaper locations. Financial institutions have also relocated data processing and call centre activities to countries such as India, as have computer manufacturers and internet service providers. Initially, firms transferred low level, unskilled or semi-skilled work to countries where labour was cheap, labour market regulation loose, and there was a low level of unionization of the work force. However, with the passage of time, firms have started to transfer higher level activities such as product design and development, as they discovered that developing countries also had pools of highly educated, technically qualified, and relatively cheap labour. In

Mini Case France—Offshoring

A growing number of French groups, including banks and tele-communications operators, have started moving their data-processing and customer relations activities to North Africa, particularly Morocco, to benefit from cheaper French-speaking staff and more flexible working hours. French business was slow to offshore in contrast to its USA and UK counterparts. This may, in part, be attributable to high levels of unemployment, and off-shoring being frowned upon by French politicians, and fiercely opposed by trade unions.

Nevertheless, by 2006, Axa, the giant French insurer, had three call centres in India employing 2,300 and serving cus-tomers in the UK, USA, Australia, and Japan. In 2006 it announced that the transfer of more operations to Argentina, India, Poland, and Morocco was under way in order to improve company competitiveness. By 2010, it intended to offshore over 5,000 jobs—resulting in savings of €100 million per annum. Axa, expecting 4,500 of its 16,000 staff in France to retire by 2012, hoped to avoid making staff redundant.

The announcement to open a call centre in Morocco employ-ing 1,500 staff triggered an angry reaction from trade unions. The unions claimed that the insurer had decided to open a call centre in Morocco after negotiations failed over company pro-posals for French staff to work later in the evenings and at weekends. Staff at Axa France work a 34-hour week. Unions promised to fight the plans.

Sources: European Works Council, Reports June and December 2006, www.amicustheunion.org; www.axa.com; *Financial Times*, 26 September 2006

India there is an abundance of well-trained programming, software-developer, and systems-engineering talent while China and Taiwan are developing world-class design expertise in specific technologies. Design is one of the most popular subjects at Chinese universities, and hundreds of design consulting firms have sprung up in cities such as Shanghai and Beijing (*CFO Magazine*, 17 March 2003; *CFO Magazine*, 29 June 2004; *Business Week*, 21 November 2005).

The savings in labour costs from offshoring can be substantial. A manufacturing worker costs, per hour: in the EU €15, in the USA well over US$20. A comparable worker in Mexico, Hong Kong, Taiwan, Portugal, or Singapore costs well under US$10 (Figure 2.6). In the computer and car industries, the Mexican production worker comes in at around a tenth of the cost of workers in the UK and the USA.

Labour savings also apply to white collar work. Project managers, software engineers, and accountants can all be much cheaper in developing countries. This is reflected in the figures produced by Mercer Consulting (Table 2.10). It is obviously much cheaper to employ staff in India and China than in the US or Europe.

The advantages of cheap labour in developing countries are likely to be offset to an extent by lower levels of productivity. As can be seen in Figure 2.7 productivity measured in terms of output (GDP) per head is much lower in the BRICs than in the USA. Russia and Brazil have productivity levels equivalent to around a seventh of the USA while China and India lag even further behind. However, productivity in manufacturing in the BRICs is likely to be higher than the figures suggest because low productivity sectors such as agri-culture are included and drag down the average.

One effect of these fast expanding economies is that wages and salaries have been increasing in countries like China and India, as demand for educated and technically

Figure 2.6 Hourly compensation costs, 2005, for production workers in manufacturing in US$

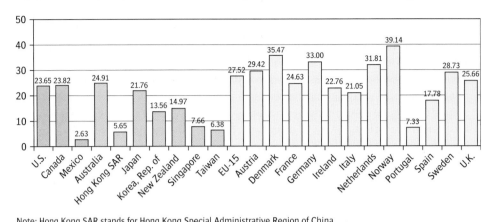

Note: Hong Kong SAR stands for Hong Kong Special Administrative Region of China.
Source: US Department of Labor

Table 2.10 Average annual pay

	China	India
Project manager	£12,173	£5,220
Software engineer	£6,998	£5,344
Accountant	£4,677	£2,956
Sales rep	£2,649	£2,464
Production worker	£1,214	£964

Source: Mercer Consulting

Figure 2.7 GDP per employed person, 1995 and 2004

(in 1990 US$ converted at PPP rates)

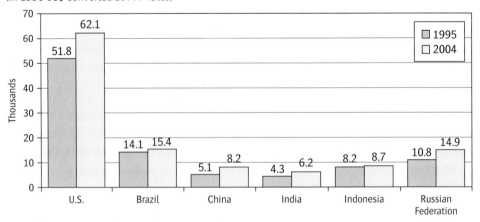

Note: Purchasing Power Parity (PPP) is the number of foreign currency units required to buy goods and services in a foreign country equivalent to what can be bought with one dollar in the United States.
Source: US Department of Labor

skilled workers starts to outstrip the supply of suitable candidates. Although the produc-tivity of Chinese workers is rising, in many industries it is not keeping pace with wages. Consequently, some MNCs may look elsewhere, like the Philippines, Thailand, and Indonesia where wages are much lower than in China or India (*The Economist*, 13 January 2007). South Korea is no longer as competitive, as far as blue-collar workers are con-cerned, but its engineers continue to be of high quality and will work up to 12 hours per day (*Financial Times*, 17 July 2007).

It has also been argued that MNCs, to avoid environmental regulations at home, have intentionally relocated polluting activities to developing countries, including China, where the authorities turn a blind eye to environmental damage (Zheng and Chen 2006). Christmann and Taylor (2001) contend that pollution-intensive MNCs have not taken advantage of lax environmental regulation in China. They found that MNCs were more likely than local firms to comply with local regulations and to adopt internationally recognized environmental standards.

Market Access

Business is interested in gaining entry to big markets or markets with the potential for growth. Thus Ernst and Young, the consultancy firm, found that France dominated UK outward investment activity because of the size of its consumer market and its proximity (*Financial Times*, 28 May 2007). The markets of the BRIC members, because of their rela-tively high rates of economic growth and purchasing power, are also attractive to MNCs. Income in China is estimated to be increasing by 11.4%, and in India by 9.2% per year (Figure 2.8).

A problem confronted by business is that attractive markets are sometimes protected from imports by barriers, such as tariffs like the USA levies on imports of steel, quotas such as those imposed by the EU on Chinese clothing and footwear, and countries such as China and Indonesia trying to ensure that a certain proportion of the cars sold there is manufactured locally. According to the OECD, there is a growing move towards protec-tionism in its member countries (OECD 2007). In order to circumvent these barriers, firms set up production facilities in the market. Another reason for locating near the mar-ket is that, for bulky, low value goods, transport costs can be prohibitive and it becomes imperative that firms produce close to their customers. Or it may be that retail firms like Tesco and Wal-Mart, construction companies, or providers of medical or education services have to be in face-to-face contact with their customers. It may also be that import-ant customers can precipitate a decision to invest abroad. When big car firms like Volkswagen and Fiat moved into Eastern Europe following the collapse of Communism, a large number of car component suppliers felt obliged to follow, given their customers' requirements for just-in-time deliveries (van Tulder and Ruigrok).

Other firms may feel the need to be close enough to respond quickly to alterations in market conditions, such as changes in taste or to provide speedy after-sales service.

Risk

Wars, hurricanes, terror attacks, uprisings, crime, earthquakes, and stock market crashes can bring companies to the brink, and sometimes tip them over the edge. Hurricanes Katrina and Rita, which in 2005 devastated Florida, Mississippi, Alabama, and gas and

Figure 2.8 Economic growth in BRIC countries

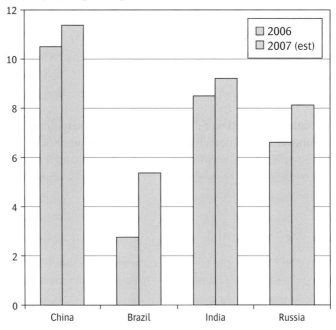

(annual percentage change in real GDP)

Source: International Monetary Fund, World Economic Outlook Database, April 2008

Mini Case FDI—Retailing in China

For foreign retailers, China offers unprecedented opportunity—the number of consumers is large and their purchasing power is expanding at a rapid rate. There is a huge and growing middle class with money to spend. Their numbers will rise from 42 million in 2005 to 200 million by 2015. Retail sales were expected to grow by 13% in 2006 to reach US$860 billion. In 2007 China had the world's seventh-largest retail market. It is forecast that annual compound growth rates of 8–10% will increase spending to some US$2.4 trillion by 2020.

And it is not simple day-to-day products selling at low prices that are in demand. There are more than one million affluent urban households who regularly buy luxury goods. Wal-Mart, in its Shenzen store, sells luxury duvets at US$14,000 and 65-inch television sets for US$15,000, and there is a high demand for Mercedes cars, BMWs, and designer goods from the likes of Dolce & Gabbana, Prada, Gucci, and Cartier. Because of this,

foreign retailers, like Wal-Mart, Tesco, and B&Q from the UK, Sweden's Ikea, Carrefour from France, and Malaysia's Parkson have scrambled to open outlets in China. Foreign retailers account for almost one quarter of the sales of the top 100 food retailers in China and more are struggling to get in. Between 2004 and 2006, the number of foreign retailers operating in China tripled to more than 1,000. The influx led to severe overcapacity and fierce price competition. Sales per square foot started to fall and profit margins shrank. Nevertheless, Wal-Mart continued to expand in China with a turnover of US$1.2 billion, but was thought to be making a loss in 2007. Carrefour was the biggest international retailer with 90 stores but China still accounted for less than 3% of group sales.

Source: *The Economist*, 5 August 2006; *Financial Times*, 13 and 14 February 2007

oil installations in the Gulf of Mexico led to the closure of a significant proportion of US oil refining capacity and to a fall of roughly 12% in oil production. BP lost 145,000 barrels of oil a day and some US$700 million in profit. The massive damage left the global insurance industry with a bill for US$80 billion. The price of insurance and re-insurance cover for areas of the world exposed to US hurricanes has also rocketed. A construction company agreed a contract in Nepal without seriously considering the implications of the uprising by Maoist rebels. Within weeks, a couple of its workers had died at the hands of rebels, and the roads on which the project relied had been blown up. The company was forced to pull out.

In today's more interconnected world, uncertainties can emerge almost anywhere as a result of product innovation, political change, changes in the law, or market deregulation.

Figure 2.9 The 23 core global risks: 10 yr horizon

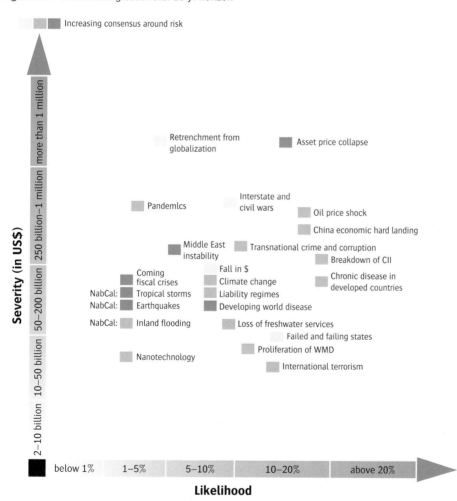

Note: Likelihood was based on actuarial principles where possible. For most risks, however, qualitative assessment was used.

Source: World Economic Forum *Global Risks 2007*

As business becomes more globalized—moving into new markets and transferring production to lower cost locations, it opens itself up to more risks, especially in countries with political instability and more vulnerability to natural catastrophes. International business needs to weigh up the risk factors when making strategic decisions on foreign direct investment (*Financial Times*, 30 August, 27 September and 5 October 2005, and 17 October 2006).

According to the World Economic Forum, the biggest risks confronting the global economy in 2007 were events associated with climate change (such as hurricanes and flooding), oil price shocks, pandemics like avian flu, and terrorism. Businesses can take out insurance against some of these risks, but this can be very costly. KPMG, the consultancy firm, estimates that only one quarter of the risks faced by a typical firm can be covered in a cost-effective way by insurance (*Financial Times*, 1 May 2007).

Risky Countries

Aon, the risk re-insurance company, regularly compiles a league table of countries in terms of the risk of doing business there with a local partner. For the three years up to 2006, the five riskiest countries were Afghanistan, Equatorial Guinea, Tajikistan, Syria, and Iraq (www.aon.com).

The oil industry, in particular, faces a very difficult and risky environment. Many countries involved in the supply chain for oil, gas, and other natural resources are volatile and politically unstable. The vast majority of the world's oil reserves, over 70%, are located in the Middle East and Africa (Figure 2.10). The authoritarian State of Saudi Arabia is the world's largest oil producer and exporter, claiming a quarter of the world's proven oil reserves, but its oil fields are off limits to the giant international oil companies because its government does not allow them to participate.

Figure 2.10 Distribution of proven oil reserves 2006

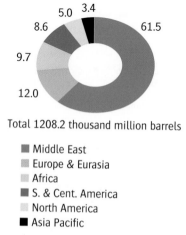

Total 1208.2 thousand million barrels

- Middle East
- Europe & Eurasia
- Africa
- S. & Cent. America
- North America
- Asia Pacific

Source: BP Statistical Review of World Energy 2007

Nigeria has vast reserves of oil but is also one of the poorest nations in the world with over 70% of Nigerians living in poverty. The oil industry remains under-developed as a result of political instability, corruption is rife, and rebel groups have declared war on foreign oil companies. This has led to a drastic reduction in production and exports. Violence and sabotage led oil companies, including Texaco and Shell, to suspend production entirely in 2006 following the murder and kidnap of industry personnel. The Chinese also encountered political problems in Somalia—an apparent power struggle between the prime minister and the president, who were members of different tribes, brought into question the oil deal signed by CNOOC (*Financial Times*, 17 July 2007).

Russia is one of the top 10 countries in terms of proven reserves and is the second largest oil exporter. Production has been rising, boosted by high oil prices. After the fall of Communism, Western oil companies were given access to Russian oil and gas resources. However, in the first decade of the 21st century, Russia has been clawing back control of its natural resources. In 2007, BP was forced to cede its controlling interest in a vast Siberian gas field to Gazprom, Russia's State controlled gas company. Shell was also obliged to concede a majority stake in its huge Sakhalin gas and oil project to the Russian company. These actions have not deterred the big oil companies, because they have found it increasingly difficult to get access to oil and gas reserves. Thus, they have been queuing up to get a stake in the Shtokman project, the world's second-biggest gas field. The oil firms are spurred on by the prospect of ever-increasing demand and higher prices and profits. The International Energy Agency foresees an oil energy crunch in the five years up to 2012, and tight gas markets by the end of the decade.

Countries like Venezuela have been tightening their grip on their oil industries, pushing to get a greater share of export earnings. In 2006 Bolivia nationalized its gas industry, and Indonesia cancelled a contract with Exxon regarding the development of South East Asia's largest undeveloped gas block in the South China Sea. Industry problems are compounded by the fact that many assets in places such as the Gulf of Mexico and the North Sea are past their peak and require massive investment to extend their lives (*Financial Times*, 30 May and 3 November 2006, 23 June, 10 and 13 July 2007).

Learning Task

Examine the map in Figure 2.11 which shows the location of Rio Tinto's current and potential operations.

1. Comment on the geographical location of Rio's operations.

2. Central Africa and Russia are virtual treasure troves of natural resources. Put forward possible reasons for Rio Tinto not having any operations in Russia or countries like the Congo.

3. Now compare and contrast the location of Rio's operation with that of BHP Billiton, another of the world's largest mining companies. Find out about Billiton's operation by going to the web site: http://hsecreport.bhpbilliton.com

Figure 2.11 Rio Tinto—location of natural resources

Source: Rio Tinto

● CHAPTER SUMMARY

In this chapter we have looked at the global pattern of wealth, international trade, and foreign direct investment. One way of comparing countries is to compare their respective GDP. This can be adjusted for purchasing power parity, which has the effect of narrowing the gap between rich and poor. The richest economy is still the USA, but China, in terms of PPP, is catching up quickly.

GDP indicates the different sizes of economies but doesn't say much about the standard of living—population has to be taken into account to give income per capita. In determining the degree of development the UNDP also looks at other indicators such as income inequality, life expectancy, literacy rates, and school enrolments. On any of these measures the world is still a very divided place when comparing the rich with the poor. Economic growth is seen as the key to raising standards of living.

All of this information is important to business in searching for new markets. Other indicators such as fixed line and mobile phone subscriptions can also be used.

International trade has increased, with exports in 1970 just 13% of world output whereas they are predicted to be 34% by 2030. Developing countries are increasing their share of trade in manufactures but this is still dominated by the triad nations. Countries trade with each other and world output increases, but history shows that the rich nations tend to benefit at the expense of the poor. There have been a number of theories put forward to explain the pattern of trade. Many countries impose restrictions, but the WTO works to liberalize trade. It has faced criticism because it is seen as a club which helps to maintain the established patterns of trade which favour the rich.

Foreign direct investment continues to grow in the quest for natural resources, lower production costs, and market access. This growth is mainly driven by cross border mergers and acquisitions. Developing countries, especially BRIC countries, are increasing sources of finance.

● REVIEW QUESTIONS

1. Why would it be useful for business to build up knowledge of the global distribution of income and wealth and how it is changing over time?

2. Analyse and explain the major trends in international trade. Discuss links between these trends and the changing distribution of world income.

3. Why is it that some firms locate their investments close to their markets whilst others appear to have the luxury of a much greater choice of location? Illustrate your answer with examples.

4. Analyse the changing importance of foreign trade and investment to the world economy. What are the implications of these changes for the level of risks faced by business?

5. What are the advantages to countries of foreign trade?
   In the light of these advantages, explain why, in 2005, the EU limited imports of clothing from China (the 'bra wars'). Which industries benefited from the limits and which lost out?
   For a discussion of the case see the article by Larry Elliott in *The Guardian*, 26 August 2005, and *Financial Times*, 7 September 2005.

6. Explain the rise of multinational companies based in developing economies.

Case Study BRICS

In a paper produced in 2003 Goldman Sachs predicted a very different looking world economy by 2050, with the possibility that the six largest economies could be, in order of size, China, USA, India, Japan, Brazil, and Russia. The triad of North America, Western Europe, and Japan has dominated world output for the last 30 years but this picture is changing. In 2005 the emerging markets accounted for nearly 50% of world output and could by 2050 account for 78% with the BRIC countries (Brazil, Russia, India, and China) accounting for 44%.

In 2005 the combined GDP of the BRIC economies was 15% of the combined GDP of the G6 (USA, Japan, Germany, UK, France, and Italy). By 2025 it could be 50% and have exceeded it by 2050. This is not to say that individuals will be wealthier in the BRIC economies than in the G6 economies, but they will be much wealthier than they are today.

China is in a league of its own within the BRIC. It already accounts for 15% of world output (measured by PPP GDP), and nearly 7% of world exports. It has overtaken Italy, France, and the UK in terms of economic size and will soon overtake Germany. It has been a magnet for FDI, attracting nearly US$240 billion between 2002 and 2005—more than Brazil (US$59.8bn), India (US$22.3bn), and Russia (US$41.5bn) put together.

Although China and India both have populations of over 1 billion they are very different. China's growth has come through manufacturing while India has grown through software systems and call centres. Russia and Brazil have much smaller populations and their growth has come from endowments of primary products—raw materials in Brazil and massive energy resources in Russia. Brazil also has a growing industrial sector, especially machinery and transport.   ➔

→ **Table 2.11** BRIC Economies 2005 and 2050

Country	2005			Growth to 2050 (% per annum)		2050		
	Pop (m)	GDP (US$bn)	GDP per head (US$)	Pop	GDP	Pop (m)	GDP (US$bn)	GDP per head (US$)
Brazil	186	1,536	8,258	.8	3.5	266	7,223	27,131
Russia	142	1,584	11,155	.2	3.4	155	7,131	45,903
India	1,103	3,666	3,324	.9	6.4	1,651	59,781	36,215
China	1,313	8,883	6,765	.5	6.0	1,643	122,271	74,402
USA	298	12,310	41,309	.7	2.7	408	40,825	100,089

Source: International Business Report 2007, Emerging Markets, Grant Thornton

The USA is currently the main export market for China, India, and Brazil but China and India are already developing strong trade links with each other. Regional trade links are important for all the BRIC economies.

Questions

Given the above scenario:

1. What are the implications for international business and its markets?

2. Explore the impact on the demand for, and the prices of, natural resources.

3. In light of your answer to question 2, analyse the effects on natural resource companies in Brazil and Russia.

4. Go on to assess what this would mean for large industrial consumers of natural resources elsewhere.

5. Multinational companies, based in the BRIC countries such as Tata and Gazprom, have been extending their international operations. What are the implications for business in other countries were many other BRIC firms to follow the example of Tata and Gazprom?

Source: www.istockphoto.com

Online Resource Centre
www.oxfordtextbooks.co.uk/orc/hamilton_webster/

Visit the supporting online resource centre for additional material which will help you with your assignments, essays and research, or you may find these extra resources helpful when revising for exams.

● FURTHER READING

For a historical account of the evolution of world trade up to the 21st century see:

● Findlay, R. and O'Rourke, K. H. (2007) *Power and Plenty: Trade, War, and the World Economy*. Princeton, New Jersey: Princeton University Press

For an in-depth analysis of the Chinese economy and its relationship with global trade see:

● Eichengreen, B., Chui, Y. and Wyplosz, C. (eds). (2008) *China, Asia, and the New World Economy*. Oxford: Oxford University Press

For an application and extension of the Porter diamond to national competitiveness see:

● Stone, H. B. and Ranchhod, A. (2006) 'Competitive advantage of a nation in the global arena: a quantitative advancement to Porter's diamond applied to the UK, USA and BRIC nations'. Strategic Change, Vol 5, Issue 6

● Özlem, Ö. (2002) 'Assessing Porter's framework for national advantage: the case of Turkey'. *Journal of Business Research*, Vol 55, Issue 6, June

Rugman has been one of the main critics of the Porter diamond. See:

● Rugman, A., Verbeke, A. and Van Den Broeck, J. (eds) (1995) *Research in Global Strategic Management: Volume V Beyond the Diamond*. Greenwich, Conn.: JAI Press

● REFERENCES

Christmann, P. and Taylor, G. (2001) 'Globalization and the Environment: Determinants of Firm Self-Regulation in China'. *Journal of International Business Studies*, Vol 32, No 3, Third Quarter

Ghazvinian, J. (2007) *Untapped: The Scramble for Africa's Oil*. Orlando: Harcourt

International Monetary Fund, World Economic Outlook Database, April 2008

Leontieff, W. (1953) 'Domestic production and foreign trade: The American capital position reexamined'.

Proceedings of the American Philosophical Society, Vol 97 November

Linder, S. B. (1961) *An Essay on Trade and Transformation*. New York: Wiley

OECD (2006) *Agricultural Policies in OECD Countries: At a Glance*

OECD (2006) *Observer*, June

OECD (2007) *Factbook*

Porter, M. (1990) 'The Competitive Advantage of Nations'. *Harvard Business Review*, March–April

Ricardo, D. (1817) *On the Principles of Political Economy and Taxation*. London: John Murray

Schneider, F. and Enste, D. (2002) *Shadow Economies Around the World: Size, Causes, and Consequences*. IMF working paper WP/00/26

Rose, A. (2004) 'Do WTO Members have More Liberal Trade Policy?', *Journal of International Economics*

Smith, A. (1776) *An Inquiry into the Nature and Causes of the Wealth of Nations*. Oxford: Clarendon Press

Subramanian, A. and Wei, S.-J. (2005) 'The WTO Promotes Trade, Strongly But Unevenly', CEPR Discussion Papers 5122

Taylor, I. (2006) 'China's oil diplomacy in Africa', *International Affairs*, Vol 82, Issue 5

US Department of Labor (2007) *A Chart of International Labor Comparisons: The Americas, Asia-Pacific, Europe*. Available at www.dol.gov

van Tulder, R. and Ruigrok, W. (undated) *International Production Networks in the Auto Industry: Central and Eastern Europe as the Low End of the West European Car Complexes*. Available at http://repositories.cdlib.org

UNCTAD (2006) *World Investment Report—FDI from Developing and Transition Economies: Implications for Development*

Vernon, R. (1966) 'International investments and international trade in the product life cycle'. *Quarterly Journal of Economics*

World Bank (2007) Global Economic Prospects: Managing the Next Wave of Globalisation

Zheng, Y. and Chen, M. (2006) *China Moves to Enhance Corporate Social Responsibility in Multinational Companies*. Briefing Series, Issue 11, August. University of Nottingham: China Policy Institute

CHAPTER THREE

Analysing Global Industries

LEARNING OUTCOMES

This chapter will enable you to:

- Distinguish between the concept of market and industry

- Identify various market structures and their implications for competition and performance

- Measure market concentration, analyse it, and explain the link with market power

- Explain and use the Porter Five Forces model for industry analysis

- Explain, compare, contrast, and interpret different official systems of Industrial classification

Case Study Worldwide Spirits Market

This case study looks at the spirits market worldwide. It identifies the products and market shares of the major players in the market and illustrates how the market power of the largest firms can vary from product to product and from one geographical area to another.

The geographical focus of the case is the Americas, both North and South, Asia-Pacific, and Europe. Spirits products include brandy, gin and genever, liqueurs, rum, speciality spirits, tequila and mezcal, vodka, and whisky. The spirits market grew slowly, at a rate of just over 2% per year, between 2002 and 2006 when total sales reached US$187.4 billion and a volume of 16.4 billion litres. The value of sales was faster than that of volume which grew at less than 1% per annum. Growth in the spirits market is expected to slow with the value of sales forecast to reach some US$217 billion by 2011.

Speciality spirits, whisky, and vodka each account for more than 20% of spirit sales and, together, hold more than two thirds of the world market. In contrast, sales of brandy account for less than 10% of the market. Europe is the largest market in the world accounting for nearly one half, followed by the Americas with around 30% and Asia-Pacific with just over a fifth.

Looking at Figure 3.1 below, it appears that the spirits market does not appear to be highly concentrated because none of the major players have big market shares. The three largest, UK-based multinational Diageo, Russia's Cristall and Jinro from

Source: www.diageo.com

South Korea together have around 13% of the world market by volume. Other important multinationals in the market are: the French firm Pernod Ricard, with brands such as Chivas Regal whisky, Beefeater, and Seagram gin; the US company Fortune Brands selling Canadian Club whisky and Sauza tequila; and the Bermuda-based firm Bacardi.

However, the picture changes significantly when the market is broken down by type of spirit and by geographical area. Leading companies have a stable of well established branded products. Diageo, for example, sells Johnnie Walker whisky, Smirnoff vodka, Captain Morgan rum, and Baileys. Whilst it only holds around 5% of the world spirits market, in the USA it has almost half of the market for blended whisky and the Smirnoff brand accounts for about one in every five bottles of vodka sold. In comparison, Pernod Ricard, with its Jameson brand, accounts for around 90% of all Irish whiskey sold in the USA and is the leading supplier of gin in that market. Fortune Brands, a relatively small player in the global spirits market has over one quarter of the world market for white spirits.

Branding is very important in this market. In the USA and Europe, suppliers are faced by large and powerful distributors like Wal-Mart, Tesco, and Aldi. Spirits producers therefore have a great incentive to spend lots of time and money on marketing campaigns to differentiate their products. Successful branding campaigns weaken the bargaining power of the big retailers who are obliged to stock the brands that customers are demanding. Effective branding also protects suppliers from competition from their rivals and acts as a barrier to new entrants.

Spirits producers face a degree of competition from other alcoholic and non-alcoholic drinks but companies such as Diageo are cushioned to the extent that they have diversified into the beer and wine markets.

Source: Datamonitor, Global Spirits, October 2007; International Wine Centre, The US Spirits Market, October 2004; *Financial Times*, 6 April 2005; www.diageo.com; www.pernod-ricard.

Figure 3.1 Global Market Share by volume 2006

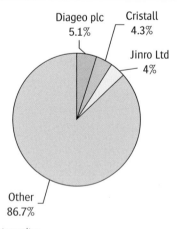

Diageo plc
5.1%

Cristall
4.3%

Jinro Ltd
4%

Other
86.7%

Source: Datamonitor

Introduction

In this chapter we develop the knowledge and skills necessary to carry out analyses of industries. We start off by examining the concepts of the market and the industry. In line with other authors we see the terms market and industry as being interchangeable. Various market structures are then explored along with their implications for the nature and intensity of competition and company performance. We go on to look at **market concentration**, how it is measured, and the implications of different levels of concentration for the distribution of market power among firms in the industry. The Five Forces of Porter's model provide a set of tools that allow a systematic and comprehensive analysis of industries. Each force is explained and applied to various industries along with a sixth force, **complementary products**. Finally, we compare and contrast the industrial classification systems used in North America, the EU, and by the United Nations. These systems lay down principles for defining an industry and then collect and classify data on each industry. The systems generate a mass of business information that can be useful in the international comparison and analysis of industries. An understanding of how the different systems classify industries is a vital element in the toolkit of the industry analyst.

The term 'global' is used liberally in this chapter. We use it on occasions where multiple countries are involved. This usage varies from other authors who interpret the word as meaning worldwide, that is covering most countries in the world.

The Market and the Industry

Analysing markets and industries involves building up a detailed knowledge of the competing firms in the industry, the goods and services they are producing, and the geographical markets where they compete.

Defining the market involves several steps:

- deciding which goods or services to include;
- identifying the firms competing in the market;
- indicating the geographical area where those firms are competing.

First, it is important to identify products or services that customers see as very similar. Economists use a concept called the **cross elasticity of demand** which measures the response of customers when one firm changes its price. If the price of a product increases and customers switch in large numbers to other cheaper products, then economists conclude that the products can be classified to the same market. In other words, there is a high cross elasticity of demand because customers see the products as being very good substitutes. One would expect to see this effect were an oil company like BP to raise the price of petrol on the forecourt to a level higher than competitors, Esso and Shell. This allows us to identify competitors because the firms making products with a high cross elasticity of demand are then defined as being part of the same industry. However, if very few customers transfer their business to the cheaper goods then the products are not seen by consumers as good alternatives and the firms cannot be classified to the same industry. The concept of cross elasticity, while neat in a theoretical sense, can be difficult to use in practice. Usually, the information required to calculate the cross-elasticity is not available. In the absence of data on cross elasticity, some observers look out for evidence that show businesses reacting regularly to decisions made by other firms. Signs of such interdependence among firms indicate that they see themselves as competitors. For example, if one firm lowers price or increases spending on advertising and others regularly follow suit, then those firms who end up pursuing similar policies could be seen as members of the same industry. Another approach is to identify firms whose actions as regards, for example, pricing, advertising, and sales promotion are constrained by others. To take the example of low cost airlines, it would be understandable were firms such as Ryanair and easyJet constrained in their pricing policies by the possible reaction of the other.

Classifying firms to a particular industry may not be as straightforward as it first appears. Car firms are often seen as operating in the same industry. But it would hardly be sensible to view the Rolls Royce as a direct competitor to a Mini or a Fiat Punto. It would make more sense, for our purposes, to consider car manufacturers as producing for a series of markets, from the most basic models to the luxury end of the market. Diversified firms also complicate the picture. Companies, producing a range of goods, may end up being classified to several industries. Take domestic appliance manufacturers such as Whirlpool, Electrolux, or LG, the South Korean multinational. They make various appliances including washing machines, dishwashers, and electric cookers—these products can hardly be seen as close substitutes, so the companies could be seen as competing in various markets, for washing machines, dishwashers, and electric cookers. Of course, the fact that diversified firms like these can offer customers like retailers the ability to source a range of products from a single company may put such firms at a competitive advantage against rivals offering a more limited range. Companies operating at several stages of production of a product can also complicate the issue of how to classify them. Examples of vertically integrated firms can be found in the oil industry where companies like Shell, Exxon, and BP drill for oil, refine it, and sell it on the forecourt. They could be classified to three industries: drilling, refining, and retailing. The media sector also provides an illustration with groups like News International producing films and distributing them through their television and satellite broadcasting companies.

Another aspect of the market that needs to be clarified is its geographical boundaries. Firms located in different places could be producing similar products, but not actually competing against each other in the same geographical market place. Geographical distance may mean that the cost of transporting goods from one area to the other is not economical so, in reality, the firms in one area are not competing with firms in the other. There are a variety of factors which keep markets separate, such as geographical distance, or poor transport infrastructure. For example, in poor countries in Africa and South East Asia the lack of road and rail networks may keep markets fragmented, whereas in the developed economies of Northern Europe improving transport links have integrated previously distinct markets. Firms may also set out deliberately to keep markets separate. Car producers do this in Western Europe. Traditionally, they have charged significantly higher prices in the UK than in countries like Belgium and the Netherlands. They hope that

British customers will not realize that prices are cheaper across the Channel and therefore will not hop across to get their cars from Belgian or Dutch dealers. UK customers who recognize that they can get a lower price on the Continent, and try to buy there, have found that distributors may claim that they are out of supplies or that they do not have access to right-hand drive cars. The EU Commission found Volkswagen guilty of discriminating in price between customers in Southern Germany and those in Northern Italy. German consumers were richer than the Northern Italians so they could afford to pay more. VW, so long as it could keep the two markets separate, increased profits by charging more in Germany than in Italy. Economists identify the geographical boundaries of the market by assessing the extent to which a price increases in one area:

- attracts competition from firms elsewhere. For example, had the high prices charged by VW in Southern Germany attracted many car dealers from Northern Italy lured by the prospect of higher profits, then the two regions could be classified as one market.

- drives customers away to cheaper areas. VW's high prices in Germany could have led many German car buyers to go to Italy to get a better deal. The two areas could be seen as part of the same geographical market had many German consumers taken that route. Such behaviour can be seen in southern England where consumers get the ferry across to France to buy cheaper alcohol and tobacco. Similarly, French buyers of alcohol and tobacco products flock to the small Spanish towns on the border where the prices of these products are much lower than in France.

Market Structures

There is a variety of market structures ranging from the pure monopoly to the perfectly competitive (see Table 3.1). In a pure monopoly, one firm dominates the market usually protected from competition by high barriers to entry (barriers to entry are explained in more detail in the discussion of Force 2, Competition from new entrants, of Porter's model). Such firms control the market and can set prices to extract maximum profit from their customers. Consumers have to pay the price because they have no alternative suppliers to turn to. In a globalizing world economy, one rarely encounters pure

Table 3.1 Types of Market Structure

Type of market structure	Number of firms	Barriers to entry	Nature of product
Perfect competition	Very many	None	Homogeneous
Monopoly	One	High	Unique
Monopolistic competition	Many	None	Heterogeneous
Oligopoly	Few	Often high	Homogeneous/Differentiated

monopoly outside the pages of basic economics textbooks although some markets, at times, may come close. For example, Wrigley accounts for around 90% of the UK chewing gum market, although only 35% worldwide while Microsoft accounts for 95% of the world market for desktop operating software (*Financial Times*, 19 October 2005; Confectionery News.com, 25 October 2006; EU Commission press release, IP/07/1567).

Market structure can be influenced by the costs incurred by business. Very high **fixed costs** can result in the creation of what is termed a natural monopoly. To survive, firms need to produce on a very large scale relative to the size of the market to generate sufficient revenues to cover their fixed costs. Examples of natural monopolies include gas, water, electricity, and telephone networks. It is very expensive to build transmission networks of pipelines for water and gas and electricity and telephone lines. The result is a market with a single producer having an overwhelming cost advantage over potential competitors. Such rivals are deterred from entering the market by the high capital investment involved and the dominant market position of the monopolist.

In perfectly competitive markets, large numbers of firms are completely free to enter and to leave the market, no individual firm can control the market, price is set by the forces of supply and demand, and buyers and sellers have complete knowledge of market conditions. Profit levels are just enough to keep firms in business. Any profits above that level are quickly eroded away by competition from entrants attracted to the market by the prospect of high profits. **Perfect competition**, where there are many firms supplying identical products with no entry barriers, is difficult to find in the real world. In reality, markets are usually imperfect—they can be costly to enter and dominated by a small number of firms who set prices, differentiate their products, earn abnormally high profits, and comprise buyers and sellers who have gaps in their knowledge of market conditions.

Another market structure is **monopolistic competition** with large numbers of firms, no barriers to entry, and only a small degree of product differentiation. The corner shop, convenience store segment of the retail market could be seen as monopolistically competitive with a large number of outlets, ease of entry, and each differentiated by their location.

In reality, most manufacturing and many service sector industries operate in oligopolistic markets where there are few firms, often protected by high entry barriers and able to exercise some control over the market. In oligopolistic markets, firms often try to differentiate their products from those of their competitors in the branding, advertising, packaging, and design of their goods and services. Firms that are successful in convincing consumers that their products are different, such as Apple with its Mac computer and the iPod, can charge higher prices and not lose custom. Oligopolists, when formulating their policies, have to take into account that their actions could affect their rivals' sales, market share, and profits and are therefore likely to provoke a reaction. For example, a price reduction by one of the players might spark off a price war where competitors try to undercut each other. The end-result could be cut-throat competition with some firms going out of business.

In order to avoid such competition, oligopolists sometimes set up **cartels**. These, usually operating in secret, aim to control competition through the firms in the market agreeing to set common prices or to divide the market geographically amongst cartel members. A UK example of this found bus companies, Arriva and First avoiding competition by dividing bus routes between them. Work by Connor (2002) suggests that global cartels are widespread. He talks of 'a global pandemic' of international cartels and a 'resurgence of global price fixing' (p 1).

Market structure can influence the behaviour of firms in the industry and the nature and intensity of competition. In perfect competition, firms cannot set their own pricing policy because price is determined by the market and there would be no point in trying to differentiate one's goods or services in a perfectly competitive market because consumers see the products as identical.

In comparison, a monopolist is free to pursue an independent pricing policy. In addition, monopolists, facing no competition, do not need to try to differentiate their products. On price, oligopolists can usually exercise some influence although they must take into account the possible reactions of their competitors. Furthermore, in oligopoly, especially when selling to the final consumer, firms make strenuous efforts to differentiate the product through, for example, their marketing and sales promotion activities. For instance, the food and drink industries in the UK spent nearly £800 million on advertising in 2006 whilst in the USA, firms producing perfumes, cosmetics, and toiletries spent the equivalent of almost 14% of their sales revenues on promoting their products. Procter and Gamble, the large producer of toiletries and other personal care products, was the leading US advertiser with an annual spend of over US$3 billion (*New Media Age*, 10 November 2007; Controller's report November 2007; Taylor Nelson Sofres Media Intelligence).

Market structure can also influence company performance. The intensity of competition can affect profitability. In very competitive markets, profits are likely to be lower than they would be were those markets to turn into an oligopoly or a monopoly.

 Learning Task

The European Commission was asked to decide whether a proposed merger between a firm producing instant coffee and one making ground coffee had any implications for competition. To come to a decision, the Commission had to determine whether the firms were competing in the same market. There was no statistical information available to estimate the cross elasticity of demand between instant and ground coffee.

Do you think consumers see these products as good alternatives?

One way to determine this is to compare the prices for both products. A major price difference could indicate that they are not good alternatives. Check prices at your local supermarket. You could also survey your fellow students to find out whether they see the two products as significantly different. An important indication that they are in different markets would be the willingness of the students to pay more for one than the other.

Market Power

The distribution of power amongst firms in an industry is measured by the level of market concentration which can be measured by looking at the market share of firms in the industry. Market concentration gives an indication of the competitive pressures in a market. High concentration levels usually indicate that competition will be of low intensity. Big firms in highly concentrated markets will be able to determine prices, the quantity and quality of output they are prepared to supply, and to force policies on reluctant customers. Thus, Coca Cola dominates the EU's carbonated soft drinks market. In both France and Belgium, Coke has 60% plus of the market compared to Pepsi's 5 or 6%. The EU found that the company had stifled competition by obliging customers to stock only Coke drinks and forced them to take less popular brands such as Sprite and Vanilla Coke (Hamouda; EU Commission press release, IP/04/1247, 19 October 2004). In the desktop software market there is a high level of concentration indicating low levels of competition. Microsoft, with its 95% market share, dwarfs its rivals and has the ability to exercise control over the market. The European Commission found that Microsoft used its market power to shut out competitors by bundling software programmes together in its Windows package and refusing to supply rivals with technical information allowing them to make their products compatible with Windows (see EU Commission press release, IP/04/382 and *The Economist*, 20 September 2007). Pure monopoly demonstrates the highest level of concentration with one firm holding 100% of the market. At the other extreme, in perfect competition, power is distributed equally amongst firms and as a result the level of market concentration is low. In oligopoly, a few firms dominate the market and the level of market concentration is usually high. The world beer market is a good illustration of this. As can be seen in Figure 3.2 eight firms account for more than half of global beer sales with the biggest, Inbev, the Belgian producer of Stella Artois beer, and SABMiller together holding more than one quarter (*Guardian*, 18 October 2007).

There are various ways of measuring market concentration. The most straightforward method is the concentration ratio (CR). This is usually calculated by taking the share of

Figure 3.2 World Beer Market Share by volume 2007

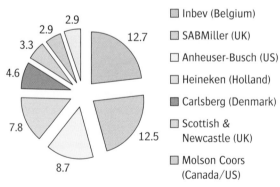

Inbev (Belgium)
SABMiller (UK)
Anheuser-Busch (US)
Heineken (Holland)
Carlsberg (Denmark)
Scottish & Newcastle (UK)
Molson Coors (Canada/US)

Source: *The Guardian*, 18 October 2007

the largest firms in industry sales or output by value or by volume. Figure 3.2 shows the market shares, by volume, of the eight largest firms in the industry, a CR8 of 55.4%. The CR4 is 41.7% with Inbev, SABMiller, Anheuser-Busch, and Heineken the four biggest firms together holding more than two fifths of the market. Were a merger to take place, say between SABMiller and Carlsberg, then the combined company would become the biggest company with a market share of 17.1% and the CR4 would increase to 46.3%.

A second method of calculating market concentration is provided by the Herfindahl-Hirschmann Index (HHI). The HHI is calculated by summing the squares of the individual market shares of all the firms in the market. The HHI gives proportionately greater weight to the market shares of the larger firms. It gives a more accurate picture than the concentration ratio because it includes all firms in the calculation. Sometimes, there is a lack of information about the market shares of very small firms but this may not be important because such firms do not affect the HHI significantly. For example, a market containing five firms with market shares of 40%, 20%, 15%, 15%, and 10%, respectively, has an HHI of 2,550 ($40^2 + 20^2 + 15^2 + 15^2 + 10^2 = 2,550$). The HHI ranges from close to zero in a perfectly competitive market to 10,000 in the case of a pure monopoly. The EU Commission sees an HHI of more than 1,000 in a market as indicating a level of concentration that could have adverse effects on competition. The Commission will be especially concerned where firms are protected by high entry barriers and where their market position faces little threat from innovation. It feels the same way when the share of largest firm in the market, that is the CR1, exceeds 40%. Consequently, in these markets, the Commission will be looking out for evidence of firms abusing their market power and will examine closely proposed mergers between firms in these markets that would raise concentration to an even higher level (see Verouden 2004; and Pleatsikas and Teece 2001).

Concentration figures can also be affected by the geographical focus of the information. For instance, Figure 3.3 shows Lenovo, the Chinese multinational, holding 8.3% of the world market for personal computers far behind that of the market leaders, HP and Dell.

Figure 3.3 Worldwide PC Market Share

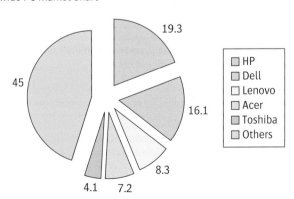

Source: *Financial Times*, 8 August 2007

However, a switch in geographical focus to the Asia-Pacific region changes the picture dramatically because Lenovo accounted for almost one fifth of the market.

What this shows is that a market can appear to be quite highly concentrated at one geographical level but fragmented at another. While Inbev holds around 13% of the world market for beer, the figure is nearer 70% in Brazil (www.bbc.co.uk).

Learning Task

1. Use the information on market shares in Table 3.2 to work out an HHI for the European beer market. Assume that the remaining firms in the beer market only hold tiny shares and that their inclusion would not significantly distort the result.

2. On the basis of your answer, discuss whether the EU Commission would be concerned, on competition grounds, were SABMiller to propose a takeover of S&N.

3. How does changing the geographical focus from the world to Europe affect the picture you get of market concentration? For example, are the same companies the market leaders in both Europe and the world? How does the CR1, 2, 3, and 4 in Europe compare with the world concentration ratios?

Table 3.2 Market Share by volume—Europe 2004

Company	% share
S&N	13.2
Heineken	11.6
Inbev	10.6
SABMiller	7.0
Other	57.6
Total	100

Source: Datamonitor, Beer—Europe, December 2006

Analysing Industries—A Framework

Porter provides a useful framework for analysing the competitive environment of an industry (Porter 1979; 2008). His Five Forces model can be used to identify and evaluate the main threats to the firms in an industry (Figure 3.4).

The Porter model is often used in combination with other complementary tools such as the PESTLE model (Chapter Four) that focuses on the wider environment or the resource-based view (RBV). While Porter focuses on the firm's external environment, the RBV tool concentrates on evaluating how the firm's internal resources and capabilities such as patents and trade marks or the success of the company in establishing a successful reputation for itself and its brands can be used to achieve and sustain competitive advantage (see Fahy 2007).

Three of the forces are concerned with competition. The first, and most important, is industry rivalry which involves competition from rivals already established in the industry. Next there is competition from new entrants to the industry. Third, the industry may have to confront competition from products which carry out the same function for customers but provide the service in a radically different way. For example, trains and planes

Mini Case Market Concentration in the Energy Market

This case concerns the high levels of market concentration in the energy markets of member states of the EU and the attempts by the Union to create a single electricity and gas market out of 27 separate national markets.

In the EU there are very high levels of market concentration in national gas and electricity markets. In 2004, the three largest firms in 10 member states accounted for more than 80% of the gas market. This indicates the low levels of competition in these markets. The UK had the lowest CR3 at 39% (see Table 3.3).

The sector had seen attempts at mergers by the already powerful national producers and also an increasing number of cross-border acquisitions such as the takeover of Scottish Power by Iberdrola, the Spanish energy company and that of Innogy, the UK's largest electricity supplier, by RWE of Germany. In certain electricity markets, there also appeared to be a tendency towards growing vertical integration between generators and distributors which would increase the power of the market leaders.

The EU as part of the Single Market programme set out to increase cross-border competition by removing barriers that were holding back the integration of separate national markets. That the markets were indeed separate was indicated by the significant price differences between the member states and the low level of cross-border trade.

Cross-border flows of electricity for instance in 2004 stood at around 10.7% of total consumption, an increase of only about 2 percentage points compared to 2000. Establishment of a single market would increase trade and competition and lead to a narrowing of the price differentials across the EU, or at least between adjacent member states or regions. The Commission found that price differences for electricity for industrial customers in the EU were more than 100% in some cases.

The main barrier to market integration in electricity was identified as a lack of interconnection capacity which made it difficult to produce electricity in one country and sell it in another. Another important obstacle was the tendency by suppliers to tie in their customers through long-term contracts. The Commission found that there had been very few new entrants to the market, hardly surprisingly, given the market power of the established suppliers and the high barriers to entry.

Table 3.3 Market Concentration in the Wholesale Gas Market

Share of the 3 Largest Producers, 2004*	
Austria	54%
Belgium	95%
Denmark	40%
Finland	40%
France	96%
Germany	72%
Greece	97%
Ireland	93%
Italy	65%
Luxembourg	88%
Netherlands	69%
Portugal	76%
Spain	74%
Sweden	40%
UK	39%
Norway	40%
Estonia	95%
Latvia	95%
Lithuania	92%
Poland	45%
Czech Rep.	76%
Slovakia	86%
Hungary	66%
Slovenia	87%

* Norway is not a member of the EU.
Source: EU Commission 2005 and 2006; *Financial Times*, 7 March 2002; Reuters UK, 23 April 2007

Figure 3.4 Porter's 'Five Forces' Model

Source: Porter 2008

both transport customers from points A to B but in a different way and consumers can get access to music by buying CDs or downloading it from the internet—it is a substitution in use. Porter calls these products, substitutes. The inclusion of this particular force helps get around problems of a precise identification of the industry. For example, in the market for luxury cars we might include firms producing Rolls Royces, Bentleys, and Mercedes because we see them as having a high cross elasticity of demand. Such a definition would exclude competition from sailing yachts or motorized vessels but these could be analysed using the substitution force in the Porter model.

The other forces are concerned with the industry customers and suppliers. We go through each of the forces in turn.

Force 1 Industry Rivalry

Industry rivalry can vary in form and intensity from one industry to the other and in particular industries over time. At one point in the 1980s, telecommunications companies like BT, France Telecom, and Deutsche Telecom in Germany were seen as national flagship companies, had very powerful market positions, and were protected by the law preventing other firms entering the industry. There was little competition to speak of. This changed in the subsequent 20 years as barriers to entry fell and they faced up to fiercer competition generated by new entrants, like Vodafone, to the industry.

Competition usually occurs in one or more of the following areas: price, advertising and sales promotion, distribution, and improvements in existing goods and services or the introduction of completely new products. This area of competition is particularly important in industries such as electronics—as illustrated in the battle between Sony with its PlayStation, Nintendo's Wii and Microsoft's Xbox. In the autumn of 2007, Sony managed to quadruple its sales and steal market share in the USA from its rivals after launching a new 40-gigabyte PlayStation 3 model and dropping price on its old models (www.FT.com, 14 December 2007). Rivalry can also take the form of a struggle for resources. In 2007, with buoyant demand from India and China, mining companies found that capacity at existing mines was stretched. Billiton, the giant Australian mining group, in an attempt to increase its capacity to supply, tried to steal a march on rivals by making a bid for a major competitor, Rio Tinto (*Guardian*, 9 November 2007). Firms in the oil industry also have to compete for reserves. In 1970 international oil companies controlled 85% of the world's oil reserves whereas, nowadays, state-owned oil companies control 80% of reserves (*Financial Times Magazine*, 15 December 2007; see also UNCTAD 2007). The difficulties that big oil firms confront in their relationships with oil-rich countries like Russia and Venezuela forces them to seek out reserves elsewhere.

Firms, especially international firms, increasingly strive for competitive advantage through mergers and alliances. UNCTAD reported that the value of cross-border M&As reached around US$880bn in 2006 which was an increase of around one quarter on the previous year. Horizontal mergers, that is between firms at the same stage of production of a product, boost market share and reduce competition. An example of this was the Air France merger with the Dutch carrier KLM which made it, in revenue terms, the largest airline in the world. Subsequently it set up an alliance with Delta Air Lines of the USA to make it one of the most powerful forces in North Atlantic aviation and posing a tough competitive challenge for other transatlantic carriers such as BA (www.bbc.co.uk; *Financial Times*, 18 October 2007). Horizontal mergers facilitate the movement into new geographical markets (see Mini Case below). Vertical mergers, where companies move closer to their supplies of raw materials or to their final customers, guarantee supplies of materials or distribution. In the late 1990s, with the internet offering new methods of distributing news, music, and film, media companies in newspaper publishing, TV, radio, and film moved to integrate different levels of production and distribution in order to place their products in the largest possible number of different platforms. The motto appeared to be 'Create Once, Place Everywhere!' This enabled companies to produce films or music, register them in DVDs or CDs and distribute them not only through retail outlets but also through the cable, satellite, or mobile telephony networks they owned. Such vertically integrated companies were in a position to exploit their products at every single level of the value chain. Thus, Time Warner the US media giant merged with internet service provider AOL and Vivendi got together with Universal. Vertical integration may also allow firms to squeeze rivals where those rivals have to come to them for supplies or for distribution (see Pleatsikas and Teece 2000).

Competition intensity can range from being cut-throat to weak and depends on the following:

- The number of competing firms—the larger the number of competitors, the more likely is rivalry to be fierce. Conversely, the lower the number of rivals, the weaker the competition is likely to be.

- The relative size of firms—where rivals are of similar size or have equal market shares, then competition can be expected to be strong. This situation can be found in oligopolies such as cars where a small number of leading firms including General Motors, Ford, Volkswagen, and Toyota compete hard for sales. By contrast, in markets where one dominant firm competes with a number of smaller rivals, competition is likely to be less intense.

- Market growth rate—when the market is growing slowly, firms, wishing to grow faster than the market, will try to take market share away from their rivals by competing more fiercely. This is the case in the traditional markets of North America and Western Europe for the beer and car industries. If a beer firm wants to grow in those markets it has to up its competitive performance or take over a rival.

- The extent of product differentiation—when firms have been successful in persuading customers that their products are different from those of their rival's then competition is likely to be less intense. In the beer market, InBev has four well-established international brands, Stella Artois, Beck's, Skol, and Leffe and more than 200 local brands while Heineken manages a large portfolio of beer brands, such as Heineken, Amstel, Cruzcampo, and Tiger.

- The importance of fixed costs—fixed costs are those which do not change with output and include, for example, depreciation, rent, and interest payments. Industries operating with large, expensive pieces of capital equipment often have high fixed costs and relatively low running, or variable, costs. Examples include oil refining, nuclear power generation, and mass car production. In such industries, firms will be under pressure to sell their output in order to generate some contribution to their fixed costs. This pressure will be particularly intense when there is spare capacity in the industry, in other words where firms are not using the resources to produce to their full potential, a situation faced by the big car producers in the traditional markets of North America and Western Europe.

- Where production capacity needs to be added in large chunks then expansion by firms can add significantly to the industry's ability to supply and could result in supply outstripping demand leading to more competition. This is a particular problem for the car industry given that new factories could add significantly to supply in an industry suffering from over-capacity. To be competitive, new factories have to be able to produce several hundred thousand units a year in order to take advantage of economies of scale.

If most or all of the above conditions are met then competition in an industry will be fierce. Conversely, if none of these conditions prevail then firms in the industry are unlikely to be competing fiercely against each other.

Often oligopolists faced with the unpalatable prospect of competition will make efforts to avoid it. There are various devices they can use to achieve this such as forming a cartel which, in many countries, is illegal. The members of the cartel agree to follow certain competition-avoiding policies. This was seen when several large multinational producers of vitamins including Roche of Switzerland, BASF of Germany, and Daiichi of Japan

Mini Case The Car Industry—The Struggle for New Geographical Markets

This case shows one aspect of Industry Rivalry (Force 1) among car firms, the struggle to tap into new geographical markets, in this case the booming Russian market. In 2005, the car market in Russia generated sales of US$12bn and it was expected to become the largest in Europe by volume, with sales forecast to reach the 4 million mark by 2015. Car ownership in Russia was only 160 cars per 1000 people compared with 508 in Western Europe.

The search for new markets by big car makers was spurred by the slow growth of car sales and the level of spare capacity in the traditional markets of North America, Western Europe, and Japan. Russia, along with other Eastern European, countries, was also attractive to car firms because of its cheap labour.

Renault, which also controls Nissan, set out to dominate the Russian car market by agreeing, in 2007, to buy a quarter of Avtovaz, the maker of the Lada, which used to be regarded as one of the world's worst brands. Renault intended to boost output to 1.5m cars a year and to improve the Lada by, for example, incorporating Renault engines and gear-boxes. The French

Source: www.istockphoto.com

company had to fight off competition from General Motors, Fiat, and Volkswagen to acquire its 25% stake in Avtovaz. The deal gave Renault and Nissan greater access to the Russian market that had already attracted GM, Ford, Toyota, VW, and other Western manufacturers.

The Russian car market was highly concentrated. In 2005, Avtovaz held more than half of the Russian market for cars but this was under threat from foreign car firms such as Hyundai and Toyota (see Table 3.4). It employed 105,000 and had a joint venture with GM producing two models. Before the deal with Avtovaz, Renault had built up a presence in Russia with a new plant in Moscow and Nissan was in the process of building a production facility in St Petersburg as was General Motors.

Source: Datamonitor, Russia—New Cars, October 2006; *Financial Times*, 5 December 2007; *The Guardian*, 10 December 2007

Table 3.4 Russian Market—Cars, % Share by volume 2005

Company	% Share
AvtoVaz	52.50%
Hyundai	6.50%
Toyota Motor Corporation	4.60%
Other	36.40%
Total	100.0%

Source: Datamonitor

agreed to charge common prices, and when Dutch brewers, Heineken, Grolsch, and Bavaria along with InBev agreed to coordinate prices and price increases of beer (EU Commission IP/07/509). The USA and the EU found that major airlines including British Airways, Air France, Lufthansa, and Japan Airlines were operating a cartel to fix the prices for carrying cargo (*Financial Times*, 22 December 2007). Some cartels may be set up to avoid competition by sharing out the market rather than agreeing common prices—this was the case with three Luxembourg brewers (EU Commission IP/01/1740). Often cartels are established by firms producing undifferentiated products where buyers will take their custom to the cheapest supplier. When supply threatens to outstrip demand in such industries firms fear the outbreak of fierce competition and sometimes set up a cartel to prevent this happening. Alternatively, competitors can avoid competition by resorting to price leadership. While cartels bring firms together in an explicit agreement, price leadership can result from implicit understandings within the industry. Under price leadership one firm raises price and the others follow suit. Price leadership takes two forms. The first is dominant price leadership where the biggest firm in the industry changes price and others, either willingly or through fear of the consequences, follow suit. Barometric is the second type of price leadership. This occurs when firms in the industry are of similar size and the identity of the price leader changes from one period to another.

Force 2 Competition from New Entrants

The entry of new firms is another threat to established firms in the industry. New entrants will be attracted into industries by the prospects of high profits and growth. It may be that established firms are not making high profits but that the entrants can see the potential for profit—this was the case with the low-cost entry to the airline industry. Entry increases the number of firms and, if it takes the form of greenfield investment, adds to industry capacity. As a result competition could become more intense. On the other hand, low growth industries with poor profits are unlikely to be threatened by a rush of new firms. Established firms are likely to leave such industries looking for more profitable pastures elsewhere.

The probability of new entrants to the industry is dependent on the height of barriers to entry. Industries protected by very high barriers face little threat of new entry. The following are examples of barriers to entry.

- Absolute cost barriers—these are advantages which established firms have over newcomers. In the world of five star hotels where location is of utmost importance, it would be difficult for a new entrant to find a sufficient number of prime sites to set up an extensive chain of hotels because many of these sites would be already occupied by established hotel chains. Similarly firms trying to enter the telecommunications, electricity generation, or rail industries could have problems because existing operators control the physical networks.

- Legal barriers—laws and regulations can constitute insurmountable barriers. Before the telecommunications and airline industries were liberalized, the legal and regulatory framework protected existing firms from new entry. In many countries, firms wishing to enter banking usually have to pass a series of legal tests to get permission to set up in business.

- Product differentiation—this can be a major barrier when firms manage to convince customers that their products are significantly different from those of their competitors. Some firms, especially in consumer goods industries like cars, food, soft drinks, and computer software, spend large amounts of money on advertising, sales promotion, and packaging to differentiate their products. Ford with its spending of US$496.9 million in the first half of 2005 was the biggest advertiser in the USA.

Table 3.5 Rank and Value of International Brands 2007

Rank	Brand	Country of origin	Value
1.	Coca Cola	U.S.	65,324
2.	Microsoft	U.S.	58,709
3.	IBM	U.S.	57,091
4.	GE	U.S.	51,569
5.	Nokia	FINLAND	33,696
6.	Toyota	JAPAN	32,070
7.	Intel	U.S.	30,954
8.	McDonald's	U.S.	29,398
9.	Disney	U.S.	29,210
10.	Mercedes-Benz	GERMANY	23,568

Source: Interbrand

Britvic, the UK soft drinks company, spends around 7% of turnover, promoting brands including Robinsons, Pepsi, and Tango (www.britvic.co.uk). And promotional expenditure in the pharmaceutical industry is one of its main areas of cost, far outweighing R&D expenditure. Total spending in the USA grew from US$11.4 billion in 1996 to US$29.9 billion in 2005 promoting products to the medical profession and directly to the US consumer (Donohue 2007; Narayanan 2004). Massive expenditures like these can build up brand loyalty and recognition to such an extent that the brands become very valuable. As can be seen in Table 3.5, it is estimated that the Coca Cola and Microsoft brands are each worth more than US$50 billion. Product differentiation can therefore be a significant deterrent to new firms entering an industry.

• Economies of scale—these occur when an increase in the scale of organization say from a small factory to a large factory leads to a fall in unit costs. In some industries, such as cars, firms need to operate on a large scale in order to compete with their rivals. If not, then they will suffer a major competitive disadvantage and some may find it hard to survive. This appears to be happening in China. A local industry has emerged selling about 1.5 million cars a year. However, the sales are divided up between a large number of companies, few of whom are anywhere near achieving the economies of scale needed to guarantee long-term survival (*Financial Times*, 9 October 2007).

Other factors deterring entry to an industry are **excess capacity**, declining demand, the ability of established firms to freeze out new entrants by controlling supply of materials and distribution through vertical integration or long-term contracts with suppliers and customers. The actual or anticipated reaction of established firms can also be an obstacle to entry especially where those companies are large and powerful. The EU found that French banks used discriminatory prices to block the entry of internet banks and supermarket chains who wished to issue credit cards (*Financial Times*, 18 October 2007).

Firms need to be ready to respond to new entrants. In the first decade of the new century, domestic banks in Singapore embarked on a frenzy of mergers when the authorities carried out further liberalization which was expected to lead to the entry of foreign competitors (Asia Pacific Bulletin, 17 August 2001). The Chinese car industry cut prices when China's membership of the WTO meant that the measures previously protecting them from foreign competition would have to be removed (Asia Pacific Bulletin, 25 January 2002).

Force 3 Substitutes

An industry may face competition from substitutes. In the Porter model, substitutes are goods or services produced by firms in an apparently different industry and delivering a similar service to the consumer but in a different way. In the airline industry, firms sell flights to transport customers from point A to B, say London to Paris. All firms selling flights, such as BA, Air France, Lufthansa, and easyJet would be seen as part of the same industry competing in the same market. But trains, ferries, coaches, and private cars could also be used by travellers to get to Paris. If the consumer sees the trains run by Eurostar as being an acceptable alternative to the services provided by airlines then it would seem sensible to include them in any analysis of an industry's competitive environment. The threat from substitutes will be influenced by the cost and ease with which customers can switch to the substitute product. For example, as oil prices rise, customers with central heating might consider switching to a cheaper form of energy. However, the costs, time and inconvenience of changing the equipment could deter switching. In addition, switching may be deterred by firms using what is called confusion pricing. This occurs where the deals offered to customers are so complicated that it is virtually impossible to compare the value of one firm's offer against another. Examples can be seen in the competitive struggle in the telecommunications sector between mobile and fixed-line telephones. Customers are offered a bewildering variety of tariffs, services, and handsets with different technical capabilities making it difficult to judge which is the best deal for them (see Leek and Chansawatkit 2006).

One problem faced by the industry analyst is that often the information is not available to assess whether customers do see different goods or services as being good substitutes, in other words, whether there is a high cross elasticity of demand.

Force 4 Customers

Firms sell their output to customers—who could be other businesses or the final consumer. For companies like Intel, business customers will be the main purchasers of its computer chips. On the other hand, supermarkets sell to the final consumer. Some firms such as Microsoft sell both to other businesses and to the final consumer. The power relationships that firms have with their customers depend on a combination of factors:

Mini Case Pharmaceuticals and the Threat from Substitutes

Substitutes (Force 3) can constitute a significant competitive threat. Big firms in the traditional pharmaceutical industry face an increasing challenge from fast-growing biopharmaceutical companies that are coming up with new treatments for diseases based on genetic science. Biotech firms use living cells to develop biotech drugs, a very different technology to that used by the traditional pharmaceutical industry. The biotech industry, while still relatively small, is expanding much faster than the pharmaceutical industry. In the USA, biotech sales of health products grew 20% to US$40.3 billion in 2006, while pharmaceutical sales grew 8% to US$275 billion. The pharmaceutical industry has recognized and responded to the growing threat. Roche, the Swiss pharmaceutical firm took over 454 Life Sciences, which makes gene-sequencing technology and NimbleGen, which makes technologies used in identifying the genetic causes of disease. Pfizer, the industry leader, bought up Vicuron, known for its anti-infective treatments while AstraZeneca acquired the Cambridge Antibody Technology Group and MedImmune. Both Abbott and Bristol-Myers Squibb both opened biotech plants while Wyeth set up what is claimed to be the biggest biotech plant in the world in Ireland. Top pharmaceutical firms like Pfizer, GlaxoSmithKline, and Merck have also gone in for large numbers of alliances with biotech companies.

Source: *The Economist*, 28 June 2007; www.CNNMoney.com, 29 May 2007; *Financial Times*, 12 January 2006; *Investors Chronicle*, 6 November 2007; AstraZeneca, *Annual Report* 2006.

- The number and size of firms—when an industry comprises a small number of large firms facing a large number of small customers then the industry will be in a powerful position. Losing a customer, in this situation, would not be very costly in terms of sales. This is the position of supermarket chains in Western Europe. They are large, few in number but have millions of customers. It is also the case for accountancy services in the Asia-Pacific region which includes Australia, China, Japan, India, Singapore, South Korea, and Taiwan. Four major players dominate the market: PricewaterhouseCoopers, KPMG, Deloitte Touche Tohmatsu, and Ernst & Young (Datamonitor, Asia-Pacific—Accountancy, August 2007).

  On the other hand, where many firms in an industry have a small number of large customers then the power switches to the buyer because loss of a single client could cause much damage to revenues and profits. Firms producing defence equipment, such as BAE in the UK or Mitsubishi and Kawasaki in Japan, are in this position. Usually their domestic governments are, by far, the biggest purchasers of arms and other defence equipment such as tanks, submarines, and aircraft carriers.

- The proportion of customer costs constituted by the product—when a product constitutes a large proportion of a business customers' total costs the more sensitive they will be to price because price increases will have a big impact on their costs and, if they are unable to pass this on, their profits. These buyers, when faced by a variety of sellers, can shop around and play suppliers off against each other in order to get the most favourable prices.

  Where customers are dealing with only a few suppliers then their bargaining power is reduced. This is the case in Europe for intensive energy users like steel makers whose energy bills are a large proportion of their total costs. As we have seen in

the Mini Case above, the EU energy sector is highly concentrated indicating low bargaining power for buyers such as those in the steel industry.

- The extent of product differentiation—the less differentiated the product the easier
  it is for customers to switch to a cheaper supplier. Farmers supplying supermarket
  chains with meat, fruit, and vegetables will be in a much less powerful bargaining
  position than firms selling branded washing powders.

- The ability of customers to integrate vertically—sellers will be at a disadvantage
  where customers are big enough to produce their own supplies either by taking over
  their suppliers or by setting up new production facilities. Wal-Mart and other supermarket chains built giant warehouses to take over the distribution of supplies direct
  from the manufacturer thereby cutting out the wholesalers that previously carried
  out this task. Comcast, the US cable company, became increasingly involved with
  the production of TV programmes. In contrast, buyers will have less power when
  they are unable to integrate vertically.

Force 5 Suppliers

Suppliers refer to businesses selling inputs such as fuel, raw materials, and components to the firms in the industry. The position of suppliers can be analysed in a similar way
to those of buyers but in reverse. The only difference, as Grant (2005a) points out, is that
it is now the firms in the industry that are the customers and the sellers of inputs that
are the suppliers. To illustrate, if the supplier industry is dominated by a few large firms,
compared to the buying industry, then the ability of suppliers to get away with price
increases, reductions in quality, and a worsening of the terms and conditions of sale will
be high. Conversely, where the supply side is more fragmented than the buying side, then
the advantage will lie in the hands of the customer. This was the case in the European
dairy industry where suppliers of milk, cheese, and yoghurt were faced by a smaller
number of big, powerful customers like Tesco, Aldi, and Leclerc. The dairy industry
responded to this inequality by consolidating. For example, in the UK, Arla took over
Express Dairies while Campina, the Dutch firm took over Germany's Sator
(www.FoodandDrinkEurope.com; www.FoodNavigator.com).

A Sixth Force: Complementary Products

The Porter model pays particular attention to the relationships between competitors'
products and also the threat from substitute products. It does not deal with the complementary relationship that can exist between products. Complementary products are
those that are used together by customers, in other words they do not compete with each
other but operate in tandem. There are numerous examples of complementary products:
mobile phones need service providers; DVDs need equipment to play them; computers
need software; cars need petrol; and printers require ink cartridges. The suppliers of complementary products can play an important role in the competitive environment for firms
in an industry, first because the firms making the products depend on the efforts of the

other, for example, in relation to product development. Second, there can be conflict over who gets most of the spoils. Such a relationship is illustrated in the case of software vendors and the producers of PCs and PC components. Most PC manufacturers want new exciting software to be developed that requires customers to upgrade to new PCs, but software providers generally prefer to target the larger market of customers with their existing computers. The schizophrenic nature of complementarity can be seen in the case of Intel, the maker of computer chips, and Microsoft. According to Casadeus-Masanell *et al.* they are 'joined at the hip' (2007, p 584) because more than four fifths of the personal computers sold worldwide contain an Intel microprocessor running Microsoft's Windows operating system. The companies are dependent on each other because consumer demand and revenues depend on how well the different software and hardware components work together. This means that the R&D programmes for both players have got to complement each other. Casadeus-Masanell reports that the two companies have been in conflict over pricing, the timing of investments, and who captures the greatest share of the value of the product. An Intel manager puts it thus:

> Intel is always trying to innovate on hardware platform and thus, always needs software. When software lags, it creates a bottleneck for Intel. Microsoft, on the other hand, wants to serve the installed base of computers in addition to demand for new computers. Therefore, a natural conflict exists between both companies. In addition, the question always remains—Who will get the bigger piece of the pie? The success of one is seen as ultimately taking money away from the other (Casadeus-Masanell *et al.* p 584).

Grant (2005b) shows how Nintendo managed to keep the upper hand in its relationships with the suppliers of games software for its video games console. Nintendo used various methods of establishing a dominant position over developers of games. It maintained control of its operating system, avoided becoming over-dependent on any single supplier by issuing licences to many developers and established a firm hold over the manufacture and distribution of games cartridges.

Other Approaches to Industry Classification

We have looked at how to go about defining an industry by identifying the firms producing products that compete against each other in a market.

However, official bodies such as governments and international agencies have industrial classification systems which can take a somewhat different approach in terms of the criteria they use to classify firms to industries and sectors. For example, firms are interested in identifying who are their competitors in the market place. In that sense they are concerned with demand-side factors. Governments, on the other hand, may view the industry as a collection of firms using the same production techniques or raw materials, that is supply-side factors. For example, manufacturers of television sets would not see themselves as competing with firms producing video recording units but the classification system used, for example, by the United Nations, groups them together.

Figure 3.5 Average annual growth rate of turnover

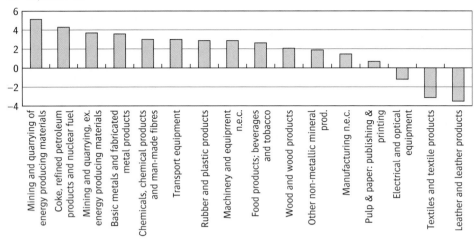

EU–25, 2000–05

Source: Eurostat Yearbook 2006–07

Variations in approach arise because firms and governments are interested in the data for different purposes. For example, governments want to know how the structure of the economy is changing, which industries and sectors are expanding, and which contracting —in terms of sales, output, occupation, and employment—and whether the statistics indicate a turning point in the business cycle. Governments are also interested in collecting information on levels of investment, expenditure on R&D, productivity, labour costs, the performance of exports and imports, and on market concentration. This knowledge is then used in the formulation of policies on education and training, science and technology, competition, and policy towards particular industries and regions. Figure 3.5 shows the broad industrial sectors used by the EU and an example of the type of information it collects on industries.

Learning Task

Figure 3.4 shows the growth rates of turnover in the EU for various industrial sectors over a six year period. Examine the figure and answer the questions below.

1. Which sectors have expanded fastest?
2. Which sectors have contracted?
3. What are the implications of your answers to both questions for firms in those sectors?
4. Discuss whether your analysis for question 3 is valid for all firms in the expanding or contracting sectors.
5. Discuss some implications of your findings for government policies towards education and training.

Benefits to Business

The data generated by governments can also be useful for firms insofar as it provides information on developments in their sector and it may also break down to a level that allows the firm to analyse the industry in which it is operating and those of its major customers and suppliers. In addition, where systems used by different countries are compatible, business can compare operating conditions and markets across national boundaries which are of major importance in a globalizing economy. Firms can assess factors affecting competitiveness such as labour costs, productivity, stock levels, the number of direct competitors, potential customers, and suppliers. Business can also use time-series data—that is where comparable statistics are available over a range of years—to make forecasts.

Being better able to assess comparative costs and benefits internationally helps business decision-making, for example whether it would be better to invest in production facilities in a country or to service that market by other means such as exporting. Comparable statistics on industries could also enhance the ability of financial institutions who will be able to analyse more accurately the risks inherent in providing credit, particularly to borrowers in other countries. For businesses wishing to borrow money, this could result in them having greater access to credit markets, and a bigger choice of credit providers.

International comparability of industrial statistics also provides significant benefits to companies making money from providing data, for example, marketing firms, research firms, and other compilers of statistics. These businesses try to compare directly prices, employment, skill levels, and other variables by industry from a variety of sources, a task made more difficult when there are underlying differences in official government statistics (epcd 2001).

Official Classification Systems

Official industrial classification systems are established for a variety of reasons:

- To ensure that different government agencies and departments collect, collate, analyse, and present information in a uniform way. It is a guarantee to users that they are being provided with consistent information.

- To provide information that can be used by government and non-government bodies as a convenient way of classifying industrial activities into a common structure.

- To provide data that is comparable over time. This allows users to identify patterns and trends in the data, for example whether an industry is in long-term growth or decline, whether it experiences violent fluctuations in the demand for its goods or services.

- To facilitate comparisons between countries. For example, the North American Industrial Classification System (NAICS) was developed to provide comparable statistics across the three NAFTA members, the US, Canada, and Mexico. In the EU, the NACE system ensures a degree of comparability in the industrial statistics produced by the member states.

Various classification systems are in force across the world. We consider ISIC established by the United Nations and the EU system NACE. Over 140 countries are using classifications of economic activities based either on NACE or ISIC which makes data highly comparable. We also look at NAICS which is used in North America and Mexico (for an overview of official classification systems, see Industrial and Economic Activities Classification Schemes at www.lib.strath.ac.uk/busweb).

ISIC

ISIC is the International Standard Industrial Classification set up by the United Nations. It provides a framework facilitating an international comparison of national statistics on industry. The EU (NACE) and many countries such as the USA (NAICS), China (CSIC), Japan (JSIC), Australia, and New Zealand (ANZSIC) use systems which are comparable, to varying degrees, with ISIC. ISIC was revised in 2006 and 2007 with many other countries following suit to maintain or increase comparability. Despite these moves, there will not be a complete convergence of systems so that problems of comparability will remain.

ISIC, along with other classification systems, collects information on establishments and groups them according to the activity they carry out. An establishment is a single physical location, such as a factory or plant, producing goods or services. It is not necessarily identical with a company or an enterprise, which may consist of one or more establishments. Multinational companies, by definition have more than one production unit, that is they are multi-plant operations. Citigroup, for instance, the giant US financial services company, has operations in more than 100 countries. Establishments are grouped according to three criteria:

- the character of the goods and services produced such as materials used in their manufacture;
- the uses to which the goods and services are put;
- the inputs, processes, and technology of production.

Establishments are classified based on their principal activity. For example, if the main sales of a bar were drinks that would be its main activity and it would be classified as serving beverages (Group 563 of ISIC revision 4). If its main sales were food then it would be classified as a restaurant (Group 561).

ISIC provides information at different levels of detail. The broadest level is the Section designated by an alphabetical letter from A to U. The Section level gives information on sectors such as agriculture or manufacturing. The next level down is the Division with two digits, followed by Groups with three digits and then Classes with four digits. The higher the number of digits the narrower is the industry focus (Table 3.6).

One can see from Table 3.7 how the system operates for Section A, Agriculture, forestry and fishing. In total, it has three divisions, seven groups and 30 classes.

To facilitate international comparability of industry statistics, there needs to be a common approach on the classification of goods and services. The UN has the Central Product Classification system (CPC) which provides a framework for international comparison of

Table 3.6 Number at each level of ISIC

Sections	21
Divisions	88
Groups	260
Classes	600

Source: UN 2006

Table 3.7 International Standard Industrial Classification

Sections are given a letter from **A to U.** Thus:

A Agriculture, forestry and fishing

Divisions have two digits.

Section A, Agriculture Forestry and Fishing has three Divisions with the digits, 01, 02 and 03. The first division is:

01 Crop and animal production, hunting and related service activities

....

Groups are given three digits.

The Crop and Animal Production Division (01) has seven groups numbered from 011 to 017. Three of the groups are:

011 Growing of non-perennial crops
012 Growing of perennial crops
014 Animal production

....

Classes give the most detailed information and have four digits.

The Group, Growing of Non-Perennial Crops (011) has seven classes, four of which are:

0112 Growing of rice
0113 Growing of vegetables and melons, roots and tubers
0114 Growing of sugar cane
0115 Growing of tobacco

Source: UN 2006a

product statistics. The CPC classifies products based on the physical characteristics of goods or on the nature of the services provided.

NACE is the industrial classification used by the European Union and its member states. It can be seen as the European counterpart of ISIC. Like ISIC, it groups establishments according to the inputs used, the production process, and the product. It has the same number of Sections and Divisions and is directly comparable to ISIC at the Division level. Each Section is given an alphabetical letter and a four digit system is used in classifying production units to divisions, groups, and classes. The product classification used by NACE, the Classification of Products by Activity (CPA) follows the UN systems but, with around 4,500 different categories, is more detailed.

Learning Task

This task requires to you to check out the Section entitled, Transport, storage and communications (if you find the revised versions, that is version 4 of ISIC and 2 of NACE the heading will be, Transportation and storage). Go to the UN web site for ISIC and the comparable EU site for NACE.

1. Identify the number, names, and digit codes of Divisions for the Section in each system. Are the industries covered by ISIC and NACE in the various divisions comparable?

2. Why might your answer be of importance to firms involved in the transport business that are interested in expanding their international operations?

Mini Case The Pharmaceutical Industry Compared

Eurostat is the EU agency responsible for the collection, analysis, and presentation of industry statistics. The information collected can be used to draw up a picture of the development of different industries and to assess their performance year on year.

This case shows the results of an investigation into a comparison of pharmaceutical prices. The pharmaceutical industry

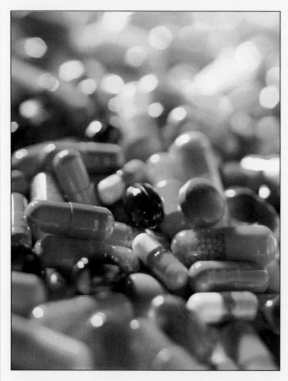

Source: Photodisc

is found in NACE Section D, sub-section DG, group 24.4, Manufacture of pharmaceuticals, medicinal chemicals and botanical products. This covers both the Manufacture of basic pharmaceutical products (class 24.41) and the Manufacture of pharmaceutical preparations (class 24.42). Eurostat reported that the industry employed more than half a million people, had a turnover of more than 170 billion euros with output growing at almost 6% per year.

In 2007, Eurostat published the results of its study of pharmaceutical prices in 27 EU and 6 non-EU countries (see Figure 3.5). It found significant differences in price levels. Fourteen countries had above-average prices. Two non-members, Iceland (IS in the chart) and Switzerland (CH) had price levels 60% and 87% higher than the EU25 average respectively. Prices in the next most expensive group of countries were between 15% and 30% higher than the EU25 average. They included EU members such as Denmark (DK), Germany (DE), Ireland (IE), Italy (IT) and a non-member, Norway (NO). Prices were below average in 19 countries, particularly in Eastern Europe where prices were significantly lower in countries like Bulgaria (BG), Czech Republic (CZ), and Poland (PL). The lowest price levels were found in Macedonia at 58% of the EU25 average.

Such information is not only useful for the EU and its member states but also for pharmaceutical companies when they are formulating pricing policies for different national markets. It could also be useful for firms or even governmental agencies purchasing pharmaceuticals and wishing to economize on the cost of drugs. For example, pharmaceutical wholesalers in high-price Switzerland might be tempted to source their drugs requirements in Macedonia.

Figure 3.6 Price level indices for pharmaceutical products, EU25=100

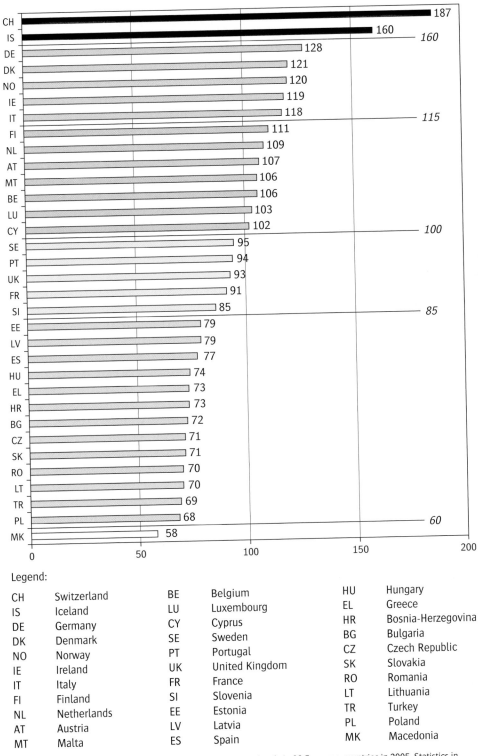

Legend:

CH	Switzerland	BE	Belgium	HU	Hungary
IS	Iceland	LU	Luxembourg	EL	Greece
DE	Germany	CY	Cyprus	HR	Bosnia-Herzegovina
DK	Denmark	SE	Sweden	BG	Bulgaria
NO	Norway	PT	Portugal	CZ	Czech Republic
IE	Ireland	UK	United Kingdom	SK	Slovakia
IT	Italy	FR	France	RO	Romania
FI	Finland	SI	Slovenia	LT	Lithuania
NL	Netherlands	EE	Estonia	TR	Turkey
AT	Austria	LV	Latvia	PL	Poland
MT	Malta	ES	Spain	MK	Macedonia

Sources: Eurostat, Pharmaceutical products—comparative price levels in 33 European countries in 2005, Statistics in focus, Economy and finance 45/2007

Table 3.8 NAICS Coding

51 Information
513 Broadcasting and Telecommunications
5133 Telecommunications
51332 Wireless Telecommunications Carriers (except Satellite)
513321 Paging

NAICS

We now look at another system of classification, NAICS which was developed by the USA, Canada, and Mexico to provide comparable statistics across the three countries. We include NAICS because it differs in certain ways from the ISIC.

There are 20 sectors in the NAICS, and 1,170 detailed industries for the USA. An example is shown in Table 3.8 which starts with sector 51, Information. It adds a further digit each time it drills down a level until the focus is on Paging with six digits.

NAICS groups establishments into industries based on the activities in which they are primarily engaged.

It provides information that is compatible, but only to a degree, with ISIC and NACE and it has been suggested that it could take anything up to 20 years to get a complete harmonization of NAICS with NACE/ISIC (ONS). Whereas NACE and ISIC operate to the four digit level, NAICS uses a six digit hierarchical coding system. NAICS also differs from NACE and ISIC insofar as it groups together industries based on a single criterion, the production process. So NAICS would not put deskjet and laser printers in the same group because the production processes differ for these products. NACE and ISIC, however, would group them together because the printers are used to perform the same function.

Establishments are classified into industries based on the activity in which they are primarily engaged. Establishments using similar raw material inputs, similar capital equipment, and similar types of labour are classified in the same industry. In other words, establishments that do similar things in similar ways are classified together.

Learning Task

NAICS provides information on the number of establishments, payroll, number of employees in an industry, and the breakdown by each US State but also shows the level of market concentration for the biggest firms.

You are a Western European advertising agency considering entry, initially on a small scale, into the USA. As a preliminary step you decide that you need information on the size and structure of your competitors in the US industry and some idea of the labour costs you would be likely to incur. You refer to the 2002 US Census and find the information contained in the following table (Table 3.9).

1. How many establishments are there in the industry?

2. What is the total revenue for the industry?

3. How concentrated is the advertising market? Look at the concentration ratio for the 4, 8, 20, and 50 largest firms.

→

→ **Table 3.9** Advertising Agencies in the USA 2002 NAICS code 541810

	Concentration Ratio*	Revenue $bn	No. of establishments	Payroll p.a. $bn	No. of employees
All establishments	100	21,881,122	12,415	9,729,113	156,648
CR4	33.7	7,363,692	611	3,464,337	44,529
CR8	41.2	9,017,313	651	4,061,544	52,087
CR20	48.3	10,560,307	799	4,753,747	61,695
CR50	53	11,606,696	886	5,206,936	68,868

* CR is the concentration ratio. It shows the proportion of industry revenues accounted for by the 4, 8, 20 and 50 largest firms in the industry.
Source: http://factfinder.census.gov

4. How many establishments on average do the four biggest firms operate? How many, on average, do the next four biggest firms run?

5. Is it possible for small firms to operate in the industry?

6. What is the pay bill, the number of employees, and the average cost of employing labour in the industry?

7. Is there anything in the information you have found that would particularly attract or deter you from setting up in the USA?

Mini Case The Reform of Industrial Classification Systems

Industrial classifications need to be periodically reviewed to ensure that they reflect the constantly changing structure of industry and business activity and that they are satisfying the data needs of users whether they be government agencies, non-profit organizations, or business. As a result, industrial classification systems are under constant review.

Reforms are necessary for a variety of reasons:

• The accelerating globalization of the world economy increases pressure to produce statistics that are internationally comparable. Some of the pressure comes from businesses searching for new markets and locations for investment. To do this it is necessary for them to compare and contrast the evolution of production and market conditions in different parts of the world.

• Changes in technology mean that new products, new raw materials, and production techniques are being introduced which change the industrial structure of economies. This sometimes requires the addition of new industrial categories and the reordering of existing groupings. For example,

new communications technologies are revolutionizing the traditional methods for sending and receiving information. Thus, there has been very rapid growth in internet publishing and broadcasting. This has generated interest in grouping together all establishments that provide information services, regardless of the information technology they employ.

• Trends such as the move towards outsourcing of activities, such as call centres and help lines, previously done in-house by financial institutions and computer manufacturers, encourages the creation of new service sector groupings.

Reforms can cause problems for users of the data. When reforms occur it may disrupt the time-series thereby impairing the ability of firms, statistical agencies, and government departments to compare statistics over a period of time, to identify trends, and to produce forecasts.

Sources: UN 2002; UN 2006b; UN 1994

● CHAPTER SUMMARY

In this chapter we set out to explain the concepts and tools that are indispensable to the industry analyst and to show how they can be used to analyse industries. We started off with the concepts of the industry and the market. It was shown that any satisfactory definition of the market needs to specify a set of products and its geographical boundaries. The next issue to be addressed was the various market structures and their implications for business behaviour and industry performance. It was shown that the more highly concentrated is the market, the more power is concentrated in the hands of a few firms able to manipulate prices, the quantity and quality of the good or service, and the terms and conditions of sale. This was followed by an explanation of the Porter Five Forces model and how this could be used to analyse industries. As part of the analysis of Porter's force of rivalry, it was demonstrated how firms sometimes make strenuous efforts to avoid price competition through the establishment of cartels and systems of price leadership. We also revealed the importance of product differentiation as a major element of competitive strategy and as a barrier to entry in certain industries. A sixth force, complementary products was added to the Porter model to make it an even more effective analytical tool. We finished off by examining the most important official industrial classification systems in the world and how they can be of use to business.

● REVIEW QUESTIONS

1. A report on the global energy market grouping together oil, gas, coal, and the energy equipment and services industries and shows that Shell has a market share of just over 9%. However, a different report, looking at oil and gas refining and marketing gives Shell more than one fifth of the market (Datamonitor, Global Energy, March 2007; Global Oil and Gas Refining, March 2007).

    Discuss which of these market definitions would be most useful to oil firms trying to analyse their competitive environment. Would it be sensible for a vertically integrated firm like Shell to include the drilling for oil in the analysis?

2. Geological maps of the world show that:

    • the greatest concentrations of metals and minerals reserves are not located in the same places as population;

    • most metal and mineral deposits are in countries with relatively low populations like Australia, Canada, South America, and Russia;

    • the most populous parts of the world, Asia, the Middle East, and Europe, have a relative deficit of resources. The USA, with its enormous market is deficient in metals, as is the fast-growing Chinese economy;

    • the rate of discovery of major reserves of minerals is in decline.

    What are the implications of this information for the competitive strategy of leading international mining groups such as Rio Tinto and Billiton?

3. The Datamonitor Report (August 2007) on Accountancy Services in the Asia-Pacific region showed that the market was dominated by four firms, PricewaterhouseCoopers, KPMG, Deloitte Touche Tohmatsu, and Ernst & Young. The report says that although these firms all provide similar services they have managed to differentiate themselves effectively. They serve thousands of business customers that are required by law to have their accounts externally audited.

Explain Porter's forces of industry rivalry, competition from new entrants, and the power of buyers. Use these forces to help you analyse the accountancy services market.

4. A report on advertising expenditure in the USA for 2007 showed that the film industry was spending around 8% of turnover on advertising while the figure for firms selling computer programming services was 0.1%.

How would you explain this? Bear in mind that the film industry is dominated by big firms while lots of small companies offer computer programming services.

5. In 2005/07 there was an upsurge in takeover activity in the media sector with 372 mergers across the world in the first quarter of 2007 worth some US$94 billion (www.CNNMoney.com). Much of the upsurge was driven by the threat from Google which had taken over YouTube. They were grabbing a huge chunk of the advertising revenues of established media companies. A prime example was News Corporation, the publisher of books and newspapers in the USA, UK, and Australia, owner of the biggest group of US television stations, and satellite broadcasters in the UK and Italy, and of 20th Century Fox studios. It had previously acquired MySpace and, in 2007, took over Dow Jones, publisher of the *Wall Street Journal*.

Explain Porter's force of substitutes (**Force 3** in the chapter) in relation to Google, YouTube, and MySpace. Analyse the implications for the media industry and its response.

6. What are the major similarities and differences in approach to the classification of industries between ISIC and NAICS?

7. Tesco, the large UK-based multinational supermarket chain, has moved into the US market, initially by setting up in California and then expanding to a chain of 1,000 stores on the West Coast (*The Guardian*, 3 December 2007).

Go to the US Government census site at http://factfinder.census.gov/, call up Section 44–45: Retail Trade, go to the five digit activity 44511, Supermarkets & other grocery stores (except convenience stores).

Find out the following information about supermarkets (NAICS code 44511) in the USA:

a) The number of establishments in the industry.

b) Total revenue for the industry.

c) Whether the market for supermarkets is highly concentrated. Look for the concentration ratio for the 4, 8, 20, and 50 largest firms.

d) The pay bill, the number of employees, and the average cost of employing labour in the industry.

e) Now look for information in the NAICS information on California. Does it give any indication why Tesco chose California as its first base in the USA?

What factors did you find that would attract Tesco to set up in the USA? Did you find any negative factors?

Case Study Global Advertising

This case study looks at the global advertising industry. It requires you to apply some concepts outlined in the chapter to the industry.

The advertising industry consists of agencies providing advertising, marketing, and corporate communications services. They advise clients on advertising and sales promotion strategies, create and produce advertising campaigns, and negotiate prices with the various media on behalf of their customers. Growing at more than 5% per year, the value of the global market comprising Asia-Pacific, Europe, and the Americas reached around US$71 billion in 2006. The Americas (USA, Canada, Brazil, and Mexico), accounting for more than half of the global market, grew faster than the average, while the European market, with almost a quarter of the market, expanded at a rate of just less than 5% per year.

The major customers for the agencies are retailers, followed by the car, and food and drinks industries with media and telecommunications firms close behind. For example in the USA, in 2006 Wal-Mart was the biggest advertiser spending some US$570 million while in the following year Motorola was committed to spending some US$400 million, Subaru, the car firm, US$200 million, and Domino's US$170 million.

The market is fragmented with the three leading multinational firms having a similar market share but together accounting for around only 17% of global market value. The leading company, with a turnover of about US$9 billion, is the US based Omnicom Group Inc., with a share of 5.7%. This is closely followed by the French firm, Publicis which holds 5.6% of total revenue and the British WPP Group with a 5.4% share. Interpublic is another important player in this market, employing more than 43,000 in over 130 countries. The picture of fragmentation at global level does not reflect the situation nationally. The advertising market in most developed countries is concentrated, following years of consolidation leaving the 'big four' agencies, Omnicom, WPP, Interpublic, and Publicis with substantial aggregate market share (see Table 3.10).

Nevertheless, competition can be intense because the leading players offer similar services to their clients. However, they try to differentiate themselves through their prestigious client list, campaign records, and also by the range of services offered. Where successful, such attempts at differentiation discourage

Table 3.10 Global Market Share by value 2006

Company	% Share
Omnicom Group Inc.	5.70%
Publicis Groupe SA	5.60%
WPP Group plc	5.40%
Other	83.30%
Total	100.0%

Source: Datamonitor

customers from switching agencies. However, strong growth in the global market takes the edge off competitive rivalry, and along with low barriers to entry, attracts new competitors.

The big players in the industry all recognize the great potential of India and China. Omnicom sees those countries as the 'markets of the 21st century' and, as a result, took over two marketing firms there (see Advertising Age Special Section, 9 October 2006 available on the Omnicom web site) while WPP sees India as the jewel in its crown (WPP World, THE Wire, November 2005).

TV, radio, and cinema form the dominant distribution channel in the global advertising market, accounting for just over half of the market's value. However, the dramatic growth in the number of media channels, for example television channels, and the increasing popularity of the internet, has worked to the benefit of advertising agencies. WPP estimated that global internet advertising revenue would overtake national newspaper ad revenue by the end of 2007. The result has been a fragmentation of markets, making it more difficult to target the final consumer in a cost-effective way. These trends reduce buyer power because they make clients increasingly dependent on advertising agencies to come up with innovative strategies for efficient ways of communicating with target markets. Fragmenting markets and the cost of developing in-house advertising expertise, make it less likely that customers will integrate backwards, for example, by setting up their own advertising units.

The capital costs of entering this market are low. However, potential new entrants could be deterred by the difficulty of ➜

→ recruiting the creative personnel on which agencies depend for their success. Furthermore, building up knowledge of client needs, expertise on the various media channels, and the variations in national regulations limiting advertising content and methods, costs time and money and could also constitute major barriers. Furthermore, the big agencies offer customers a comprehensive range of advertising and marketing services which newcomers might find difficult to match. Finally, leading agencies have got well established brands and track records which clients might be reluctant to forgo in favour of untried newcomers to the market.

Sources: Datamonitor, Global Advertising, October 2007; *Adweek*, 19 June 2006, 22 Oct 2007; *Campaign*, 28 July 2006; www.omni-comgroup; www.wpp.com; www.interpublic.com

Questions

1. How concentrated is the global advertising industry? Does the global level of market concentration reflect the situation in national markets?

2. Industry rivalry can take various forms. Explain what these different forms are and indicate which you would expect to be important in this industry.

3. Assess the bargaining power of buyers in the industry. How has this changed with the development of new communications technology?

4. With reference to the barriers to entry to this market, discuss the likelihood of new entry.

5. Why are India and China so attractive to the big advertising agencies? Why might merger and acquisition be an attractive way for big firms like Omnicom and Publicis to enter the Indian and Chinese markets?

 Online Resource Centre
www.oxfordtextbooks.co.uk/orc/hamilton_webster/

Visit the supporting online resource centre for additional material which will help you with your assignments, essays and research, or you may find these extra resources helpful when revising for exams.

● FURTHER READING

For further discussion of market definition and market power see:

- Pleatsikas, C. and Teece, D. (2000) 'The Competitive Assessment of Vertical Long-Term Contracts' presented at the Trade Practices Workshop, Business Law Section, Law Council of Australia, Queensland, 12 August

  and

- Pleatsikas, C. and Teece, D. (2001) 'The analysis of market definition and market power in the context of rapid innovation'. *International Journal of Industrial Organization*, Vol 19, Issue 5, April

  and

- Verouden, V. (2004) 'The role of market shares and market concentration indices in the European Commission's Guidelines on the assessment of horizontal mergers under the EC Merger Regulation'. FTC and US DOJ Merger Enforcement Workshop, Washington, DC, February 17–19

Porter's Five Forces Model has come in for some criticism. See:

- Coyne, K. P. and Balakrishnan, S. (1996) 'Bringing discipline to strategy'. *The McKinsey Quarterly*, No 4 and

- Miller, A. and Dess, G. G. (1993) 'Assessing Porter's (1980) model in terms of Generalizability, Accuracy, and Simplicity'. *Journal of Management Studies*, Vol 30, Issue 4, July

For an extension of Porter's Five Forces Model see:

- Nalebuff, B. J. and Brandenburger, A. M. (1996) *Co-opetition*. London: Profile Books

● REFERENCES

Casadesus-Masanell, R. and Yoffie, D. B. (2007) 'Wintel: Cooperation and Conflict'. *Added Management Science*, Vol 53, Issue 4, April

Connor, J. M. (2002) *The Food and Agricultural Global Cartels of the 1990s: Overview and Update*. Purdue University Staff Paper #02-4, August

Donohue, J. M., Cevasco, M. R. and Meredith, B. (2007) 'So A Decade of Direct-to-Consumer Advertising of Prescription Drugs'. *New England Journal of Medicine*, Vol 357, Issue 716, August

epcd (2001) 'Convergence of industrial classification between NACE and NAICS'. Second report of the working group, October. Available at www.census.gov

EU Commission (2005) Report on progress in creating the internal gas and electricity market. Communication from the Commission to the Council and the European Parliament, COM (2005) 568

EU Commission (2006) Corrigendum, Commission Communication on Progress in Creating the Internal Gas and Electricity Market, COM (2005) 568 and Technical Annex, SEC (2005) 1445, 12 January

Fahy, J. (2007) *The Role of Resources in Global Competition*. London: Taylor and Francis

Grant, R. (2005a) *Contemporary Strategy Analysis* (5th edn). Oxford: Blackwell

Grant, R. (2005b) *Cases in Contemporary Strategy Analysis*. Oxford: Blackwell

Hamouda, H. M. Agreement with Coca-Cola ends the European Union's Five Year Inquiry into a Potential Abuse of a Dominant Position. Available at www.luc.edu

Leek, S. and Chansawatkit, S. (2006) 'Consumer Confusion: The Mobile Phone Market in Thailand'. *Journal of Consumer Behaviour*, Vol 5

ONS (2007) Operation 2007—Key Issues. Available at www.statistics.gov.uk

Narayanan, D., Ramarao, C. and Pradeep, K. (2004) 'Return on Investment Implications for Pharmaceutical Promotional Expenditures: The Role of Marketing-Mix Interactions'. *Journal of Marketing*, Vol 68, Issue 4, October

Porter, M. E. (1979) 'How Competitive Forces Shape Strategy'. *Harvard Business Review*, March–April

Porter, M. E. (2008) 'The Five Competitive Forces That Shape Strategy'. *Harvard Business Review*, Vol 86, Issue 1, January

UN (1994) Economic Classification Policy Committee, Services Classifications. Issues Paper No 6, March

UN (2002) Criteria for Determining Industries, Economic Classification Policy Committee. Issues Paper No 4, 16 September

UN (2006a) International Standard Industrial Classification of All Economic Activities (ISIC), Revision 4, 20 November

UN (2006b) UN Statistics Division, Classifications Newsletter No 18, December

UNCTAD (2007) World Investment Report

CHAPTER FOUR

The Global Business Environment

LEARNING OUTCOMES

This chapter will enable you to:

- **Explain the nature of the global business environment**

- **Understand and apply the PESTLE analytical framework**

- **Undertake an external environmental audit**

- **Analyse the impact on business of changes in the external environment**

- **Assess the attractiveness of countries as places to do business**

Case Study BP

This case demonstrates the difficulties multinational companies face in dealing with the diverse political, legal, and regulatory environments.

In 2007, BP, a global integrated oil firm and the world's fourth largest company, announced the loss of 5,000 jobs in a cost cutting exercise to try to restore profits which had slumped by 22% to just US$17.2 billion. The US operations had been a continuing source of problems. In 2005, a huge explosion in BP's biggest American refinery at Texas City killed 15 people and injured 500 in and around the facility. An investigation by the US Chemical Safety Board (CSB) found that cost cutting had helped compromise safety at the plant. Another investigation found that BP had failed to provide adequate resources to ensure safety at its US refineries. One of the themes of the report was the gap between the rhetoric and high ideals of the senior management and the day-to-day practice of its operations.

In February 2008 the CSB returned to the Texas City refinery to investigate the third fatal accident following the 2005 explosion. The explosion cost BP US$373 million in civil and criminal penalties and an increase in investment of US$1.7 billion per year from 2007–2010 in its US refineries. With sales revenues of US$274 billion this was a drop in the ocean. More important was the loss of reputation to a company which promoted itself as an ethical leader in the oil industry. It had re-branded itself 'Beyond Petroleum' and introduced a new logo, the Helios, inspired by the sunflower and supposed to reflect a commitment to cleaner ways of producing energy.

In March 2006, an oil pipeline in the Prudhoe Bay oilfield leaked, spilling 270,000 gallons of oil. As a result BP faced criminal charges. In April, BP was fined US$2.4 million for safety violations in Ohio, and in June of the same year the US authorities charged BP with manipulating the price of propane resulting ➔

Source: www.istockphoto.com

➜ in higher prices for consumers. By August, BP had decided to shut the Prudhoe oilfield. It claimed that it had found 'unexpectedly severe corrosion' in a pipe but whistleblowers had for years been warning of poor maintenance and widespread corrosion.

Another issue for oil companies is that the largest reserves of oil are located in countries like Russia, the Middle East, Africa, and South America where there are political problems in gaining access. TNK-BP, for example, is an Anglo-Russian joint venture in danger of falling victim to Russia's determination to gain control over its oil and gas industry.

BP's decision to extract oil from the tar sands of Canada has also been controversial. Environmental pressure groups claimed that the operation would greatly increase carbon emissions. This seems to be a move away from the clean image portrayed by the 'beyond petroleum' logo. The company responded to criticism arguing that it would be using technology that was less damaging than open cast mining, and declaring that the sands would have been developed anyway.

Sources: *BP issues Final Report on Fatal Explosion*, and *Annual Report and Accounts*, both at www.bp.com; Chemical Safety and Hazard Investigation Board Investigation, report No 2005-04-I-TX Refinery Explosion and Fire; *Financial Times*, 8 February 2008; *The Independent*, 10 December 2007

Introduction

In this chapter we are going to examine the global macroenvironment and the tools which firms use to analyse it. The external environment is changing radically and becoming much less predictable due to:

- the accelerating rate of globalization;
- the information technology revolution;
- the increasing economic and political weight of countries such as China, India, and Russia;
- international institutions like the WTO and the EU becoming increasingly important influences on the global environment, as have NGOs with their vocal opposition to free trade and investment, and their success in getting environmental issues, such as climate change onto the political agenda of national governments and international agencies.

Firms face great difficulty in monitoring, analysing, and responding to an external environment subject to literally thousands of different forces, both domestic and international. Massive waves of globalization in recent decades have made the task of monitoring the external environment much more complex and turbulent. Firms can find themselves operating in countries with very disparate histories, political and legal institutions and processes, economic, financial, socio-cultural environments, and physical and technological infrastructures. Firms have to be prepared to cope with various languages, different trading rules and currencies, and volatile exchange rates. Given this complexity, organizations may find it difficult to identify forces that could have a critical impact, as opposed to those that can be safely ignored. This ability to evaluate the external forces is vital because the environment creates opportunities for firms to achieve crucial objectives, such as profits and growth. However it can also pose dangers to firms that could result, ultimately, in their failing. At the global level, the external environment can force organizations to alter policies on prices, modify products, and adapt promotional policies. It may oblige them to restructure the organization, and to change strategies regarding moves into new product or geographical markets, and it can make them vulnerable to takeover. These can be seen as indirect costs for business when operating abroad.

The External Environment

The external environment of the firm comprises all the external influences that affect its decisions and performance. Such influences can vary from firm to firm and industry to industry and can change, sometimes very rapidly, over time. According to many observers, the environment for international business is changing faster than ever in two particular aspects, complexity and turbulence. Complexity relates to the increasing diversity of customers, rivals, suppliers, and of socio-cultural, political, legal, and technological elements confronting international business. Complexity is increased by the forces in the external environment continuously interacting with, and impacting on, each other. An increasingly complex external environment makes it more difficult for firms to make sense of, and to evaluate, information on changes in the environment and to anticipate their impact on the business. This, in turn, makes it more of a problem to formulate an appropriate response. The problems created by complexity are aggravated by the growing turbulence of the environment. A turbulent environment is one where there is rapid, unexpected change, in contrast to a stable environment where change is slow and predictable. Turbulence has increased with the rapid widening and deepening of the political, economic, socio-cultural, and technological interconnections brought about by globalization, and facilitated by advances in telecommunications.

What was a fairly static environment may become turbulent and subject to violent change. In the 1990s, the relatively tranquil environment faced by EU airlines like BA, Air France, and Lufthansa was disturbed by the decision made by the EU to liberalize entry into the industry. New aggressive rivals in the form of the low cost airlines like Ryanair, easyJet and Air Berlin entered the industry competing away the established firms' market shares on short and medium-haul flights. Business operating on a purely domestic basis is likely to confront a safer environment than its international counterparts. Some firms, like corner shops, face a relatively simple and certain environment whereas multinationals, like Nestlé, operating in almost 100 countries have to deal with one that is much more dynamic, complex and in some cases, dangerous and uncertain.

Growing complexity and turbulence in the environment makes it more difficult for firms to predict demand. It leads to competition becoming more disorderly, shortens the time available to make decisions, increases the risk of product obsolescence, and forces business to speed up the innovation process. Mason (2007) suggests that most managers have not been trained to cope with an environment of complexity, uncertainty, and turbulence and goes on to claim that such an environment is not conducive to traditional authoritarian, top-down, command and control styles of management.

Mini Case Complexity and Turbulence—China is Changing the World

This case shows how political and economic developments in China have affected, in expected and unexpected ways, the international business environment. After the decision by the Chinese Communist Party to move towards a more open economy, it has become the fastest growing economy, the world's second largest exporter of goods after Germany, the biggest exporter of capital, and the largest emitter of greenhouse gases.

Source: www.istockphoto.com

China's entry into the world economy had a big impact on global prices. With its low unit costs of production feeding into low export prices, it helped to lower world prices of exports, putting manufacturers, particularly in the developed economies under great competitive pressure. On the other hand, its booming demand for commodities such as steel, copper, and oil has caused their prices to rise. Between 2003 and 2008 the world price of metals rose by 180% and energy by 170%—good news for mining companies, such as Billiton and Rio Tinto, but bad news for car manufacturers and transport companies who are big consumers of these commodities. It is forecast that, were Chinese oil consumption to continue to grow at the same rate, deposits of oil and natural gas would be rapidly exhausted and the implications for climate change would be catastrophic.

There are fears that China's development will provoke a political backlash from other countries. Continued growth in China's trade surplus could trigger protectionism by governments in North America and Europe which could have a serious impact on importers and retailers of Chinese goods. Political tensions are also rising with Chinese efforts to secure supplies of raw materials in Africa and South America. State-backed organizations, using China's vast foreign exchange reserves, are also taking stakes in industry and commerce in the West.

Sources: *Financial Times*, 3 January, 23 January and the supplement on Africa-China Trade on 24 January 2008; *The Economist*, 26 July 2007

However, it would be unwise to see firms as simply being the subject of the macroenvironment (see Chapter Seven). Business, especially big businesses like Microsoft, General Electric, ExxonMobil, and Deutsche Bank, can exercise influence over their macroenvironment. The US presidential election in 2000 shows how firms attempt to do this. Large oil companies in the USA, along with other energy interests, gave around US$50 million to the Republican Party in the run up to the Presidential election. George W. Bush was elected with Dick Cheney as Vice President. Both Bush and Cheney had previously been involved in the oil industry. Cheney had been the CEO of Halliburton, the world's largest oil field services company (www.bbc.co.uk, 1 May 2001). On his election, the President abandoned the Kyoto protocol on global warming and moved to allow oil drilling in the Arctic National Wildlife Refuge in Alaska. Just before the EU was about to slap a €300 million fine on Microsoft for abusing its dominant position in computer operating systems, US diplomats lobbied the EU to take a softer line (*EU Observer*, 27 September 2006).

Opportunities and Threats

Globalization, associated with the increased cross-border movement of goods, services, capital, and people, is creating a more closely interdependent world characterized by growing networks and has been a major influence in shaping the external environment of business. The widening and deepening of globalization means that local environments are not solely shaped by domestic events. Equally, increased interdependence causes local, regional, or national events, such as the 2007 credit crunch which originated in the USA, and bird flu with its origins in South East Asia to become global problems. Increasing interconnectedness means that threats and opportunities are magnified, especially for organizations operating internationally.

Opportunities

Globalization generates opportunities for business to enter new markets, take advantage of differences in the costs and quality of labour and other resources, gain economies of scale, and get access to raw materials. Over the last decade China and India have opened up their economies to foreign trade and investment. Foreign companies including Tesco, Heineken, Disney, General Motors, and Toyota have taken advantage of the opportunity to invest in China and India.

Many firms have responded to the new environment by globalizing production and reorganizing their supply chains to take advantage of low cost labour, cheap international transport, and less regulated operating environments. Wal-Mart, the largest retailer in the world purchases many of its supplies of toys, clothes, and electronics goods from China. In 2004, it purchased US$18 billion worth of goods from China. Other large retail multinationals like Carrefour and Auchan of France, Metro in Germany, Makro of the Netherlands, UK-based B&Q, IKEA of Sweden, and the US firm Home Depot also source extensively from China (Coe *et al.* 2007). Boeing is another example, with the three million parts in a 777 being provided by more than 900 suppliers from 17 countries around the world (*Guardian*, 18 January 2008). An implication of this trend is that the fates of these companies, and their customers, become intertwined with their foreign suppliers and subject to the external environments in which they operate.

Threats

Globalization is also accompanied by threats which can have devastating effects on business, causing long-term damage or even leading to the collapse of the business. In the past, threats for international firms tended to be seen as country-specific, arising from:

- financial risks, for example, currency crises, inflation;
- political risks associated with events such as expropriation of assets by foreign governments or unwelcome regulations; and
- natural disasters such as earthquakes and tsunamis.

For example, the 1999 earthquake in Taiwan cut the supply of computer chips to HP, Dell, and Compaq, and the Chinese earthquake in 2008 forced Toyota to halt production there. But now there is an additional set of threats—these include terrorism, hacker attacks on computer networks, and global diseases such as AIDS and bird flu.

Terrorists are more likely to attack business than other targets, particularly US business. Two-thirds of terrorist attacks are against US businesses in the Middle East, South America, and Asia (*Financial Times*, 25 April 2006; Enderwick 2006).

As firms become more international they become more vulnerable to threats. For example, with the move towards global sourcing, supply chains can become stretched as they straddle multiple borders and involve more parties (see Braithwaite 2003, for a discussion of global sourcing and its risks). This leaves the supply chain more liable to disruption.

According to Lee (2004), increasing world trade in goods has resulted in 20 million container trips each year with 17,000 containers arriving at US ports each day. The 9/11 terrorist attacks led the USA, along with other governments, to tighten up on security at ports. This resulted in a more rigorous inspection of cargoes, which led to increased delivery times. As a result, costs rose for firms who, often facing fiercer competition as a result of globalization, were trying to reduce delivery times and minimize stockholding through the introduction of just-in-time. It also raised costs for shipping firms as it increased the time taken to turn round their vessels. The takeover of P&O by the Arab firm Dubai Ports was delayed by concerns raised in the USA as P&O owned several American ports and there were concerns about port security.

Another effect of 9/11 was to make it more difficult, and sometimes even impossible, to get insurance cover. Enderwick (2006) reports that Delta Airlines' insurance premium against terrorism in 2002 rose from $2 million to $152 million after the attack.

Increased international sourcing of supplies means that firms need to pay particular attention to the maintenance of quality standards. In 2007, the giant US toy firms Mattell and Hasbro had to recall millions of toys made for them in China because of hazards, such as the use of lead and small magnets that could be swallowed by children (*Financial Times*, 30 August, 10 September 2007).

Threats for some firms and industries can be opportunities for others. In 2005, the US States of Florida and Louisiana, along with the Gulf of Mexico were devastated by several hurricanes—the city of New Orleans had to be evacuated. Oil firms, operating in the Gulf, suffered extreme losses as a result of extensive damage to oil rigs and onshore pipelines and refineries. The supply of oil was adversely affected, and prices rose hitting big consumers of oil such as shipping and airline companies. On the other hand, some firms benefited. With power lines down, and many houses destroyed, producers of portable power generators experienced a surge in demand, as did producers of mobile homes. And in 2006, Shell, which had only suffered limited hurricane damage, announced its largest profits ever.

Financial risks have become increasingly important because, over the last 40 years, there have been increasing levels of volatility in financial markets. Unexpected movements in exchange rates, interest rates, and commodity and equity prices are major sources of risk for most MNCs. Surveys show that many large MNCs see the management of foreign exchange risks to be as important as the management of other risks.

There are various overlapping risks associated with exchange rate movements that need to be managed. Contractual risk occurs when firms enter into contracts where the revenues or outgoings take place in a foreign currency. A Eurozone firm may agree to buy a good from

Mini Case Global Threats—Cybercrime

Increasing global interconnectedness has been accompanied by the development of new threats which can have a devastating impact on business. Advances in communications technology have made it easier to commit crimes using computers and the internet. This fast-growing threat is called cybercrime. It is attractive because it can be done at a distance and with anonymity. It includes identity theft where personal information, for example, from customers is stolen. Users are lured to fake web sites where they are asked to enter personal information such as usernames and passwords, phone numbers, addresses, credit card numbers, and bank account numbers. The information can be used to drain bank accounts or to buy goods and services using fraudulently obtained credit card details. It also includes hacking into computers to get access to confidential business information, and the creation and distribution of viruses and worms on business computers. Companies may find themselves being blackmailed by cybercriminals threatening to use the information they have stolen to attack their systems. An example of this was seen when Russian gangsters tried to blackmail gaming companies with threats to attack their online operations.

It is estimated that, in Britain alone, six million people illegally download films and music every year costing film and music companies billions of pounds in lost revenues.

In the UK, cyber-attacks are estimated to be costing businesses £10 billion a year. In the USA, the FBI estimated that cybercrime costs US businesses £33 billion a year (*Financial Times*, 5 May 2006).

International banks like HSBC receive thousands of virus attacks. Research from IBM showed a significant increase in virus attacks. In January 2004, one in 129 e-mails was virus-ridden, but by June 2005 that proportion had grown to one in 28 emails. Traditional viruses are spread by e-mail, while worms detect and infect computers by simply wriggling around the computer network. While globalization has offered opportunities in China, it has also created challenges for business because the spread of the internet has meant that a lot of cybercrime originates in China. It was estimated that China accounted for as much as 42% of cybercrime in the Asia-Pacific and Japan region.

Sources: *Financial Times*, 9 November 2005; *The Independent*, 17 September 2007; *The Timesonline*, 18 March 2005 and 12 February 2008; www.techterms.com. For an update on the incidence of cybercrime go to Symantec's Risk Management report at www.symantec.com

---

a US supplier and pay in dollars, or may accept dollars in payment from US customers. If the dollar falls against the Euro then purchasers in the Eurozone benefit because they need to exchange fewer euros to buy the goods. On the other hand, French champagne producers, selling to the US, will lose out because the dollars they receive will buy fewer euros.

The next risk arises when firms earn money abroad and have to translate that into their domestic currency for the purposes of the reports and accounts. Movements in the exchange rate could have a major impact on the profit and loss account and on the balance sheet value of assets held abroad. After 2002, the US dollar declined in value against other currencies (see Figure 4.1). Unilever reported, in the fourth quarter of 2007, that sales in the Americas had grown but that the movement in exchange rates had reduced the Euro value of turnover by 6%.

Fluctuations in exchange rates make it difficult to evaluate company performance. Some companies get round this by stripping out the effects of movements in rates by translating the current year's turnover and operating profit using the previous year's exchange rate, or stating the sales and profits in the appropriate foreign currencies or, like Unilever, stating how much sales or profits were reduced or increased as a result of exchange rate changes.

Figure 4.1 Euro–US Dollar Exchange Rate 2007/08

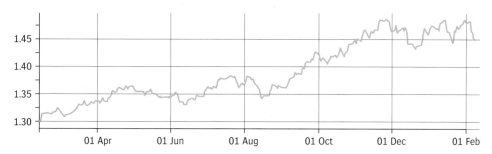

Learning Task

The Economist magazine provides information on currency movements at: www.economist.com. Call up a graph of the movement of the exchange rate of the Euro against the dollar for the past year.

1. How many dollars could you get for one Euro at the start of the period and how many at the end? Calculate the percentage change.

2. Typically the exchange rate fluctuates on average by 10–15%.
   How does the result of your calculation compare with the typical change?

3. Analyse the possible impact of the change in the dollar rate for European car makers like VW which do not have manufacturing facilities in the USA (that was the case until 2008).

4. What would be the likely effect on European airlines buying aircraft from the US firm, Boeing?

Mini Case Volatility in Financial Markets

Over the last 40 years there has been increasing levels of volatility in financial markets. As regards currencies, there was a system of fixed exchange rates up to the early 1970s. Since its collapse, exchange rates have become increasingly volatile. Between 1970 and 2000 the dollar appreciated by two thirds against sterling but fell by more than 70 per cent against the Japanese yen. In 2000 one dollar bought 107 yen but subsequently the dollar rose in value and by mid 2007 was worth almost 130 yen. As can be seen in Figure 4.1, in March 2007 a Euro was worth US$1.30 but by November it had gone up by about 14% to around US$1.48. For every one yen rise against the dollar, Toyota suffers a fall in profit of more than US$300 million while a one yen increase against the Euro knocks profits down by around US$5 billion. Exchange rates vary on average by 10–15% per year which is enough to eliminate the average profit margin of a typical MNC.

Sources: Bowe and Dean (2003); *The Guardian*, 10 March 2005; www.just-auto.com.

Scanning the Environment

Big international firms spend time and resources regularly scanning their environment in order to identify forces that will have a major influence on them. In particular, they will be looking out for changes in the environment that could have an impact on their operations in terms of helping or hindering them achieving their objectives. These objectives for industrial and commercial firms usually include profits and growth, and they may also set themselves targets with regard to market share or becoming the leading brand. Thus, firms will be particularly sensitive to aspects of the external environment that will affect their ability to achieve their objectives.

Taking profit as an example, this is determined by the ability of the firm to generate sales revenue and control costs. So they will seek to identify external forces that generate major opportunities to increase revenue or to cut costs. On the other hand, business will also endeavour to spot significant threats that might reduce revenues and increase costs. Firms then evaluate these forces in terms of:

- the most probable opportunities and threats;
- their potential impacts on the organization;
- the ability of the business to deal with them.

For example, firms can assess the impact of an outbreak of war or hackers breaching their IT systems and work out the effects on the various functional areas of the business, their ability to deliver to their customers, and on their share price.

This impact analysis, when done early enough, allows firms the time to consider a range of responses to exploit the opportunities and defuse the threats. This helps organizations recognize and adapt policies and strategies to their changing regional, national, and global environments. Because of increasing volatility and turbulence in the external environment, firms have got to expect/prepare for the unexpected.

Firms like Shell do this by spending lots of time and energy trying to anticipate possible changes in the external environment and coming up with alternative strategic responses. It has developed a tool called Global Scenario which it uses to explore various scenarios relating to the legal environment, the role and importance of the market and the State, non-governmental organizations in society, forces bringing about global integration, and the factors leading to fragmentation and economic growth. It is also interested in the impact of the growing concerns about environmental issues, such as global warming, on the demand for fossil fuels such as coal, oil, and gas (Figure 4.2).

Figure 4.2 Scenario Planning

Global frameworks
In the next ten years, social and political responses to globalisation will become clearer. How will they challenge globalisation and what will the reaction be? How do people, as individuals or collectively, view the international system? How do governments and inter-governmental organisations build legitimacy and act effectively in the international system? What is the role of regulation in the operation of global markets?
States and markets
States and markets are natural complements, and the mixed economy is an enduring 20th century legacy. But how will the composition change? How will states govern markets—or will markets discipline states?
Corporation of the future
How will competition shape innovation and vice versa? Will innovation be incremental or monumental? How will contractual relationships be affected, particularly as regards flexibility?
Energy
Themes explored included the impact of environmental concerns on fossil fuel demand and on the development of new and unconventional fossil fuel sources, as well as the future of renewables, oil price behaviour, and the link between gas and oil prices.

Source: Scenarios: An Explorer's Guide at www.shell.com

The Macroenvironment

Macroenvironmental forces comprise the wider influences on the business environment. They can be classified under the headings of political and legal, economic and financial, socio-cultural, technological, and ecological. While each of these can be examined as independent elements, often changes in one area of the external environment can have an impact on others. For example, a government may take a policy decision to carry out a big expansion of public spending on infrastructure. This could influence the economic environment by increasing the total demand for goods and services in the economy and boost the rate of economic growth. If the economy is close to operating at full capacity then it could also lead to an increase in inflation and/or suck in more imports or divert exports to the domestic market. The balance of payments could suffer, which could result in a fall in the exchange rate. Another instance of the interconnection between the various elements in the external environment occurred when the Chinese and Indian authorities made a decision to open up their economies to foreign trade and investment. These decisions changed the political environment and helped transform the economic environment as their rates of economic growth soared. This, in turn, had an impact on the microenvironment of business because rapid growth of income and demand for goods and services in China and India made them very attractive markets for foreign firms. On the other hand, the microenvironment can lead to changes in the macroenvironment—the credit crunch of 2007/08 is likely to lead to tighter government regulation of financial services.

We are going to examine each element of the macroenvironment in turn, looking in particular at their potential impacts on business. For this we use PESTLE as an analytical framework. PESTLE is an acronym for the Political, Economic, Social, Technological, Legal, and Ecological factors which fashion the environment within which business operates. It is often used to identify opportunities (O) and threats (T) which can be combined with an analysis of a firm's strengths (S) and weaknesses (W), to produce a SWOT analysis.

Political and Legal Environment

The political and legal environment is made up of the various political and legal systems under which business operates. We treat these together here because political institutions, such as governments and parliaments, pass laws and establish regulations which shape the legal environment within which business operates. The courts, the police, and prisons ensure that the laws are enforced and lawbreakers are punished. Political regimes range from the liberal democratic systems of North America and Europe, to the Communist regimes of China and Vietnam, to military dictatorship in Burma (Chapter Seven deals with this in more depth).

Some industries, like oil, need to pay particular attention to their political environment because they operate in a very politically sensitive sector, energy. Politicians and civil servants need to be kept on-side because they are the people who decide whether oil companies are given the opportunity to search for, and exploit, oil reserves. Like other areas of the external environment, the political environment can turn nasty. Countries such as Russia, Venezuela, and Bolivia have been taking back control of their energy reserves from the oil majors. BP is a company with many reasons to nurture relationships with political institutions, and the people within them—it was nationalized in Iran, Iraq, and Nigeria, fined millions of dollars for illegally fixing propane prices in the USA, and for oil spills in Alaska.

Business also often looks to its domestic government to protect it from threats abroad (see next Learning Task). Governments in powerful countries such as the USA can exercise their influence over other countries to provide protection for US firms. This is particularly reassuring for MNCs given that the majority of the largest multinationals are based in the USA. However, commentators such as Haass (2008) see the USA losing position as the dominant world power. After the collapse of the Soviet Union, the USA was the dominant economic, political, and military power in the world. But in the 21st century, US dominance is being challenged economically and politically by countries such as China whose share of the world economy is growing rapidly (for conflicting views of change in the global balance of power see Walllerstein and Wohlforth 2007). Going along with this line of reasoning would suggest that the USA will not be able to offer the same degree of protection to its international companies.

Learning Task

Examine the chart below which shows the average level of tariff protection afforded by the authorities in LDCs (Lesser Developed Countries) and Developed Economies.

1. Why do countries, both rich (Developed Economies) and poor (Lesser Developed Economies), protect industries like agriculture and textiles?

2. Compare and contrast the level of protection given by developed as opposed to LDCs. Advance some reasons for the differences between rich and poor countries.

3. Vietnam provides a very high level of protection (44%) to its processed food sector.

   What are the implications of that level of protection for domestic producers of processed food products in Vietnam?

4. The level of protection on textiles in Malawi is equivalent to 36% of the world price.

   Discuss what a foreign textile manufacturer would need to do to penetrate the market in Malawi.

Figure 4.3 Import Protection as % of World Price

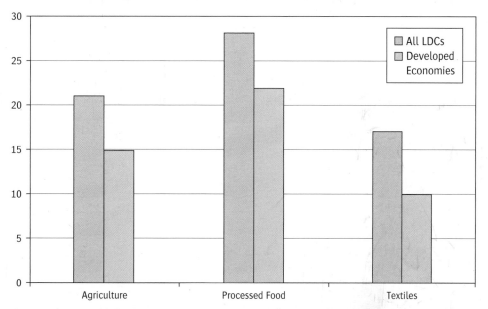

Sources: *Short- versus Long-Run Implications of Trade Liberalization for Poverty in Three Developing Countries.* Hertel, T. W., Ivanic, M., Preckel, P. V., Cranfield, J. A. L. and Martin, W. *American Journal of Agricultural Economics*, Dec 2003, Vol 85, Issue 5

Firms also have to take account of the increasing importance in the political and legal environment of international institutions like the World Trade Organization (WTO), the EU, and the substantial number of regional trading blocs that have been established, and bodies such as the International Accounting Standards Board that has the task of setting international accounting standards. Countries get together in the WTO to agree the rules

Mini Case Political Change and Market Opportunities

1989 saw a major change in the political environment in Europe. Communism collapsed, and countries in Eastern Europe such as Poland, Hungary, and Bulgaria freed themselves from control by the USSR. This major upheaval in the political environment opened up trade and investment opportunities in these economies to Western firms. Now if you go to any capital city in Eastern Europe whether it is Moscow, Budapest, or Prague you will see designer shops and people with a wide range of international luxury brands like Gucci, Armani, and Mercedes-Benz —these businesses quickly recognized the market potential in the growing number of rich people. However, companies producing mid-market brands were slow to exploit the market provided by consumers with lower incomes. This meant that a potentially lucrative market was being neglected. There are about 200 million people in central Europe with incomes of US$500 to US$1,300 a month, with most of it concentrated in just three countries—Poland, Ukraine, and Russia. This is a much larger market than the 50 million people on top incomes that multinationals have already successfully reached. There are signs that companies have seen the potential and have moved to exploit these market opportunities. Firms like Ryanair, Pepsi, Tesco, Scottish and Newcastle breweries, and MTV have all penetrated Eastern Europe markets. And even in lower income economies in Eastern Europe there are market opportunities. Car producers have seen the potential: Renault, for example, in 2004 produced and launched its low cost Logan car in Romania selling initially at €5,000. This was a great success with sales over three years of around 600,000 and Renault announced its intention to produce the car in Russia as well. Ford announced in 2007 the purchase of a Romanian car plant where it planned to make more than 300,000 vehicles and engines a year.

Source: *Financial Times*, 6 August, 13 September 2007; *Automotive News Europe*, 10 March 2003

Photo by Gina Policelli

and regulations around international trade and investment. The WTO then acts to ensure respect for the rules. In 2008, a WTO panel ruled, in a case brought by the USA, the EU, and Canada, that China had broken the rules by using tax policy to restrict imports of car parts. Saner and Guilherme (2007) point out that the common approach used by the International Monetary Fund and the World Bank towards developing countries included:

- reducing budget deficits by raising taxes and cutting public expenditure;
- giving up control of interest rates;
- reducing barriers to trade and foreign direct investment;
- setting a stable and competitive exchange rate; and
- privatizing public enterprise.

All of these could have significant effects for domestic and foreign firms on the intensity of competition, market shares, prices, costs, and profits.

Economic and Financial Environment

The economic and financial environment comprises forces that affect large areas of the economy like the rate of economic growth, interest rates, exchange rates, and inflation and the policies of domestic and international institutions that influence these economic variables. The rate of economic growth is important for business because it indicates

Figure 4.4 Real GDP Growth

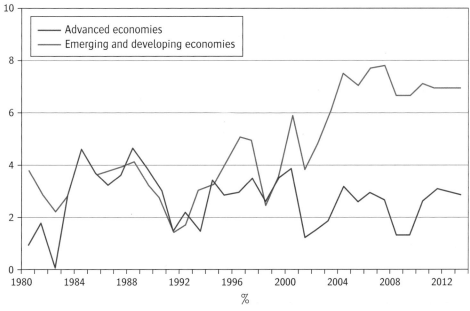

Source: International Monetary Fund, World Economic Outlook Database, April 2008

the speed at which the total level of demand for goods and services is changing. In fast-growing economies income and purchasing power is increasing, leading to an expansion in demand. By contrast, slow growth means that markets are not expanding so quickly and are therefore not so attractive for business. Institutions like the IMF produce information on the world economy and its component parts. Its figures show that advanced economies have been growing relatively slowly whilst developing countries are expanding at a more rapid rate—Chinese growth, for example, topped 11% in the first half of 2007, while India and Russia were growing at rates of 9 and 8% respectively (IMF 2007). The IMF also makes predictions of growth rates which could be of use for business trying to identify which markets will be fastest growing. Figure 4.4 indicates that markets in developing countries will continue to grow faster than those in advanced economies (see Chapters Two and Nine).

Despite the higher rates of economic growth in poorer countries they still account for a relatively small proportion of world income and purchasing power, indicating that the biggest markets continue to be located in richer regions. IMF estimates (2008) show that the advanced economies generate more than three quarters of global income, the USA alone leading the way with around 27% of world GDP. Japan, Germany, the UK, and France together make up a further quarter of income (Table 4.1). GDP measures the size of an economy—it represents the value of all goods and services produced within the geographical boundaries of a country. Dividing total GDP by the country population gives the level of output or income per head.

Business can also be affected by volatility in the economic and financial environment. In the 20 years after the late 1980s, there were seven periods of turmoil in financial markets:

Table 4.1 Total Gross Domestic Product 2006

Ranking	Economy	$US mills
1	USA	13,194,700
2	Japan	4,377,053
3	Germany	2,915,867
4	China	2,644,642
5	UK	2,402,003
6	France	2,252,108
7	Italy	1,858,336
8	Canada	1,275,283
9	Spain	1,231,733
10	Brazil	1,072,360
	World	48,144,470

Source: International Monetary Fund, World Economic Outlook Database, April 2008

- the US stock market crash of 1987;
- the crisis in the European Monetary System in 1992 when sterling and the Italian lira were removed and several other currencies had to be devalued;
- Russia defaulting on debt repayments and the collapse of Long Term Capital Management in 1998;
- the financial crisis in East Asia of the late 1990s;
- the dotcom crash of 2000;
- the impact of the attacks on the Twin Towers in 2001;
- the 2007/08 credit crunch.

Such events cause a sudden and, because of globalization, geographically widespread increase in uncertainty in business and finance. Markets become volatile and make the assessment of risk more difficult. As a result, there is a flight from, what are deemed to be, risky to safer assets. Lenders steer away from providing credit to the private sector into lending to governments. It can become more difficult and costly for business and financial institutions to borrow money. Confidence takes a hit, which has a knock-on effect on economic growth because business and consumers become less willing to invest or buy goods and services. The inability to borrow, combined with contracting markets, could result in companies going out of business. These effects can be alleviated, to an extent, when institutions such as central banks, take action to boost confidence by, for instance, reducing interest rates and providing credit to banks, as happened in the USA and the UK during the 2007/08 credit crunch (see IMF 2008 for a more detailed impact analysis of these events).

Socio-cultural Environment

The socio-cultural environment is concerned with the social organization and structure of society. This includes many social and cultural characteristics which can vary significantly from one society to another. Social aspects include the distribution of income and wealth, the structures of employment and unemployment, living and working conditions, health, education, population characteristics including size and breakdown by age, gender and ethnic group, social class, the degree of urbanization, and the provision of welfare for the population in the form of education, health care, unemployment benefits, pensions and so on. The cultural components cover areas like language, religion, diet, values and norms, attitudes, beliefs and practices, social relationships, how people interact, and lifestyles (for more discussion of the socio-cultural framework see Chapter Five). Responding to cultural differences, whether that is producing packaging in various languages or changing ingredients in food products due to different diets, can incur costs for firms.

Technological Environment

In simple terms, technology refers to the know-how or pool of ideas or knowledge available to society. Business is particularly interested in advances in knowledge that it can exploit commercially. Technology offers business the prospect of:

- turning new ideas into new or improved products or production techniques;
- entering new markets;
- boosting revenues;
- cutting costs;
- increasing profits.

However, technological advance has been a fundamental force in changing and shaping the patterns of business as regards what it does and how it does it. The advent of microelectronics is a good illustration. In the production process it has cut down the amount of labour and capital required to produce a certain level of output, allowed firms to hold fewer components in stock, improved product quality by increasing the accuracy of production processes and facilitating quality testing, and reduced energy use by replacing machinery with moving parts with microchips (see Chapter Six for more detailed discussion of the technological framework).

However, technology involves much uncertainty. Firms can pump lots of resources into research and development, be at the cutting edge of technology with new products that technically excel those of their competitors, but that does not guarantee success. Sony found this out when its Betamax video system lost out to VHS (see Mini Case, The Battle between Sony and Toshiba in Chapter Six for information on the battle between Sony's Blu-Ray and Toshiba's HDVD systems). Big pharmaceutical companies have increased their spending on research and development significantly but have found that the number of new drugs being generated has fallen. As a result, they have had to rely on old drugs for their revenues, look for ways of cutting costs and go for mergers (PriceWaterhouseCoopers 2007). These technology uncertainties make it more difficult for business to carry out long-range planning.

The Ecological Environment

In recent decades there has been increasing concern, both nationally and globally, about the interaction between human beings, the economic systems they establish, and the earth's natural environment. Business forms a major part of economic systems that impact on the environment by using up resources and altering the ecological systems on which the world depends. The damage to the ozone layer, the impact of global warming, and the rise in sea levels due to greenhouse gases emitted by power generation, industrial, transport and agricultural sectors, have been of growing concern (for more discussion on the ecological environment see Chapter Ten).

Environmental challenges are a global phenomenon. Global warming is not confined within national borders but affects the whole world. There is widespread recognition that economic growth is harming the environment irrevocably, and that we need to move towards a system that values the natural environment and protects it for future generations.

There is growing pressure on the political authorities to respond to these ecological threats. There are a number of possible policy responses all of which have implications for business:

Mini Case ExxonMobil versus the Environmentalists

This case illustrates attempts by a giant oil major to defuse threats to its business by influencing the debate around global warming.

In 1997, the US president, the Democrat Bill Clinton, agreed to the Kyoto Treaty that would reduce greenhouse gas emissions and prevent climate change. ExxonMobil, the giant US oil company, feared that the treaty would be approved by the US Senate and the result would be greater controls on emissions from fossil fuels, oil, coal, and natural gas. It came up with a plan to stall action on global warming. It set out to raise doubts among the public, and in the media, about the uncertainties in the scientific evidence for global warming. Exxon argued that the theory behind climate change was based on forecasting models with a very high degree of uncertainty. It claimed that there was no convincing evidence that climate change was occurring and that, if it was, there was no convincing evidence that humans had any influence on it.

Its plan was to recruit and train a number of independent scientists who had not been publicly involved in the debate on climate change and to depict supporters of action on global warming as out of touch with reality. A proposal was made to set up a Global Climate Science Data Centre which would undermine the evidence of scientists arguing for measures to be taken against global warming. The Centre would inform and educate members of Congress, the media, business, and educational institutions about climate change. The company spent millions of dollars spreading its message worldwide. It pumped hundreds of thousands of dollars into organizations that also questioned global warming like the American Enterprise Institute and the American Council for Capital Formation. In the event, and much to the joy of Exxon, the US Senate which had fallen under the control of the Republican Party, failed to ratify the Kyoto Treaty.

However, by 2007, with the Democratic Party in control of Congress, the company had changed its position. It had withdrawn funding from bodies sceptical of climate change and claimed that its position on climate had been widely misunderstood.

Sources: Environmental Defense at: www.environmentaldefense.org; Exxon internal memo available at www.edf.org; *The Guardian*, 20 March 2002 and 12 January 2007; *The Independent*, 8 December 2005

- tax the polluter;
- subsidize firms who manage to reduce activities that harm the environment, for example by switching to non-polluting sources of energy;
- use regulations to control the amount of pollution generated by business;
- promote the creation of environmentally friendly technologies.

Screening and Evaluating Foreign Markets

Companies seeking to expand abroad do so in order to increase sales, or to access resources, or both. They can do so in a number of ways—from exporting to setting up production facilities overseas. Whatever method they choose they are faced with the complex task of screening and evaluating foreign markets.

What makes an attractive market or production location? Countries differ in terms of their attractiveness as a result of variations in the economic environment, growth rates, political stability, disposable income levels, available resources, government incentives, level of competition, and the associated risk. The decisions about which markets companies will serve and how they source the goods for those markets are highly interdependent. In some cases, such as food retailing, car servicing or gyms, which require face-to-face contact with customers or where the cost of transport is prohibitive, location must be where the market is.

For others, such as microchips, production can take place anywhere in the world and be shipped to markets elsewhere. Firms may want to use their existing production facilities wherever they are located, because there is spare capacity, to serve new markets or they may want to establish new local production capacity.

In this section we are going to build on the general macroenvironmental analysis already established in this chapter together with the industry analysis of Chapter Three, to provide a framework to assess 'attractiveness'. Entry into any market must begin with an understanding of how that market is structured, because this will determine the opportunities to make profits. To what extent this is sustainable will depend on an understanding of the macroenvironment and how this affects the structure of the industry now and in the future. For example, the size and growth of the market is determined by a combination of factors in the economic, socio-cultural, and political environments or technological environment. The internet, for example, can increase the size of the market or make it easier to control foreign operations.

Figure 4.5 Country Attractiveness

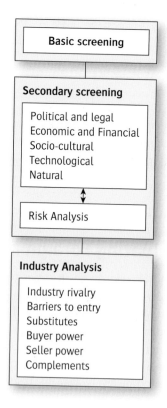

Organizations such as the Economist Intelligence Unit (EIU) assess countries for a variety of risk and sell the results to business. One table produced is an assessment for 150 countries of the degree of operational risk. Country ratings are based on 10 categories of risk:

- security;
- political stability;
- government effectiveness;
- legal and regulatory;
- macroeconomic;
- foreign trade and payments;
- financial;
- tax policy;
- labour market;
- infrastructure.

The least risky countries tend to be the most advanced economies, whilst poorer countries dominate the ranks of the most risky. Switzerland heads the table as the least risky with a score of 8 (out of 100), closely followed by Denmark (9), Finland, Singapore, and Sweden (all 10). At the other end of the scale Iraq comes in at 150th with a score of 85. Myanmar is 148th (78), Venezuela 144th (75), Ecuador 141st (68), and Kenya 139th (66) (www.Economist.com, 28 April 2008).

Basic Screening

The first stage in any screening process is to assess whether there is a basic demand for the company's products or if the basic resources required are present. This is a fairly obvious first step which can eliminate many countries from the search. For example a country's climate can be a significant influence on the pattern of demand. There is no demand for heating in Malaysia, a tropical country with an average year round temperature above 30 degrees Celsius, but a great demand for air conditioning. This makes screening fairly straightforward for specialized goods of this nature but less so for other more widely consumed products such as confectionery, computers, and games.

One way is to use trade statistics, such as the United Nations' International Trade Statistics Yearbook, to look at the goods and services a country is importing from abroad, or to identify to which countries your domestic competitors are exporting. Simple screening of countries can also be undertaken by access to basic statistics on GDP, GDP per capita, and other indicators of wealth such as the ownership of cars, televisions, and telephones. If you are selling digital cameras, flat screen televisions, and DVD recorders then Japan, with a per capita income of US$38,410, is a better starting point than Haiti with a per capita income of only US$480 (World Development Indicators database, World Bank, 1 July 2007). Another way is to look at the domestic output of an economy to see what local producers are selling.

Similarly, companies intending to produce abroad can do a quick scan of what they consider are essential resources to undertake production. Availability of raw materials is one such consideration, but access to labour and finance are other important considerations. A lot of information is freely available from organizations such as the United Nations, the World Bank, the International Monetary Fund (IMF), the International Labour Office (ILO), and the Organisation for Economic Co-operation and Development (OECD).

Detailed Analysis

Once the list of possible alternatives has been reduced by basic screening, companies will need to start a much more detailed analysis of opportunities and threats, now and in the future, through an examination of the forces outlined in Figure 4.5 and discussed earlier in the chapter.

In assessing the national business environment of countries companies will be primarily concerned with the ease of operations and the risk involved. For this reason the first move for many will be to countries whose business environment is much like their home base. Carrefour, a French company, is the world's second largest retailer with 12,500 stores in 30 countries. The Carrefour name came into being in 1959 but it wasn't until 1969 that it took its first venture outside France, and that was in Belgium—a country, in terms of its business environment, very similar to France. Its next venture was to Spain and then in 1975 to South America. It wasn't until 1989, when it entered the Taiwanese market, that it ventured into a very different business environment. However, by 2007, more than 80% of turnover was still being made in France and other European countries (www.carrefour.com).

In the next section we see how the elements of PESTLE are applied in a country analysis.

Political and Legal Environment

The main factors in any assessment of the political and legal forces are government regulation, government bureaucracy, political risk, and law and order.

Governments can erect barriers to trade and investment, or encourage it through a regime of incentives. One feature of increasing globalization is the competition for business. UNCTAD report that over the period 1991–2002, 95% of FDI policy changes were aimed at encouraging greater FDI. In 2002 96% of the 248 changes made created a more favourable climate (UNCTAD 2004).

Typical of the type of incentives are:

- Financial incentives—investment grants or credit guarantees.
- Fiscal incentives—reduced corporation tax.
- Regulatory incentives—easing of health and safety or environmental regulations.
- Subsidized services—water, electricity, communications.
- Market privileges—preferential government contracts.
- Foreign exchange privileges—special exchange rates.

Other features of the regulatory and legal regime to consider are the tax regime, employment laws, health and safety laws, environmental policy, and competition policy.

Government bureaucracy, in relation to business, refers to the difficulties faced by business in day to day operations because of the number of regulations that they have to comply with, and the rigidity with which they are enforced, commonly referred to as 'red tape'. For example, how long does it take to obtain licences to operate and how many forms have to be completed and submitted to government, how often, and in how much detail?

The Heritage Foundation in the USA, a libertarian think-tank, assesses countries according to various measures of freedom—freedom to trade, freedom from tax, regulation and corruption, the strength of property rights, and labour, financial, and investment freedom. It then ranks countries according to their scores out of 100. Those scoring between 80 and 100 are classified as free, from 70–79.9 mostly free, 60–69.9 moderately free, 50–59.9 mostly unfree and less than 50 repressed. Hong Kong with a score of 90.3 was ranked 1st. The USA with a score almost 10% below Hong Kong was ranked 5th, and North Korea with a score of 3 was ranked 157th (see Table 4.2 below for the scores of a selection of countries).

Learning Task

From Table 4.2, select one country in the top 10 and one ranked above 100. Using any secondary data you can obtain to explain the differences in the rankings.

Secondary data is available in World Development Indicators on the World Bank web site. The IMF produces country reports and the OECD carries out country surveys, reviews, and guides which are available on their web sites.

Political risk refers to the possibility of the business climate changing in such a way as to negatively affect the way in which business operates. Sources of risk include:

- Change in political leadership.
- Radical change in philosophy of political leadership.
- Civil unrest between ethnic groups, races, and religions.
- Corrupt political leadership.
- Weak political leadership.
- Organized crime.
- Poor relationships with other countries.
- Wars.
- Terrorism.
- Piracy.

Table 4.2 Economic Freedom Index 2008 (%)

Country	Rank	Score	Country	Rank	Score
Hong Kong	1	90.3	Italy	64	62.5
Singapore	2	87.4	Nicaragua	81	60.0
Ireland	3	82.4	Kenya	82	59.6
Australia	4	82.0	Poland	83	59.5
United States	5	80.6	Pakistan	93	56.8
New Zealand	6	80.2	Brazil	101	55.9
Canada	7	80.2	India	115	54.2
Chile	8	79.8	Indonesia	119	53.9
Switzerland	9	79.7	China	126	52.8
United Kingdom	10	79.5	Lesotho	132	51.9
Japan	17	72.5	Russia	134	49.9
Germany	23	71.2	Vietnam	135	49.8
Sweden	27	70.4	Angola	143	47.1
Austria	30	70.0	Venezuela	148	45.0
Spain	31	69.7	Bangladesh	149	44.9
Botswana	36	68.6	Burma	153	39.5
Uruguay	40	68.1	Libya	154	38.7
Mexico	44	66.4	Zimbabwe	155	29.8
France	48	65.4	Cuba	156	27.5
Malaysia	51	64.5	Korea, North	157	3.0

Source: www.heritage.org

One source of risk is a change in political leadership. Elections take place every four or five years in all of the advanced industrialized economies of the world, and with this can come relatively minor changes in attitude to business. This might result in changes in trade agreements or general changes in policies and regulations towards business. This is risk which is fairly predictable and shouldn't therefore be a problem. It is risk which is unpredictable that is the bigger problem. Although past patterns can be analysed to assess the risk, this also has its dangers. Kenya was generally considered as one of Africa's more politically stable countries with a thriving tourist industry bringing in about US$1 billion per year. Controversial elections in December 2007 triggered a wave of violent unrest resulting in more than 1,000 deaths and 250,000 forced from their homes. The World Bank was predicting growth in real GDP of 6.5% for Kenya in 2008 (Global Economic Outlook—October 2007), but the violence has hit the economy by reducing the number of tourists to a trickle. Horticulture was Kenya's other big earner but this also depended on the tourist industry as did the many local handicraft sellers.

It is the other sources of political instability which form the biggest risk. The possible consequences are

- Property seizure by
  - confiscation—assets seized by government without compensation
  - expropriation—assets seized with compensation.
  - nationalization—takeover by government of an entire industry.
- Property destruction.
- Freezing of funds.
- Kidnapping of employees.
- Market disruption.
- Labour unrest.
- Supply shortages.
- Racketeering.

Mini Case Piracy

This case illustrates the increased risks of global business operating in unfamiliar territory with lengthening supply chains.

12 March 2008: en route from Calabar to Port Harcourt, Nigeria. Armed pirates, in three speedboats boarded a tug, underway, kidnapped six Nigerian nationals and took them ashore. The kidnappers are demanding a ransom for the safe release of the hostages. The kidnappers claim to be the 'protectors of the Bonny River'.

Source: www.icc-ccs.org—weekly piracy report

Piracy is defined by the International Maritime Bureau as:

An act of boarding or attempting to board any ship with the apparent intent to commit theft or any other crime and with the apparent intent or capability to use force in the furtherance of that act.

In 2007 there were 263 reported acts of piracy, up 10% from 2006. 75% of these attacks were against container ships, general cargo ships, bulk carriers, and tankers. The increase was attributed to a greater number of attacks in Nigeria (42) and

Somalia (31) (Figure 4.6). Many attacks in Nigeria were by heavily armed groups with political grievances, particularly in the Niger delta region where there are tensions between foreign oil corporations and a number of the Niger Delta's minority ethnic groups who feel they are being exploited. In other piracy hotspots, Indonesia and Bangladesh, the number of incidents is down as national authorities have cooperated to tackle the problem (see Comparative Index).

Figure 4.6 High Risk Areas 2007

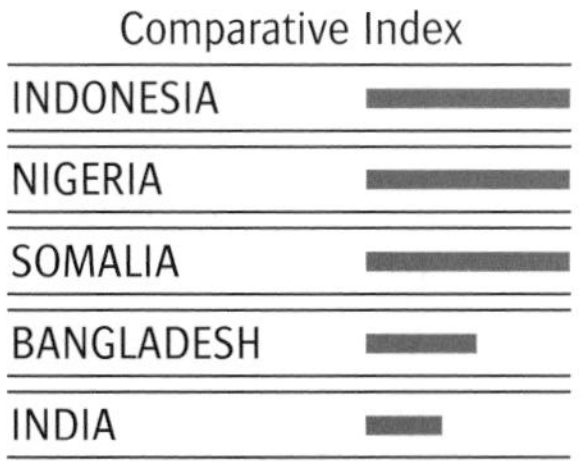

Comparative Index	
INDONESIA	■■■■
NIGERIA	■■■■
SOMALIA	■■■■
BANGLADESH	■■
INDIA	■■

Source: ICC-IMB Piracy and Armed Robbery Against Ships Report, Annual Report 2007 ➔

Source: www.istockphoto.com

Economic and Financial Environment

The major financial considerations will be rates of inflation, interest rates, exchange rates, credit availability, financial stability, and returns on investment. High and variable rates of inflation reduce the value of earnings and make forecasting and planning difficult, adding to the risk of operations. Similarly, exchange rate volatility adds to the uncertainty surrounding the value of any repatriated earnings, and how much capital is needed for investment. On the other hand some firms in the financial sector depend on volatility to make a living. Large industrial and commercial firms quite often have Treasury departments not only trying to protect earnings, but also trying to make money out of movements in exchange and interest rates.

Table 4.3 Country Risk

Selected countries and territories, May 2007					
Least risky			**Most risky**		
Rank		Score*	Rank		Score
1	Singapore	15	92	Iraq	90
2	Hong Kong	21	91	Zimbabwe	83
3	Chile	23	90	Myanmar	75
4	Botswana	24	89	Sudan	68
	Kuwait	24	88	Nicaragua	67
	Taiwan	24			
			87	Cuba	66
7	Oman	26	86	Kenya	64
8	Israel	27		Ecuador	64
9	Australia	28	84	Uzbekistan	62
	Bahrain	28		Jamaica	62
	Qatar	28	82	Venezuela	61
12	Saudi Arabia	30		Lebanon	61
	United Arab Emirates	30		Côte d'Ivoire	61
14	South Korea	31	79	Moldova	60
15	Malaysia	33	78	Syria	59

*Out of 100, with higher numbers indicating more risk. Scores are based on indicators from three categories: currency risk, sovereign debt risk and banking risk.
Source: *The Economist*, 22 August 2007

Table 4.3 shows an EIU country assessment of financial risk. Countries with good records on economic policy making such as Singapore, Hong Kong, and Chile tend to do well. Those with poor payment records, institutional failings, and civil violence are the worst rated.

Learning Task

Carry out a basic screening of Venezuela for firms involved in:

• the production of newspapers and magazines

or

• oil production.

Use Tables 4.2 and 4.3, and any other information you can access, to comment on the conditions to be faced by foreign businesses considering setting up operations in Venezuela.

The major imperative is to develop a number of indicators which help firms evaluate the relative strengths and weaknesses of markets. This assessment often uses broad economic, social, or infrastructural indicators as proxy measures for market potential.

This is not intended to assess the size of markets for particular products but to be an overall assessment of the market potential of a country. In particular companies will want an indication of:

- Market size—the relative size of the overall economy. Population size can be a useful indicator of the number of potential customers while GDP per head and disposable income per head indicates whether there is a sufficient level of purchasing power—the overall buying power of those within the economy is referred to as market intensity. The distribution of income tells us about whether purchasing power is evenly spread.

- Market growth—size is important but the rate at which the market is growing is also important so that markets which are large but shrinking or growing very slowly can be avoided and those which are small but growing rapidly can be targeted. Growth in population and GDP are often used to assess market growth.

- Quality of demand—refers to the socioeconomic profile of the customers within a market.

Other popular indicators are:

- Energy consumption.
- Televisions per head of population.
- Mobile phones per head of population.

Learning Task

Using Table 2.1 in Chapter Two, select a high income, a middle income, and a low income country. Using the statistics in that table, and any other secondary data you can obtain, compare the potential markets of the three countries.

Socio-cultural Environment

In assessing countries for markets and industrial locations socio-cultural factors also have to be taken into account. The availability and skill level of labour is important as is the motivational basis of work, levels of pay, working hours, the level of trade unionization, language, religions, and customs. These also play a role in market assessment, but the distribution of wealth and social class which determines the quality of demand referred is probably more important.

The growth of a 'middle class' in many emerging markets is boosting world demand for mass consumer goods and is making these countries the target for global multinational companies. China is at the forefront of this, although estimates of the growth of its middle class vary. What all seem to agree is that during the next 20 years a huge middle class with enormous spending power will emerge. Wal-Mart, Carrefour, Tesco, IKEA, and Kingfisher's B&Q are already well established in China.

Technological Environment

Another key feature of country attractiveness is how well developed the infrastructure is. An efficient transport and communications network is necessary for markets to function properly, and if the intention is to export a well developed port infrastructure is also necessary. Key elements to assess in the infrastructure are:

- Science and technology infrastructure.
- Extent and quality of road network.
- Extent and quality of public transport network.
- Telephony network.
- Internet capacity.
- Water supply.
- Air transport.
- Quality of ports.
- Electricity production and certainty of supply.

Countries with well-developed infrastructures are attractive to business because they facilitate market growth and offer cheaper and better transport and communication networks. Developing countries with poorer infrastructures in Africa, Asia, or Latin America are less appealing.

Ecological Environment

The natural environment is the source of essential raw materials which are part of any basic screening but the natural environment is also the source of major but difficult-to-predict risks. Natural catastrophes such as earthquakes, flooding, and hurricanes are all unpredictable, although certain areas are more prone to these occurrences than others.

Competitive Forces

Once the national business environments have been screened and the risks assessed, the final element is to analyse the competitive environment in particular product markets (see Chapter Three for an in-depth discussion of how this can be done). This should also include an assessment of how the macroenvironmental forces might affect the competitive environment in the future.

This analysis should follow that explained in Chapter Three and would include an assessment of:

- The size of the market.
- The growth rate of the market.
- The number and size of competitors.
- Marketing strategies.

- Production capacity.
- Cost structure.
- Ease of entry into the market.
- Substitutes.
- Power of buyers.
- Power of suppliers.

The Global Competitiveness Report

The World Economic Forum (WEF) produces a Global Competitiveness Report. This measures national competitiveness taking into account the microeconomic and macroeconomic foundations of national competitiveness based on the ideas outlined in Porter's diamond and the stages of development (see the section on The Competitive Advantage of Nations in Chapter Two). The WEF identifies '12 pillars of competitiveness' as:

- Institutions—the legal framework, government attitudes to markets and freedom, excessive bureaucracy, overregulation, and corruption.
- Infrastructure—quality roads, railroads, ports, airports, electricity supply, and telecommunications.
- Macro-economy—economic stability.
- Health and Primary Education—a healthy workforce with a basic education.
- Higher education and training—higher grade skills necessary for the economy to move up the value chain.
- Goods market efficiency—sophisticated customers and competitive domestic and foreign markets.
- Labour market efficiency—flexible labour markets with appropriate reward systems.
- Financial market sophistication—with savings channelled to productive investment.
- Technological readiness—access to information and communications technology.
- Market size—domestic and foreign markets allow economies of scale.
- Business sophistication—quality of business networks and individual firms' operations and strategy.
- Innovation—high levels of R&D expenditure, collaboration between universities and industry, protection of intellectual property.

According to the WEF these 12 pillars are the key to national competitiveness but they are only separated in order to be measured (Figure 4.7). They are interdependent and re-inforce each other. For example the 12th pillar of innovation is impossible without an advanced higher education system, or without the protection of intellectual property rights.

The WEF identifies three stages of development linked to the pillars and identified as the factor driven stage, efficiency-driven stage, and the innovation driven stage. The WEF allocates countries to each stage according to two criteria. The first is the level of GDP per

Figure 4.7 The Twelve Pillars of Competitiveness

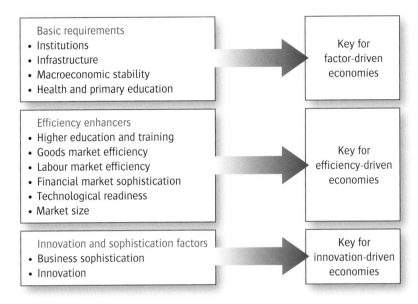

Source: The Global Competitiveness Report 2007–2008, World Economic Forum

capita (see Table 4.4) and the second is the share of exports of primary goods in total exports with the assumption that countries with a ratio of 70% or more are factor driven. Those falling in between are said to be 'in transition'.

In 2007–08 the USA topped the overall ranking of the 131 countries included in the report with Switzerland in second position. The rankings are calculated from secondary data, plus a survey the WEF carries out among 11,000 of the world's business leaders (Table 4.5).

Table 4.4 Income thresholds for establishing stages of development

Stage of Development	GDP per caplta (in US$)
Stage 1: Factor driven	<2,000
Transition from stage 1 to stage 2	*2,000–3,000*
Stage 2: Efficiency driven	3,000–9,000
Transition from stage 2 to stage 3	*9,000–17,000*
Stage 3: Innovation driven	>17,000

Source: The Global Competitiveness Report 2007–08, World Economic Forum

Table 4.5 Global Competitiveness Index rankings

Country	Rank	Score/7	Country	Rank	Score/7
United States	1	5.67	Italy	46	4.36
Switzerland	2	5.62	Hungary	47	4.35
Denmark	3	5.55	Barbados	50	4.32
Sweden	4	5.54	Mauritius	60	4.16
Germany	5	5.51	Sri Lanka	70	3.99
Netherlands	10	5.4	Syria	80	3.91
Belgium	20	5.1	Georgia	90	3.83
Kuwait	30	4.66	Senegal	100	3.61
Saudi Arabia	35	4.55	Cambodia	110	3.48
Portugal	40	4.48	Uganda	120	3.33
Latvia	45	4.41	Burundi	130	2.84

Source: The Global Competitiveness Report 2007–08, World Economic Forum

Mini Case Investing in Italy

Italy is the world's seventh largest economy with a GDP of US$1,858 billion (see Tables 2.1 and 4.1), and a per capita income of US$31,802. It has a history of weak political structures and, recently, a declining economic base. In 2007 inward investment into the EU grew by 15% to US$610 billion, but in Italy inward investment fell 28% to a very low US$28 billion. In contrast, inward investment into France grew by more than 50% to US$123 billion.

Why? The World Economic Forum lists inefficient government bureaucracy and inadequate supply of infrastructure as the most problematic obstacles to doing business in Italy. In the WEF rankings Italy comes 46th and scores poorly in macroeconomic stability, labour market efficiency, and financial market sophistication.

Many tourists will see the Italian towns which retain their traditional shops as quaint, unlike many other European towns and cities which look very much alike with global retail chains and their familiar facades. But the reason for the absence of these chains is not that they don't want to be there,

it is because it is made so difficult to invest there. Italy is ranked 64th in the Heritage Foundation's Index of economic freedom.

According to the *Financial Times* (22 January 2008) there are no KFC outlets in Italy and only 37 Burger Kings. McDonalds have managed to open 360 outlets but have battled bureaucracy, nationalism, and corruption to even get that far. The article goes on to say that AT&T pulled out of an investment, in 2007, in Telecom Italia because of political interference from the government. There is a mass of regulations, selective application, and long drawn out processes for settling disputes.

All this means that Italy is not an attractive country in which to invest, with the consequence being economic growth below the European average, and estimated by the Economist Intelligence Unit to be a lowly 0.8% for 2008, rising only slowly to 1.7% in 2012.

Sources: Global Economic Forum; *Financial Times*; Economist Intelligence Unit, Heritage Foundation

Learning Task

Your company is looking for investment opportunities abroad and wishes to evaluate various country locations. Select three countries, one from South America (not Venezuela), and one from Africa, and one from Asia: compare the attractiveness of these countries for foreign direct investment.

● CHAPTER SUMMARY

In this chapter we examined the global external business environment. The factors in this environment are highly interdependent but can usefully be analysed in the following categories: political and legal, economic and financial, socio-cultural, technological, and ecological, the various elements that make up the PESTLE model. This environment is increasingly complex, dynamic, uncertain, and can be hostile. Firms need to scan the environment constantly in order to identify opportunities for new markets, for cost reductions, and for new sources of supply. They also need to look out for the many threats, not just from competitors but from economic and financial volatility, political instability, new technology, and natural disasters.

Firms can systematically screen countries to assess their attractiveness as new markets and/or production locations. This should include a macroenvironmental analysis of potential countries, as well as an assessment of the associated risks of doing business. The final stage in this process is to link this analysis with analysis of the product market as outlined in Chapter Three. Many commercial organizations specialize in country and market analysis.

● REVIEW QUESTIONS

1. Globalization has provided significant opportunities for firms to reconfigure their supply chains and globalize production systems. Explain what is meant by this and illustrate your answer with examples.

2. Discuss the risks associated with firms outsourcing supply to China.

3. Imax is a company producing cinema projectors in the USA that can show 3D films in its chain of cinemas in the USA and Europe. What are the implications for Imax of a decline in the dollar against the Euro?

4. In the early years of the new century, the EU provided protection for domestic manufacturers of T-shirts and bras, shoes, and energy-saving light bulbs against competition from cheap Chinese imports. In 2008, The European Candle Institute, representing four EU candle makers, complained of unfair competition from China, arguing that hundreds of jobs were being threatened. The EU agreed to investigate (see *The Guardian*, 19 February 2008).

   a) How would you expect wholesalers and retailers in the EU to react to these actual or potential changes in their external environment? Give reasons for your answer.

   b) The EU stated an intention to phase out the import on protection on low-energy bulbs. Try to find out why big manufacturers like Osram, a subsidiary of the German company Siemens, opposed the removal while Philips supported it. Which side prevailed in the argument? (See *The Guardian*, 25 July 2007; *Financial Times*, 27 July 2007.)

5. The WEF produces a rank and scores for the 12 pillars for each country it assesses. Access the WEF web site and look up the rank and scores for the USA, Italy, and Nigeria. Construct a table to show these and explain how the three countries differ in their attractiveness to foreign investment.

Case Study The Credit Crunch

This case shows how a change in an obscure corner of the finance sector in the USA had worldwide repercussions on the business environment.

In the USA in the years up to 2007, there had been a boom in house prices. Financial institutions lent money to high-risk borrowers with low or uncertain incomes, high ratios of debt to income, and poor credit histories. These became known as sub-prime loans.

Borrowers were lured into taking loans by what Feldstein calls 'teaser rates', unrealistically low rates at the start of the loan which, when they subsequently rose, became too expensive for customers to pay. Borrowers took the loans to cash in on the boom in US house prices. They were only obliged to pay back a minimum amount each month which neither covered the interest or paid back any of the capital sum. The result, in many cases, was that the size of the debt increased. This was not a problem when interest rates were low, but became one when they went up.

Lenders repackaged these poor quality mortgages with more traditional and less risky financial products like bonds and sold them on to other US and foreign financial institutions. These institutions then used them as security to borrow more money. The fact that these finance companies did not need to show these assets on their balance sheets meant that there was a lack of information and transparency on the level of risk and on which institutions were carrying most risk. When house prices fell in the USA and teaser rates expired, the rate of default on loans by sub-prime borrowers ballooned and the value of the assets held by the institutions plummeted. There was a widespread flight from risk and a drying up of credit for risky investment. Financial institutions faced a shortage of liquidity* because they could not turn their products into cash. To regain liquidity, hedge funds had to conduct fire sales of other assets which put downward pressure on prices in equities and foreign currencies like the Japanese yen.

The impact was felt worldwide. The New York, Tokyo, London, and other European financial markets became extremely volatile with share prices fluctuating violently. Bad sub-prime debts and the drying up of liquidity led to the collapse of Bear Stearns, a big US investment bank. The crisis was not confined to the USA. Germany's banking market was the worst hit by the credit market turmoil. Two banks collapsed and had to be rescued by the government with financial support of over £17 billion. There was a run on institutions, even those with no direct connection to the US sub-prime market. Northern Rock, the fifth largest British bank, had to be taken into public ownership (see the Mini Case Northern Rock—A Credit Crunch Casualty in Chapter Nine). The crisis even touched China, with Bank of China left holding nearly £5 billion of securities backed by US sub-prime mortgages.

The European Central Bank responded to the crisis by making massive amounts of credit available to the banking system, as did the Federal Reseve, the US central bank, and the Japanese authorities. The Federal Reserve also reduced interest rates because of fears for the US economy as a result of the crisis.

The IMF estimated potential losses to the world banking system from the credit crunch at around a trillion US dollars. UBS, the Swiss bank, and HSBC together wrote off almost US$30 billion. As the UK Chancellor saw it, 'the time was when a small bank in a US State got into trouble, it was bad news for that town or State but nowhere else. But today, when a Florida householder defaults on their mortgage, the effects are felt across the world' (cited in *The Observer*, 23 September 2007).

* Liquidity reflects the ease with which assets can be turned into cash

Source: Martin Feldstein, 'Housing, Housing Finance and Monetary Policy', 1 September 2007 www.kc.frb.org; IMF, Global Stability Report, April 2008; *Financial Times*, 18 August 2007 gives an overview of the crisis   →

→ Questions

1. What is the link between the globalization of finance and the spread of the credit crisis from the USA to other countries?

2. Find out whether the credit crunch was followed by a major slow-down in the rate of economic growth in the USA or European economies in 2008 and 2009.

3. The Federal Reserve, the European Central Bank, and the Bank of England all intervened to relieve the liquidity crisis. What would have been the effects on business had the Central Banks simply allowed the financial system to be starved of funds?

4. It was envisaged that the turmoil on the stock market could lead to a major loss of jobs in the City of London in 2008. Why do you think that might be the case? Try to find out whether there were major pay-offs in the City in 2008.

5. This question requires you to examine the impact of the crisis at Northern Rock on some of its stakeholders.

The Northern Rock share price was around 640 pence and its work force numbered 6,000 when it approached the Bank of England for emergency funds in September 2007.

What did the shareholders eventually receive for their Northern Rock shares? How does that compare with the September price?

Find out what happened to the number of people employed by the company.

6. The credit crunch gave opportunities to government controlled foreign banks from China and the Middle East, the so-called sovereign funds, to pick up shares cheaply in major Western financial institutions.

Discuss why Western governments might be concerned about government-controlled sovereign funds taking large stakes in major Western financial institutions.

Consult the following articles: *Financial Times* 23 December 2007, 18 January, two articles on 24 January 2008, 23 February 2008; *The Economist*, 26 July 2007.

Online Resource Centre
www.oxfordtextbooks.co.uk/orc/hamilton_webster/

Visit the supporting online resource centre for additional material which will help you with your assignments, essays and research, or you may find these extra resources helpful when revising for exams.

● FURTHER READING

For a very readable view of possible political, social, economic, and technological developments in the global economy see:

● Moynagh, M. and Worsley R. (2008) *Going Global: Key Questions for the 21st Century*. London: A&C Black Publishers

The next two articles give alternative views on the changing world power of the USA:

● Wallerstein, I. (2007) 'Precipitate Decline'. *Harvard International Review*, Spring, Vol 29, Issue 1

● Wohlforth, W. (2007) 'Unipolar Stability'. *Harvard International Review*, Spring 2007, Vol 29, Issue 1

For the issues around doing business in China:

● Xiaowen Tian (2007) *Managing International Business in China*. Cambridge: Cambridge University Press

The World Bank, the International Monetary Fund, and the United Nations provide information on global developments as well as producing country assessments. OECD publications give an international perspective in addition to looking at individual countries.

Business Monitor International produces country risk assessments for various areas of the world: Asia, South East Asia, Latin America, the Middle East, and so on. The Economist Intelligence Unit also produces valuable country reports. The CIA World Factbook is a useful source of information on countries. The US Department of State publishes Country Reports on Terrorism.

For information on how Shell analyses the environment and the various scenarios it envisages for the period up to 2025 see:

● Royal Dutch Shell Group (2005) *Shell Global Scenarios to 2025: The Future Business Environment— Trends, Trade-offs and Choices*. US: Institute for International Economics

● REFERENCES

Bowe, M. and Dean, J. W. (2003) 'International Financial Management and Multinational Enterprises' in *Oxford Handbook of International Business*, A. M. Rugman and T. L. Brewer (eds). Oxford: Oxford University Press

Braithwaite, A. (2003) *The Supply Chain Risks of Global Sourcing*. Stanford Global Supply Chain, October

Coe, N. M., Kelly, P. F. and Yeung, H. W. C. (2007) *Economic Geography*. Malden: Blackwell

Enderwick, P. (2006) 'Managing the Global Threats'. *University of Auckland Business Review*, Vol 8, Issue 2, Spring

Grant, R. (2005) *Contemporary Strategy Analysis*. Oxford: Blackwell

Haass, R. (2008) 'A political education for business: An interview with the head of the Council on Foreign Relations'. *McKinsey Quarterly*, February

Lee, H. L. 'Supply Chain Security—Are You Ready?'. Stanford Global Supply Chain SGSCMF-W1-2004, Management Forum, 3 September 2004

Mason, R. B. (2007) 'The external environment's effects on management and strategy: A complexity theory approach'. *Management Decision*, Vol 45, Issue 1

Porter, M. (1990) *The Competitive Advantage of Nations*. London: Macmillan Business

PWC (2007) 'Pharma 2020: The vision: Which path will you take?'

Saner, R. and Guilherme, R. (2007) 'The International Monetary Fund's Influence on Trade Policies of Low-Income Countries: A Valid Undertaking?'. *Journal of World Trade*, Vol 41, Issue 5, October

UNCTAD (2004) Series on Issues in International Investment Agreements UNCTAD/ITE/IIT/2003/5— E.04.II.D.6, 10 February

PART TWO

Global Issues

CHAPTER FIVE

The Socio-cultural Framework

LEARNING OUTCOMES

This chapter will enable you to:

- Explain the importance of the social and cultural environment for business

- Understand and explain major social and cultural elements such as demography, urbanization, religion, and language

- Analyse the implications of various social and cultural elements for business

- Compare and contrast the liberal, conservative, and social democratic social models

Case Study China—The Importance of Guanxi

Firms from the West and Japan, attracted by fast growing markets and low production costs, have been rushing to do business in China. To be effective, it is important for business to have a knowledge and understanding of Chinese culture. In this case study we look at guanxi, an aspect of Chinese culture that is particularly important for firms wishing to be successful in China.

Guanxi refers to the networks of social connections based on trust and the reciprocal exchange of favours and mutual obligations. The exchanges taking place amongst members of the guanxi network are not solely commercial, but can involve gifts and banquets and can extend into other areas of social life such as helping a member of the network avoid loss of face or social status which is very important in Chinese society. The network members have an obligation to return favours and if this does not occur then the culprit loses face and incurs damage to their reputation. The degree of obligation is determined by one's ability to help—the weaker party expects to receive more, in exchange for less. Guanxi creates mutual dependence and indebtedness amongst the network members. In the business world, networks can involve customers, suppliers, competitors, partners in joint ventures, and other forms of alliance, research institutes, politicians, and civil servants. Western firms wishing to do business in China need to create effective social

networks. McDonalds came to grief in a site in Beijing because of inadequate guanxi. Despite holding a lease on the site, it was evicted in favour of a newcomer with stronger guanxi.

Guanxi has been embedded in Chinese society for thousands of years and is also an important feature of business life in Chinese communities overseas, Taiwan, Korea, and Japan. It is used by business to overcome competitive and resource disadvantages and the problems arising from an underdeveloped legal framework, for example contract law.

There is some debate amongst commentators as to whether guanxi is becoming more or less entrenched. While Guthrie argues that it is on the wane, Park contends that it has become more deeply rooted and that firms, particularly foreign firms, need to understand and use guanxi. He argues that effective use of guanxi is critical to business performance because it can give firms a competitive advantage, facilitate flows of resources, and generally make it easier to deal with the external environment. Li gives some support to this as he found a positive link between the performance of high technology new business ventures in China and political networking by their managers.

Sources: Guthrie 1998; Li and Zhang 2007; Ordóñez de Pablos; Park and Luo 2001; Xin and Pearce 1996; *Financial Times*, 27 November 2000

Introduction

Why did the merger between two big pharmaceutical companies run into trouble? Why did McDonalds have to employ a queue monitor to control customers in Hong Kong? In a nutshell it comes down to culture. Following the merger between American pharmaceutical company Upjohn and the Swedish firm Pharmacia, it became clear that the cultures of the two parties were incompatible. Upjohn executives did not like the gradualist style of management practised by the Swedes, which favoured consensus. The Americans were harder driven, preferred taking the decisions themselves and their main focus was on results. There were also smaller irritations. The Americans found it difficult to understand why the Swedes went on holiday for the entire month of August. On the other hand, the Swedes could not see why the Americans banned alcohol at lunch (*Financial Times*, 10 November 2006). McDonalds want customers to carry their own tray, queue up in an orderly fashion, pay, seat themselves, eat quickly, help clean up afterward, and depart. In Hong Kong, customers, following local custom, crowded round the tills and pushed their money over the heads of the people ahead of them. McDonalds appointed an employee to act as a queue monitor, and within a few months, regular consumers began to enforce the system themselves. But McDonalds also had to accept that customers, rather than paying a brief visit, used the outlets as leisure centres (Watson 2000).

Business operating at the international level has to face a variety of social and cultural environments where social characteristics, structures, and institutions may differ significantly. Societies across the world can differ enormously in terms of demography, health, class structures, the composition by ethnic group, the incidence of corruption, the importance of pressure groups, and in norms and values. To be successful, business has to be aware of the differences that could be important to it as regards the level and pattern of demand, the quality and quantity of labour, and the policies and strategies it has to adopt.

This chapter examines the social and cultural environment. This encompasses a vast range of social and cultural characteristics which can vary significantly both within societies and between one society and another. Social aspects include the distribution of income and wealth, the structures of employment and unemployment, living and working conditions, health, education, population characteristics including size and breakdown by age, gender, and ethnic group, the degree of urbanization, and the provision of welfare for the population in the form of education, health care, unemployment benefits, pensions and so on. The cultural components cover areas like language, religion, diet, values and norms, attitudes, beliefs and practices, social relationships, and how people interact. There are links between certain aspects of culture and social conditions, for example between diet and certain types of disease, values, and norms and the role of women in society, religious beliefs, and attitudes to contraception and their effect on birth rates.

There are far too many elements to be addressed comprehensively in a single chapter. Therefore, the chapter focuses on a limited number of social and cultural aspects. We start off by considering culture and then go on to consider some important elements in the social environment.

Culture

Culture can be seen as a system of shared beliefs, values, customs, and behaviours prevalent in a society and that are transmitted from generation to generation (Bates and Plog 1990). Hofstede (1994), the management scientist, described these elements of culture as the software of the mind, 'the collective programming of the mind which distinguishes the members of one category of people from another'. The values in the culture are enforced by a set of norms which lay down rules of behaviour. These rules are usually supplemented by a set of sanctions to ensure that the norms are respected. Culture comprises a whole variety of different aspects, including religion, language, non-verbal communication, diet, dress, and institutions to ensure that the values and beliefs are transmitted from one generation to another. Culture is dynamic, in other words, it changes over time not least due to the process of globalization with the increasing cross-border movement of goods, services, capital, and the migration of people (Dahl).

Different cultures can have significantly different attitudes and beliefs on a whole range of issues. As we will see later, when discussing the various social models, there is a significant divide between the USA and Continental Europe on attitudes to social issues such as poverty. In the USA poverty tends to be seen as the fault of the poor whereas in Europe the poor tend more to be seen as victims of the system. Cultural attitudes can also vary towards issues such as, corruption, women at work, sexuality, violence, suicide, and time.

Cultural attitudes can have important implications for business. Some of the most influential research on culture and the workplace was carried out by Hofstede (1991; 2001). His study, the largest that had then been conducted, surveyed over 100,000 workers in IBM subsidiaries in 40 countries looking for cultural explanations of differences in employee attitudes and behaviour. He concluded that the norms and values embedded in national culture were a very powerful influence on the workplace, and that different approaches would be necessary when managing people from different cultural backgrounds. Hofstede (1994) concludes that the workplace can only change people's values to a limited extent (see Mini Case). The message for multinational companies was that they would be unwise to assume that an organizational culture that was successful in the cultural context, for example of the USA, would be equally successful in a completely different cultural context in, say, China. Hofstede's work (2007) also contains another message for multinationals. He contends that countries, especially big countries like China, India, Indonesia, and Brazil do not have a single national culture but a variety of cultures that can vary significantly from region to region. A similar point could be made for smaller countries, in Western Europe for instance, where different cultures may be based on ethnic group rather than region.

Research has revealed fundamental cultural differences between East and West that have important implications for Western executives trying to do business in the East. Psychologists have shown that Eastern and Western cultures can vary significantly in terms of perception, logic, and how they see the world around them. Apparently, Westerners focus more on detail while Easterners tend to look at things in the round. For example, when American students were asked to look at a picture of a tiger in a forest, they focused on the tiger while Chinese students concentrated more on the background, that is, the context within which the tiger was located.

Researchers attribute this to different social environments. In East Asia, social environments are more complex, collective, and constrained. As a result, Easterners need to pay attention to the social context if they are to operate effectively. On the other hand, Western societies prize individual freedom and there is not the same need to pay heed to the social environment. With their focus on the individual, Westerners tend to view events as the result of specific agents, while those raised in the East set the events in a broader context.

Cultural differences influence the way firms in the East and West do business. For example, when an applicant for a job appears uneasy, Westerners are likely to see that as an undesirable characteristic of the interviewee which makes them unsuitable for stressful jobs. In the East, they will tend to view the uneasiness in the context of a stressful situation, the interview, and thus be less likely to attribute it to the character of the applicant. Similarly, North Americans, when posing a question, expect a trustworthy person to respond immediately, with any delay inspiring mistrust. In contrast, the Japanese view more favourably individuals who take time to ponder before giving a reply. Attitudes towards contracts also vary. Once a contract is signed, Westerners regard them as agreements set in stone while Easterners, such as the Japanese, take a more flexible view.

Mini Case National Culture Matters

National cultures can vary significantly from one country and the differences can be reflected by employees in the workplace and by consumers in the market. Such variations in the psychology of work and organizations and in the market place have major implications for management. Managerial systems and approaches that work well in one country may be inappropriate for another.

Geert Hofstede, when working with IBM, noted that, while the company promoted an organizational culture in the form of common values, assumptions, and beliefs, there remained differences in attitudes and behaviour among IBM's international subsidiaries. He concluded that organizational culture is less influential than the attitudes and values prevalent in the national culture.

In his research, he considered four dimensions of culture: the extent to which people accept an unequal distribution of power; the extent to which people try to avoid uncertainty; the extent to which people stress individualism over collectivism; the extent to which people value material goods over quality of life. Hofstede found the USA to have an individualistic society, with a low power distance and a low need to avoid uncertainty, whilst collectivist-oriented societies in Asia scored highly on both these measures.

In some societies such as India, Mexico, Thailand, and Arab countries, hierarchies are very important and power is distributed very unequally. Less powerful members of organizations, those on the lower rungs of the hierarchy, expect and accept the unequal distribution of power. In other countries such as Israel, Sweden, and Ireland there is low acceptance of differences in power and a greater desire for equality. Money, incomes, promotion, and status are highly valued in countries such as Japan, USA, Mexico, Australia, and Malaysia. Hofstede labelled these societies as masculine. Other countries which he characterized as feminine, saw the quality of life and human relationships as more important—they included Sweden, the Netherlands, Singapore, and Taiwan.

Research has found that in feminine societies advertisements tend to display fewer differences in the portrayal of women and men in the type of roles they play. In masculine societies, advertising portrays men and women in very different roles. These findings have important implications as to how workers are managed and how consumers are targeted in different cultures.

Hofstede subsequently added a fifth dimension, long-term versus short-term orientation, that is the degree of importance of the past, the present, and the future in different cultures. He found that Brazil, India, and some East Asian countries had a long-term orientation. At the other extreme, the USA, Britain, Spain, Nigeria, and Pakistan focused on the short term while most European countries lay somewhere in the middle.

Sources: An and Kim 2007; *Financial Times*. 26 August 2003; Hofstede 1991, 2001, 2007

Source: www.hsbc.com

They are quite happy to renegotiate if circumstances change. They look at the situation of their customers or suppliers in the round and may renegotiate in order to maintain a long-term relationship. In the East there is a desire for consensus and harmony. Westerners sometimes perceive Japanese managers as incompetent or indecisive because, in pursuit of consensus, they continually consult their team and are usually reluctant to challenge the decisions made by others (Nisbett 2005; *Financial Times*, 27 November 2000). One of the authors came across an example of this during an interview with the Scottish executive put in charge of Mazda, the Japanese car company, by the parent company, Ford. Coming from a Western culture, he was used to debate, discussion, and disagreement when arriving at decisions. In Mazda he found the reluctance to disagree among his senior managers extremely frustrating.

Meetings in North America or Europe have formal agendas setting the order in which items are discussed, and each item is resolved prior to proceeding to the next. The Japanese, rather than deal with agenda items in a rigid sequence, may prefer a more flexible approach which enables them to get a better overview. To Westerners, meetings in Japan may appear unstructured, chaotic, and even threatening. However, Japanese managers are well used to such ambiguity.

Differences in approach can also be seen in negotiations. Westerners expect to focus on contentious issues and try to achieve the most beneficial outcomes for themselves. In contrast, the Japanese prefer to discuss areas of agreement, with the expectation that harmony will lead to the resolution of details. Such differences can lead to bad feeling in negotiations. Lee quotes a senior South Korean official involved in trade negotiations with Australia. Even though Australia was running a large trade surplus in agricultural products with South Korea, which was of serious concern to the Koreans, 'Australia,

Mini Case Culture and Management

Surveys of executives in various different countries indicate that management styles are influenced by national cultures and can vary enormously.

A survey, carried out on 700 managers in the UK, Sweden, the Netherlands, the USA, Hong Kong, India, and Australia found that American managers, like the Upjohn executives in the merger with Pharmacia, wanted to act quickly and get things done. They were more than happy to take risks and to face the consequences. A quarter of USA managers admitted having lost £10,000 or more as a result of unwise decisions, compared with just 2% of Hong Kong managers and 7% of British executives.

Swedish executives came out as caring for their employees and being prepared to invest heavily in training and staff development. On average Swedish managers judged half of their employees as truly exceptional at their jobs. This compared with a little more than 20% in Australia and the UK.

In the UK, executives were found to be somewhere between the USA and Swedish models. They were judged to be of strong character, operating in an environment that was risk-averse, but where it was important to get the job done.

A very distinctive culture was found in Hong Kong. Managers operated in a highly collectivist way and spent large amounts of time micro-managing employee output in organizational structures that were very hierarchical. Those at the top of the hierarchy such as the chief executive were highly valued while staff lower down were viewed as more dispensable.

Another survey of 200 British, French, and German chief executives, chairmen, and directors looked at the decision making process. The findings indicated that British managers were happy to have their decisions challenged. The Germans stressed the importance of humility while the French manager enjoyed wielding power without having to consult first.

Source: *Financial Times*, 15 October 2004 and 9 January 2006

nevertheless, continuously puts pressure on Korea to buy more of them...they are self-centred, one-sided, only concerned with self-interest, not in considering another's situation or position' (2004, p 76).

The upshot is that business has to take cultural differences into account when considering entry to foreign markets through exports, joint ventures, or through takeover or greenfield investment. Similarities between the domestic and foreign cultural norms and values may make entry for a firm easier whereas large differences may cause major difficulties due to misunderstandings and conflict where social groups do not want to give up valued elements of their culture (Oudenhoven and van der See 2002).

Learning Task

A survey was carried out in 14 countries where Muslims are either the overwhelming majority or a prominent minority. Questions were asked about attitudes to women and work. The responses are shown in Table 5.1 below. Examine the tables and answer the questions.

1. Which countries are most/least favourably disposed towards women working outside the home?

2. In which countries are attitudes most/least favourable to women working alongside men in the workplace?

3. Do men have widely different attitudes to women and work? Illustrate with some examples from the tables.

4. In the light of your answers, which countries would be a suitable location for a textile factory employing both men and women?

5. A firm would like to give one of its female managers experience of working abroad. Which countries would appear to be most/least accepting of this?

Table 5.1 Women and the Workplace

Women Should Be Permitted to Work Outside the Home				Separation of the Sexes in the Workplace			
	Men %	Women %	Diff.		Men %	Women %	Diff.
Bangladesh	36	57	+21	Bangladesh	20	36	+16
Lebanon	58	75	+17	Turkey	21	30	+9
Pakistan	24	41	+17	Nigeria	32	40	+8
Uzbekistan	64	77	+13	Tanzania	15	21	+6
Turkey	60	72	+12	Pakistan	35	36	+1
Senegal	60	68	+8	Indonesia	5	6	+1
Nigeria	32	38	+6	Lebanon	25	23	−2
Mali	51	56	+5	Uzbekistan	48	42	−6
Indonesia	20	24	+4	Senegal	17	11	−6
Jordan	13	16	+3	Jordan	18	14	−4
Tanzania	47	47	0	Mali	44	32	−12

Percent 'completely agree' within each category.
Question not permitted in Egypt.

Percent 'completely agree' within each category.
Question based on Muslims.
Question not permitted in Egypt.

Source: Speulda and McIntosh (2004)

Religion

A core element of the culture in many societies is religion. In such societies religion is a major influence on the attitudes and beliefs that regulate behaviour. Christianity has the ten commandments, Islam has five pillars, and Buddhism has eight precepts. Each religion has a system of rewards for those who are good and punishment for those who are evil.

Learning Task

The map below (Figure 5.1) shows the geographical location of major world religions (note that space limitations make it impossible for the map to represent the large number of Muslims in areas like Western Europe and North America).

1. Comment on the geographical spread of Christianity, Islam, and Judaism.

2. Discuss the implications for fast food retailers such as McDonalds or Burger King of expanding in the Middle East.

3. Where are the major markets for firms producing goods specifically aimed at Jewish consumers?

Figure 5.1 Major Religions of the World

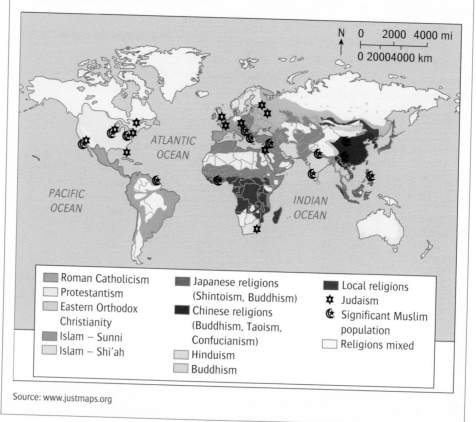

Source: www.justmaps.org

Although there are hundreds of religions in the world, five of them, accounting for around 75% of the world population, predominate. Christianity with 2.1 billion followers has the greatest number of adherents, followed by Islam with 1.3 billion, Hinduism at 900 million, Buddhism with 376 million, followed a long way behind by Judaism with 14 million. Christianity and Islam together account for more than half of the world's population and operate in more regions of the world than all the other religions (Adherents; McFaul 2006). Even in China, where religion declined after the Communist revolution, it is estimated that around 400 million Chinese practise some religion, with 100 million of them Buddhists and 20 million Muslims (*The Economist*, 1 February 2007).

Some religions lay down rules about which foods can and cannot be eaten, and how they should be prepared. For instance, Muslims are not supposed to consume pork, alcohol, foods that contain animal fats, tinned vegetables that include animal fat, frozen vegetables with sauce, particular margarines, and bread or bread products containing dried yeast. Animals have to be slaughtered in a particular way. In Judaism, meat from cattle, sheep, goats, and deer can be eaten but not from pigs and there are rules forbidding the mixing and consumption of dairy products with meats. As in Islam, animals must be slaughtered in a certain way. Only fish with scales and fins can be eaten. Hindus do not eat meat, but dairy products including milk, butter, and yoghurt are considered to enhance spiritual purity, and most Buddhists are vegetarian. There can be differences in dietary rules among faiths of the same religion. Some Christian faiths, such as Protestantism, do not have dietary rules while others, such as the Mormons, avoid alcohol and caffeinated drinks like coffee, and most Seventh Day Adventists do not eat meat or dairy products. The various rules and rituals around eating help religions reinforce their identity and distinguish them from other religions. These rules have implications for food manufacturers and retailers wishing to operate in countries with large numbers of practising Muslims, Jews, Hindus, and Buddhists (Better Health Channel).

Growth of Secularism

For a long period it seemed as if religion was a declining force in world affairs. This fitted in with the view that religion was irrational and associated with low levels of socio-economic development and ignorance. It was thought that the influence of religion would diminish with growing levels of prosperity, higher levels of education, and the spread of democracy. But in the 21st century, religion appears to be gaining force in society, whether that be reflected in the growth of radical Islam, the spread of evangelical Christianity, the opposition by George W. Bush, the US President, to scientific research on stem cells, or the claims by Russian Presidents Gorbachev and Putin to be adherents of the Orthodox church.

Language

Another important distinguishing feature for many cultures is language.

There is no agreed total on the number of languages spoken in the world today. Estimates vary from between 3,000 and 10,000 with Ethologue suggesting a figure of about 7,000 (Gordon 2005). Estimating the number of speakers is complicated because it

Mini Case Secularism versus the Church

In many developed countries, and particularly in Western Europe, there has been a trend towards secularism shown by people moving away from religious beliefs and practices. Secularism is seen as a threat to the influence of the Church because it rejects religiously prescribed rules, advocates the separation of the church and the State, the freeing of education from church authority, the rejection of church prescriptions about divorce, birth control, abortion, and sex before marriage.

Source: www.istockphoto.com

Decisions according to the secularists should be made on scientific and rational grounds. Moves towards secularism indicate a decline in the power of religion and religious institutions.

Italy, the home of the Vatican, is a good example for it has one of the world's lowest birth rates despite the opposition of the Catholic Church to contraception, and the incidence of abortion is similar to that of countries in North West Europe. A quarter of young cohabiting couples are unmarried and the share of Italians attending mass at least once a month has been in long-term decline.

But even in Western Europe, religion can still play an important role in politics. In Italy it managed to stop the government extending legal rights to unmarried couples including gays and restricted the scope of a law on the treatment of infertile women.

While secularization spread all over Europe in the post-war decades and grew in pace after the 1960s, in other areas of the world, such as the USA and Latin and Arab countries, there has been a resurgence in the power of religion and religious institutions. In the USA evangelical Christian values have played a prominent role in the policies pursued by President George W. Bush.

Source: *The Economist*, 31 May 2007; Swatos; Falk 2006

can vary widely from one decade to another, due to factors such as population growth and armed conflicts. The Asian population is forecast to grow by 25% to over 5 billion in the half century up to 2050, while the number of European inhabitants is expected to fall by some 64 million (UNa). As a result the number of speakers of Asian languages like Chinese, Hindi, and Bengali will increase dramatically while those speaking German, French, and Italian will fall. War, civil unrest, abuses of human rights, political instability, and people moving across borders to find work can also cause the figures to change significantly. This is illustrated by UN estimates putting the number of refugees at more than 10 million people in 2020 with the vast majority coming from Asia and Africa. More than 2.5 million people fled from the conflict in Afghanistan to neighbouring countries such as Pakistan and Iran, and around 400,000 went from Iraq to Iran, Germany, the Netherlands, and Sweden (UNHCR). It is obvious from the figures given that major changes are occurring in the number and location of speakers of a language.

While estimates vary of the most commonly spoken languages, most research identifies Mandarin/Chinese, with over 1 billion speakers, as first in the rankings. Other languages in the top five are Arabic, Hindi, English, and Spanish. The top languages are spoken across many countries. Chinese is spoken in 10 countries, English in 29 and

Spanish in 20, mainly Latin American, countries (see www.ethnologue.com; CIA World Factbook 2007).

Business will be interested in the speakers of a particular language especially when they congregate together in large enough numbers to constitute a market worth exploiting or present an attractive pool of labour. In the past, language speakers, even where there were lots of them, were not attractive to firms when they were widely dispersed geographically because of the high marketing and distribution costs.

Learning Task

Greece has a population of over 11 million but the total number of speakers globally is some 12 million people. It is also spoken in Cyprus, USA, Germany, UK, Poland, Australia, Russia, Canada, Ukraine, South Africa, Egypt, Albania, Sweden, Kazakhstan, Georgia, Italy, Austria, and Bulgaria.

How might the internet make small foreign communities of Greek speakers a commercial proposition for Greek firms producing traditional products?

Countries Speaking the Same Language

Even where a single language is the mother tongue in several countries, business may still encounter certain difficulties. English is the mother tongue in the UK, the USA, Australia, and the major part of Canada but that does not mean that communication is always straightforward. Words used in one country may not be understood in another. The British talk about multi-storey car parks while the Americans refer to a parking garage and the Canadians to a parkade. Similarly, Americans go to a convenience store, the British to a corner shop, and the Canadians go to a depanneur. Australians, like Americans, drive on freeways while the British drive on motorways. And some words have completely different meanings. American cars run on gas but British vehicles run on petrol. In the UK mufflers are scarves that are put round the neck for warmth but in the USA it is part of the car exhaust system that deadens noise (see Linguist). Similar concerns are likely to arise with Spanish which is also spoken in many Latin American countries.

Issues also arise in countries where English is an official language, for example in India, Pakistan, and South Africa or where it is widely spoken as a second language. Firms would be foolish to assume that they can conduct business effectively in English because levels of proficiency in the language can vary dramatically. Some may only have the ability to read the language but may have difficulties speaking or listening to it. Even where people have a good level of proficiency, it does not figure that they can understand it to the required level, especially where the topic of discussion is technical or legal, for instance around product specifications or patents and copyright.

Facing such difficulties, business will often turn to translators and interpreters. However, according to Crystal, translation always involves some loss of information because it is impossible to get an exact equivalence. One can see some rather extreme examples of this in the UK where lists of instructions accompanying imported products have been translated from the source language unintelligibly into English—electrical products from East Asia give some good examples. Crystal gives several specific illustrations of this problem. The slogan 'Come alive with Pepsi' appeared in a Chinese newspaper as 'Pepsi brings your ancestors back from the grave' (2003, p 347).

Even big multinational companies can slip up with language. One of the most well-known gaffes was when General Motors sold the Nova model in Spain. Nova means, it does not go, in Spanish. Toyota offered the MR2 in France which, when pronounced, means excrement. Estée Lauder produced a hair spray for its German customers called Country Mist. Unfortunately, mist in German means manure (*The Times*, 9 November 2002).

For a long time, British and American firms have come in for much criticism for their linguistic insularity, their assumption that English is the global language of business, and that foreigners will be happy and able to communicate in English. Therefore, for them building up competence in foreign languages is not a priority. The situation may have improved to a degree, but one US senator said that the country was 'linguistically malnourished' (Eric Digests). International surveys of language skills across Europe tell a consistent tale: the UK is bottom of the league in terms of competence in other languages. A survey of 28 countries published by the European Commission aggregated all non-mother tongue languages spoken and produced the results given in Figure 5.2.

The British Chambers of Commerce survey in 2004 found that 80% of export managers could not competently conduct dealings in even one foreign language. A survey by consultants, Grant Thornton, showed a similar picture. The proportion of UK executives capable of negotiating in more than one language was half the EU average, and well below

Figure 5.2 Language skills of Europeans

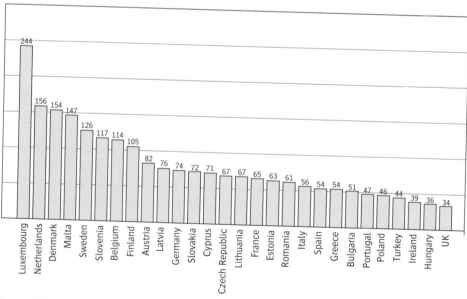

Source: CILT

Figure 5.3 Language and Trade

Where English is the language of our customers, we sell more than we buy:

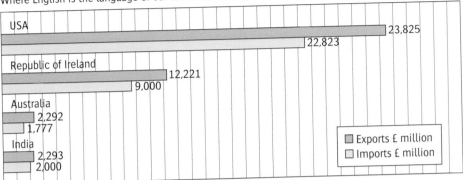

However, where the language of our customers is not English, we buy more than we are able to sell:

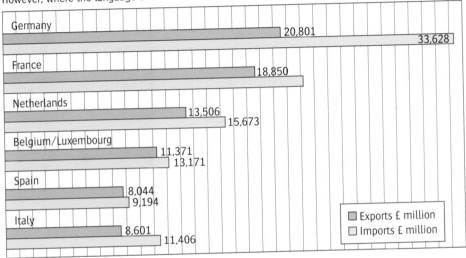

Source: CILT

the global average. The fact is that only 6% of the world's population are native English speakers. Three quarters speak no English at all (CILT).

While English is the most widely spoken foreign language throughout Europe and can be seen as the global language of business, it does seem as if competence in foreign languages is essential for international commerce. The evidence in Figure 5.3 suggests that if companies want to buy anything from anywhere in the world, they can manage with only English; if they want to sell something abroad, they need to learn the language of their customers.

Time

Different cultures vary in their attitudes to time. In some cultures the clock directs behaviour, in others behaviour is determined by the natural course of events in which people find themselves. In cultures where people follow the clock, they are careful to turn up on time for meetings and are likely to be irritated and frustrated if others do not. In other cultures, people behave according to event time which means that they organize their time around various events and participate in one event until it reaches its natural end, and then begin the next event. It has been found that the clock directs behaviour in North America, Western Europe, East Asia, Australia, and New Zealand. Event time is often found in South America, South Asia, Mediterranean countries, and in developing economies with big agricultural sectors—in which people operate according to the seasons rather than the clock, and clock time is not yet fully part of people's work habits. North Americans will schedule a meeting for 9am, turn up on time and apologize if they are a few minutes late. In countries like Saudi Arabia, people may turn up 20 minutes late and feel no need to apologize. It may be that in cultures where status is important, this is demonstrated by the high status participants turning up late. In event time countries a higher proportion of time at work is likely to be devoted to social activities such as chatting, having cups of tea or coffee. People from clock time cultures will often get frustrated by this behaviour, seeing it as time-wasting or an inefficient use of resources. However, these activities could be useful for a business because they may help to build up supportive groups so that when someone comes under pressure, colleagues will be happy to help out on a voluntary basis. Also it may be that important business relationships are made during what appears to be aimless social activity (Brislin and Kim 2003).

The Social Environment

In this section we move on to examine various elements of the social environment. We start off by examining social divisions and then go on to compare three social models which show how the State looks after the welfare of its citizens. Subsequently we consider demography, the process of urbanization, and then health and education.

Divisions within Societies

All countries are characterized by social divisions. In some societies the major dividing lines are based on social class whilst in others it might be caste, ethnic group, age, or gender. Such divisions are often associated with inequalities between the various social groups in income, wealth such as land, property, shares and so on, levels of health and education, and lifestyles. Such social inequalities are important to business insofar as they can affect the pattern of demand for goods and services. For example, countries where a relatively small social group control most of the income and wealth and the rest are relatively poor will have very different levels of demand for luxury goods compared to countries where wealth and income are more evenly spread. Similarly, great inequalities in health and education could affect the quality of the labour force.

Examining one of the areas of inequality, income, Brandolini and Smeeding (2007) found in their study of industrialized nations that, in terms of disposable income (income after deduction of income taxes and social security contributions) the US, among rich countries, had the highest level of inequality with the highest earners earning around six times more than the lowest. Only Russia and Mexico had higher levels of inequality. Most European countries have lower levels of inequality than the USA. The most equal societies were the Scandinavian countries, along with Finland and Holland. Japan and Taiwan lay somewhere in the middle of the rankings.

Social Models

In different countries, the State takes on varying degrees of responsibility for the welfare of its citizens. Today in most developed economies the State spends more on welfare than all other programmes. This spending takes the forms of benefits to the elderly, the disabled, the sick, the unemployed, and the young. It also usually involves spending on health care and education. Welfare policies may vary from country to country in terms of their aims, the amount of money spent on them, the priority given to different programmes, and the identity of the beneficiaries. In some countries the State intervenes only to provide a limited level of support to those who are regarded as deserving of help. This tends to be the dominant system in Anglo-Saxon countries. In others, such as in Scandinavia, benefits are universal, relatively generous, and open to the entire population. In poor countries the provision of welfare is often left to the family. Influences on the various approaches are the levels of economic wealth, different attitudes towards poverty, and towards the proper role of the State.

In the West, there are three social models in operation, the liberal, the corporatist, and the social democratic. Trying to classify different welfare states neatly into separate pigeon-holes is not straightforward, because they are continually adjusting to factors like globalization and to demographic change such as the ageing population, or to the feminization of the labour force. And sometimes a country will contain elements of several models. For example, the UK has aspects of both the liberal and the social democratic models. On one hand, as in the USA, unemployment benefits are not tied to incomes and require those out of work actively to seek employment or training or perform community service. On the other hand, the provision of universally provided social services in the UK such as the National Health Service and more generous in-work benefits for those who take low-paid jobs, a policy underpinned by a minimum wage, are more akin to the social democratic model prevalent in countries such as Denmark and the Netherlands.

The Liberal Social Model

The liberal social model found in the USA, Canada, and Australia and also, to an extent, the UK, is based on a clear distinction between the deserving and undeserving poor, with limits on the level of benefit payments. In liberal welfare states like the USA and the UK there is a sharp cut-off in unemployment benefits to discourage dependency and to force people back to work.

There is a commitment to keep taxes low and to encourage people to stay in work. While everyone is treated equally, there is a low level of welfare provision as expressed in the level of social expenditure (see Figure 5.4). There is a belief that people can better

Figure 5.4 Public social expenditure (as a percentage of GDP, 2003)

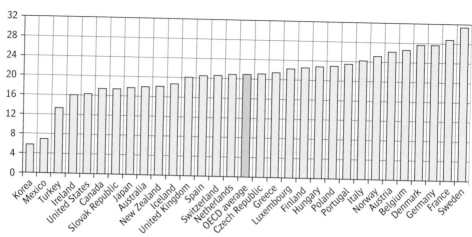

Note: Public social expenditure comprises cash benefits, direct 'in-kind' provision of goods and services, and tax breaks with social purposes.
Source: OECD

themselves through their own efforts, and that they may be poor because they do not try hard enough. In the USA, and to a lesser extent in the UK, there is scepticism about the State's effectiveness in tackling poverty. The welfare system, by giving benefits to single parents, is also believed to discourage marriage and to encourage single motherhood (see Lang 2007 on the US system).

Even in countries operating the liberal model, there can be major differences in the level and nature of welfare provision. For example, in the UK and Canada publicly funded health care is provided free to all at the point of delivery. All citizens qualify for health coverage, regardless of medical history, personal income, or standard of living. By contrast, the US system is a combination of private insurance paid for by workers through their employer, publicly provided insurance for the elderly (Medicare), the military, veterans, the poor, and disabled (Medicaid). The implementation of Medicaid varies greatly State by State. In the USA around 43 million people do not have private health insurance, which makes it the only developed country that does not provide health care for all of its citizens (University of Maine 2001).

Now we look at the corporatist and social democratic models operating in many European countries. They share certain distinctive characteristics. There is a commitment to social justice. Neither system abandons those who fail. They aspire to high levels of employment, universal access to health care and education, adequate social insurance for sickness, disability, unemployment, and old age and have a well developed system of workers' rights. These systems seem better at tackling poverty than the liberal model operating in the UK and the USA (Hemerijck).

The Corporatist Model

The corporatist model is typical of continental European countries such as Germany, France, Austria, and Italy. Japan and Southern Europe also display elements of the corporatist model but spending is not as generous as in France or Germany (see Figure 5.4). In the past, the Church played an influential role on the model with its commitment to the preservation of the traditional family. Thus, wives who were not working were excluded while family benefits were paid to those having children. The model emphasizes the importance of work and benefits are based on individual contributions. Benefits are generous relative to those provided in countries operating under the liberal model. In contrast to the liberal model, poverty is viewed as either inevitable or as a result of social injustice. This is why in Germany and the Netherlands, political parties of both the right and the left support an extensive welfare state. While around one in five households in Britain are poor the rate for Germany is one in eight.

In corporatist systems, there is a belief in the value of partnership and dialogue between the government and the various interest groups in society (sometimes called the social partners) such as trade unions and employers' associations. This is seen as a way of avoiding and reconciling conflicts over economic and social policy. It emphasizes solidarity between the various social groups and gives an important role to voluntary organizations such as churches and charities. In Germany, for example, church bodies are important providers of welfare services to groups such as migrants and young people.

The Social Democratic Model

The social democratic model, found in Scandinavian countries, has several defining characteristics. Sweden, where total State spending makes up 60% of the economy, spends almost twice as much on social welfare as the USA (see Figure 5.4). Britain falls between the low-spending USA and the high-spending continental European countries.

There are much lower levels of poverty in Sweden compared to the UK and the USA. According to UNICEF, less than 5% of Swedish children live in poverty while more than one in five are in that position in the USA.

Support is provided through generous welfare benefits for all those who are poor, old, young, disabled, and unemployed, and there is universal access to education and health care. There is a heavy commitment to helping families and to mothers wishing to work. This is financed by high levels of taxation. Secondly, unlike the liberal model, governments usually commit themselves to generating and maintaining high levels of employment and low levels of unemployment. There is an emphasis on taxation and spending policies that redistribute income from the rich to the poor and an active approach is taken to finding jobs for the citizens. As in the corporatist model, dialogue between the social partners is valued (UNICEF).

Learning Task

Health is regarded as a good indicator of the quality of life. Examine Table 5.2 which shows some health indicators in the USA, France, and Sweden.

1. How does the health of the USA population compare with that in France and Sweden?

2. Use your knowledge of the different social models to come up with explanations for your findings.

3. What other explanations might be advanced?   →

→ **Table 5.2** Health Indicators for the USA, France, and Germany 2005

	Life expectancy (years)		Adult mortality rate*		Infant mortality rate #
	Male	Female	Male	Female	Both sexes
US	75	80	137	81	7
France	77	84	128	58	4
Sweden	79	83	78	50	3

* probability of dying aged 15–60 years per 1,000 of population
# per 1,000 live births
Source: World Health Organisation

Mini Case The Clash of Social Models

Critics have launched bitter attacks on the social democratic and corporatist social models of Western Europe and blame them for the inferior economic performance of Europe compared with the USA, for example as regards economic growth.

They attribute high and persistent unemployment in France and Germany, declining productivity growth, growing fiscal strains, and the mediocre and inflexible services provided by the state, to high tax and spend policies and over-zealous interference with market forces, for example, the setting of a minimum wage. The essence of the argument is that high taxes and benefits discourage people from seeking employment and working hard and businesses from taking risks. The result is mediocrity—people who do well are penalized by high taxes while nobody is allowed to fail. The answer is to move towards a liberal regime where market forces are allowed much freer rein. Critics accept that the free market can result in undesirable outcomes but it leads to a more creative, flexible, and productive economy. In their view people should take responsibility for their lives and not be protected by the State from the consequences of their own decisions. Thus, if individuals decide not to buy health insurance then they, not the State, must bear the consequences when they become ill.

Defenders of the social democratic model challenge claims of superior US performance. They argue that growth of GPD per head has grown at roughly the same rate in the USA and the majority of European countries, and that European countries such as Sweden are richer than the USA as measured by per capita income, even though its economy is more highly regulated and has a larger welfare state. They also claim that French and German productivity levels are higher than in the USA. In addition, they say that inequality, poverty, and crime rates are much higher in the USA, and point to the large proportion of the US population not covered by private health insurance.

Sources: *Financial Times*, 1 March 2006; *The Economist*, 7 September 2006; Navarro and Schmitt 2005

East Asia

Some authors have noted that some East Asian societies do not fit in with any of the models outlined above. In Japan and the four 'tiger' economies of Hong Kong, Singapore, South Korea, and Taiwan, priority has been given to economic growth and welfare policies have been subordinated to that. They do engage in social policy but only after attending to their main objective of growth, and social policies are often geared to the achievement of economic objectives. While welfare arrangements do vary in each of these countries, there are some common elements. In these societies, there is hostility towards the concept of the welfare state, public expenditure on social welfare is low, social rights and benefits tend to be limited, and the family is expected to play a central role in social support.

The Japanese Constitution accords its citizens a minimum standard of healthy civilized life. They have a right to basic health care, and pensions are almost universal. However, benefits are limited and the family is expected to play a role (Holliday 2000). Compared with other OECD members, Japan ranks very low in the level of social assistance it provides (see Figure 5.4). The level of income inequality and relative poverty among the working-age population in Japan has been rising and is higher than the OECD average (Jones 2007). In Hong Kong, around half the population live in rented housing provided by the authorities, and rights to health care and education are universal but limited. The State does not provide pensions, unemployment benefit, or child benefit. In Taiwan, the bulk of welfare spending predominantly goes to groups in the armed forces, State bureaucrats, and teachers while the less fortunate, the poor, the handicapped, the old, and the young receive almost nothing (Holliday 2000). A lot of resources have been put into the education system in pursuit of the country's economic objectives (Chow 2001).

Demography

Demography is the study of population. It looks, amongst other things, at the size of the population, its rate of growth, the breakdown by age, gender, ethnic group, and the geographical distribution of the population.

World population was 6.6 billion in 2007, half a billion more than in 2000. More than 80% of the world's population live in poorer regions, and just less than one fifth in the more developed regions—by contrast, in 1950 almost one third of the world population lived in rich countries (Table 5.3). Poorer countries have increased their share of world population because they have been growing almost three times as fast as the more developed regions (UN, World Population Prospects: The 2006 Revision).

The number of people and their geographical location are of interest to business. Large populations may indicate that markets are there to be exploited. However, to be attractive to business, incomes in such populous areas need to be high enough for consumers to be able to afford to buy goods and services.

The most highly populated countries tend to be found in the less developed regions of the world. China and India are the most populous each with over one billion people. Together they account for more than one fifth of the world population. The USA and Japan are the only rich countries to make the top ten in terms of population (Table 5.4).

Urbanization

Another long-term trend in demography is the move by people from rural areas into towns and cities. This process is called urbanization. The developed world is already highly urbanized with three quarters of the population living in towns and cities, the

Table 5.3 World Population 1950, 1975, 2007

Motor area	Population (million)		
	1950	1975	2007
World	2,535	4,076	6,671
More developed regions	814	1,048	1,223
Less developed regions	1,722	3,028	5,448
Least developed countries	200	358	804
Other less developed countries	1,521	2,670	4,644
Africa	224	416	955
Asia	1,411	2,394	4,030
Europe	548	676	731
Latin America and the Caribbean	168	325	572
Northern America	172	243	339
Oceania	13	21	34

Source: UN, World Population Prospects The 2006 Revision

Table 5.4 The 10 Most populous Countries 2007 (millions)

1. China	1.331
2. India	1.136
3. US	304
4. Indonesia	228
5. Brazil	191
6. Pakistan	165
7. Bangladesh	147
8. Russia	142
9. Nigeria	137
10. Japan	128

Source: UNFPA, State of the World Population 2007: Unleashing the Potential of Urban Growth

corresponding figure for other areas of the world being less than half. According to the UN, more than half of the world's population will be living in urban areas by 2008 (Figure 5.5). While the more developed regions had reached this figure by the 1950s, it was not expected to be attained in the less developed regions until around 2019.

The pace of urbanization is particularly fast in Africa, Asia, and Latin America. Currently the proportion of people living in urban areas is 42% in China and 29% in India. The UN estimates that by 2030 the number of urban dwellers in Asia will almost double to

Figure 5.5 World Urban and Rural Population

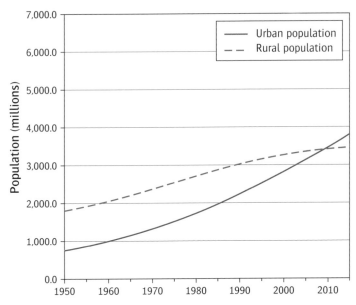

Source: UN, World Urbanization Prospects The 2007 Revision

2.6 billion and will increase by some 440 million in Africa, and by 200 million in Latin America and the Caribbean. The rural population is expected to fall by 28 million people.

At present, in the USA more than four out of every five people live in urban areas while the proportion is even greater in the UK, Australia, Argentina, Brazil, and South Korea. The process results in an increasing geographical concentration of people in cities. Tokyo has a population of around 33 million, New York 22 million, Seoul in South Korea 23 million, and London has 12 million. The great wave of urbanization, occurring in the last 50 years has affected poorer countries disproportionately. Large cities like Sao Paulo in Brazil, and Bombay and Delhi in India have more than 20 million inhabitants (UNFPA).

The implications of this process are manifold. It raises concerns in urban areas about increasing crime rates, lack of clean water and sanitation, sprawling ghettos of slums, and the ability of the infrastructure, for example road, rail, and energy networks to cope with such a large influx of people. Associated with the process of rapid urbanization is an increasing interest in new religious movements. This comes as a surprise to those who expected urbanization to accelerate the trend away from religion and towards rational values. Thus radical Islam has grown in popularity in the Arab region, whereas Pentecostal Christianity has expanded in Latin America and parts of Africa. Religious movements are also gaining hold in the fast-growing cities of China. Urbanization can also have repercussions on firms employing workers who have moved into cities from rural areas because people bring their rural ways with them. An executive of a UK firm producing soap in Accra the capital of Ghana, told one of the authors that their workers would not come to work when it rained because that was what they did on the farm.

Mini Case Slum Dwellers in Cairo

Source: www.istockphoto.com

Cairo is the capital of Egypt and, with just over 11 million inhabitants, is the largest city in Africa. Cairo's population almost doubled in the 30 years up to 2005. Incomers from the countryside congregate in 67 unofficial areas, some within garbage dumps, which circle the city. Some of these squatter communities have a million people living there. They are crowded into self-made tiny rooms in tenement blocks of slums with makeshift roofs or no roofs at all. Open sewers line the streets and the air is polluted by fumes from burning rubbish. Not surprisingly disease is rampant, poverty is rife and on the increase, and illiteracy is the order of the day. Thousands live and work on the city's rubbish tips, cleaning, recycling, and selling trash in order to feed their families. All family members, including children, are obliged to work to survive. Some are forced to sell personal belongings for cash, beg, or become prostitutes. The slums are a breeding ground for radical Islam. This, along with a high crime rate, pollution and noise, and fear of civil unrest drive the rich to protect themselves behind the walls of gated compounds.

Sources: UNFPA; *Times Educational Supplement*, 23 March 2007; *Financial Times*, 13 December 2006

Furthermore, the firm had to provide transport to bring their employees to work because they were used to walking to the farm from the village.

Changes in Population Size

Population size is affected by the death rate, the birth rate, and net migration.

With increasing prosperity, advances in sanitation, diet, and medical knowledge, death rates have been declining, not only in the richer countries of the developed world but also in Asia, Latin America, and the Caribbean. However, in some former communist countries, like Russia and the Ukraine, rates have been increasing—largely as a result of deteriorating social and economic conditions, and in some African countries due to the spread of HIV/AIDS.

Birth rates at a world level have been falling. By 2010 they were expected to be at 2.55 children per woman—half the level they were in the 1950s. Women in less developed countries have twice the number of children as their counterparts in the rich world (UN Population Prospects: The 2006 Revision). Birth rates tend to fall as countries become richer. In poor countries, where incomes are low and there is minimal or no welfare provision, people have large families to support them in their old age. Increasing incomes in these countries reduces the need for large families. The OECD suggests that the changing role of women also has a big influence on the number of children they have. As the level

Figure 5.6 Immigrants Share of Host Population by Level of Development, 1975–2005

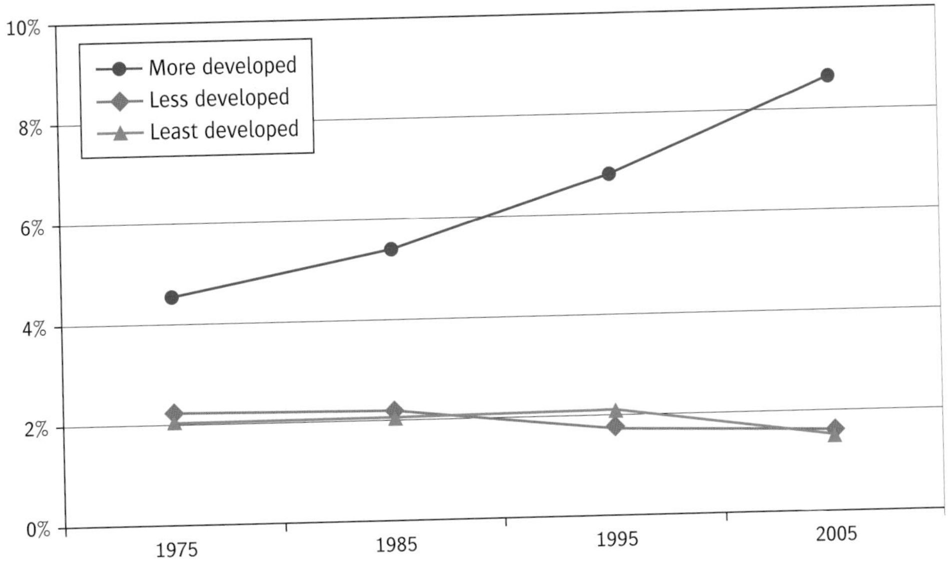

Source: Martin 2008

of education of women increases, along with their greater participation in the work force, so the birth rate declines. The attitudes of women, especially in the developed world, are changing away from their traditional role as a bearers and nurturers of children. Even in supposedly Catholic countries such as Poland, Italy, and Spain, where the Church condemns contraception, there have been significant declines in the birth rate (d'Addio 2005).

As regards international migration, it has been increasing since the 1970s. Estimates put the number of people living outside their country of origin at about 185 million in 2005, or 2.9% of the global population. At first sight, this seems fairly insignificant. However, as Martin points out, the picture changes if the inflow of migrants is measured as a proportion of the increase in the labour force. On that calculation, migration accounts for 30–40% of the growth of the labour force in the developed economies.

As can be seen in Figure 5.6 migrants have moved in their greatest numbers to the more developed countries. By 2005, migrants accounted for more than 8% of the population in those countries. In 2005, about 60% of the world's stock of migrants lived in Europe and North America, followed by 26% in Asia, leaving only 15% in the other major regions of Africa, Oceania, and Latin America (Martin 2008).

The Ageing Population

Increased life expectancy and falling birth rates means that the average age of the population in many countries will rise, and this has become a major demographic concern. This will lead in some countries to stagnation and even decline in the population. Europe is the first region in the world to experience demographic ageing. By 2050 it is expected that the

Mini Case　Hispanic spending power in the US

One of the major demographic changes in the USA has been the increase in the Hispanic* population. In 2005 there were more than 40 million Hispanics in the USA. According to the US Census Bureau, the number of Hispanics is projected to rise by 188%, which will double their proportion of the population from 12.6% in 2000 to 24.4% by 2050. In four States—New Mexico, California, Texas, and Arizona, Spanish is spoken by more than a quarter of the population.

For business this means that the Hispanic market is one of the fastest growing in the USA. The spending power of these consumers is estimated to rise to more than US$1,000 million by 2008, a much faster increase in consumption than that of non-Hispanic groups. Business, particularly from the car, food and drink, personal care, and telecommunications industries, has responded by spending millions of dollars advertising in Hispanic media. Companies like Procter and Gamble have moved to exploit the lucrative Hispanic market. In 2003, P&G spent around US$90 million on advertising its top 12 brands to Hispanic consumers. In addition, it increased the smell factor of its Tide Tropical Clean detergent because of the Hispanic predilection for strong scents. Unilever aimed advertising of Ragu, its pasta sauce brand, specifically at Hispanic consumers. The language used in the advertisement is Spanish while the setting is Argentina.

*the US authorities define Hispanics as persons of Mexican, Puerto Rican, Cuban, Central or South American, or other Spanish Culture (US Census Bureau)

Source: *Financial Times*, 25 March 2004; US Census Bureau, National Population

population in the EU will fall by nearly 10 million people, while the number of those over 80 years of age will increase by some 34 million (EU Commission). The populations of other regions in Europe, Africa, the Middle East, and Asia will start to age later because their populations are much younger.

Learning Task

Examine the bar chart in Figure 5.7 that shows birth rates in a number of European countries in 2006. Bear in mind that 2.1 is the replacement rate—the rate required to keep populations stable. In other words each woman needs on average to produce 2.1 children to prevent the population from falling.

1. In which countries would the population increase were the birth rate to continue at its 2006 level?

2. Discuss the implications of low birth rates on demand for the following sectors:
   • Retailers specializing in clothing and toys for babies and young children?
   • Universities training school teachers?
   • Amusement parks?

3. What are the implications of an increase in the number of older people on demand for:
   • Pharmaceuticals?
   • Travel companies specializing in cruises?
   • Providers of nursing homes?

Figure 5.7 European Birth Rates 2006

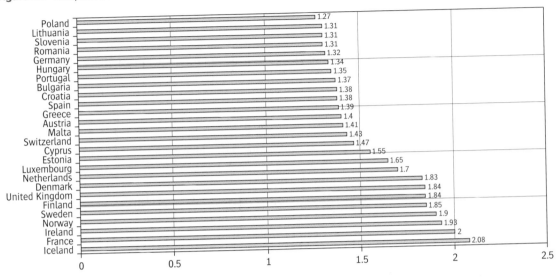

Source: Eurostat

The OECD reckons that the ageing population could lead to shortages of labour, wage inflation, increased pressures on taxation and public expenditures, and a fall in the rate of economic growth. Unless something is done to alleviate the problem, taxes will have to rise to meet the increasing cost of pensions and health care, or public expenditure and benefits will have to be cut. Global growth could fall to less than 2% per year, which is

Mini Case Ageing and the Restructuring of the Welfare State

All welfare systems have been facing pressures for retrenchment in recent years. The strain on public expenditures has been rising as people live longer and retire earlier. This process causes an increase in the dependency ratio i.e. an increase in number of older people who are not working relative to the number of people in work or available for work. The situation has been exacerbated by low fertility rates, meaning that there are fewer young people available to enter the workforce. A rising dependency ratio is a concern in many countries because the older generation contribute less in taxes but, at the same time, put extra pressures on pension and social security systems. In addition, economic crises since the 1970s have made it harder to expand welfare. The problems are particularly acute on generously-funded pension and health care systems in

France and Germany. To cope, some Scandinavian countries have switched from universal tax-funded pensions to pensions dependent on individual contributions and linked to statistics on longevity. The UK and the USA began pension restructuring in the 1980s. But no country is finding it easy to restructure its systems of State support. There is strong popular resistance to change in France and Germany where plans for cut-backs have led to mass demonstrations with citizens fearing that their generous unemployment benefits and pensions could be slashed and replaced by the far less beneficial pay-outs prevalent in the USA and the UK.

Source: *Financial Times*, 21 October 2005

almost one third less than for the period from 1970 to 2000. One response would be to encourage older people to work longer. This could be accompanied by a rise in the age of retirement, as has occurred in the public services in the UK. However, employers would need to change their negative attitudes to the employment of older workers. There would need to be more opportunities for flexible working and training for older people to help them develop new skills.

Health and Education

Global levels of health and education are associated with the level of socio-economic development defined by factors like income, socio-economic status, and living conditions. People in poor countries generally have lower levels of health and education than those in rich countries. In poor countries there is a clear relation between growth in GDP per head and life expectancy.

According to the World Health Organization (2002), poverty is the single largest determinant of ill health. High levels of poverty are associated with high rates of malnutrition, lower life expectancy, high infant mortality, and a higher risk of contracting infectious diseases such as tuberculosis and HIV infection. In rich countries in 2004, 16 people in every 100,000 caught tuberculosis while the rate for Sub-Saharan Africa was 17 times more—at 281. Significant disparities can also be seen in education levels between rich and poor regions. The global literacy rate, that is the ability to read and write, is getting on for 90% (UNESCO 2008). However, in Southern Asian countries like India the figure is 61% and for Pakistan around 50% (CIA).

Implications for business

It has long been generally accepted that economic development is a key determinant of health. This is because poor countries do not have adequate means to provide health care, or for their citizens to buy enough food or good quality food. Poor diet increases vulnerability to disease. This susceptibility is increased due to bad housing conditions and a lack of clean water and sanitation. Lower levels of education are usually associated with poor health because people have not been taught about health risks and how to cope with them. Now it is suggested that the causation may also operate in the other direction, that is that health and education levels can influence business performance through their effects on labour productivity and the supply of labour—which are both key determinants of economic growth. One would expect healthier, and more highly educated workers to produce more output because they would be stronger physically and mentally, and be more able to work more effectively with machinery and equipment. Better health could also have a beneficial effect on the quantity of labour, insofar as it results in workers losing fewer days through absenteeism, and to the extent that it increases the life expectancy of the labour force. Suhrcke, Rocco and McKee (2007) claim that a reduction in adult mortality of 2% per year would generate a gain equivalent to between 25% and 40% of a country's annual income. Finally, it is claimed that a better educated labour force is likely to make it easier for business to train and retrain their workers making it easier for them to improve performance and to respond to the changing external environment. Firms need to take into account levels of education when developing goods and services for particular markets. Thus, it would not be sensible to sell technically advanced products in markets where education levels are low and where the technical expertise is lacking to set up and maintain the products. Similarly, firms selling products normally accompanied by complicated instructions might need to consider how those instructions could be conveyed visually in markets where literacy levels are low.

● CHAPTER SUMMARY

We can see from our analysis that the international social and cultural environment offers major opportunities but also poses many threats and challenges to business.

One conclusion to be drawn is that business ignores cultural differences at its peril. As we have seen, in China, and in other countries with large Chinese speaking communities, a knowledge and understanding of guanxi in China is imperative. Hofstede has pointed out that, for companies, culture more often leads to conflict than synergy and that cultural differences can be a nuisance at best and are frequently a disaster. Firms need, as a matter of course, to take into account the varying national attitudes to such factors as hierarchy and power distance when considering entry to foreign markets through exports, joint ventures, takeover or when setting up completely new production facilities. To be successful abroad, firms need to be aware of the impact of culture on the conduct of business meetings, how negotiations are carried out, and on attitudes to contracts. Different national cultures may require business to respond to the local culture by changing their approach to the management of personnel, to the products they produce, and to the methods used to market their products. Failure to do so can lead to higher costs, lower levels of productivity, and poor sales and profits.

Our examination of the social environment demonstrated how social models vary from one country to another, from the less generous liberal approach in the USA to the more generous Swedish social democratic model. The debate continues to rage between the supporters of these models as to which model provides the best environment for business and which promotes economic performance and social cohesion. We have seen how changes in the social environment can be of importance for business. Demographic changes, for example, population growth in Asia and Africa but decline in Europe along with an ageing population, the process of urbanization, and different national levels of health and education all have implications for the quantity and quality of the labour supply as well as for the economic growth rate and the pattern of demand for goods and services.

● REVIEW QUESTIONS

1. The table below (Table 5.5) shows social spending as a percentage of GDP from 1990 to 2003.

   a. What is the trend in social spending over the period from 1990 to 2003? To answer this, look first at the EU and OECD averages. Do any countries buck the trend?

   b. Which countries were the highest spenders in 2003 and which the lowest?

   c. How would you explain Sweden's high levels of expenditures compared to those of the US?

Table 5.5 Public social expenditure (as a percentage of GDP)

	1990	1991	1992	1993	1994	1995	1996	1997	1998	1999	2000	2001	2002	2003
Australia	14.1	15.2	16.2	16.5	16.2	17.1	17.2	17.0	17.0	16.9	17.9	17.4	17.5	17.9
Austria	23.7	23.9	24.5	26.0	26.6	26.6	26.6	25.5	25.4	25.6	25.3	25.4	25.8	26.1
Belgium	25.0	25.8	25.9	27.0	26.5	26.4	26.9	25.8	26.1	25.9	25.3	25.7	26.1	26.5
Canada	18.4	20.6	21.3	21.2	20.2	19.2	18.4	17.7	18.0	17.0	16.7	17.3	17.3	17.3
Czech Republic	16.0	17.3	17.6	18.1	18.1	18.2	18.3	19.1	19.5	20.0	20.3	20.4	21.0	21.1
Denmark	25.5	26.3	26.8	28.6	29.4	28.9	28.2	27.2	27.0	26.8	25.8	26.4	26.9	27.6
Finland	24.5	29.6	33.6	29.9	29.2	27.4	27.1	25.2	23.2	22.8	21.3	21.4	21.9	22.5
France	25.3	26.0	26.6	28.1	28.1	28.3	28.6	28.5	28.7	28.8	27.6	27.5	27.9	28.7
Germany	22.5	23.7	25.7	26.1	26.1	26.6	27.1	26.4	26.7	26.7	26.6	26.7	27.4	27.6
Greece	18.6	18.0	18.1	19.1	19.1	19.3	20.0	20.0	20.6	21.4	21.3	22.3	21.3	21.3
Hungary	—	—	—	—	—	—	—	—	—	21.6	20.6	20.7	21.9	22.7
Iceland	14.0	14.5	15.0	15.3	15.2	15.5	15.2	14.9	14.9	15.4	15.3	15.6	17.3	18.7
Ireland	15.5	16.3	17.1	17.1	16.8	16.3	15.4	14.3	13.4	14.2	13.6	14.4	15.5	15.9
Italy	19.9	20.1	20.7	20.9	20.7	19.8	22.0	22.7	23.0	23.3	23.2	23.3	23.8	24.2
Japan	11.2	11.4	11.9	12.5	13.1	13.9	14.1	14.2	14.9	15.4	16.1	16.8	17.5	17.7
Korea	3.0	2.8	3.1	3.2	3.2	3.5	3.6	3.9	5.5	6.3	5.1	5.4	5.4	5.7
Luxembourg	21.9	22.3	22.7	23.1	22.9	23.8	23.5	22.5	21.6	21.7	20.4	19.8	21.6	22.2
Mexico	3.6	4.0	4.4	4.7	5.2	4.7	4.5	4.5	5.8	5.8	5.8	5.9	6.3	6.8
Netherlands	24.4	24.4	24.9	25.1	23.6	22.8	21.8	21.2	20.6	19.9	19.3	19.5	19.9	20.7
New Zealand	21.8	22.2	22.0	20.3	19.5	19.0	18.9	19.9	20.0	19.3	19.1	18.4	18.4	18.0
Norway	22.6	23.5	24.4	24.3	24.0	23.5	22.7	22.2	24.5	24.6	22.2	23.2	24.6	25.1
Poland	15.1	21.5	25.5	24.9	23.8	23.1	23.3	22.7	21.5	22.2	21.2	22.4	23.0	22.9
Portugal	13.7	14.7	15.5	17.0	17.2	18.1	18.7	18.6	19.0	19.5	20.2	20.9	22.2	23.5
Slovak Republic	..	..	..	..	..	18.9	18.7	18.2	18.2	18.8	18.1	17.8	17.9	17.3
Spain	20.0	20.7	21.8	23.2	22.1	21.5	21.4	20.8	20.7	20.4	20.4	20.2	20.2	20.3
Sweden	30.5	32.1	35.0	36.2	34.9	32.5	32.1	30.7	30.5	30.1	28.8	29.3	30.4	31.3
Switzerland	13.5	14.5	16.0	17.4	17.3	17.5	18.1	18.8	19.0	18.8	18.0	18.7	19.4	20.5
Turkey	7.6	8.2	8.5	8.3	7.9	7.5	9.7	10.8	11.1	13.2	..	..	..	..
United Kingdom	17.2	18.6	20.3	21.0	20.5	20.4	20.1	19.2	19.3	19.0	19.1	20.1	20.1	20.1
United States	13.4	14.4	15.1	15.3	15.3	15.4	15.2	14.9	14.8	14.6	14.6	15.2	16.0	16.2
EU15 average	21.9	22.8	24.0	24.6	24.2	23.9	24.0	23.2	23.0	23.1	22.5	22.9	23.4	23.9
OECD avarage	17.9	19.0	20.0	20.4	20.1	19.9	20.0	19.6	19.7	19.8	19.4	19.7	20.3	20.7

Source: OECD

d. Is there any evidence of convergence among developed countries in terms of the proportion of the national income spent on social expenditure?

e. Some commentators have argued that globalization is leading to a 'race to the bottom' with regard to welfare spending. Do the figures lend support to that argument?

2. You are an engineering company struggling to survive in a fiercely competitive environment. Intense competition compels you to hold down costs by keeping stock levels of materials and components at a minimum, and to deliver to customers on time. Consequently, you are looking for ways to cut costs. One possibility is to set up in a cheaper location abroad.

Your research indicates that the cheapest locations by far are found in countries with a culture that operates on event time rather than clock time. Explain what is meant by event time and clock time. Explore some of the implications for the company of setting up in an event time environment.

3. It is often claimed that UK business loses out abroad because of the inability of British managers to communicate in languages other than English. Discuss.

To help answer this question, have a look at the CILT publication, 'Talking World Class: The impact of language skills on the UK economy' available at www.cilt.org.uk

4. Obesity is on the rise in the developed world and governments are becoming increasingly concerned about the health implications.

- What are the possible implications of this for companies in the fast food and drinks industries?

- Investigate how the industries are responding. The quality press regularly publish articles on the topic. For example, have a look at the *Financial Times* of 10 January 2005, 13 March, 22 December 2006 and 5 February 2007

- What might be the implications of the rise in obesity for productivity?
  See the short article on this in the *Financial Times* of 5 February 2007.

5. Tease out some of the implications of an ageing population for:

- car manufacturers such as Ferrari and GM

- financial institutions such as pension funds

- medical schools

- companies running holidays for 18–30 year olds

Case Study Social Divisions in India

India, a vast country with a relatively young population of over one billion people, has been described by *Business Week* as, 'part Silicon Valley; part Stone Age'. This tells us that India is a country of great contrasts. On the one hand, it has a relatively small corps of people, around 4% of the population, who are university educated, English speaking, IT literate, and entrepreneurial concentrated in cities like Mumbai and Bangalore—which is known as the Silicon Valley of India. Its economy, in the first decade of the 21st century, has been very dynamic with economic growth rates averaging more than 7% per year. On the other hand, millions live in great poverty and a majority of its labour force still work in traditional agriculture. Of the 202 million children who enrol in the country's 1 million schools every year, barely 15% make it to high school, and only half of them successfully complete their schooling. There is a great shortage of drinking water and infant mortality rates and rates of child malnourishment are amongst the highest in the world. Corruption is widespread.   →

→ Socially, India is a very divided country. An important basis of social division is the caste system which divides India's mainly Hindu society into four orders. Historically, Brahmin priests and scholars were at the top of the hierarchy, wielding enormous power over other castes. Next in line were rulers and soldiers who conquered and controlled kingdoms, then came the wealthy merchants, followed by peasants and labourers. Intermarriage and even socializing between these various castes was forbidden. In addition to these four orders were the untouchables, or Dalits. They were called untouchables because their touch was seen by other castes as enough to cause impurity and pollution. The caste system persists to this day and is particularly strong in rural areas. The Dalits who number some 170 million, are at the bottom of India's social hierarchy. They have the worst jobs such as cleaning sewers, the lowest incomes and face discrimination and social exclusion—they are, for example, not permitted to share drinking water sources or to participate in religious worship and festivals with other castes.

Officially, the caste system was abolished when India achieved independence from British rule in 1947. In 1950, the Government provided a certain quota of jobs in government and places in education for Dalits. Despite this, the caste system persisted. In the 1990s, India extended the system of reserving of government jobs and places in State schools and colleges for castes marginally above the Dalits in the hierarchy. The rationale for this affirmative action was that it was the only way to level the playing field between the various social groups. However, whilst lower castes have formed strong voting blocs and gained much political power, discrimination continues to be rampant. The upper castes still dominate the best jobs in Indian society.

As a result, in 2006, the Government came up with a proposal to reserve a further share of places in colleges and universities for members of lower castes. It also raised the possibility of forcing private companies to reserve half their jobs for these groups. Some businesses are concerned about this, arguing that their inability to appoint people on merit will harm their ability to compete in the global economy.

There are also great social divisions between men and women. While the Indian Constitution grants equal rights to men and women, strong patriarchal traditions persist. Women generally continue to occupy a lower social status than men and suffer the effects of poverty disproportionately. Regarding education, women in India are much less likely than boys to go to school and college. While almost three quarters of men are literate, female literacy is less than 50%. Very few women, only 1.5%, have a college education. A large number of women die when giving birth. In rural areas, women work longer hours than men and carry out more arduous tasks. Usually women do not own land or other assets, nor do they inherit those from their families. Violence against women is commonplace. Dalit women are in a particularly poor position in society because, not only are they subject to the patriarchal power of their own men, but also to that of the upper caste. Sooryamoorthy calls them the 'oppressed of the oppressed'.

Finally, India is divided by language. There are 22 official languages. Hindi is the national language and is spoken by 30% of the population. English, the language of the middle classes, enjoys joint status with Hindi and is the most important language for national, political, and commercial communication.

Sources: CIA Factbook; *The Economist*, 27 May 2006, 10 June 2007; *Business Week*, 11 February 2006, 11 March 2006; *New Internationalist*, October 2006; World Bank, India; Data and Statistics, World Health Organization, Reproductive health indicators database

Questions

1. Explain why India could be portrayed as 'part Silicon Valley; part Stone Age'?
2. Explain the major social divisions in India.
3. Analyse the attractions of India as a market for Western firms.
4. Foreign firms have been queuing up in recent years to invest in India. For example, many firms in the finance and IT sectors have relocated their call centres.

What issues might they expect to encounter concerning the labour force due to:

- The caste system?
- The divisions between men and women?
- The large number of official languages?

5. How would you expect the upper castes to react to government attempts to impose quotas on university places and jobs in the public and private sectors? (See the *Economist*, 27 May 2006 and *Business Week*, 22 May 2006)
6. Explore the advantages and disadvantages for business of the Indian Government expanding educational and job opportunities for the lower castes.

Online Resource Centre
www.oxfordtextbooks.co.uk/orc/hamilton_webster/

Visit the supporting online resource centre for additional material which will help you with your assignments, essays and research, or you may find these extra resources helpful when revising for exams.

● FURTHER READING

Hofstede and McCrae carried out further research correlating personality traits with cultural dimensions in 33 countries. See:

- Hofstede, G. and McCrae, R. R. (2004) 'Personality and Culture Revisited: Linking Traits and Dimensions of Culture'. *Cross-Cultural Research*, Vol 38, February

The following article looks at demographic and health data from six countries in Latin America to determine whether there is a link between increasing inequality in income and inequality in aspects of health and education.

- Sahn, D. E. and Younger, S. D. (2006) 'Changes in Inequality and Poverty in Latin America: Looking beyond Income to Health and Education'. *Journal of Applied Economics*, Vol 9, Issue 2, November

Damodaran's book examines the entry into commerce of castes in India previously having no history of engagement in business activity.

- Damodaran, H. (2008) *India's New Capitalists: Caste, Business and Industry in a Modern Nation-State*. London: Palgrave Macmillan.

The following book is a comprehensive examination of important aspects of globalization and has a section devoted to culture.

- Goldblatt, D., Perraton, J., Held, D. and McGrew, A. (1999) *Global Transformations: Politics, Economics, Culture*. Stanford: Stanford University Press.

Global Health introduces the reader to changes in the health of the world's population and the reasons for those changes.

- Rosling, H. (ed.) (2006) *Global Health: An Introductory Textbook*. Stockholm: Studentlitteratur AB

● REFERENCES

d'Addio, A. C. and d'Ercole, M. M. (2005) 'Trends and Determinants of Fertility Rates in OECD Countries: The Role of Policies'. OECD Social, Employment and Migration Working Papers 27, November

Adherents available at www.adherents.com

An, D., Kim, S. (2007) 'Relating Hofstede's masculinity dimension to gender role portrayals in advertising: A cross-cultural comparison of web advertisements'. *International Marketing Review*, Vol 24, No 2

Better Health Channel. Available at www.betterhealth.vic.gov.au

Brandolini, A. and Smeeding, T. M. (2007) 'Inequality Patterns in Western-Type Democracies: Cross-Country Differences and Time Changes'. Luxembourg Income Study, Working Paper Series, Working Paper No 458, April

Bates, D. and Plog, F. (1990) *Cultural Anthropology*. Maidenhead: McGraw-Hill

Brislin, R. W. and Eugene, K. (2003) 'Cultural Diversity and People's Understanding in the Uses of Time'. *Applied Psychology: An International Review*, 52(3)

Central Intelligence Agency (2007) *World Factbook*. Available at www.cia.org

Chow, P. C. Y. (2001) Social Expenditures in Taiwan (China). World Bank Institute, January

Crystal, D. (2003) *The Cambridge Encyclopedia of Language*. Cambridge: Cambridge University Press

Dahl, S. 'Communications and Culture Transformation: Cultural Diversity, Globalization and Cultural Convergence'. Available at www.stephweb.com

Encarta available at http://encarta.msn.com/media

Esping-Anderson, G. (2006) 'Three Worlds of Welfare Capitalism' in Pierson & Castles (eds) (2nd edn). *The Welfare State Reader*. Cambridge: Polity

EU Commission (2005) Europe's changing population structure and its impact on relations between the generations, memo/05/96, Brussels, 17 March

Eric Digests available at www.ericdigests.org

Falk, R. (2006) 'The Christian Resurgence and World Order'. *The Brown Journal of World Affairs*, winter/spring, vol xii, issue 2

Gordon G. R. (ed.) (2005) *Ethnologue: Languages of the World*, 15th edn. Dallas, Tex.: SIL International. Available at www.ethnologue.com

Guthrie, D. (1998) 'The Declining Significance of Guanxi in China's Economic Transition'. *The China Quarterly*, No 154, June

Hemerijck, A. 'The Self-transformation of the European Social model'. Available at www.fas.umontreal.ca

Ho Park, S. and Luo, Y. (2001) 'Guanxi and organizational dynamics: organizational networking in Chinese firms'. *Strategic Management Journal*. Vol 22, Issue 5, April

Hofstede, G. (1991) *Cultures and Organizations: Software of the Mind*. New York: McGraw-Hill.

Hofstede, G. (1994) UNESCO Courier. April, Vol 47, Issue 4

Hofstede, G. (2001) *Culture's Consequences: Comparing Values, Behaviors, Institutions and Organizations Across Nations*. Thousand Oaks, Calif.: Sage

Hofstede, G. (2007) 'A European in Asia'. *Asian Journal of Social Psychology*, 10

Holliday, I. (2000) 'Productivist Welfare capitalism: Social Policy in East Asia'. *Political Studies*, Vol 48, September

Jones, R. S. (2007) 'Income Inequality, Poverty and Social Spending in Japan'. OECD Economics Department Working Paper no 556, June

Lang, K. (2007) *Poverty and Discrimination*. Princeton and Oxford: Princeton University Press

Lee, H.-S. (2004) 'Outstanding issues in bilateral economic relations between Australia and South Korea', *Australian Journal of International Affairs*, Vol 58, Issue, March

Li, H. and Zhang, Y. (2007) 'The Role of Managers' Political Networking and Functional Experience in New Venture Performance: Evidence from China's Transition Economy'. *Strategic Management Journal*, Vol 28, Issue 8, August

Linguist. Available at http://australianenglish1.narod.ru and http://canadianenglish1.narod.ru

Luxembourg Income Study. Available at http://www.lisproject.org

Martin, J. P. (2008) 'Migration and the Global Economy: Some Stylised Facts'. OECD, 29 February

McFaul, T. (2006) 'Religion in the future global civilization: globalization is intensifying religious conflicts. What will happen in the years ahead?'. *The Futurist*, 1 September 2006

Navarro, V. and Schmitt, J. (2005) 'Economic Efficiency versus Social Equality? The U.S. Liberal Model versus the European Social Model'. *International Journal of Health Services*, Vol 35, No 4. Available at www.vnavarro.org/papers

Nisbett, R. E. (2005) *The Geography of Thought: How Asians and Westerners Think Differently—and Why*. London: Nicholas Brealey

OECD (2007) Factbook. Available at http://dx.doi.org

Ordóñez de Pablos, P. undated. '"Guanxi" and Relational Capital: Eastern and Western Approaches to Manage Strategic Intangible Resources'. Available at www.iacmr.org

Pierson, C. and Castles, F. (eds) (2006) *The Welfare State Reader* (2nd edn). Cambridge: Polity

Pierson, P. (ed.) (2001) *The New Politics of the Welfare State*. Oxford: Oxford University Press

Speulda, N. and McIntosh, M. (2004) 'Pew Global Attitudes Project: Global Gender Gaps'. Available at http://pewglobal.org

Suhrcke, M., Rocco, L. and McKee, M. (2007) 'Health: a vital investment in eastern Europe and central Asia'. World Health Organization. Available at www.euro.who.int

Swatos, W. H. Jr (ed.) *Encyclopedia of Religion and Society*. Available at http://hirr.hartsem.edu

UN (2006) *World Population Prospects: The 2006 revision*

UNESCO (2008) Sixth Edition of *World Data on Education*, 2006/07

UNFPA. 'State of the World Population 2007: unleashing the potential of urban growth'. Available at www.unfpa.org

UNHCR (2003) 'Refugees by Numbers'. Available at www.unhcr.org.uk

UNICEF. 'Child Poverty in Rich Countries, 2005'. *Innocenti Report Card* No 6. available at www.unicef.org.uk

University of Maine (2001) 'The US Health care System: The Best in the World, or Just the Most Expensive?'. Available at http://dll.umaine.edu

van Oudenhoven, J. P. and van der See, K. I. (2002) 'Successful International Cooperation: The Influence of Cultural Similarity, Strategic Differences and International Experience'. *Applied Psychology, An International Review*, 51, 4

Watson, J. L. (2000) 'China's big Mac attack', *Foreign Affairs*, Vol 79, Issue 3, May/June

World Bank. Available at www.worldbank.org/governance

World Health Organization (2002) 'The European health Report'. Available at www.euro.who.int

World Health Organization (2007) 'Health status: Mortality'. Available at www.who.int

Xin, K. R. and Pearce, J. L. (1996) 'Guanxi: Connections as Substitutes for Formal Institutional Support'. *The Academy of Management Journal*, Vol 39, No 6, December

CHAPTER SIX

The Technological Framework

LEARNING OUTCOMES

This chapter will enable you to:

- Explain the meaning of technology and concepts associated with it

- Identify and explain the sources of technology and how firms go about innovating

- Explain why the intensity of technological activity varies by firm size, sector, and country base

- Analyse the importance of the technological environment, both domestic and foreign, for business decisions and performance

- Explain how the external environment allows business to protect its technology in an international context

Case Study Samsung

The case illustrates the importance of technology as a competitive tool. It shows how one company, Samsung, used technology to turn itself from a relatively small company, with products imitating those of its rivals, into one of the world's innovative leaders in consumer electronics.

Samsung is a South Korean company with assets valued in excess of US$280 billion, sales of more than US$159 billion, profits around US$13 billion, employing nearly 140,000 people (2006 figures). Its profits put it alongside the likes of giants such as General Electric and Exxon Mobil. Samsung is best known around the world as a consumer electronics brand but is also the world's largest producer of two of the main components used in digital devices—liquid crystal displays (LCDs) and memory chips.

Samsung faces fierce competition domestically from LG Philips and from Japanese rivals such as Sharp and Sony, western technology companies such as Nokia, a handful of Taiwanese companies and rivals emerging in China. Samsung's aim is to be ahead of its competitors in manufacturing technology, costs, and new product development. The company has done this by investing in technically advanced state-of-the art plants making chips, flat screens, mobile phones, and other digital devices. Company management decided that it would no longer compete on price at the low end of the market but would improve its brand, design, and technology so it set up creative design centres in London, Tokyo, San Francisco, and Seoul.

As a result, the company has emerged over the past few years as one of the world's most powerful and fastest-growing technology companies. Its consumer electronics products, once dismissed as cheap imitations of more sophisticated Japanese products and produced with second-hand Japanese technology, have come to be regarded as some of the most innovative and desirable on the market. Helped by the growing popularity of its stylish handsets, it is fighting hard to overtake Motorola as the world's second-largest maker of mobile phones after Nokia, and is challenging the Japanese for leadership in flat-screen TVs and computer equipment.

The Industrial Design Society of America which awards the equivalent of the Oscars for design, awarded Samsung medals for its portable printer, two flat-screen monitors, and a microwave oven. Only Apple, the US technology company, has won more design Oscars than Samsung. As regards branding, Samsung has become one of the most valuable in Asia trailing just behind Sony.

Source: Samsung Annual Report 2007; *Business Week* at www.businessweek.com; *Financial Times*, 25 April 2008

Introduction

New technology is most visible in personal computers, mobile phones, portable digital audio players like the iPod, digital cameras, and high definition flat panel TVs produced by the information and communications industry but can also be seen in the products of other high-tech industries such as pharmaceuticals and biotechnology. Technology has become internationalized. Thus, consumer goods like mobile phones and BMWs can be seen on the streets of Mumbai as well as those of Berlin and Tokyo. Multinational companies, such as Microsoft, General Motors, and Fujitsu, transfer production technologies from their domestic base to foreign operations and many like Nokia and Lucent take opportunities offered by the international environment to develop global research strategies, carrying out research and development both at home and abroad.

Technology is a double-edged sword for business offering many opportunities but also challenges. On the one hand, it opens up a variety of opportunities for business in terms of new products, processes, and markets. On the other, it leaves firms more open to a range of competitive threats such as takeover, increased competition and even to the theft of their technologies. The rapid internationalization of technology means that firms need to monitor both their domestic and their foreign technological environments. For many industries, technology is of the utmost importance and can determine whether firms prosper or fall by the wayside.

What is Technology?

In simple terms, technology refers to the know-how or pool of ideas or knowledge available to society. Some is codifiable, meaning it can be written down and transferred easily to others but there is also tacit knowledge which is carried about in the heads of a firm's employees and therefore not easy to transfer.

Learning Task

Examples of tacit knowledge at work would be the car mechanic who can tell the health of an engine machine from the sound it makes, or the bank manager who, through years of experience, develops a gut feeling for clients who would be a bad credit risk or the nurse knowing how tight to make a bandage.

Try to come up with some other examples of tacit knowledge either from the world of work or from your own experience as a student.

Technological advance comprises new knowledge or additions to the pool of knowledge and can lead to changes in how businesses behave: for example changes in how goods and services are produced, how production processes are managed, the characteristics of the good or service, and how products are distributed and marketed. Technical change can refer to both ground-breaking advances in knowledge or simply to minor modifications of products and processes.

There are a number of terms associated with technology and it is useful to have an understanding of these. Research and Development (R&D) refers to the discovery of new knowledge (research) about products, processes, and services, and the application of that knowledge to create new and improved products, processes, and services that fill market needs (development).

Basic research is the pursuit of knowledge for the sake of it. In other words, it is carried out to push back the frontiers of knowledge with no thought of its commercial application. Such research is commonly funded by governments and is most often undertaken in universities or research institutes. It can be very expensive, take an inordinate length time to yield results and it may produce no results at all.

An example of basic research was that carried out by Crick and Watson at Cambridge University. In 1953 they announced the most important biological discovery of the twentieth century, the structure of deoxyribonucleic acid, DNA, the chemical of life. Crick and Watson's discovery of DNA spawned the biotechnology industry producing new treatments for genetic diseases such as cancer, multiple sclerosis, and cystic fibrosis. It led to numerous scientific discoveries that have changed our lives, from the food we eat to the seeds that farmers use in their fields and to the DNA testing used by the police to help identify criminals. While there are businesses, for example in the electronics and pharmaceuticals industries, helping to fund basic research in the hope that some commercially exploitable ideas will be generated, firms, as a rule, do not usually get involved.

Companies are normally more interested in applied research, that is, activities intended to lead to new or improved products and processes with clear and more immediate commercial uses. Even in applied research, there is no guarantee that results will be exploitable commercially. Scientists at General Electric (GE), one of the biggest companies in the world with interests ranging from jet engines to nuclear power stations to financial services, estimate that around 20% of the company research projects are scrapped each year.

Innovation is the commercial exploitation of new knowledge, in other words, developing new ideas into products and production processes and selling them on to customers. It is often measured by R&D spending or by the number of patents—a patent gives its owner the exclusive right to exploit the idea and gives it the legal right to stop others from using it. But innovation can also arise through investment in new machinery and equipment, market development, skills, brands, new ways of working, new business processes, and linkages with other organizations. It can involve the implementation of major advances in technical knowledge such as the digitization of electronic equipment, or small incremental changes such as a minor improvement in a production process. When firms come up with new ideas for products, processes, brands, and so on these become part of their intellectual property.

The spread of innovation from one firm and industry to another, nationally and internationally is known as technological diffusion. Diffusion has been growing at a rapid pace as is shown by the growth of high technology exports, foreign licensing agreements, and the foreign ownership of patents. After 1990, high-technology exports worldwide grew very rapidly with Chinese manufacturing industries performing particularly well increasing its share to more than 10% by 2005. By contrast the shares of the USA and Japan had declined while that of the EU was relatively stable (Gatelli 2007) (Figure 6.1).

Although the intensity of cross-border technological diffusion has been increasing, it has not affected all countries equally. Taking patent ownership as a measure, countries such as Luxembourg, Russia, Hungary, Singapore, and China show high levels of foreign ownership, with more than half of domestic inventions being wholly or partly owned by foreigners (Figure 6.2). On the other hand, less than 5% of patents in Japan and South Korea are foreign-owned. The foreign owners, predominantly MNCs based in the triad of the USA, the EU, or Japan, have a tendency to own patents in countries with close historical and cultural links as well as geographical proximity to their home country (OECD 2006).

Figure 6.1 World Market Shares (exports) of countries on total trades in High Tech

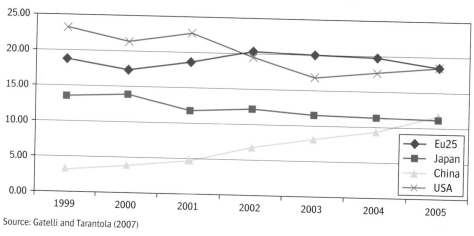

Source: Gatelli and Tarantola (2007)

Figure 6.2 Foreign Ownership of Domestic Inventions 2000–2002

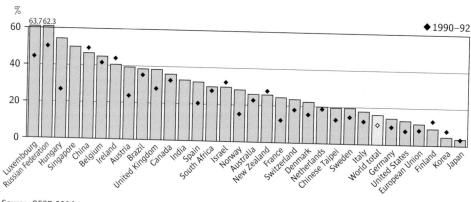

Source: OECD 2006

The OECD (2006) reports that the degree of internationalization varies across different technologies. Information and communication technologies are more internationalized than other technologies with Russia, Brazil, China, and India showing relatively high levels of foreign ownership of patents in this area. Biotechnology is another area with high levels of foreign ownership.

Furthermore, some countries are dependent on foreign companies for their R&D capabilities, with foreign MNCs accounting for a significant proportion of R&D spending in Hungary, Ireland, Spain, Canada, and the UK as compared with the USA and Japan. According to UNCTAD (2005a), West European MNCs show the highest levels of R&D internationalization.

Globalization in general, and multinational companies in particular, are important vehicles for the international diffusion of new knowledge through their trading, investment, and competitive strategies. Their influence is illustrated by the international spread of lean manufacturing in the car industry. This sets out to eliminate waste and to decrease the time between receipt of a customer order and delivery. It was pioneered by car makers in Japan and subsequently adopted by western companies such as GM, Ford, and VW as a result of the fierce competition they faced from their more efficient Japanese rivals.

Waves of Innovation

History has seen waves of major innovations:

- The Industrial Revolution, starting in Britain in the second half of the 18th century, involving machines such as water-driven spinning jennies and looms.
- The next wave saw steam power being used to drive the machines used in the production of manufactured goods in the second half of the 19th century particularly in Britain.
- The third wave occurred at the end of the 19th century with enormous expansion in chemical industries with the introduction of products such as synthetic dyestuffs and high explosives. An important advance in communications occurred with the invention of the telephone.
- In the first half of the 20th century we moved into the age of oil and the application of electricity to industrial processes.
- The second half of the 20th century saw rapid developments in electronics, communications, computers, aerospace, pharmaceuticals, biotechnology, petrochemicals, and synthetic materials.

In this last wave information and communications technology (ICT) has become increasingly important. ICT is a term that encompasses all forms of technology used to create, store, exchange and use information in its various forms whether that be business data, voice conversations, still images, motion pictures, or multimedia presentations. It involves the use of machines such as computers, telephone exchanges, robots, satellites, automatic cash dispensers, cable TV along with the software installed in them. ICT is all-pervasive affecting the home, the office, the factory and it has major implications for business both large and small from the small corner shop with its computerized accounts to supermarket chains such as Wal-Mart and Tesco which use electronic links with their suppliers to ensure that their shelves are always stocked with sufficient quantities of the appropriate goods. It has led to Sony being a dominant force in consumer electronics for decades with products such as the Walkman music player, the Playstation games console, and the Trinitron television.

The pace of change in ICT has been extraordinary due to a variety of factors. The needs of the military have been a major impetus for developing computers to solve problems related to encryption, decoding, and missile trajectory. The development of microelectronic technologies owes much to the space race between the USA and the USSR because US rockets were smaller than Soviet rockets, they could not carry as much computer equipment. Miniaturization provided the solution and led to the computer chip.

With the power and speed of computer chips doubling every 18 months and their cost falling by 50%, many new products have emerged from laptop computers to mobile phones to global positioning systems and satellite TV. An important development has been the internet which is an enormous international computer network initially developed in the US defence sector. It links a vast number of pages of information and is expanding at an exponential rate. It has led to the emergence of auction companies like eBay and search engines such as Google. In 2002, it was estimated that about 10% of the world population was using the internet. By 2007, at over a billion people, this had risen to around a fifth. The highest number of users was in Asia, with well over 400 million followed by Europe with more than 300 million, North America with 200+ million, Latin America with just over 100 million and Africa with between 30 and 40 million (www.internetworldstats.com).

In the 21st century, a further wave could be caused by advances in biotechnology. Scientists have mapped the entire sequence of human genes which promises to improve our understanding and ability to treat a wide range of diseases and illnesses that are linked to the genes which will change how medical conditions are treated. Research on embryonic cells could lead to drugs that induce damaged organs to repair themselves. There have also been major advances in body imaging technology embodied in scanners using

Mini Case Dot.com boom . . . and dot.com crash

The dot.com boom started around 1995 when people started to become aware of the big increase in internet users, and the commercial opportunities this offered. Numerous dot.com companies were set up to exploit these opportunities and many were floated on the stock exchange. Investors, on both sides of the Atlantic, flocked to buy their shares blithely ignoring the fact that many of the dot.coms had been set up by people with little or no business experience, had never earned any profits or owned any tangible assets and often had no serious business plan, share prices soared and the most unlikely people became rich overnight. For example, dozens of students of mathematics and computer programming at MIT became millionaires because of part-time jobs they held at an internet start-up company.

Some companies, such as Google and Amazon, went on to be a success but many made huge losses and fell by the wayside—sometimes only months after being launched on the stock exchange. One example was the British-based Boo.com which was set up in late 1999 to sell clothing on-line to fashion-conscious consumers world-wide. It was founded by a book critic and a fashion model and backed by LVMH, Europe's largest luxury goods group, the US finance companies, JP Morgan and Goldman Sachs, and the Benetton family. Technical issues delayed its launch which led the company to bring in expensive consultants to remedy the problem. In 18 months it ran through some US$185 million. Around US$6 million was spent on fashion clothes which were unfashionable by the time the site went live. By May 2000, the company had collapsed after it failed to secure extra funding from investors.

Source: *Financial Times*, 10 December 1999, 3 May 2007; www.Investopedia.com; for discussion of the dot.com boom see Cassidy 2002

ultrasound, gamma rays, or X-rays. These permit scientists to obtain detailed pictures of areas inside the body, the pictures being created by a computer linked to the imaging machine. Surgeons can identify potential tumours, the damage following a stroke and signs of incipient dementia. Firms such as Coca Cola and BMW have used this new technology to examine areas of the brain that are used when confronted with new designs or brands or when choosing between competing products on supermarket shelves. Nanotechnology will have major implications for the pharmaceutical industry and firms providing medical technical breakthrough equipment.

Some commentators, like Wonglimpyarat (2005), suggest that another wave could be sparked by nanotechnology, the science of the ultra-small. Nanotechnology is the ability to manipulate and manufacture things using individual particles of materials when the dimensions of the particles are 100 nanometres or less. The width of a human hair is about 100,000 nanometres (Woodrow Wilson Centre www.nanotechproject.org). This is already having a big impact on firms producing computer chips, integrated circuit boards, flat displays in products like computers, televisions, and mobile phones and in textiles and biotechnology.

Developments in the sequencing of the genes and in nanoscale machinery are accelerating, and internet connectivity and telecommunications bandwidth are growing ever faster, and bringing on still further waves of innovation. When the rate of innovation

Mini Case Nanotechnology

This case looks at developments in nanotechnology and the product opportunities that it is creating for a range of industries.

According to the Woodrow Wilson Centre in Washington, more than US$30 billion in products incorporating nanotechnology were sold globally in 2005. By 2014, it was estimated that this figure would grow to US$2.6 trillion. The technology accounts for around 1% of all patents and has attracted the interests of 3,000 businesses world-wide. Research is being undertaken in 65 countries, 37 of which are developing countries and up to now most research effort has been geared to the needs of rich countries. However, nanotechnology offers great opportunities to confront some major problems faced by poor countries such as providing clean drinking water or combating tropical diseases.

In 2007 it was reported that the number of consumer products based on nanotechnology had doubled in the previous year. There were 475 products including cosmetics, clothing, health and dietary supplements, bedding, and sporting goods. Clothing was the top category with 77 products, followed by cosmetics with 75, and food and beverages with 61. New products included an ice axe for mountaineers containing a steel alloy said to be 60% stronger and 20% lighter than normal steel and a nutritional supplement that claimed to protect against hundreds of diseases.

Research is also going on apace in the field of nanomedicine. Scientists are working to create new kinds of drugs for treating cancer, Parkinson's, and cardiovascular disease. They also are seeking ways to engineer nanomaterials for use as artificial tissues that could replace diseased kidneys and livers, and even repair nerve damage. Work is also under way to come up with therapies for conditions such as Alzheimer's, nerve injury and brain damage from stroke.

The Woodrow Wilson Centre runs a Project on Emerging Nano-technologies: www.nanotechproject.org/consumerproducts. Log on to see the latest developments in nanotech products.

Source: *Financial Times*, 18 May 2007; Woodrow Wilson International Centre ➡

Photograph: David Hawxhurst

accelerates it has the effect of shortening the length of the product life cycle. The period of time from conception to the death of the product is reduced and this increases pressure on business to innovate to stay ahead of the competition.

Theorists, like Schumpeter (1976), have attempted to explain why technological innovation occurs in cycles. He built on the work of the Russian economist Kondratieff who had noted a tendency for economies to go through cycles of expansion and then contraction, each cycle or wave lasting around 50 years. Schumpeter argued that the growth phase of the cycle arose from a bunching of innovations that brought about a technological revolution and led to the creation of completely new markets and industries through the invention of new products, production processes, or the discovery of new sources of raw materials or energy.

For the waves to occur, there have to be people willing to take the risks of exploiting the new ideas commercially. Schumpeter saw the entrepreneur as playing this vital role. Nowadays, we look to firms to carry out that function.

Who Innovates?

According to Moore (1999), a Silicon Valley consultant, only a very small proportion of firms are prepared to run with a risky untried technology. Using the technology adoption model developed by Rogers (1995), he studied the diffusion of innovation among the customers of high tech companies and found significant differences in their reasons for innovating.

He classified companies into five categories:

- Innovators—3% of companies who are risk takers and technology enthusiasts always keen to be the first to try out a new technology.

- Early adopters—15% of companies who are enthusiastic about new ideas because they want to gain a competitive advantage.

- Early majority—a third of companies. Pragmatists taking up new technologies when they are convinced that they can deliver solid benefits.

- Late majority—another third who are extremely cautious and want to see concrete benefits before they accept a new idea.

- Laggards—about 1 in 6 who are resistant to new ideas and only adopt new technology when failure to do so would cause major damage to the organization.

Moore's is a useful tool for firms trying to sell new technologies. They would be well advised to concentrate their initial marketing efforts on getting the new technology established firstly with the small number of customers who are the innovators, followed by the early adopters in the expectation that success with them would lead to a take-up by the late majority and even eventually by the laggards. But which firms are most likely to innovate?

Research shows that the rate of innovation varies from sector to sector, industry to industry, by size of firm, and by geographical location. The European Commission found that a larger proportion of manufacturing firms than service sector firms were technological innovators, but these proportions varied widely between countries. Innovation activity seems to be relatively high in countries such as Ireland, Denmark, and Germany but low in Belgium and Spain.

By industrial sector, innovation across the EU is high in the coke and chemicals, electrical and optical equipment, and machinery and equipment industries and low in the textile and leather industries. In terms of firm size, the larger the firm, the more likely it is to be an innovator even in low tech industries. Big manufacturing firms spend a much larger proportion of their turnover on innovation activities than small firms. However, using measures of innovation other than R&D and patents shows that small and medium sized firms can also be important innovators. Historically manufacturing firms have carried out most R&D. However UNCTAD (2005b) suggests that research activity in the service sector is on the increase probably due to the increasing use of ICT by firms in areas such as finance and transport.

However, industries are not all equally affected by the competition arising from technological change and the opportunities and threats that it poses. Firms operating in industries where technology evolves and diffuses rapidly need to stay very aware of their technological environment. Such high technology industries include aerospace, computers and office equipment, radio, TV, and communications equipment and pharmaceuticals. A firm in these industries failing to respond, effectively to its technological environment runs the risk of falling sales, market share, and profits and even takeover or bankruptcy. This is particularly so in markets where, due to customer preference, only the latest product sells.

There are some industries that are less sensitive to technological change. These are classified as medium technology industries and include motor vehicles, electrical (other than communications equipment), and non-electrical machines, chemicals excluding drugs, cars, rubber and plastics products, and shipbuilding and repairing.

Finally, there are the low tech industries that are relatively unaffected by competition in the area of technology such as paper products, textiles, non-fashion clothes and leather goods, food, beverages and tobacco, wood products, and furniture.

The high and medium-high tech sectors together usually account for most R&D and contribute a disproportionately large share of sales of new and improved products (see Figure 6.3).

The share of total turnover generated by new or improved products varies widely between manufacturing sectors being high in the transport equipment and electrical and optical equipment sectors but low in the wood, pulp, and printing, and basic and fabricated metals sectors.

Figure 6.3 Share of R&D accounted for by high, medium, and low technology sectors

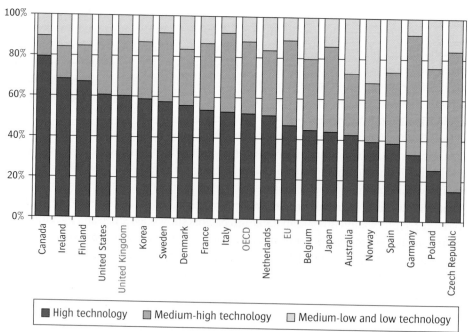

Source: HM Treasury 2004

Learning Task

The top 10 companies by expenditure on R&D 2006

Rank	Company	R&D Expenditure £bn
1.	Pfizer	3.9
2.	Ford Motor	3.7
3.	Johnson & Johnson	3.6
4.	Microsoft	3.6
5.	DaimlerChrysler	3.5
6.	Toyota Motor	3.5
7.	Siemens	3.4
8.	General Motors	3.4
9.	Samsung	3.1
10.	Volkswagen	2.9

Source: DTI 2008, The 2007 R&D Scoreboard

Globally, it is the largest companies, in the richest countries, in a limited number of sectors that account for the vast majority of the money spent on R&D. R&D spending also shows that companies based in the USA are strong in both IT hardware and software and Japanese firms in vehicles and electronics. Examine the list and answer the questions below to test the validity of this claim.

1. Are the 10 companies amongst the biggest multinationals in the world? Figure 1.3 in Chapter One would be a good starting point. If you cannot find the company name there go to the latest World Investment Report at www.unctad.org

2. In which countries are these companies based? Are they all rich countries?

3. How would you explain the presence of Samsung in the list? Referring back to the case study at the start of the chapter would be a good idea at this point.

4. Which industries are their main areas of operation? Give some reasons for your answer.

Measure of Innovation: Geographical Location of R&D

R&D expenditure is geographically concentrated, with the 10 largest spenders accounting for more than four fifths of the world total. Eight of the 10 are developed countries, with China and South Korea making up the remainder (Table 6.1). North America, with around a 40% share, is the leading spender on R&D, hotly pursued by Asia in second place with just over 30% and then Europe with over one quarter. Latin America and Africa together account for only tiny shares, less than 4% (UNESCO 2005).

Sources of Technological Advance

Technological advances can come from a variety of sources both inside and outside the organization. New ideas for commercial exploitation may be generated in the wider environment by scientists and technologists working in universities or research centres, or from individual inventors. Scientists at Bristol University invented and developed a new and simpler form of dental implant and set up a company to exploit the idea commercially. The new product is simpler to use and easier and cheaper to transport. This development had significant implications for the dominant firms, Nobel Biocare of Sweden and Straumann of Switzerland in this fast growing market estimated to be worth around £1 billion. Novartis, the Swiss multinational pharmaceutical firm, bought out NeuTec

Table 6.1 R&D expenditure in the World and in Developing Economies
(ranked by their 2002 values and in $billions)

Rank	Economy	1996	2002
	World	575.6	676.5
1	United States	197.3	276.2
2	Japan	138.6	133.0
3	Germany	52.3	50.2
4	France	35.3	32.5
5	United Kingdom	22.4	29.3
6	China	4.9	15.6
7	Korea, Republic of	13.5	13.8
8	Canada	10.1	13.8
9	Italy	12.6	13.7
10	Sweden	9.8	9.4
	Total	495.8	587.6
	Share in world (%)	86.1	86.9
	Developing economies, South-East Europe and CIS	44.5	57.1
1	China	4.9	15.6
2	Korea, Republic of	13.5	13.8
3	Taiwan Province of China	5.0	6.5
4	Brazil	6.0	4.6
5	Russian Federation	3.8	4.3
6	India	2.1	3.7
7	Mexico	1.0	2.7
8	Singapore	1.3	1.9
9	Turkey	0.8	1.2
10	Hong Kong, China	0.7	1.0
	Total	39.1	55.4
	Share in developing economies, South-East Europe and CIS (%)	88.0	97.0

Source: UNCTAD 2005b

Pharma a biotech company set up by Manchester University. NeuTec had developed new treatments for a number of life-threatening infections such as the superbug MRSA. Sometimes businesses establish research links with universities to give them first call on new ideas generated by the university. Haier of China, the fourth largest global producer of white goods such as fridges, freezers, and washing machines has entered into R&D contracts with several US universities.

Big firms in industries such as pharmaceutical and electronics have their own R&D facilities which generate ideas for new goods and services. GE spends billions of dollars annually on R&D in the US, India, China, and Germany (www.ge.com/research). As part of its research effort, it runs a Global Research Centre in the USA employing 1,000 PhDs and with a budget of £272 million a year. The centre pioneered very successful breakthroughs in lasers, optical lenses, and digital X-rays which allowed doctors a more accurate view of organs and bones and did away with the need for film and light boxes.

Business can also look to the more immediate environment as a way of facilitating the innovation process. For example, firms may cooperate with domestic or foreign rivals where the costs of innovation are high or to improve their ability to innovate. Collaboration can help lower the costs and risks of innovation as well as facilitating the commercialization of new scientific and technical knowledge and can therefore be an attractive strategy for small and medium-sized firms. The Italian furniture and textile industries, comprising mainly small firms, have formed networks of producers that allow them to cooperate on technology and ensure that they maintain their competitive edge in the market place. Examples of cross-border collaboration can be seen in the car industry where even financially powerful big car producers feel obliged to cooperate to develop costly new models and components—GM had a joint venture with DaimlerChrysler to develop new transmission systems while Peugeot had a joint venture with BMW to develop new car engines. Technology, particularly the internet, facilitates the process of collaboration—it is easy, speedy, and cheap for R&D units based in different countries to exchange information in the form of text, graphics, design drawings, video images, and so on.

Firms often try to involve suppliers, distributors, and customers (the supply chain in other words) in the innovation process to develop and share innovative ideas or to share in the development of new products or processes. In the aerospace sector, Supply Chain Relationships in Aerospace (Scria) is an example of such networking.

Some companies, particularly Japanese firms such as Nissan and Toyota, look to stakeholders such as the employees to come up with ideas for improving products and processes. Every year Toyota, a Japanese car company that has outdone its western rivals for years, receives literally thousands of suggestions from assembly line workers about how it could do things even better. Workers are encouraged to find ways of shaving as little as

Learning Task

This task gets you to compare and contrast how firms in various countries use different forms of co-operation to help them innovate.

The Institute of Fiscal Studies carried out research on the extent to which innovative firms in four EU countries engaged in cooperative activity.

Draw on Table 6.2 to answer the questions below.

1. What conclusions can be drawn regarding cooperation in manufacturing and services across the four countries?

2. Compare the level of cooperation in the high-technology and low technology sectors.   ➡

➜ **Table 6.2** Percentage of innovative firms with cooperation agreements by sector 1998–2000

Sector	France	Germany	Spain	U.K.
Manufacturing	29%	19%	13%	25%
High-technology sectors	36%	28%	22%	32%
Low-technology sectors	25%	13%	10%	20%
Services	18%	17%	15%	20%
Total	26%	18%	14%	23%

Source: OECD 2006

Table 6.3 shows the percentages of innovative firms undertaking different types of cooperative agreement. It covers three types of cooperative activity: with customers and suppliers (vertical cooperation); with competitors (horizontal cooperation); and cooperation with universities or research laboratories (cooperation with the research base).

3. According to Table 6.3 what is the most common type of cooperation in the four countries?

4. Which is the least frequent type of cooperation in all countries? Why might that be the case?

Table 6.3 Percentage of innovative firms with different types of cooperative agreements 1998–2000

Type of co-operative agreement	France	Germany	Spain	U.K.
Agreements with the research base				
Manufacturing	18%	13%	12%	16%
Services	10%	9%	10%	10%
Total	16%	11%	12%	14%
Agreements with suppliers or customers				
Manufacturing	21%	13%	7%	21%
Services	14%	11%	13%	18%
Total	19%	12%	9%	20%
Agreements with competitors				
Manufacturing	7%	6%	4%	4%
Services	5%	8%	6%	6%
Total	7%	7%	5%	5%

Note: calculations in tables 3 and 4 are weighted to be representative of the population of innovative firms in each country. Populations are innovative firms with 20 or more employees.
Sources: Abramovsky *et al.* (2005), Understanding co-operative R&D activity: evidence from four European countries, IFS Working Papers, W05/23

one-tenth of a second off routine tasks. Most suggestions involve tiny modifications to existing practices, for example performing a particular task while standing up rather than sitting down. If the modifications work, they are adopted throughout Toyota's factories.

Finally, the acquisition of new machinery and equipment can be an important source of product or process innovation for small and medium-sized enterprises. The new equipment may require the business to change the way it produces the product or to produce new or improved products.

What Motivates Business to Innovate?

Technical advance is driven by a complex combination of factors in the firm's external environment: the intensity of competition, relationships with customers and suppliers, and government policies.

The Intensity of Competition

Since the mid 1980s the pace of globalization in the world economy has accelerated. The reduction in the barriers to the movement of goods, services, and capital across borders has meant that markets have become increasingly integrated, innovation has diffused much more quickly and technological competition has grown more intense. Increasing competition from emerging economies such as China and India has also contributed to the process. Competition means that when one firm innovates, competitors may be forced to react, often in creative ways. This could involve major ground-breaking advances or, more likely, improvements and innovations around the first innovator's design, for example, 'me-too' drugs in the pharmaceutical industry. Technological competition may drive firms to launch new products and at a faster rate, add features, enter, or even create, new markets. In this way technological competition begets more innovation and more competition. The increase in technological competition makes life more risky for business because one of the persistent characteristics of innovation is that most attempts to innovate fail in the marketplace.

Customers and Suppliers

Some industries may find that the pressure to innovate comes from customers or suppliers. Car components producers, hoping for contracts with big manufacturers like Nissan, get business on condition that they change their mode of operation to meet Nissan's cost and quality requirements. Nissan advises suppliers on how to go about changing their production processes in order to increase efficiency. In the North East of England, where Nissan manufactures cars, it has set up a high-tech learning centre which suppliers use to develop their skills and to improve their productivity. For example, through the centre, suppliers can find out about Kaizen, a Japanese management technique embracing the concept of continuous improvement.

On the other hand, suppliers can be the instigators of innovation. Taking health care as an example, we can see that advances in body imaging has led to new and much more sophisticated scanning techniques being used in hospitals which has implications for the treatments offered but also for the training of staff. Similarly, keyhole surgery means that the methods of operating on patients has had to change while new drugs, developed to treat disease such as cancer or stomach ulcers, has led to a decline in the use of surgery in the treatment of these conditions.

Government Policy

Increasingly governments have become aware of the importance of technical progress to the performance of their economies. To this end they can pursue policies which remove or mitigate the effects of some of the barriers or give a positive impetus to innovation. Some innovations never get started or suffer serious delays because of their cost, or the inability to secure finance for what financial institutions view as too risky projects. This is a particular problem for small firms who may also suffer because they are often unaware of the information that is being generated elsewhere, for example in universities and research institutes that could be commercially exploited. Lack of qualified scientific and technical personnel can be another barrier to the development and exploitation of new ideas as can the high cost of protecting intellectual property rights (IPRs) or where the degree of protection awarded to intellectual property is low. On the other hand the regulatory framework can also be a positive influence. For example, stringent environmental and consumer regulation as found in several EU countries, can force firms to raise their game regarding innovation. Labour laws making it difficult to fire employees may cause firms to innovate by forcing them to search for less labour intensive production methods.

Thus in 2000, the EU embarked on its Lisbon strategy, a 10-year plan to improve competitiveness, with innovation and the knowledge economy as two of its central planks. Member states agreed to pursue policies that would help reduce some of the important barriers to innovation with the aim of making the EU the most competitive economy in the world. To that end, the EU agreed to aim for an increase in R&D spending to 3% of GDP per year, with two thirds of that coming from private sector firms, and to coordinate R&D programmes across the members of the union. The Strategy also saw education and training as crucial in providing a workforce capable of creating knowledge-intensive industries and services. However, a mid-term review in 2005 found that progress had been slow. EU leaders reasserted their commitment to the strategy but in 2007, the Commission still felt the need to urge member states to face up to the need for change (EU Commission 2005; www.europa.eu; http://cordis.europa.eu).

Businesses operating in developed economies are likely to be at an advantage because of the well developed school and higher education, and training systems which means that a high proportion of the population is literate and numerate. Conversely, firms operating in poor countries will be at a disadvantage, although countries like China and India, focusing on closing the innovation gap with richer economies, are producing increasing numbers of highly skilled and technically qualified graduates. China, in 2002, counted more researchers than Japan and estimates suggest that by 2010 it will have the same number of science and engineering graduates as the USA. India is also intent on establishing an IPR regime which protects and promotes innovation (for more discussion on education see Chapter Five and Chapter Eleven).

Governments, following the prescriptions of Michael Porter for improved competitiveness, promote the emergence of industrial clusters of associated firms including suppliers, customers, competitors and other related institutions that rivals in other locations do not have access to. Clusters allow firms to boost their competitiveness by taking advantage of the intimate knowledge of, and interaction with, other businesses located in the cluster. These are visible in countries like Italy where a textile cluster comprises not merely fabric and garment manufacture but also supporting industries like textile machinery and design, all located within a compact 200–300 square km. In Andhra Pradesh in India, the State has, through public-private partnerships, encouraged the creation of clusters in the IT, biotechnology, pharmaceutical, and textile sectors. Similar attempts to develop clusters have occurred in Latin America and in the Basque country in Spain.

Governments can pursue tax, subsidy, and equity support regimes that make finance more easily available, and cut the costs and risks associated with innovation. Almost all rich countries provide tax incentives and subsidies for innovation, although the focus is usually on promoting research which tends to favour big business and to discriminate against SMEs.

Why Technology is Important for Business

Technology opens up all sorts of domestic and foreign opportunities for businesses who are ready to take advantage of them. On the other hand, it can also pose many threats to firms who are unaware of, and unprepared for, technical change. It can, as we will see from the example of the internet, erode boundaries between markets and industries.

Technology can be a principal factor determining the size and growth of firms, the structure of industry on a global scale, its location and ownership and the organization of production. According to Held, technology has played a part in the global restructuring of production. It has helped MNCs slice up the value chain by facilitating the location of segments of the production process to lower cost countries or to subcontract production activities to cheaper suppliers in Asia or Latin America.

Competitive advantage regarding productivity, costs, and products can all be heavily influenced by new ideas and knowledge. Those ideas and knowledge can result in new inventions, designs, trade marks, literary, and artistic works. These are the firm's intellectual property. In reality not many companies invent wholly new products; most of them adapt and extend ideas that others have already tried. Apple's iPod was not the first MP3 player, but the company added enough to make its version innovative. Similarly, drugs companies often build on each other's breakthroughs to produce 'me-too' drugs.

Opportunities

New goods and services—firms can create new and improved goods and services, revive tired products and consequently penetrate new markets, and, as a result, can end up with powerful market shares and controlling valuable processes, products, designs, and brand names. Danish firm Lego is a good example of a firm using technology to revive a flagging product, the toy building brick. The brick is now sold with electronic technology allowing customers to build a range of moving robots.

Global organization—technology makes it increasingly easy to extend globally and to integrate economic activity in many widely separated locations. Technology has thus facilitated the rapid growth of the multinational corporation with subsidiaries in many countries but with business strategies, production, and distribution still being determined and controlled by head office in a single nation. So MNCs like Unilever are able to employ around a quarter of a million people in 100 countries and sell its products in 150 countries.

Learning Task

This task requires you to assess the link between R&D expenditure and company performance.

Improved performance arising from technology can enhance a company's share performance. The R&D Scoreboard suggests that share prices (and sales growth) in companies with the highest R&D intensity perform better than the average. In the 2007 R&D Scoreboard, the top 10 UK-based companies were:

- GlaxoSmithKline
- AstraZeneca
- BAe Systems
- BT
- Unilever
- Rolls Royce
- Royal Bank of Scotland
- HSBC
- Vodafone
- BP

1. Choose two of the top 10 UK-based companies in the latest R&D Scoreboard and construct a graph of changes in their share prices (growth in sales) over the last five years. Now find out how the FTSE 100 (their competitors) has performed and chart the figures in your graph.

2. Comment on the relative performance of the research intensive companies with the FTSE 100 (sales growth of the competitors). Identify a range of technological and other factors that could have influenced their share price.

Small firms—technology can make it easier for small firms to compete with large. The internet, for example, enables all firms to communicate with customers both at national and at international level and to sell goods and services at relatively low cost. Small companies can design their own websites for as little as a few thousand pounds. Firms, producing for niche markets, can use the web to reach customers who are of little interest to conventional distributors such as Wal-Mart. The Abebooks web site, for example, brings together around 14,000 independent booksellers worldwide holding over 80 million new, used, rare, and out-of-print books. In the USA the biggest music retailer is Wal-Mart. Given the need to make a return on its shelf space, it is only interested in carrying the biggest hits and cannot afford to carry a CD or DVD that sells only a handful of copies a year. The web offers firms the opportunity to tap into customers interested in the 'non-hits'. And in some areas non-hits can often be a bigger market than the best sellers. In the USA in 2004, books selling more than 250,000 copies each sold 53 million copies in total. Those selling fewer than 1,000 copies totalled 84 million.

Freezing out competitors—exclusive control of technology can give firms the ability to freeze out their rivals by excluding them from using the same knowledge or techniques. That is why in industries such as pharmaceuticals, IT hardware and software firms readily apply for patents which, if granted, will give them control of a technology. Microsoft, by 2005, was applying for around 3,000 patents when in 1990 it received a mere five, while IBM took out more patents than any other US company between 1999 and 2003. Companies may deliberately set out to hoard patents purely to frustrate rivals by preventing them from getting access to new technology. This can be a very powerful competitive tool in certain sectors such as IT software and hardware where there has got to be technical compatibility, sometimes called interoperability, between programs and equipment. In the telecommunications industry, compatibility is vital for a firm to be able to connect to the network.

Apple was particularly effective in freezing out competition when it set up iTunes. The company made it technically impossible for songs bought on iTunes to be played on competitor's equipment. Shortly after Apple launched its service in Europe it announced that it had sold 800,000 songs in the first week of operation. Both iTunes and the iPod won a market share of about 80% in the USA and the UK, as well as a substantial market share in many European countries. The iPod's strong market position gave Apple the bargaining power to strike a deal with the four biggest record companies to sell songs through iTunes for around 54p each. The agreement was widely seen as a defeat for record companies.

Another tactic used by firms to exclude rivals is to get their technical standards accepted as the norm. Microsoft has done this very successfully by managing to get Windows accepted as the standard computer operating system, and then bundling in additional software such as Internet Explorer which makes it very difficult for rival browsers to get a foothold in the market. And success breeds success, because people buy Microsoft Office because they know they can take their knowledge anywhere, and because they want to be able to share their work with other users. The number of other users is vital (Microsoft's dominance in operating systems has been subject to intense scrutiny by regulatory bodies—see the case study at the end of Chapter Seven).

Licensing—can be used to control the diffusion of a firm's technology and also to generate significant additional income streams. In America alone, technology licensing revenue accounts for an estimated US$45 billion annually; worldwide, the figure is around US$100 billion and growing fast. IBM earned over US$1 billion annually from its intellectual-property portfolio (on the other hand, IBM also earns a lot of money by providing open-source services, that is free-to-use-and-adapt software, but then makes money by designing and tailor-making that software into commercial packages for customers who are unable or unwilling to do that for themselves) whilst HP's revenue from licensing quadrupled in less than three years, to over US$200 million (*The Economist*, 20 October 2005). Microsoft went in for extensive licensing of its patented technology when growth in its core products started to slow down. This move by Microsoft also allowed the company to counter charges of abusing its monopoly by claiming that it was making its technology available to competitors.

Related products—a firm with a powerful technological position in one product may be able to oblige purchasers of that product to buy related products thus generating additional income. For example, a manufacturer of photocopying machines could require the

Mini Case HD-DVD The Battle between Sony and Toshiba

This case illustrates the importance to firms of getting their technical standards accepted by their customers as the industry norm if they are to capitalize on their innovations.

Establishing one's standards as the industry norm can provoke fierce struggles such as occurred in the high definition DVD sector where Sony with its Blu-ray format and Toshiba with its HD-DVD were competing to become the high-definition replacement for DVD. Initially both companies attempted unsuccessfully to agree on a unified set of standards. Sony was particularly mindful of the last great format war in the 1980s, when its Betamax videotape lost out to VHS, even though it was widely considered a superior technology. It lost that battle and, as a result, its Betamax technology was made redundant. One reason for the defeat was that Sony failed to build a base of potential customers.

Sony and Toshiba embarked on a ferocious struggle to get their standards accepted by major customers such as Hollywood studios, TV, PC, and video console manufacturers. Toshiba managed to recruit Microsoft and Intel to its camp and intended to steal a march on Sony by being first to the market place with its new player. Sony, along with partners Philips and Pioneer, persuaded Dell, the world's biggest personal computer maker, and Disney, and most of the other Hollywood studios, to back the Blu-ray format it had been developing for more than a decade. Its players were expected to go on sale a few months after HD-DVD and to cost twice as much. Sony hoped to secure a boost from the launch of the PlayStation 3 video game console which was fitted to play Blu-ray discs.

The outcome is crucial for Sony because it was facing increasing competition in portable music players and TV from Apple, and from Korean and Chinese rivals. The Toshiba format

Source: Photodisc

was an evolution of current DVD technology. It was a simple and low-cost step to go from manufacturing standard DVDs to producing HD-DVDs. Blu-Ray was a new and much more expensive technology.

Source: *Financial Times*, 9 April 2007, 7 and 8 January 2008

customer to take its own brand of ink or toner, or a computer maker could ensure that its own peripheral equipment was used with its machines. Microsoft consumers can only use Microsoft games in their Microsoft Xbox but these games cannot be used in a Sony PlayStation (such activities could be seen as anti-competitive and attract the interest of the regulatory authorities—see the section on Competition Law in Chapter Eight).

Increased productivity—there is empirical evidence indicating that those countries and companies more rapidly adopting information and communication technologies tend to show higher levels of growth in productivity. For example, US companies have invested more in ICT than their European counterparts and consequently have experienced particularly strong productivity growth in sectors that make intensive use of ICT.

Reducing costs—telecommunication operators such as BT or France Telecom have also been major beneficiaries of technology. Automation of the exchanges permitted reductions in the work force whilst the miniaturization of computer equipment created savings in the amount of floor space required. The replacement of mechanical by electronic parts in the equipment economized on maintenance because electronic parts are more reliable than mechanical components and also because electronic machinery is now constructed in modules—any problems can be diagnosed electronically, the faulty module identified, removed, and replaced by another. As regards new products, technology enabled telecoms firms to offer a plethora of new services to their customers, such as, ring back, answering services, and the ability to use wireless-free telephones and computers.

One can also see this in the driverless metros in cities such as Hong Kong, and in airport trains like those in Stansted airport in the UK. Another advantage is that technology could help firms deal with labour shortages. John Smedley, a medium-sized British manufacturer of luxury knitwear, had a costly labour intensive production process and faced a shortage of textile workers. The company could have cut costs and dealt with its labour shortage by getting its sweaters made in south-east Asia. But it was reluctant to do this because this would mean sacrificing the Made in England label, the hallmark of John Smedley knitwear and the reason why the company could demand high margins on its products. The company solution was to invest in new technologically advanced knitting machinery that did away with the labour needed for panel stitchers. It enabled more of its workers to focus on the design and hand finishing of its products and, additionally, allowed the company to manufacture patterned designs which allowed it to tap into new markets. The previous technology only allowed it to produce single colour items (*Financial Times*, 24 September 2005).

Job design—technology can facilitate the redesign of jobs and change the pattern of skills required by business. ICT, in the newspaper industry, has led to a disappearance of the traditional skills of the printer and a reduction in wage costs. Printing was a job traditionally done by a highly unionized workforce with skills being built up over a period of five or more years. These days news information is keyed in by the journalist via the computer whilst photographs and advertisements are input by less highly unionized and lower paid workers with computer skills which can be learned much more quickly. In this way, technology can reduce the skill levels required which means that employers do not have to pay the same levels of wages and salaries.

Monitoring and control—ICT also enhances the ability of business to monitor and control what is going on in the workplace. In call centres, employers can monitor the number of calls workers take, how long it takes to deal with customers, what is said in the conversation with clients, and the outcomes, for example, how successfully staff exploit sales opportunities and the length of time staff are logged off on breaks. They can use the data to evaluate the performance of individual employees, or teams, and also for the call centre as a whole. Additional information can be gathered on the average length of time a caller has to wait before he or she is put through and the number of callers who ring off before they are put through. Similarly, such technology can make it easier for firms to monitor employees who are working from home (BT employs around 12,000 home workers—*Financial Times*, 21 June 2006) or workers whose job entails them moving from one location to another such as salesmen or lorry drivers.

Internal communications—ICT can be used to improve internal communications. E-mail or blogging (a blog is an online diary or journal) can be used cheaply and easily to reach thousands of employees simultaneously. Investment banks like Dresdner Kleinwort and law firms such as Allen & Overy introduced blogging to facilitate communication and to allow online collaboration. Some firms, such as Motorola and Apple, use their technology as a tool to improve competitiveness. Workers are encouraged to use computers to exchange information. As a result the workforce becomes more knowledgeable and more willing to accept and adapt to new ideas and change. Businesses who are successful with this approach are called learning organizations (for more on the learning organization see Senge 2006).

Threats and Challenges

While technology offers many opportunities for business to meet the objectives of generating sales and profits, it can also pose many threats and challenges. Burton Malkiel, an economics professor at Princeton and a company director in the biotechnology industry described the risk rather colourfully, calling biotechnology a 'crapshoot' and going on to say that, 'Even biotech companies themselves don't know which one is going to make it' (*Financial Times*, 3 July 2007).

Business organizations have to prepare for, and learn to cope with, new technology and to take advantage of the opportunities offered by technology to devise new consumers' goods and new methods of production and distribution, to create new markets, and to take advantage of new forms of industrial organization. Innovation involves change in products or processes and it can be risky especially for firms who are not good at managing change effectively because new products may not catch on in the market place and new production processes may not deliver the expected benefits. Most product innovations fail as do a significant proportion of process innovations. In IT projects, the failure rate in the UK has been estimated by Standish, the reputable analysts of project success, at more than 80% and that rate has not changed much since the mid 1990s.

If firms are not prepared then new technology could result in them going out of business. Schumpeter called this the process of creative destruction. He argued that innovation over a period of time, by bringing in new products, new sources of supply, and new types of organization could create a form of competition that strikes not simply at profits and market shares but at their very existence. Schumpeter's notion of creative destruction is neatly encapsulated by the chief executive of Procter & Gamble who said, 'People ask me what I lose sleep over. If somebody announced an alternative to solution chemistry (i.e. washing powder) for laundry, all of a sudden I've got an US$11 billion business that's at risk (*Financial Times*, 22 December 2005). HMV, the UK music retailer, underestimated the threat from online competition both in terms of physical CDs and in music downloading. Its sales fell sharply and its share price was undermined.

Mini Case Creative Destruction—The Kodak Case

The case is a good illustration of Schumpeter's concept of creative destruction. It shows how Kodak was severely punished for its slow reaction to important advances in photographic technology.

Kodak, in the 1990s, was a leading producer in the world of traditional cameras, film, and photographic paper. It was one of a handful of manufacturers operating in a capital-intensive multi-million pound industry and enjoying very high profit margins. In the early years of the new century, disruptive digital technology began to wreak havoc on Kodak's business threatening its very existence. Demand for its products took a nose dive as it began to lose customers at twice the expected rate to new digital cameras. At first, Kodak management saw falling sales as part of a slowdown in the economy. However, by 2003, the company had realized its mistake and belatedly embarked on its own digital strategy. It announced tens of thousands of job cuts at its film factories and started to produce a range of digital equipment.

Following this near disaster, the company did go on to make some successful innovations. It was one of the first to identify one of the biggest flaws of the new technology. Customers were frustrated with digital pictures that could not easily be printed out at an acceptable quality or price. Self-service kiosks were installed in thousands of shops. An online printing service was set up offering cheap prints to those with broadband internet connections. The company also pioneered easy-to-use home printers which can be linked with cameras by even the most technologically-challenged.

Source: *Financial Times*, 29 November 2006

Source: www.istockphoto.com

Even firms sitting on comfortable monopoly positions can find such positions threatened by new technology. The telecommunications industry is a case in point where national monopolists such as BT, Deutsche Telekom, and France Telecom who owned networks of telephone lines, found themselves under severe attack from mobile phone companies and from firms using satellite systems.

As in telecommunications, such competition may not arise from within the existing boundaries of an industry. Companies like Amazon, using the web as a new business model, have made a significant impact on traditional book retailers like Waterstones. Not only does Amazon provide a greater choice of books in its 800,000 titles, it also uses digital technology that permits customers to read excerpts from 33 million pages of 120,000 volumes. In the travel business, one of the most successful forms of e-commerce, the internet has pitted travel agents and established airlines against online providers in an intense battle to win customers. Online agents such as Expedia and Travelocity have shaken up the travel booking business while low cost airlines like Ryanair and easyJet have used the internet to cut the costs of their reservation systems. This has made them even more price competitive, and has forced their established rivals, such as BA, Air France, and KLM, to extend their online reservation service. As a consequence, more and more flights and trips are being booked over the internet rather than through call centres or high-street travel agents. Some commentators estimated that online booking would accounted for a third of the USA US$200 billion travel market in 2005. US railway and airline customers book almost half of their trips online (*The Economist*, 29 September 2005).

R&D—No Guarantee of Success

Conventional wisdom assumes that company spending on R&D is a good thing, with the implied assumption that it will lead to innovative success. According to this view, the more a company spends on research the better the result is. However, the counterview to this is that R&D is an input and its impact, like any other input such as labour and machinery, depends on how efficiently it is deployed. The productivity of R&D expenditure in terms of new products and processes is determined by the quality of the inputs, and those who are managing it. Consequently, there is no automatic correlation between high R&D spending and company performance.

A survey of the world's top 1,000 R&D companies by consultants Booz Allen failed to find any significant relationship between R&D spending and business success as measured by growth in sales, profit, the value of the firm on the stock market, or total shareholder return. The top 10% of R&D spenders enjoyed no consistent performance advantage over companies that spend less on R&D. Firms such as Reckitt Benckiser, the leading Anglo-Dutch producer of consumer cleaning products, spends a very low proportion of its turnover on R&D but enjoys a reputation both for innovation and for relatively high margins. Apple Computer, a very successful innovator with the AppleMac, iPod, iTunes, and iBook also challenges the conventional wisdom because it spends less on R&D than the computer industry average, and much smaller amounts than competitors such as Microsoft or Sony. However the survey did find that companies spending relatively little on R&D significantly under-performed their competitors (*Financial Times*, 8 November 2005).

Protecting Technology

Bill Gates reflects the importance of technology when he claims that, '. . . it has become imperative for chief executives to have not just a general understanding of the intellectual property issues facing their business and their industry, but to have quite a refined expertise relating to those issues' (*Financial Times,* 12 November 2004). The globalization of markets means that firms have to look for protection not just at home but also abroad.

Technology can be so important to company performance that business often spends much time and effort in ensuring that its intellectual property is protected and in pursuing those who infringe it. The external environment offers organizations the possibility of protecting their codifiable technology.

Methods of Protection

In richer countries the owners of intellectual property rights are normally accorded the protection of the law. Legally, the intellectual-property system covers five areas and aims to provide legal protection against counterfeiters and copiers and is vital in many fields, such as music, film, biotechnology, nanotechnology, and in consumer goods where branding is important in gaining and retaining competitive advantage.

Patents—a patent can be taken out on inventions—when firms come up with a commercially exploitable idea for a new product such as the iPod, they will often apply for a patent. Patents can be granted on new inventions for a period of up to 20 years in the UK, Germany, Japan, and the USA.

Designs—designs comprise the characteristics of the product such as the shape, pattern, and colour and the law allows companies to prevent others using their designs.

Trade marks—brand names like Perrier or Persil, or logos such as the Nike swish can also be protected. Trade marks comprise any signs capable of being represented graphically particularly words, designs, letters, numerals, the shape of goods, or of their packaging provided that such signs are capable of distinguishing the goods or services of one firm from those of other businesses.

Copyright—book publishers, film, television, and music companies can take out a copyright on original literary, dramatic, musical, artistic works, sound recordings, films, and television broadcasts that they have produced and, more controversially, firms can also copyright information on genetic data. So music by U2 or Coldplay, and television programmes such as Friends and Frasier can be protected, as can cartoon characters such as Disney's Mickey Mouse and Donald Duck.

Industrial espionage—involves the theft of a firm's secret information. A striking example of attempted espionage concerned Coca-Cola which treats its product formulae as closely guarded secrets. An employee at its headquarters tried to steal a sample of a secret new product with the intention of selling it to Coke's bitter rival, Pepsi. Pepsi, refusing to take advantage of this, reported the approach to Coke who called in the police. Undercover FBI officers, posing as Pepsi executives, launched a sting operation and arrested the employee who subsequently ended up being charged with unlawfully stealing and selling trade secrets (*The Guardian,* 7 July 2006).

The OECD (2006) reports a steady growth in patenting activity particularly in the areas of ICT, biotechnology and nanotechnology. Business is also increasingly looking to protect their intellectual property abroad. In 2003, the USA accounted for more than a third of the patents filed at the European Patent Office while Japan had a share of 15%.

Problems in Protecting Technology

Even though rich countries usually provide a degree of legal protection for technology, firms, particularly small and medium-sized enterprises, may still encounter problems in protecting their IPRs.

Cost—the cost of filing a patent can be high and can vary considerably from one country to another. It is, for example, much more expensive to obtain patent protection across Europe than in the USA.

Multiple applications—these must be made in different countries to get legal protection. Patent applications usually have to be translated into the language of the country where the patent is to be registered. Getting highly technical application documents translated into various languages such as Chinese, Portuguese, Hungarian, and so on could be a very costly exercise.

In 2006, the European Commission estimated that the cost of registering patents in EU member states typically varied between €37,500 and €57,000. This is up to six times greater than the cost of registering a patent in the USA or Japan. China, on the other hand, is relatively cheap—costing a tenth of that in the richest countries.

Differing protection periods—in Japan designs are protected for 15 years but in Germany the period is 20 years. In the USA owners of copyright are given 95 years, while the period in the EU is 50 years. The situation is further complicated by the situation in some countries, including Australia and Germany, where firms can be granted minor patents which allow them to apply for protection for a shorter time than a full patent.

Application time—the entire procedure from application to grant will generally take over 12, and in many cases over 18 months and that time period may be further extended where the law provides for other parties to oppose the granting of the patent.

Enforcement problems—firms may have to pursue infringements through various national courts which could also be time-consuming and expensive. Once again the cost can vary country by country. In China the cost of enforcing a patent through the courts is between US$60,000 and US$120,000 compared with about US$100,000 in Germany, US$500,000 in the UK, and US$5 million in the USA.

While the issues outlined above can pose challenges for big firms, it can make it virtually impossible for poorer small and medium-sized firms to protect their technology. The consequence of all these issues is that the system excludes small businesses because they cannot afford to defend their intellectual property in court.

In some countries the level of legal protection is either low, or non-existent, or the authorities do not enforce the law. China is a particular source of concern in this regard being seen as the counterfeiting capital of the world and berated regularly by the US authorities for its lax enforcement of IPRs. Many MNCs have filed law suits against Chinese competitors. Intel took action for infringement of a sound card patent claiming around US$8 million compensation. German company Bosch had a dispute with Chinese white-goods maker, the Hisense Group, on their similar 'HiSense' trademarks. Concern over IPRs has been particularly high in the car industry with legal suits being launched by Japanese car companies, such as Toyota, Honda, and Nissan, and by General Motors against Chinese car companies for breach of intellectual property rights. General Motors sued a Chinese carmaker, Chery, for allegedly copying the Matiz, a car designed by its South Korean subsidiary, Daewoo and has taken action in several countries. The US company claimed that the two vehicles shared remarkably identical body structures, exterior designs, interior designs, and key components and that the vast majority of parts in the Matiz and Chery QQ were interchangeable. GM also tried to stop Chery registering its name as a trademark for exports to the USA, claiming it is too similar to Chevy, the shortened version of GM's Chevrolet brand. GM took nearly two years to decide to take action against Chery, a State-owned carmaker. It had extensive talks with the Chinese government on the issue and was advised to sue if mediation with Chery failed. Following two years of mediation, the lawsuits were withdrawn. Perhaps this outcome is not surprising given the concerns about the ability to pursue the culprits effectively through the Chinese legal system. GM knew that Chery's majority owner, the city government in Wuhu, Anhui, was certain to fight the case and, if it lost, the enforcement of any penalty.

● CHAPTER SUMMARY

In the chapter we have shown how technology refers to ideas and knowledge that business can exploit commercially. The sources of new ideas on which companies can call are many and varied, ranging from universities and research institutes to competitors, customers and suppliers, and to employees.

Globalization and technology make foreign sources of new ideas more accessible and have made it easier for business tap in to foreign sources through, for example, cross-border R&D partnerships.

Innovations tend to be concentrated in big firms operating in the high-tech manufacturing sector. The rate of innovation varies from firm to firm, sector by sector and country to country. Companies in Japan generally spend more on R&D and take out more patents than firms based elsewhere. Firms are motivated to innovate by increasingly fierce competition from rivals, both domestic and foreign, other elements in the supply chain, developments in the ICT sector, and the policies pursued by governments.

Technology offers opportunities to business organizations to increase their profits and growth through the introduction of new and improved goods and services and through changes to their production processes. Technology also helps firms to restructure their global patterns of production through investment in low cost locations or by sub-contracting to cheaper suppliers. However, as we have seen with Kodak, technology can also pose threats and challenges for firms particularly if they allow themselves to fall behind their competitors. Technological advance, because it involves change in products or production processes, is a risky business particularly for firms that do not manage change well.

Finally the external environment offers business the means to protect its intellectual property although the degree and cost of protection can vary significantly from one country to another. In countries like China and some other South East Asian countries, where the level of protection is low, there are significant problems with the theft of IPRs, the counterfeiting of goods and the piracy of films, music, and books. Attempts to provide protection internationally haven been slow to progress and are relatively underdeveloped.

Industries and firms differ to the extent to which they protect their intellectual property with companies in the IT and electronic sectors having a high propensity to protect their technology compared with firms in the car industry.

● REVIEW QUESTIONS

1. Review your understanding of the following terms:
   - technological advance;
   - applied research;
   - innovation;
   - technological diffusion;
   - intellectual property.

2. Discuss how multinational companies could contribute to the international diffusion of technology. Illustrate your answer with examples.

3. Explain why innovation is important for big firms in the consumer electronics/pharmaceutical industry.

4. Discuss, with examples, how customers or suppliers could result in a firm innovating.

5. According to the R&D Scoreboard, car firms do not take out many patents compared to other industries. Give some explanations for this.

6. What problems does business encounter when trying to protect its IPRs?
   Use examples from China to help you answer this question.

7. Why do small firms find it difficult to protect their technology?

Case Study Counterfeiting and Piracy

Counterfeiting is now a booming industry and is costing companies around the world billions of pounds a year. The products affected range from fake designer handbags to sportswear, CDs, DVDs, computers and video software, car parts, cigarettes, and pharmaceuticals. It has been calculated that European Union companies could be losing up to US$62 billion a year to counterfeiting, while the annual worldwide impact is more than US$200 billion. In addition to this loss of revenue, firms may also suffer a decline in the value of their brand due to the dilution of their reputation for quality or reliability.

The worst offenders for large-scale counterfeiting of videos and DVDs are China and some South American countries, where it is relatively cheap and easy to set up large manufacturing facilities. China is the worst culprit because laws are not very supportive of brand owners, disc-burning technology is readily available, and labour is cheap.

Portugal, India, and Pakistan are foremost in clothing and textile piracy, for example, while Latin America is noted for pharmaceuticals and the Middle East turns out a lot of fake car parts.   →

→ The reaction to piracy varies from one industry to the other. The music and film industries have been pouring resources into the fight against piracy for years and have coordinated industry-wide strategies for dealing with the problem and have lobbied governments across the globe. Music firms such as Universal, Warner, and EMI have been pursuing the Russian music website allofmp3.com claiming that the site, which offers downloads for as little as 5p, was illegal because it paid no royalties to record companies or musicians. Allofmp3.com was the UK's second most popular download site, accounting for 14% of downloads. It was envisaged that were the industry to obtain a verdict that the website was illegal in the British courts, it might still find it very difficult to enforce the ruling in Moscow. The industry has also exerted pressure on internet providers, Tiscali and Cable & Wireless to suspend broadband access to customers who were making copyrighted music available over file sharing networks. Sony BMG tried including secret software that would prevent illegal copying of its CDs. Unfortunately for Sony the software made customers' computers vulnerable to viruses and the company had to stop using it after it settled a series of law suits initiated by aggrieved customers.

Music companies use teams of ex-police officers, forensic accountants, and computer specialists to tackle the pirates by monitoring websites, internet newsletters, and mailing lists to track down the worst offenders and gather evidence for civil or criminal legal actions.

In contrast, some luxury goods providers apparently do not regard counterfeiting as a serious threat because they feel that they are not really losing out since their true customers would not be tempted by counterfeit goods. This could be a mistake because counterfeiting can damage the reputation of the company and its brands because quality is poor. The result could be lost sales and profits.

The pharmaceutical industry takes a different view of piracy. It does not want people to know about it because the implications for public confidence in the drugs could be enormous.

Source: *Financial Times*, 30 April 2003; http://news.bbc.co.uk; *The Guardian*, 20 July 2006

Questions

1. Advance a case for firms making efforts to protect their intellectual property.

2. Why are the music and film industries particularly vulnerable to counterfeiting?

3. What would you see as the main intellectual property of luxury goods firms? Discuss the pros and cons of such firms failing to protect their IPRs.

4. Why is counterfeiting more prevalent in some countries than in others?

5. Explore the reasons for the pharmaceutical industry wishing to keep quiet about counterfeiting of its products.

 Online Resource Centre
www.oxfordtextbooks.co.uk/orc/hamilton_webster/

Visit the supporting online resource centre for additional material which will help you with your assignments, essays and research, or you may find these extra resources helpful when revising for exams.

● FURTHER READING

Anderson shows how the internet helps products that in previous eras would have failed because of low demand, survive and prosper.

● Anderson, C. (2006) *The Long Tail: Why the Future of Business is Selling Less of More.* Hyperion Books

Cantwell and Janne examine the internationalization of technology in Europe by MNCs using patents as a measure.

- Cantwell, J. and Janne, O. (2000) 'The Role of Multinational Corporations and National States in the Globalization of Innovatory Capacity: The European Perspective'. *Technology Analysis & Strategic Management*, Vol 12, Issue 2, June

Edgerton analyses the importance of technology to 20th century society at the global level.

- Edgerton, D. (2007) *The Shock of the Old: Technology in Global History Since 1900*. London: Profile Books

The book by Rogers cited in the references below is now in its fourth edition and is a classic text in the field of the diffusion of innovation, London.

● REFERENCES

Abramovsky, L. *et al.* (2005) 'Understanding co-operative R&D activity: evidence from four European countries'. IFS Working Papers, W05/23

Cassidy, J. (2002) *Dot.con: The Greatest Story Ever Told*. London: Penguin

EU Commission (2005) 'Mobilizing the brainpower of Europe: enabling universities to make their full contribution to the Lisbon Strategy'. SEC 518

Gatelli, D. and Tarantola, S. (2007) 'High-tech trade Indicators 2006: EU-25 vs. USA, China and Japan'. Institute for the Protection and Security of the Citizen, Econometric and Statistical support to Antifraud

Held, D. *et al.* (1999) *Global transformations: Politics, Economics and Culture*. Stanford: Stanford University Press

HM Treasury (2004) 'Science and Innovation Investment Framework 2004–2014'. July. Available at www.hmtreasury.gov.uk

Moore, G. A. (1999) *Crossing the Chasm, Marketing and Selling High-Tech Products to Mainstream Customer*. New York: HarperCollins

OECD (2006) *Compendium of Patent Statistics*

Porter, M. E. (1998) *The Competitive Advantage of Nations*. Basingstoke: Palgrave MacMillan

Rogers, E. M. (1995) *Diffusion of innovations*. New York: The Free Press

Schumpeter, J. A. (1976) *Capitalism, Socialism & Democracy*. London: Routledge

Senge, P. M. (2006) *The Fifth Discipline: The Art and Practice of the Learning Organization*. London: Random House

UNCTAD (2005a) *UNCTAD survey on the internationalization of R&D: Current patterns and prospects on the internationalization of R&D*

UNCTAD (2005b) *World Investment Report 2005: Transnational Corporations and the Internationalization of R&D*

UNESCO (2005) *UNESCO Science Report*

Wonglimpiyarat, J. (2005) 'The nano-revolution of Schumpeter's Kondratieff cycle'. *Technovation*, Vol 25, Issue 11, November

CHAPTER SEVEN

The Political Environment

LEARNING OUTCOMES

This chapter will enable you to:

- Explain what is meant by the terms, political system and State

- Analyse the characteristics of different political systems and understand their importance for business

- Identify and explain the functions performed by the institutions of the State

- Evaluate the arguments regarding the demise of the nation-State

- Assess the importance of the State for business

- Analyse how business can influence the State

Case Study China—A Society in Transition

This case looks at how political decisions to liberalize the economic system can open up multiple opportunities for business. It also examines some of the challenges that confront firms trying to take advantage of those opportunities.

In the late 1970s the Chinese leadership began moving the economy from Soviet-style central planning to a market-orientated system. While the system continues to operate within a political framework of strict Communist planning and control, the economic influence of domestic and foreign private sector organizations and individual citizens has been steadily increasing.

China is important for foreign companies for a variety of reasons. Firstly, it is attractive to foreign business as a location for labour-intensive industries like clothing and textiles because resources in China are relatively cheap—the average wage rate in the USA is 50 times that of China. It is also an appealing location for highly polluting industries for example, chemicals, because China does not strictly enforce its environmental laws. With a quadrupling of GDP since the late 1970s China has become an attractive market. The population is 1.3 billion, the majority being poor and consequently with little purchasing power. However, there are enough rich people with an apparently insatiable appetite for the luxury goods produced by companies such as BMW cars and Rolex watches. In addition, there is a large and growing middle class which constitutes an important market for firms such as General Motors and British American Tobacco. The rapid industrialization of the Chinese economy has created a lucrative market for foreign suppliers of raw materials, capital equipment, and components. Finally, there is vast market potential. Income and purchasing power in the Chinese economy has been expanding at just below 10% per year, a very rapid rate which is forecast to continue.

Regarding politics, the People's Republic of China is a one-party Communist State. The Politburo, comprising the leadership of the Communist party, is the focus of power. It sets policy and controls all administrative, legal, and executive appointments.

The National People's Congress is the parliament or legislative body. The delegates are not elected by the general populace but are selected by the 22 provinces, 4 municipalities, 5 autonomous regions and the armed forces. The Congress elects the President and Vice President.

The State Council is the executive body, the equivalent of a cabinet and is headed up by the President. Its members are appointed by the Congress (see diagram below).

The judicial system in China poses challenges for foreign business. While the Chinese authorities have made efforts to improve the civil, administrative, criminal, and commercial law, the criminal law remains complex and the civil and commercial law tend to be rudimentary. Legislation is loosely worded and there is a maze of regulations. As a result, foreign businesses ➡

Figure 7.1 Political System in China

Source: www.istockphoto.com

→ can find it difficult to use the law, for example, to enforce contracts, and prevent others forging their products or infringing their patent rights. Furthermore, the courts are not independent of the executive, are firmly under the sway of the Communist party and also often corrupt.

Opening up its economy to the outside world has created problems for the Chinese Communist party. It has attempted to continue its long-established policy of exercising a high degree of control over its citizens whilst at the same time gaining the benefits of globalization. Take the internet as an example: it provides a cheap and easy way of communicating with the outside world. China's wish to obtain the economic benefits of networked computing conflicts with its desire to restrict freedom of speech, and the information available to its citizens. With 94 million users, the internet is seen by the Chinese authorities as a particularly important challenge and there is evidence that they regularly censor the internet and spy on users. Such controls raise important issues for foreign internet service providers, portals, and media companies wishing to operate in the Chinese market.

The political system operating in China does not apply in Hong Kong. When Britain handed the colony over to China in 1997, the Chinese authorities agreed to an arrangement under which the territory was granted more freedoms and democracy than the mainland. That is why China is described as being 'one-nation, two-systems'. While the mainland is communist, Hong Kong is seen by some as a glittering showpiece of capitalism.

Sources: CIA World Factbook; Zittrain and Edelman 2003

Introduction

Why do newspapers and radio and television news programmes regularly feature presidents and prime ministers like Barack Obama, Gordon Brown, Nicolas Sarkozy, Valery Putin, and Silvio Berlusconi? Why does business spend so much time and money trying to influence them? It is because they are major decision-makers in a powerful entity called the State. Knowledge of where decision-making power lies in the State is very important for business whether that be a firm wishing to influence the process of formulating laws or regulations, or to get permission to drill for oil, or a contract for building roads and airports.

The political environment has major implications for both the macro and micro environments of business. State institutions establish and enforce the legal and regulatory framework within which business operates. They can have a significant influence on a whole range of business decisions. They can stop firms doing what they want to do or force them to do things they do not want to do. For example, they can give or deny permission for one firm to take over another. The EU Commission did not allow General Electric to take over its rival Honeywell. An EU recycling directive will increase car manufacturers' costs by forcing them to take responsibility for disposal of their products when they come to the end of their useful life. The political environment is significant for business because the decisions emanating from it can generate important opportunities for firms and also pose significant threats, not only domestically but also abroad. The ability of the State to wage wars, pursue diplomacy, agree treaties and alliances, establish policies as regards migration, taxation, interest rates, the exchange rate, the balance of payments, inflation, education, health, the environment, maintaining law and order, and guaranteeing the right to buy and sell private property all have important implications for business.

As globalization proceeds, business, even when it is not involved in exporting, importing, or producing abroad, increasingly finds itself affected by political events outside its home base. It is important that firms build up an understanding of the diverse nature of different political systems and how they operate. This knowledge will make it easier for business better to grasp the opportunities the systems provide as well as coping with the challenges they pose.

In this chapter we examine the different types of political system, the size of the State and how it has grown. We also consider the impact the political environment can have on business and, in the final section, we look at how firms go about influencing their political environment.

What is the Political Environment?

An important entity in the political environment is the nation-State where political parties fight elections, form governments and make laws and enforce them. National governments are indeed an important part of the political environment but they are only one element of a much broader concept called the State. As you will see later, the State comprises institutions such as the civil service and the judiciary as well as governments. Governments come and go but the other elements of the State tend to be more permanent. Basically the political environment is made up of those institutions which make political decisions and implement them. The political environment not only comprises institutions operating at the national level but also, as we will see, bodies at local, regional and supranational (above the nation-State) levels.

The Institutions of the State

The core of the State can be seen as a set of institutions having the legal power, ultimately backed up by coercion (the power to make people do or stop doing things), to make decisions in matters of government over a specific geographical area and over the population living there. The State comprises the following institutions:

- the legislative branch which includes those institutions which make the laws, e.g. Parliament in the UK, Congress in the USA, the Diet in Japan. An important role in such bodies is played by the leading politician, the president in the USA, France, Russia, the prime minister in the UK, Japan, Italy, Spain, the chancellor in Germany, along with cabinet members, ministers, and senior civil servants because they determine and direct government policy.

Parliaments pass policies, laws, and regulations which are then implemented by the executive branch. The EU Parliament is an example of a legislative body but at the supranational level (see Mini Case):

- the executive branch puts the laws into effect and ensures the desired outcomes. It gives policy advice to government ministers. This branch includes administrative bodies, such as the civil service in the UK and the European Commission in the EU—uniquely the Commission has the power to initiate policy. Regulatory agencies, which operate, to an extent, separately from central government also form part of the executive branch. Examples include the Federal Communications Commission in the US, and the Office of the Communications Regulator (OFCOM), the water regulator (OFWAT), the energy regulator (OFGEM) in the UK. In Britain, they are known as Quasi Autonomous Non-Governmental Organizations, often referred to as Quangos. In developed countries the executive branch is usually large, running to thousands of people. Heads of government, such as the US President or the British Prime Minister, are commonly the chief executive of this branch.

- the judicial branch interprets and applies the laws—this branch comprises the judiciary, the police, and the armed forces which give the State its capacity to enforce the laws that it makes. Businesses operating in the geographical area are required to accept that the State has the authority to make decisions and to maintain order. If they are not prepared to accept this authority then the State can try to compel them to do so through the judicial system of police, courts, and prisons. At the EU level the Court of First Instance and the European Court of Justice interpret and apply the laws of the Union (for more discussion of EU law see the section on the EU in Chapter Nine).

Mini Case EU Institutions and Decision-Making

The case identifies and explains the decision-making power of institutions in the EU. Various institutions participate in EU decision-making. The most important are:

- the European Commission: this is the civil service of the EU with powers that are wide and varied. It is the only institution having the power to initiate laws and is responsible for enforcing them. It negotiates international treaties on behalf of the EU as well as the entry of new members. It is headed by a President and a number of Commissioners each with responsibility for a particular area such as the internal market, trade, and transport. While the Commission proposes new legislation, it is up to the Council of the European Union and the Parliament whether those proposals are made law. The Commission seeks to uphold the interest of the EU as a whole.

- the Council of the European Union: this represents individual member states and comprises ministers from national governments. It meets on a regular basis and is arguably the most important decision-making institution. It plays a vital role in the development of EU law. It has to approve

all laws and budget proposals but cannot make new laws on its own. It must get the agreement of the Parliament. The Council has the power to sign international agreements with non EU countries.

Each country's voting power in the Council is based on its population size with the smaller less populous countries, like Malta and Cyprus, being given more votes than their population would warrant. In some areas such as common foreign and security policy, taxation, asylum and immigration policy, Council decisions have to be unanimous. In other words, each member state has the power to veto any new proposals in these areas. On most issues, however, the Council takes decisions by qualified majority voting (QMV). QMV requires around three quarters of the votes to be cast in favour of a proposal. In addition, a member state may ask for confirmation that the votes in favour represent at least 62% of the total population of the Union. If this is found not to be the case, the decision will not be adopted.

- the European Parliament (EP): this is made up of representatives elected by the citizens of each member state. Each member state has a number of seats allocated on the ➡

➡ basis of the size of its population. The EP does not have the same powers as national parliaments. For example, it cannot propose new laws nor has it the power to legislate on matters of taxation, agricultural policy (which accounts for around 40% of the EU budget), or industrial policy. Instead, it can only discuss and vote on laws proposed by the Commission. In order for a new EU law to pass, it has to have the support of both the Parliament and the Council of the European Union. The EP also has the power to accept or reject Commissioners and to sack the entire Commission through a vote of censure.

There are two other important institutions. The first is the European Council. This brings together the heads of government and the Commission President four times a year. They map out the overall direction of the Union, for example as regards enlargement and deal with issues that have not been resolved because of their contentious nature such as the size of the budget and how it is to be spent. It decides who will be President of the Commission. Like the Commission, the council also has a President. Under the Lisbon Treaty, a politician will be chosen to be president of the European Council for 2.5 years, replacing the previous arrangement where countries took turns at being president for six months.

The second institution is the European Court of Justice (ECJ). The Court upholds EU law and, in EU matters, is the highest court in all of the member states. It arbitrates between member states, institutions, and individuals in cases relating to EU law. There is no right of appeal against ECJ judgments.

Sources: Europa, European Institutions and other bodies. Available at http://europa.eu; Civitas, http://www.civitas.org.uk

Learning Task

This task lets you review your understanding of the different branches of the State. Allocate the following people to the appropriate branch of the State.

	Legislative	Executive	Judicial
President of France			
The Cabinet Secretary (UK)			
President of the EU Commission			
The chief of police			
Local authority politician			
Supreme Court judge in the USA			
Member of the US Congress			
Commander of the armed forces			
The Queen of Britain			

Different Political Systems

We start off by considering the political environment at the level of the nation-State. If we take membership of the United Nations as an indicator of the number of independent countries in the world then there are 191. These nations operate under a variety of political systems but in each of them a national government exercises the right to make laws and to ensure that they are enforced in society. In some countries, power is concentrated in the hands of one or a few people while, in others, power is spread over a large number of different groups.

No two countries have identical political regimes.

We examine four different types of political system, liberal democracy, authoritarian and absolutist, communist, and theocratic. You will see that in the real world these regimes sometimes do not exist in their pure form. Subsequently, we go on to look at the differences between unitary states and federal states.

Liberal Democracy

There are two main characteristics of liberal democracies. The first is the right of citizens to elect governments to represent their interests. The second is the right to individual freedom. More specifically, such societies comprise:

- governmental institutions based on majority rule with members drawn from a variety of political parties winning their positions through free elections. This occurs, for example, in the countries of Western Europe, North America, Latin American countries such as Argentina and Brazil, and Asian countries like India and Japan where voters have the choice of candidates from several political parties. The party that wins the majority of votes or seats usually becomes the party of government;

- State institutions which are constrained in their powers by other institutions. In the USA this is reflected in the separation of powers amongst different bodies. Power and responsibility is divided between the President, the congress, the executive, and the judges. Each acts as a check and a balance on the others in the exercise of power. So the President may wish the USA to join a regional trading area—for example, George W. Bush in 2005 wanted the US to be a member of the Central American Free Trade Association (CAFTA) but he had to get the approval of Congress to do so;

- governments that are accountable to the electorate. This means that citizens can vote governments out of office if they do not like what they are doing. In the UK, India, and Japan, the electorate have the opportunity to do this in national elections that are held every four or five years;

- the right to personal freedom and to express views freely. In liberal democracies, television, radio, and the press are not under the sole control of the State so a range of views can be expressed. There is also the right to assembly which means that people can gather peacefully and demonstrate to make their views known. This right was exercised when more than a million people demonstrated in London in 2003 against the Iraq war. These rights are guaranteed by an independent judiciary;

- a permanent, skilled, and impartial public service, for example, the civil service, responsible to the government and through it to the electorate;

- most liberal democracies operate a mixed economy. That is true whether one looks at the countries of North America, Europe, and nations such as Argentina, India, and Japan. In these nations, the majority of economic activity is carried out in the private sector with business and the consumer having the freedom to buy and sell goods and services. However, the State can also play an important economic role through taxation and public expenditure and ownership of, or significant shareholdings in, certain industries. It can also limit the freedom of business to trade and to make profit through the laws and regulations that it passes.

Of the 191 nations in the UN it seems that less than half are full liberal democracies. Liberal democracy is more likely to be found in rich, politically stable countries such as those in North America and in Northern and Western Europe and in Japan. This is obviously of interest to business because stability and, prosperity make liberal democratic economies and their markets very attractive for business. It is therefore no surprise to find that the vast bulk of trade and foreign investment takes place among liberal democracies. Liberal democracy is found less often in countries with a low level of income per head of population. Such countries frequently experience political instability and this can be a deterrent to business getting involved in their economies. While there are countries that are clearly liberal democracies, there are others like Russia that are moving, sometimes rather unsteadily, towards it.

There is a debate as to whether prosperity leads to the creation of liberal democratic systems or whether countries are rich because they are liberal democracies. Commentators such as Fukuyama take the former view arguing that when a country gets past a certain level of economic development the citizens will increasingly demand democratic participation and democratic political institutions. Others, such as Wright, disagree, for she has found that public demands for democracy in China have fallen as the economy has prospered.

Authoritarian and Absolutist Systems

A relatively small number of countries operate under authoritarian or absolutist regimes. These are forms of government in which one person or a group of people exercise power unrestrained by laws or opposition. These countries are usually characterized by:

- restrictions on the activities of political parties. It may be that only one political party is allowed to operate which gives total support to the ruler. Iraq, under Saddam Hussein, was a good example of this;

- the State is headed by one or several people who have unbridled power to make decisions. Myanmar (formerly known as Burma) is run by a small number of military officers;

- an absence of checks and balances on the power of the ruler. In Saudi Arabia, the royal family holds power with little constraint from parliament or the judiciary;

- a system where support for the ruler is based on patronage. Patronage, or clientelism, as it is sometimes called, occurs where favours are doled out in return for political support. Such favours can take a variety of forms such as money, jobs in government offices, or public contracts. Alternatively, the system could be based on inheritance where power and privilege is passed on from one member of the ruling family to another—once again Saudi Arabia is a good example of this. Saudi law declares the country to be a monarchy ruled by the sons and grandsons of King Abd Al Aziz Al Saud. So when King Fahd died in 2005, his crown passed to his half-brother, Abdullah.

Of course patronage is not confined to authoritarian and absolutist regimes. It also occurs in some liberal democracies. In the USA the slang expression, 'pork barrel politics' is often used to describe this behaviour. It occurs when members of congress lobby to get publicly funded projects that bring money and jobs to their own districts as a political favour to local politicians or citizens. Examples include infrastructure projects such as the building of dams, improvements to harbours, and the construction of bridges and roads.

In Italy, there has been a history of Christian Democrat governments distributing State jobs, tax relief, and preferential pensions treatment to blocs of reliable supporters. Fiat was a particular beneficiary because, after the Second World War, the Agnelli family, its owners, enjoyed a privileged relationship with the Christian Democrats. In return for political support, various Christian Democrat-led governments helped Fiat by building motorways, keeping the price of petrol low, minimizing investment in public transport, and protecting the domestic car market from foreign competition.

So some characteristics of authoritarian regimes may also be present in liberal democracies.

Countries operating under authoritarian or absolutist regimes only constitute a small proportion of the world's population and income. Thus, as far as business is concerned, their markets are not that important. However, firms may be interested in producing goods and services in these countries because resources like labour are often cheap. And for some primary sector industries a number of these countries are vital because they are rich in natural resources. For example, several countries in the Middle East are sitting on vast reserves of oil. Saudi Arabia is the world's single largest oil producer and has, by far, the biggest oil reserves. This makes it attractive to the big multinational oil companies such as Exxon, Shell, and BP. Oil companies need to be aware of the identity of those exercising power in these nations. Such knowledge is invaluable for these companies because it indicates where they need to apply influence when, for example, they are trying to obtain permission to drill for oil (for more on the oil industry and its political environment see the section on the political and legal environment in Chapter Four).

Communist Regimes

Communist regimes tend to have the following characteristics:

- the production of most goods and services is owned and controlled by the State. In China, even though companies such as VW and General, have been allowed to invest there, the State continues to exercise a very significant degree of economic control over what is produced, how much is produced, where it is produced, and who will produce it; the system is dominated by one political party. Vietnam is another example of a one-party State where the Communist Party has a tight control of the political system.

- in addition to controlling the economy, the Party controls the legislative, executive, and judicial branches of the State as well as trade unions and the media. In North Korea, for example, the Communist Party controls television and the press (Chapter Six discusses some of the difficulties confronted by firms in dealings with the Chinese political and legal system).

Unlike liberal democracies, communist regimes do not value so highly the right to personal freedoms. They put more emphasis on meeting the needs of society as a whole.

Theocratic regimes

In theocratic regimes:

- religion or faith plays a dominant role in the government;
- the rulers in government are normally the same people who lead the dominant religion;

Mini Case Equatorial Guinea

This case looks at a country that, in 1991, declared itself to be democratic. However, it fails to qualify as a liberal democracy on a number of grounds.

Equatorial Guinea is a former Spanish colony located on the West coast of Africa. Since it gained independence in 1968, it has been ruled by two men from the same family.

Large oil and gas deposits were discovered offshore in the mid-1990s, and Equatorial Guinea is now one of sub-Saharan Africa's biggest oil producers. But few ordinary people benefit from the oil revenues. Little of the money from oil is spent on health, education, or on improving the infrastructure. Opponents of the regime complain that President Obiang Nguema and his supporters use the money for their own enrichment. It was reported that the President's family had amassed US$800 million in a US bank. Despite international calls for greater financial transparency in the sector, President Obiang has said oil revenue figures are a State secret.

In 1996 Equatorial Guinea's first multi-party presidential election was held amid reports of widespread fraud and irregularities, returning the President with 99% of the vote. The President exercises almost total control over the political system and suppresses political opposition. There are only two members of parliament who openly oppose the regime.

His Government has been accused of widespread human rights abuses. The main broadcasters are State-controlled and there are only a few private newspapers. Mild criticism of public institutions is allowed but criticism of the leadership is not tolerated and self-censorship is widespread.

Source: CIA, World Factbook; www.bbc.co.uk; *El Pais*, 7 August 2005

Source: www.istockphoto.com

- policies pursued by government are either identical with, or strongly influenced by, the principles of the majority religion, and typically, the government claims to rule on behalf of God or a higher power, as specified by the local religion.

There are no more than a handful of theocratic states. Iran is one example of a theocratic regime where the political process is heavily influenced by Islam. The policies of the Islamic political parties are founded on the Koran and the ayatollahs and mullahs, the religious leaders, are very influential in the formulation of policies. They, along with Islamic lawyers, sit on a council that has the power of veto over laws proposed by parliament. A priority in Iran is to resist what is seen as the corruption inherent in western materialism which makes it difficult for big western MNCs to operate there given that they are seen as the agents of the materialist culture.

The Vatican City is another example of theocracy. It is an independent, sovereign State with the Pope as its elected head. Its policies are based on the teachings of the Bible. Power is concentrated in the hands of the Pope who holds supreme legislative, executive, and judicial power.

Unitary and Federal Systems

Political regimes may also be classified according to the distribution of power at different levels. The regime may be unitary where most decision-making power is held by the institutions of central government and where the regions and localities have little or no autonomy. In unitary states the institutions of central government normally are responsible for important policy decisions, for the majority of public expenditure and for the raising of taxes with the regions having fewer powers in this regard. The great majority of countries in the world have a unitary system. France, Italy, Japan, and China are examples of unitary states.

On the other hand the system may be federal where power is shared between the centre and the component regions. In such systems regions may have significant decision-making powers in relation to areas such as spending and taxation. Friction between the centre and the regions in federations is not unusual. In 2005, it was reported that a number of States in the USA intended to break away from the environmental policy of the Federal Government. They announced plans to freeze carbon dioxide emissions from big power stations. This was a departure from the stance of the government in Washington which had withdrawn from the Kyoto protocol on climate change in 2001 arguing that mandatory emissions targets would devastate the US economy.

More than 2 billion people live in federal states and they comprise half the world's land area. Examples of federations are the USA, Germany, Brazil, and India. The implications for business are that, in unitary systems, those who award contracts for goods and services and decide rates and levels of tax are located at the centre of the regime. Thus, firms wishing to be given government contracts or to influence taxation decisions have to be in a position to affect the decision-making process at the centre. In federal systems businesses may find themselves dealing with decision-makers at both the centre and in the various regions of the federation.

Learning Task

The chart below shows the share of tax revenues raised by different levels of government. It shows that, in some countries, the national government has much greater tax raising powers than regional or local governments. In some countries tax raising powers are more decentralized.

1. Explain why the tax raising powers in the UK appears to be much more centralized than either the USA or Germany.

2. Assuming that public spending is similarly decentralized, what are the implications for businesses wishing to sell to the public sector:

   a. in the UK?

   b. In the USA?

Figure 7.2 Share of Tax Revenues 2001

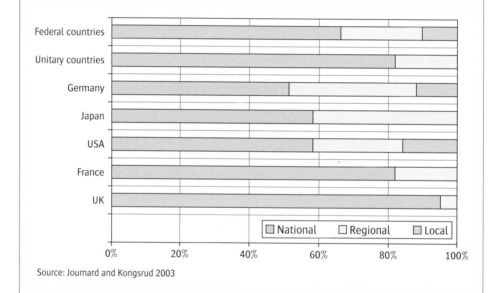

Source: Joumard and Kongsrud 2003

The Size of the State

In this section we examine the size of the State relative to the economy. This is most commonly done by looking at the amount of money the State is spending and what it takes in tax as a proportion of the total income generated in the country i.e. gross domestic product. As we will see, the size and importance of the State varies from one country to another.

Public Expenditure

At the start of the 20th century, government spending in today's large industrial countries accounted for less than 10% of their GDP. Governments confined themselves to a limited

Figure 7.3 Total Government Expenditure as % of GDP

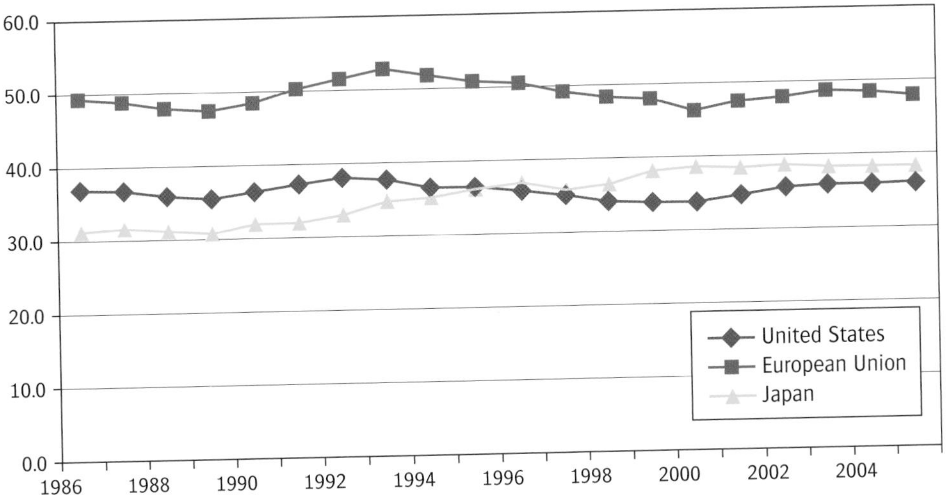

Source: OECD

number of activities such as defending the country against external threats, maintaining law and order within their borders and controlling the amount of money in circulation.

However, the First World War, 1914–18, changed things. High taxes were introduced by the protagonists to pay for the war and the tax revenues allowed governments to maintain higher spending afterwards. By the 1920s public spending had risen to an average of 15% of GDP. Following the wave of welfare spending designed to combat the Great Depression in the early 1930s, the average rose again; by 1937 it had reached almost 21% of GDP.

The three decades after the end of the Second World War in 1945 saw the biggest increase historically in public spending. This mainly reflected the fact of governments taking on responsibility for maintaining high levels of employment and adequate living standards. One result of this was a major expansion of the welfare state. Spending also increased significantly on defence arising from the cold war between the West and the Communist bloc of countries. By 1980, the State's average slice of the economy had leapt to 43% (in America the percentage topped 30%; in many small European countries it breached 50%). During the 1980s and despite the anti-government rhetoric of some countries, it continued to grow, hitting 47% of EU GDP in 1994 (see Figure 7.3). At the beginning of the 21st century, spending in the EU15 accounted for the equivalent of around half of GDP while for the USA and Japan it was lower, but still significant, at more than a third (see Figure 7.4). Countries such as Sweden, Denmark, and France with highly developed welfare states top the list with the USA, Japan, Australia, Korea, and Mexico at the bottom.

Where does the Money go

The largest amounts of public spending go on subsidies and transfers, for example, pensions, social security, and unemployment benefits. This is followed by spending on

Figure 7.4 Public Expenditure as % GDP 2006

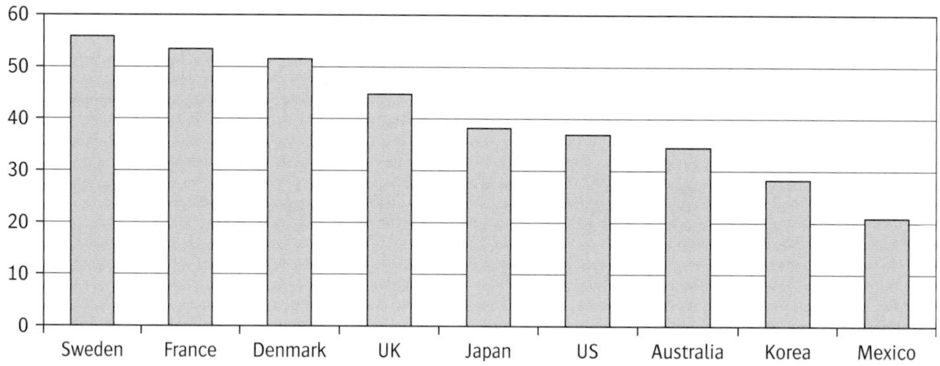

Source: OECD

defence, law and order, education and health, often referred to as public or government consumption (in the UK this represents about 21% of GDP at current prices).

How the Money is Raised—Taxation and Borrowing

A clear trend since the mid 1970s was a steady increase in the proportion of total income taken by taxes. The tax-to-GDP ratio across most of the developed economies rose despite many countries cutting tax rates on personal and company income (see Figure 7.5). This reflected the effects of stronger economic growth which generated higher company profits. Some countries have also tried to offset the effects of cuts in tax rates by drawing more sectors and people into the tax net and reducing the degree of tax evasion and avoidance. The tax take tends to be higher in Western European countries. In Sweden and Denmark, it is equivalent to about half of GDP while it exceeds 40% of GDP in Italy, Austria, France, Norway, Finland, and Belgium. Mexico had the lowest tax ratio at around 18% followed by South Korea, the USA, Japan, and Switzerland with ratios in the 20–30% range (Figure 7.6).

More than 90% of the tax revenues raised in the developed economies come from three main sources: direct taxes on the income of individuals and business, indirect taxes on goods and services such as VAT and excise duties, and another form of direct tax, social security contributions.

Businesses pay tax on their net income i.e. their profits. There has been a widespread tendency for tax rates on profits to drop in the advanced economies (Figure 7.7). Devereux and Sorenson describe the reduction in the tax rate on profits as remarkable. In 1982, they reported that 15 countries had tax rates in excess of 40%. In Germany, Sweden, Finland, and Austria the rate was around 60%. By 2006, rates had fallen significantly across all countries. Only Japan, the USA, and Germany had rates of more than 40%. This trend may be due to the spread of globalization and the wish by countries to attract and retain foreign direct investment. A further reason is that host countries want to encourage those businesses to retain their earnings in the host country.

Figure 7.5 Percentage Changes in tax to GDP ratio 1995–2005

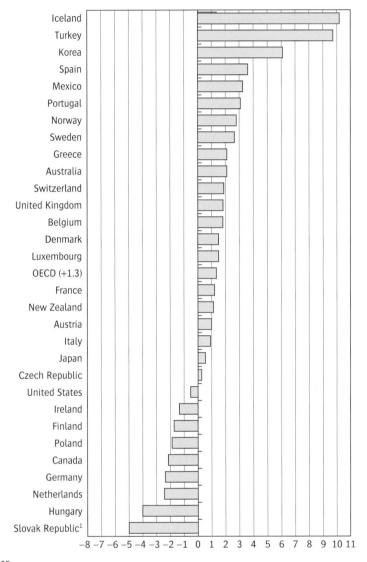

¹ 1998–2005
Source: OECD 2007b

When spending is greater than the taxes raised, governments usually borrow to cover the deficit. The USA has, for a number of years, been running large budget deficits. In 2007, it was US$163 billion while the figure for the UK was expected to be around £40 billion. On the other hand, India and China were running significant budget surpluses showing that tax receipts were higher than public expenditure (*The Economist*, 14 February 2008; HM Treasury 2008).

Figure 7.6 Total Tax Revenue (as a percentage of GDP, 2004)

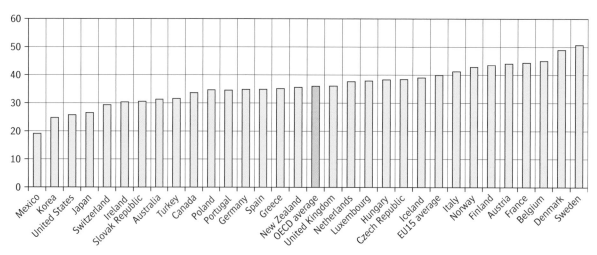

Source: OECD Factbook 2007

Figure 7.7 Tax rate on Company Profits 1982–2006

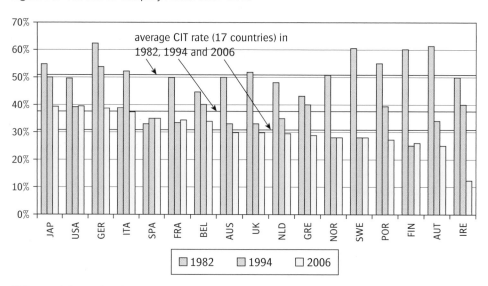

*CIT: corporate income tax rate
Source: OECD 2007a

The Demise of the Nation State?

Some commentators including Ohmae and, to some extent, Held have argued that the State has become increasingly powerless in the face of globalization. They contend that the increasing and all-pervasive interconnectedness of national economies is fatal to the effective power of individual States. It is claimed that national governments can no longer manage their domestic economies because they are subject to the forces that shape the

Learning Task

Examine Figures 7.3 to 7.7 and answer the following questions:

1. Give some evidence of the increase in the size of the State in industrialized countries in the period after 1945.

2. Come up with explanations for the increase in the size of the State.

3. What could be the reasons for France and Sweden being the largest public spenders and the USA and Japan among the lowest?

4. Explain why governments wish to attract and retain foreign direct investment. Why might globalization cause them to reduce company taxation?

international economy. So if an individual government wanted to set profit tax on business at a much higher level than other countries then firms would relocate or ensure that their profits were earned in countries with a lower profits tax. Tax revenues would fall and the government would be obliged to revert to a lower level of profit tax. Similarly, if a government wanted to have a relatively low rate of interest then this would be undermined by investors moving their money out of the country to take advantage higher rates elsewhere. This would reduce the supply of money available for borrowers and put upward pressure on interest rates. A government wanting to prohibit dangerous or undesirable working practices might find that the affected industries move abroad or shut down, because the new regulation would put domestic firms at a disadvantage in competition with foreign producers. Some commentators supported their arguments with the case of Germany where welfare benefits were high relative to other countries. Generous benefits meant that, for each worker, employers had to pay a high level of social security tax on top

Learning Task

Commentators such as Ohmae argue that governments must bow down before worldwide competition. In other words, governments cannot buck global market forces. For example, a government announcement of expensive reforms to its health or education systems might be deemed too costly by the big financial institutions. Anticipating higher taxes to finance the reforms, they might move money out of the country punishing the country with higher interest rates or a collapsing currency. This would deter the government from increasing public expenditure to finance its reforms.

  An implication of this argument is that the market will enforce a convergence of taxation and public expenditure among countries; in other words, there will be a race to the bottom.

1. Examine Figures 7.3 to 7.6. Is there any evidence of public expenditure or taxation converging at the lowest levels?

2. What does your answer to question 1 suggest about the claim that governments cannot buck the global market?

of wages. This pushed up labour costs and made the German economy less competitive internationally. As a result Germany suffered from slow growth and high levels of unemployment. It was thus no surprise to the commentators that Chancellor Schroeder decided to cut back on the welfare benefit system. They saw the reforms as an indication that countries cannot buck global market forces.

Critics of Ohmae's view, such as Hirst and Thompson (2005) and Scholte (2005), argue that the demise of the nation-State is much exaggerated. Hirst and Thompson point out that the actual net flows between major economies are considerably less than a century ago. They contend that the main test of globalization is whether world economic trends confirm the existence of a single global economy. In this respect, they suggest, the evidence falls far short of any such claim. Others argue that globalization has not weakened the most powerful States such as the USA, Japan, and those in Western Europe who are the parent States and political voices of most of the major multinational corporations (MNCs). These countries, powerful in their own right, are also able to exercise influence through their continued domination of decision-making in the international financial institutions and forums such as the IMF, World Bank, and G-7. Scholte says that the most one can argue is that globalization has severely constrained the bargaining positions of smaller and weaker States, mainly in the underdeveloped world. This is hardly a new situation since small and poorer States have always had to consider the potential responses of more powerful States to the policies they adopt.

Functions of the State and their Importance for Business

Earlier on we looked at the different branches of the State. However, the boundaries of the State are not always clear-cut and, as we now discover, they can extend much further than the narrow description given above. Modern governments perform many functions besides the traditional ones of maintaining law and order and protecting the country from external attack.

A crucial role for the State is the preservation of the economic and financial system. A striking example of this occurred with the 2007/08 credit crunch when the USA and European banking systems were in turmoil. Financial institutions, unable to borrow money, went bust, or, like Northern Rock in the UK, were taken into public ownership. In the USA, JP Morgan Chase took over the about-to-fail Bear Stearns bank at a bargain basement price, but only after the US central bank, the Federal Reserve, had extended credit of US$30 billion to Bear Stearns. Stock markets gyrated wildly and the dollar plunged against other currencies. Governments could not allow the global financial system to crash because the money and credit provided by banks is a vital lubricant for business in a modern economy. Central banks in the USA, the UK, and the Eurozone intervened to prevent a collapse by making hundreds of billions of dollars of loans available to financial institutions (*Financial Times*, 22 March 2008; see Case Study at end of Chapter Four; government intervention in trade is discussed in Chapter Two).

We are now going to look in more detail at a number of functions that can have a significant impact on the external environment of business. By carrying out these functions, State institutions can make decisions that constrain the ability of business to meet its objectives such as making profits and increasing sales or market share. On the other hand, they can also provide opportunities which firms are able to exploit for commercial gain.

Law of Contract

The State has a major part to play in establishing the wider environment within which business operates. It passes laws and adopts regulations that set the legal framework or rules of the game for business, some of which are especially important. For example, in liberal democracies the State usually guarantees the right to own and to buy and sell capital assets, goods and services, the lifeblood of all commercial businesses. One particularly important aspect is the law of contract, where the State lays down and enforces rules and obligations relating to transactions around the buying and selling of goods and services. The law of contract ensures that if a business sells goods or services, it will be able to use the law to pursue the customer for payment, were that to be necessary. Similarly, a firm contracting to buy a certain quantity and quality of goods wants to be sure that it is able to use the law to remedy any shortfalls or deficiencies on the part of the supplier. Business will be reluctant to operate in countries where it is not able to enforce the terms of its contract. A good example of such a country is the Congo, in Africa, which the big oil multinational, Shell, classifies as a country where State institutions are ineffective. The absence of an effective judicial system makes it virtually impossible for firms to enforce the law of contract (for more on contract law see Chapter Eight).

Law and Order and External Attack

Another function of the State is to protect its geographical area from both external and internal threats. It usually has the army, navy, and air force to deal with external threats, for example, military threats from other countries, and the police, courts, and prisons for helping to maintain law and order within the geographical frontiers of the State. States that can effectively protect themselves from external threat and maintain law and order internally are seen by business as providing a more stable and attractive operating environment.

Spending and Taxation

Economically, the State is the largest and most important single player in developed countries. This is reflected in the amount of money governments spend and take in tax in relation to the whole economy. Governments spend money on buying goods and services, paying the wages of State employees and providing welfare benefits. Taxation takes the form of direct taxes, those on incomes, and indirect taxes which are levied on expenditure

Mini Case   Minimizing the Tax Burden

This case shows how firms go about minimizing the amount of money they hand over to governments in taxes. One approach is to evade paying taxes, which is illegal, or to exploit a legal loophole to avoid tax.

Tax Evasion

Globalization makes it easier for companies, especially big MNCs, to minimize their global tax burden. They can do this in several ways. One of the most commonly used is transfer pricing which involves the mispricing of cross-border trade. Firms may, for example, sell goods from subsidiaries in high-tax countries to other group companies in low-tax countries at below market prices. The goods can then be re-sold at market rates, thereby ensuring that the profit attracts less tax.

In 2003, GlaxoSmithKline, the giant pharmaceuticals company, was presented with a US$5.2 billion bill for extra taxes and interest by the US Government over revenues dating back to the late 1980s. In the UK, the tax authorities questioned the transfer pricing policy of Nissan going back to the date of its incorporation in 1990.

The cost of tax evasion by firms can be substantial. It has been estimated that mispricing cost the American taxpayer US$53 billion in 2001.

Tax Avoidance

Big retailers in the UK, including Tesco, Woolworths, and Amazon avoid VAT by setting up subsidiaries in the Channel Islands of Jersey and Guernsey to sell products online. They were, quite legally, exploiting an EU law that allowed them to offer discounts on products such as CDs and DVDs. The British Treasury estimated that such schemes were costing it some £80 million a year in lost revenues.

Source: *Financial Times*, 22 July 2004; *The Observer*, 28 August 2005

Source: www.istockphoto.com

(there are a variety of welfare regimes in operation across the world with very different implications for the size and character of government spending and taxation—see the section on social models in Chapter Five).

The State can use its spending on goods and services and welfare benefits and taxing along with other policies towards interest rates and the exchange rate to influence the level of total demand for the goods and services produced by business. When the economy is going into recession, the State can increase demand by raising its own spending on goods and services, or it can cut taxes or lower interest rates to encourage consumers and business to increase their spending. Alternatively, when the economy is booming and there is a danger of inflation going out of control, the State can cut spending, or raise taxes and interest rates to reduce spending and relieve inflationary pressures.

Such decisions can have major implications for business. For example a decision to raise interest rates increases the cost of borrowing for firms and is often greeted by them with dismay. The higher cost of borrowing may also cause consumers to cut back on spending on goods such as consumer durables which they would normally buy on credit. On the other hand, organizations such as the retail banks may welcome such an increase in rates because it allows them to charge their customers more for loans. Rising interest rates often mean that banks can widen the gap between the interest they pay their customers on their current accounts and the income they can earn on their depositors' money.

The State can raise taxation revenue from business through direct tax on income such as profits or by levying indirect taxes on expenditure such as VAT, or excise duties which are usually imposed on a limited number of industries such as oil, alcoholic drinks, and tobacco.

Negotiator

The State also acts as a negotiator with other States. Negotiations can be bilateral where two countries are involved, or multilateral where more than two participate. The WTO is a multilateral body where important negotiations take place on reductions in barriers to trade and to the movement of capital across borders. Such negotiations can be very good for business particularly when they open up new markets. On the other hand, they can remove barriers that protect domestic firms from foreign competition.

Regulator

Regulation can affect a very wide range of business activities. For instance, regulations could constrain the ability of the firm to take out patents or set its own prices e.g. in the telecommunications and water industries in the UK. It could also affect the level of competition, and market entry. For example, in both the EU and the USA the authorities liberalized entry into the civil aviation market which led to new entry and a much fiercer degree of competition (for a more detailed discussion of barriers to entry, see Chapter Three).

Regulations could increase a firm's costs by stipulating requirements relating to consumer health and safety, to employment contracts and to the natural environment or by requiring companies to fill in certain forms and to meet certain administrative formalities i.e. red tape (for more discussion of the impact of regulations on business see Chapter Eight).

In its role as a regulator the State can take the power to grant or refuse a firm a licence to operate or to guarantee it a monopoly. In the developed world, banks and other financial institutions usually need to get a licence to sell financial services. HSBC, one of the world's biggest banks, claims that compliance with the rules and regulations in 79 different national markets cost it more than £200 million (*Financial Times*, 2 March 2004). Regulations can also determine whether or not firms can merge—the US Federal Trade Commission blocked a merger between Staples and Office Depot, the big office supplies companies.

Firms may also find that regulations lay down the technical specifications to which their products must conform. There are examples of drugs regulators, concerned about safety, demanding more rigorous testing, prohibiting the launch of a new drug or ordering pharmaceutical companies to withdraw products from the market place. Wyeth, the big US pharmaceutical company, complains that regulation is the single most important factor driving up its costs. It claims that regulators are demanding more costly, complex and longer running trials using more patients. According to the company, it is not uncommon to spend up to US$20,000 per patient in a single test phase and for cancer, it could be anything up to US$100,000 per patient. As a result it wants governments to reduce the burden of regulation (*Financial Times*, 15 April 2005).

The main forms of regulation are at the national level but supranational regulation is becoming increasingly important through bodies such as the World Trade Organization or the EU.

Deregulator

Just as the State can regulate so can it deregulate, or liberalize. Thus the USA and EU have liberalized their civil aviation sectors. Now EU airlines have the freedom to set their own prices, to fly over the territory of member states, to operate flights within those countries and to set up routes between them. As a result, numerous low cost airlines emerged, such as easyJet and Ryanair, that caused all sorts of competitive problems to the established national carriers like British Airways and Lufthansa. The EU also deregulated the telecommunications sector leading to the establishment of major competitors such as Vodafone to national monopolists such as France Telecom, Deutsche Telecom, and British Telecom.

Arbitrator

The State also acts as an arbitrator or referee between firms who are in dispute with each other. Thus business may look to State institutions, such as the courts, or other regulatory agencies, to resolve disputes with other firms or to take action against them.

Such disputes could relate to a whole range of issues such as breach of contract, abuse of market power and patents and so on.

Microsoft's competitors have complained on numerous occasions to the competition authorities in both the USA and the EU about how Microsoft abuses its market power making it very difficult for them to compete in the software market. The President of the

Computer and Communications Industry Association, which represents computer firms has argued that the only way to stop Microsoft acting unlawfully is for governments to enforce vigorously the decisions made by the courts (Ed Black, president of the Computer and Communications Industry Association, cited in *The Guardian*, 25 November 2004).

Customer for Goods and Services

The State can also play a vital role as a customer for business. The UK State spends over £100 billion on goods and services every year. For example, each year the NHS spends £11 billion and the Ministry of Defence £13 billion. So for some industries, such as pharmaceuticals and armaments, the single most important customer is the State and the purchasing policies pursued by the State towards those industries is of paramount importance. This can be seen in those countries with ageing populations where the State is trying to control public expenditure through pressure on pharmaceutical firms to lower prices and by turning to lower priced generic drugs.

It is similarly important in the IT sector where, in 2001, the State accounted for 55% of IT spending in the UK while in the construction industry it accounted for more than a third. It was also the second biggest single customer for professional services (*Financial Times*, 6 February 2004).

The State can also be a major client for the financial sector. When governments run budget deficits they borrow from financial institutions in exchange for financial instruments such as bonds and Treasury Bills. This can make governments major customers for lending institutions—the UK Government in 2008/09 was expected to borrow the massive sum of £43 billion (www.guardian.co.uk, 21 May 2008).

The purchasing strategies pursued by the State can have important implications for suppliers. For example, there are claims in the UK that government procurement policies favour large companies at the expense of small and medium sized enterprises. There is also much evidence that many States pursue nationalistic purchasing policies, favouring domestic producers over their foreign counterparts even when the foreign firms offer better value.

Supplier of Goods and Services

In many countries the State takes on the job of producing and selling goods and services. Sectors where the State often carries out these activities are energy, water, sanitation, transport, postal services, and telecommunications. The organizations responsible for producing in these sectors are frequently publicly owned and controlled. Other areas of production where the State is usually heavily involved is in the provision of welfare services with health and education services being two prime examples. In many developed economies the State exercises a high degree of control over the finances and policies pursued by schools, universities, and hospitals. The policies pursued by governments in those areas could be important for business since they could have implications for the quality of the labour force in terms of health and education levels.

As we have seen, the State supplies some goods and services essential for private sector production. For business to operate effectively, there has got to be a transport infrastructure in the form of road and rail networks, ports, and airports. Usually the State is involved in providing these and also some of the services associated with them such as rail or air travel. Similarly, State agencies can be suppliers of such vital elements as energy and telecommunications as well as basic research and development, and economic statistics. Financial services may also be provided by State agencies. For example, in the UK the Export Credit Guarantee Department (ECGD) insures exporters against the risk of not getting paid by their overseas buyer for reasons such as insolvency, war, or lack of foreign exchange. In the six years up to 2004, the agency paid £645 million to arms firms for failed deals with Indonesia of which £400 million went to BAE, Britain's biggest arms firm. The ECGD also guarantees loans provided by banks to overseas borrowers who want to buy from the UK and it can arrange loans at favourable rates of interest.

The policies pursued by these State-owned suppliers as regards pricing and investment can have a significant impact on the performance of their customers in the private sector. For example, big energy consuming firms in the steel and chemicals industries in France will be very sensitive to the prices charged by the State monopoly suppliers, Electricté de France (EDF), or Gaz de France (GDF), because energy counts for a large proportion of their costs (see OECD 2005 for information on public ownership in OECD countries).

Competitor

State organizations may be important competitors for private sector firms in, for example, energy, transport, and telecommunications and in areas such as health and education. Often private sector firms complain that they face unfair competition from their State rivals. This can take several forms. The State firm may be subsidized allowing it to charge artificially low prices or it may be able to raise finance at much lower rates of interest than its private sector rivals simply because it is a State agency and is regarded as less risky by the financial markets. Foreign private sector energy companies wishing to enter the French market could face formidable competition from their State-owned rivals, EDF, one of the world's largest electricity companies and GDF. EDF has entered markets in both Western and Eastern Europe, but foreign energy firms trying to penetrate the French market have run up against barriers to entry put up by the French State despite EU efforts to liberalize the energy market. Even if entry was possible, new firms would find themselves competing with a heavily protected domestic producer. EDF is the largest producer of electricity in France. Most of France's electricity is produced by nuclear power which receives great dollops of subsidy from the French government.

Subsidizer

The State often subsidizes business in the form of grants, tax reliefs, and cheap loans to maintain or generate employment or to maintain the production of goods and services regarded as important to the national economy (see Figure 7.8). The French Government in the 1990s, in fierce competition with the UK authorities for investment from Toyota, reportedly offered the company tax breaks, waived some social security contributions and gave money to help train the work force in its car plant. When, in 2005, EuroDisney, operator of two theme parks outside Paris was experiencing financial problems, the

Figure 7.8 Total State aid by sector, EU–25, 2006

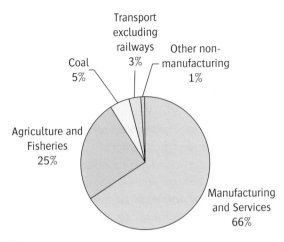

Source: EU Commission 2007

French Government came to its aid with US$500 milllion in investments and cheap loans through a State-owned bank.

According to the European Commission, Boeing from the mid-1980s had, or would, receive subsidies worth around US$28 billion. In 2006, EU States subsidized business to the tune of more than €49 billion with manufacturers being the main beneficiaries. The breakdown by sector is shown in Figure 7.8.

In summary we can see that the exercise of the functions outlined above can have an impact on industry structure, ownership and control, for example, through the control of mergers and acquisitions or through policies to remove barriers to entry in industries such as airlines and telecommunications. It can also have a significant influence on the decisions organizations make in areas like pricing, product, and investment. Such influences may then have important implications for the performance of a company, in areas such as profit performance, market share, and growth rate.

How Organizations Influence the State

As trade, overseas investment, and foreign competition have grown in importance, so firms, particularly those with international operations, have perceived the increasing importance of their relationships with State institutions. While decades of international negotiations may have made trade and the movement of capital freer, companies in many sectors confront increasing competition in their domestic markets and still face barriers in foreign markets. To protect themselves against foreign competition, to get the barriers removed, or to keep them in place for that matter, companies often appeal to forces in their political environment that could help. As the chief executive of BP said 'We've always got to be in a position to turn to the government in power' (*Financial Times*, 2 August 2002).

Because the State can have such an important impact, firms often make big efforts to try and influence the decisions it makes and are often prepared to devote very large amounts of resources to ensure a successful outcome to their attempts to do so. Thus, big firms such as Ford and Microsoft, often have global political strategy overseen by a senior executive with a substantial budget usually reporting directly to the chief executive. Where very important public policy issues arise, the chief executive often intervenes to represent and advocate the company's interests to the State. For example, both Bill Gates and the chief executive officer of Microsoft lobbied the European Commission intensively in the run up to the decision on whether the company was abusing its Windows monopoly (see case study at the end of the chapter).

Big firms are in the best position to exercise an influence on the State. One reason for this is the possible reluctance of the State to cause hostility in businesses whose decisions on pricing, production, investment, employment, imports and exports can have a major influence on the ability of the State to achieve its goals of economic prosperity, high levels of investment and employment, low inflation, and a healthy balance of payments. Some industries, by their nature, are also well positioned to influence the State. For example, governments may be averse to taking decisions that will provoke a critical reaction in the press or on television. This gives the people who run the media the power to influence politicians especially in the run-up to national elections. The authorities may be reluctant to incur the wrath of firms operating in high technology, high growth industries for fear of losing their contribution to jobs and to economic growth. Such sensitivities may cause governments to consult business before embarking on new policies. As a lobbyist for Enron the large American MNC put it, 'We have many friends in (the UK) government. They like to run things past us some days in advance to get our view' (Karl Milner, lobbyist for Enron and a former aide to Gordon Brown, *Financial Times*, 29 January 2002). He could also have made a similar claim for Enron's network of contacts and influence with the Bush administration in the USA.

The pharmaceutical industry is a good example of an industry that is often treated with care by State institutions such as the UK Medicines and Healthcare Products Regulatory Authority (MHRA). Pharmaceutical firms are major suppliers to the National Health Service (NHS). The NHS depends on the industry for providers of existing and new medicines that are important in the provision and quality of healthcare. The UK Government is very keen to promote innovation by encouraging firms to invest in research and development. The pharmaceutical industry is a major source of R&D and innovation within the UK. It invests about £3.5 billion per year in R&D in the UK which is about a quarter of the total R&D carried out by manufacturing industry. The government is also interested in increasing exports. The industry is a major exporter with export sales of around £11.8 billion per year, with a £3.1 billion trade surplus. Finally, pharmaceutical firms directly employ some 83,000 people in the UK (www.abpi.org.uk).

Methods of Influencing the State

Business employs a variety of methods to influence decision-makers in the institutions of the State to protect and promote their interests. We will now examine some of these methods.

Lobbying

Businesses try to exert influence over the State by lobbying individually or collectively with other firms (see Nownes 2006). To do this they set up offices or employ professional lobbyists in the cities where State institutions make their decisions. Washington in the USA, where the institutions of the federal government are located, is such a location. It is said that the pharmaceutical industry alone has more lobbyists in Washington than the number of elected representatives in congress. It wields considerable power over its regulator, the Food and Drugs Administration, and donates millions of dollars each year to members of congress sitting on important safety committees. So effective has it been that the close links between the industry, its regulator, and the congress has been called the iron triangle.

Where businesses succeed in getting the regulator to serve their interests rather than that of the wider society they are said to have captured the regulator—a situation of so-called regulatory capture. According to some commentators, the pharmaceutical industry has been one of the more effective in this regard with the regulatory agencies appearing to identify their interests very closely with the industries they are supposed to regulate (see the Mini Case below).

Mini Case The Pharmaceutical Industry

This case shows an example of an industry trying to influence its political environment through the development of a very close relationship with its regulators.

The UK pharmaceutical industry, through its trade association, The Association of the British Pharmaceutical Industry, has developed a cosy and harmonious relationship with its watchdog, the Medicines and Healthcare products Regulatory Agency (MHRA). The agency is financially dependent on the industry with pharmaceutical firms providing all of its funding. The industry lobbies the agency at regular meetings and dinners and it has argued that the aims of the agency and the industry are similar, that is, to ensure that medicines are as effective and as safe as possible. They operate in tandem having jointly lobbied the European Commission and other EU governments to influence a review of the laws governing drugs companies.

The MHRA is advised on which drugs are safe and effective by the Committee on the Safety of Medicines (CSM) which is composed of independent medical and scientific experts. Records show that that almost half the members of the CSM had personal financial links to the industry while others declared that they had received research grants from the industry.

Sources: Health Select Committee, Minutes of Evidence, September 2004, HC 1030-i; Pharma Marketletter, 19 October 2004; Abraham 2002

Learning Task

Explain the powerful influence of the pharmaceutical industry on State institutions.
Assess whether this influence is good or bad for NHS patients.

Brussels, as the location for many EU institutions, is another major lobbying focus for business. Hundreds of trade associations have offices there, ranging from the International Federation of Industrial Energy Consumers, to the Liaison Committee of European Bicycle Manufacturers, to the International Confederation of European Beet Growers, to the Union of European Railway Industries. Many individual companies also have representative offices.

Companies such as Microsoft, Intel, Procter & Gamble, General Electric, and General Motors have offices in Brussels to lobby the Commission, the European Parliament, and the Council of Ministers—the three important decision making institutions in the EU capital. Their desire to influence the political and regulatory process in Brussels has swelled the ranks of the professional lobbyists in the city. It is now estimated that around 15,000 to 20,000 lobbyists compete for the attention of the EU institutions (www.europarl.europa.eu; see Greenwood 2003).

When deciding how to lobby, businesses have to take a number of factors into account. They must choose whether to act alone or in alliance with others in the industry, the State institutions to be influenced, the amount of pressure to be exerted on the agencies and the degree of publicity that is advisable.

Big firms are usually powerful enough to lobby on their own account. Boeing is an example of this being the world's largest manufacturer of aircraft. It spends a lot of time and resources on lobbying. For example, it has lobbied the US Government to take action to protect it from its main European competitor, Airbus. It urged the US Government to take action on Airbus which it argues has been unfairly subsidized by European countries. Likewise, Airbus looks for support to the EU authorities contending that Boeing receives large subsidies from the US taxpayer.

Small and medium-sized firms, on the other hand, often find it more effective to lobby along with other firms in the same industry through, for example, trade associations operating either at national or supranational levels. At the national level in Britain, for example, the trade association for the consumer electronics industry is the British Radio and Electronic Equipment Manufacturers' Association (BREMA). BREMA is also associated with the European Association of Consumer Electronics Manufacturers (EACEM) which represents the industry in the EU.

In addition to lobbying on an industry basis, firms can also lobby through national bodies which represent business more generally, like the Confederation of British Industry (CBI) in Britain or the Bundesvereinigung der Deutschen Arbeitgebervebaende (BDA) in Germany when trying to influence the State at the country level. Or they may subscribe to supranational associations, such as the Union of Industrial and Employers Confederation of Europe (UNICE) or the European Round Table (ERT) at the European level.

State Consultation with Business

Frequently, business does not need to spend time and money lobbying, because it expects the State to seek its views on proposed policies, regulations, and laws. In the UK, government departments, as a matter of course, consult bodies representing the construction and vehicle industries on draft regulations. The obligation to consult business is written into the EC Treaty. It requires the Commission to consult firms when preparing proposals particularly in the areas of social policy such as employment rights, working conditions, and equal opportunities, and in public health legislation relating to fields like biotechnology. The intention in the EU is for business to play a substantial role both in drafting and in implementing new measures (see the europa web site for examples of business being consulted by the EU).

Promises or Threats

Occasionally, firms try to influence the State by using promises or threats. Big MNCs are able to offer countries the attractive prospect of large investment projects generating much income and many jobs. It is no surprise that governments fall over themselves in their attempts to attract such MNC investment especially in times of high unemployment.

When Disney announced that it was seeking a location for a theme park in either Spain or France, both governments competed very fiercely for the investment because it was expected to generate around 40,000 jobs and attract large numbers of tourists. Spain's offer to pay 25% of the construction costs was seen off by the French commitment to extend the Paris railway system to the site at a cost of US$350 million, to provide the land at a very favourable price, and to lend Disney a substantial proportion of the construction costs (Packman 1999).

On the other hand, if business does not like the current or proposed policies of a particular country, it can threaten to cut down investment or relocate production, thereby reducing the number of jobs. For example, the chairman of Ford Europe issued such a warning stating that his company would not hesitate to close down major assembly operations in countries wishing to give workers longer holidays or a shorter working week. Another possibility is for the firm to refuse to supply goods and services. This occurred when Pfizer, unhappy with the French Government's attempt to hold down drug prices, threatened to withhold the supply of new drugs from the French market until the government allowed higher prices. It also tried to enlist the support of other drugs giants such as GlaxoSmithKline and Eli Lilly in its campaign (www.bbc.co.uk).

Direct Access to Government Ministers and Civil Servants

Firms, especially large ones, are often able to get representation on government advisory committees where the concerns of business can be aired with the other committee members, civil servants, and government ministers. In the EU, business has representation on the European Economic and Social Committee which is consulted by the various institutions of the union, the Commission, Council, and the Parliament. Over and above these formal structures, big business is also in a good position to get informal access to civil servants and ministers. A refusal would be highly unlikely were Ford or Shell to ask for a meeting with a government minister or high-ranking civil servant.

Employment and Exchange of Personnel

Commentators often refer to the revolving door between industry and the State in terms of personnel. Some companies see major benefits in offering jobs to ex members of the legislative or executive branches of the State such as former government ministers and high ranking civil servants. The reason given is that such people bring invaluable knowledge of how the State operates and therefore could be very useful when companies are trying to win contracts or influence policy. Others suspect that the jobs may be pay-offs for past favours to the company or that the new employees will be able to exploit their links with the State to gain improper advantage for the firm.

Defence companies are some of the largest recruiters of civil servants. Between 1997 and 2004, Lockheed Martin in the USA was one of the largest contributors to the campaign funds of political parties of any federal contractor and had hired 57 senior government officials as executives or lobbyists. Boeing came second on the list of top 20 contractors that had taken on senior officials, followed by Northrop Grumman, Raytheon, and General Dynamics—all defence companies (*Financial Times*, 6 December 2004).

Mini Case Defence Contractors and the Pentagon

The case study illustrates the relationship that can develop between business, in this case Boeing, and a major customer, the US defence department.

In 2004, Senator John McCain, a member of the US Congress investigated the apparently close links between defence contractors and the Pentagon.

He claimed to have found evidence of serious failures, and even corruption, in procurement procedures in one of the biggest procurement deals by the US Air Force, a US$23.5 billion order for 100 aircraft refuelling tankers from Boeing.

The purchasing officer was a civil servant who had been responsible for nearly every important purchase by the air force between 1993 and 2002. She acknowledged steering contracts worth billions of dollars to Boeing over a four-year period, influenced by hopes of a job with the company. The officer had also got Boeing to give jobs to her daughter and son-in-law. She also admitted boosting the price paid to Boeing for the tankers, describing it as a gift to the firm. After leaving her job at the Pentagon, she was employed by Boeing. She ended up being sentenced to nine months in prison. Boeing's former finance director was charged with illegally hiring the civil servant and the chief executive of the company resigned.

Source: *Financial Times*, 7 December 2004

Learning Task

1. Why should defence companies, in particular, be among the largest hirers of ex civil servants?
2. Discuss the pros and cons for companies of employing civil servants previously involved in negotiations with them.

In some countries, the UK for example, there is a well developed arrangement for the temporary exchange of managers and civil servants. Here, managers give up their jobs to work for a time in the civil service while senior civil servants move in the opposite direction. The benefits for business are that managers can learn how the civil service operates, shape policy advice to ministers, make useful network of contacts in the administrative branch, while civil servants who have transferred to private firms can be persuaded of the values and methods of the business community which they take back to the civil service.

Giving Money or Gifts

Companies donate money openly to political parties particularly in the run up to elections. Firms often justify this support by insisting that they are helping those parties who will create a better environment for the effective functioning of the market economy. Historically, in the US the party traditionally favoured by business has been the Republicans, in the UK the Conservatives and in Japan the dominant LDP.

During the 2000 American presidential election the oil and gas industry supported the republicans to the tune of nearly US$13 million. Some commentators suggested that the industry hoped that a republican presidency, under George W. Bush, would allow it freedom to explore for oil in Alaska and to influence how the electricity industry was regulated. The finance, insurance, and real estate sectors contributed almost US$40 million to the coffers of the Republican Party. The motive here, according to some observers, was to ensure continued deregulation of financial markets. The now bankrupt US energy firm Enron donated money to the Republican cause and to both the Labour and the Conservative parties. In the UK, Enron executives were able to meet ministers, civil servants, and MPs and press their case for the overturning of the Government's block on building new gas-fuelled power stations.

Firms may also give money illegally to political parties or State officials. The Christian Democratic Party in Germany was forced to admit that the party had taken US$6.1 million in undeclared contributions between 1989 and 1998 in violation of Germany's strict political funding laws. International arrest warrants were issued for two former officials of the giant French oil company Elf Aquitaine. The suspicion was that the money had been paid to facilitate Elf's purchase of an oil refinery and a chain of petrol stations, assets of the former East Germany that the Kohl Government sold to the French company in 1992. Pei claims that Chinese political officials could be receiving in total up to US$86 billion each year (Chapter Four examines the issue of corruption in more depth).

BAE, the Britain's biggest arms manufacturer, has regularly been accused of paying bribes. A BBC investigation revealed that the company had a 'slush fund' which made £60 million of corrupt payments to Saudi officials, including providing prostitutes, Rolls-Royces, and Californian holidays. Saudi Arabia is a major purchaser of defence equipment. *The Guardian* reported that BAE had been identified as secretly paying more than £1 million through American banks to General Pinochet, the former Chilean dictator in return for defence contracts (the case study at the end of Chapter Eleven looks in more detail at the allegations of corruption against BAE).

● CHAPTER SUMMARY

In this chapter we examined the characteristics of various political systems, the liberal democracies of Europe and North America, Communism in China, the authoritarian regime in Saudi Arabia, and the theocratic system in Iran. We saw how the political organization of countries into unitary or federal systems can have significant implications for business as regards the locus of important political decisions, for instance regarding taxing and spending. We identified and explained the different functions carried out by the State and showed how important they can be, for example, in preventing the collapse of the economic and financial system and in setting the legal and regulatory rules of the game for business. We also considered the arguments for and against the thesis that globalization had led to the demise of the nation-State. Finally, we considered the variety of methods, from lobbying to the donation of money that firms use to influence their political environment.

While relationships between business and the State can be difficult there is a great degree of interdependence between the two. On the one hand, governments depend on business to deliver economic growth, low inflation, a healthy balance of payments, and to create jobs. On the other hand, business depends on the State to create and maintain an environment that provides opportunities to produce and sell goods and services and to make profits.

● REVIEW QUESTIONS

1. What is the State? Why is it important for the pharmaceutical industry? Explain with examples.

2. Compare and contrast the characteristics of liberal democratic and theocratic states. Which of these types of State would be more attractive for a Western MNC?

3. Why do businesses prefer to operate in countries that are politically stable? Discuss how businesses might feel about producing in countries where there is political stability but also a dictatorship.

4. To what extent do you agree that globalization has undermined the power of the nation State? Give evidence to support your arguments.

5. Find an example of a firm or industry that has tried to influence government policy. Identify the methods used and evaluate how effective they have been.

Case Study Microsoft and the State

Over the last 20 years Microsoft has had a difficult time with regulators in both the USA and in the EU. This case study focuses on the company's dealings with the European competition authorities.

In March 2004, after more than five years of investigation, the European Commission fined Microsoft almost €500 million (the biggest ever fine imposed by the EU in a competition case) for abusing its Windows monopoly by trying to shut out competitors. Microsoft broke European Union competition law on two grounds: it failed to provide the information needed by rivals in the market for computer servers in order for them to compete with it; it excluded competitors by making the supply of Windows conditional on the inclusion of its Media Player programme. This 'bundling' together of software meant that consumers were not given the possibility of choosing a different Media Player.

In addition to the fine, the EU ordered Microsoft to disclose the information that it had previously refused to supply to its competitors and to offer a version of Windows which did not include Windows Media Player.

Microsoft contended that the information was its own intellectual property and maintained it was merely meeting consumer demand for more functions. It spoke out against the fine and applied for an immediate court injunction against the Commission's decision, and launched an appeal. One can see the attraction of an appeal to Microsoft. This could take years, a very long time in the fast-changing world of computer software.

The European case was sparked by a 1998 complaint by Sun Microsystems, which alleged that Microsoft was not sharing the source code of its PC operating systems. This made it difficult for Sun to make servers that interacted smoothly with Windows, the operating system installed on some 90 per cent of computers worldwide. At that time, Microsoft was itself trying to enter the server market.

The case was later broadened to include the bundling of application software—in this case, Windows Media Player—with the Windows operating system. RealNetworks, then the dominant maker of PC audio-visual software, claimed that this wiped out demand for its product, which many considered to be better than Microsoft's. RealNetworks' share of this market has since fallen behind that of Windows Media Player. The European case was further broadened to include bundling of any future products. The move reflected fears at the European Commission that the pace of high-tech innovation might leave it fighting yesterday's battles.

Before the Commission made its final decision on the case, Mario Monti had a three-way phone call with Steve Ballmer, the chief executive of Microsoft and Bill Gates. Mr Ballmer flew to Brussels to continue the discussions in person reflecting the company's keen desire to settle.

Many competition regulators welcomed the Commission decision arguing that Microsoft had wriggled out of too many agreements in the past. Ed Black, president of the Computer and Communications Industry Association said, 'The facts of this case . . . have focused on Microsoft's anti-competitive behaviour and illegal tactics, which they have used to steamroller companies, and force unwanted business deals on most, crushing the few who would not bend to their will'.*

The Commission's decision not to agree a settlement was driven by its desire to set a precedent. However, the Commission's requirement that Microsoft open access to its operating code applied only to Windows 2000, not to Windows XP, which is being dealt with in a separate case.

The Court of First Instance, in its 2007 ruling on the appeal, upheld the Commission decision commenting that Microsoft's arguments were, 'scarcely credible' 'purely semantic' or 'wholly unsubstantiated'. Microsoft agreed to comply fully with the Commission decision.

However, in the autumn of 2007, Opera Software, a Norwegian company filed a new complaint with the Commission, in which it accused Microsoft of abusing a dominant position by tying its Internet Explorer browser to the Windows operating system.

Sources: *Financial Times*, 24 March 2004, 18 September, 14 December 2007; *The Economist*, 23 March 2004 and 20 September 2007; European Commission (2007), Commission adopts Decision in the Microsoft case, Competition Policy Newsletter, Number 2, Summer

*cited in *The Guardian*, 25 November 2004

Questions

1. What are the implications of the Commission decision for Microsoft?

2. What opportunities does the decision give to Microsoft's rivals?

3. How effective was Microsoft in its attempts to lobby the Commission?

4. Give reasons for Microsoft's appeal against the Commission decision.

5. Prepare a short defence of Microsoft's bundling of its software products.

6. Now argue the case against Microsoft's bundling policy from the point of view of its competitors.

 ## Online Resource Centre
www.oxfordtextbooks.co.uk/orc/hamilton_webster/

Visit the supporting online resource centre for additional material which will help you with your assignments, essays and research, or you may find these extra resources helpful when revising for exams.

● FURTHER READING

For a treatment of important changes and trends see:

- Mansbach, R. W. and Rafferty, K. L. (2007) *Introduction To Global Politics: A Journey From Yesterday To Tomorrow*. London: Taylor & Francis

For a useful overview of different political regimes see:

- Derbyshire J. D. (1999) *Political systems of the world*. London: Helicon

The Georgetown University website focuses on the politics of the 35 nations comprising North and South America:

- Georgetown University. 'Political Database of the Americas'. Available at http://pdba.georgetown.edu

The Keele guide is more wide-ranging covering the Americas, Europe, Asia, Africa, and Oceania:

- Keele University. 'The Keele Guide to Latin American Government and Politics on the Internet'. Available at www.keele.ac.uk

● REFERENCES

Abraham, J. (2002) 'The pharmaceutical industry as a political player'. *The Lancet*, Vol 360, 9 November

Devereux, M. P. and Sørensen, P. B. (2005) 'The Corporate Income Tax: International Trends and Options for Fundamental Reform'. October. Available at www.sbs.ox.ac.uk

European Commission (2007) Antitrust: Commission ensures compliance with 2004 Decision against Microsoft. 22 October. IP/07/1567

Fukuyama, F. (1993) *The End of History and the Last Man*. London: Penguin

Greenwood, J. (2003) *Interest Representation in the European Union*. London: Palgrave MacMillan

HM Treasury (2008) *Forecasts for the UK economy: a comparison of independent forecasts*. March, No 251

Hirst, P. and Thompson, G. (2005) *Globalization in Question: The International Economy and the Possibilities of Governance*, 3rd edn. London: Polity Press

Joumard, I. and Kongsrud, P. M. (2003) 'Fiscal Relations across Government Levels'. OECD Economic Studies No 36, 2003/1

Nownes, A. J. (2006) *Total Lobbying: What Lobbyists Want (and How They Try to Get It)*. Cambridge: Cambridge University Press

OECD (2005) *Corporate Governance of State-Owned Enterprises: A Survey of OECD Countries*

OECD (2007a) *Fundamental reform of Corporate Income Tax*

OECD (2007b) *Revenue Statistics 1965–2006*

Ohmae, K. (2005) *The Next Global Stage: The Challenges and Opportunities in Our Borderless World*. Wharton School Publishing

Packman, H. M. and Casmir, F. L. (1999) 'Learning from the Euro Disney Experience: A Case Study in International/Intercultural Communication'. *International Communication Gazette*, December, Vol 61

Pei, M. (2007) 'Corruption Threatens China's Future'. Carnegie Endowment, Policy Brief No 55, October

Scholte, J. A. (2005) *Globalization: A Critical Introduction*. London: Palgrave MacMillan

EU Commission (2007) State Aid Scoreboard

Wright, T. (2006) 'Why Hasn't Economic Development Brought Democracy to China?'. Available at www.eastwestcenter.org

Zittrain, J. and Edelman, B. (2003) Empirical Analysis of Internet Filtering in China, IEEE Computing, March

CHAPTER EIGHT

The Legal Environment

LEARNING OUTCOMES

This chapter will enable you to:

- Explain the importance of the legal environment for business

- Compare and contrast the different systems of law and their implications for international business

- Assess the importance of contract, tort, and criminal law for business behaviour

- Appreciate the significance of international law for firms involved in international trade and investment

- Understand the lack of development of the law around the internet and the difficulties this raised for firms involved in e-commerce

Case Study Internet Gaming and the Criminal Law

The case study shows the devastating impact on the gaming industry of a decision by the US authorities to enforce the law.

Internet gambling in the USA, in the run-up to 2006 had been booming, to the benefit of a small group of companies, BetonSports, PartyGaming, SportingBet, Empire Online, and 888. Some internet gaming companies were making up to 80% of their revenue and profits on bets from the USA.

In 2005, PartyGaming floated on the London Stock Exchange (LSE) despite the fact that most of its revenue was generated by online gamblers in the USA. The company's view was that on-line gambling was not illegal in the USA. That position changed when the Unlawful Internet Gambling Enforcement Act was passed in October 2006, and PartyGaming immediately ceased taking bets from US customers.

Other companies followed PartyGaming in launching on the LSE. Investors took up the shares with such gusto that the online gaming firms entered the FTSE top 250 companies. The profits to be made were enormous. When PartyGaming floated, the shares could have been sold three times over. At its peak the stock exchange valuation of the company reached an astonishing £7 billion, greater than Marks and Spencer and British Airways. It was reported that directors of PartyGaming made hundreds of millions of pounds between them selling some of their shareholdings.

High share prices and burgeoning profits allowed some betting company entrepreneurs and the managers who ran them, to lead a very high life, travelling in private jets, owning second homes in Costa Rica, drinking Dom Perignon champagne, and wearing Savile Row suits.

The party came to an abrupt end however, when, in the summer of 2006 and before the law came into force, the Department of Justice started to arrest online gaming executives. En route to his headquarters in Costa Rica, the chief executive of BetonSports was arrested by FBI agents at Dallas airport and taken to prison. He has yet to come to trial and faces a possible sentence of 20 years. The following year the founder of the company was arrested and charged with fraud, racketeering, and tax evasion.

The enforcement of the US law deprived the companies of the lucrative US market and their share values collapsed. In a single day the value of PartyGaming's shares fell by £2.48 billion. It also provoked industry restructuring through, for example, mergers and acquisitions, such as the takeover of Empire Online by PartyGaming.

Sources: *Mail on Sunday*, 18 November 2006; *Financial Times*, 30 December 2006 and 31 March 2007

Source: www.partygaming.com

Introduction

In this chapter we examine the legal environment within which international business operates. We show the importance of the legal framework and how its rules and regulations can impinge on business literally from the cradle to the grave. The law can have a major influence on business behaviour, for instance when it wishes to form a company or to negotiate a contract. It can require firms to compensate those whom they injure and it can forbid business, under the threat of penalty, from undertaking certain types of behaviour such as mergers and acquisitions, colluding with competitors and polluting the environment. We go on to consider the major systems of law prevailing across the globe and we conclude by outlining some important aspects and institutions in international law and their implications for the business community.

Changes in the legal environment can provide business opportunities but can also generate risk. The firm may find itself the subject of a claim by, for instance, a rival, a customer, or a supplier which could result in loss. This could take the form of a financial loss and it could also result in damage to the company reputation. Companies may feel that they are protected by the law only to find that judges put a different interpretation on the law, or it may be that the law is not rigorously enforced (see the opening Case Study to the chapter). Finally, changes in the law could leave the company exposed to legal action for actions previously regarded as permissible.

Knowledge of different legal and regulatory systems operating at national and international levels is invaluable for business in a world where foreign trade, investment and outsourcing, and international e-commerce are growing rapidly.

The Importance of Law for Business

The legal environment forms a vital element of the external environment of business. Firms producing everything from laptop computers, mobile phones, air flights, toys, cosmetics, financial products, drugs, fertilisers, food and drink are all subject to requirements laid down by the law. The legal environment sets the rules of the game within which business operates. It can influence a business from its inception, by laying down certain legal steps which must be undertaken to set the business up, to its death with rules relating to the winding up of the company. When the firm is up and running, the law cannot only tell it what to do but also what not to do. The law is a double-edged sword for business because it offers both threats and opportunities. On the one hand, it can leave firms open to legal action but, on the other, it also gives them the possibility of pursuing others to protect and promote their interests. Business is also subject to regulations. These are not laws as such but rules that take their authority from statutes and are usually issued by governmental agencies at all levels, national, regional, local. In most developed countries, utilities companies in the energy sector and in telecoms and water are regulated. In the UK, for example, OFWAT regulates the water industry and OFGEM the energy sector, whilst in the USA the Federal Aviation Administration (FAA) deals with aviation and the Federal Trade Commission (FTC) is responsible for protecting the consumer and dealing with monopolies.

The legal environment can influence the whole process of production and sale as regards:

- Production techniques: how firms produce goods and services can be influenced by laws and regulations. For example the EU specifies production practices which producers and processors of organic food, such as Green & Black's the chocolate firm owned by Cadbury Schweppes, must follow (Defra available at www.defra.gov.uk).

  Firms using heavily polluting production techniques like the steel industry or coal fired power stations, emitting gases and other chemical pollutants that cause acid rain and ozone depletion, can find their activities being controlled by the law. While their production benefits them, it also creates externalities in the form of pollution of the environment and imposes costs not only on people living next to the plants but on the world as a whole. Examples of Governments using the law to control emissions occurred in the passage of Clean Air Acts in the UK in 1956, the USA in 1963, and Canada in 2006. In the EU, the Clean Air for Europe programme fixes targets for the emission of polluting gases such as sulphur dioxide and nitrous oxide. By limiting emissions, the law attempts to forces the polluters to carry the cost, that is to ensure the costs previously borne by parties outside the firm are internalized.

- The characteristics of the product: the law can determine product characteristics from the materials used to the product specifications—the USA along with many other developed economies has banned most uses of asbestos since it was found to cause lung cancer and other respiratory diseases.

- The nature of the packaging and the contents of the labels: most major economies like the USA, EU, Japan, and China have rules relating to the packaging and labelling of products such as food and hazardous chemicals.

- The content and placement of advertising and sales promotion: tobacco and alcohol are two industries that are heavily regulated in this regard. Tobacco advertising is banned on radio and television in the USA and EU with the EU ban extending to print media and the internet. It is not allowed at all in Canada and New Zealand. Tobacco firms like British American Tobacco and Philip Morris, in order to counter the effects of the advertising bans on sales, have had to find other ways of promoting their products. They have made more use of billboards and direct mailing, got their products placed in films, and sponsored music-oriented events particularly attractive to young people, for example discos, 'raves', and concerts.

- How firms treat their workers: many countries, the USA, the UK, China, Japan, and Russia prescribe a minimum wage. The EU has a longstanding commitment to equal pay for equal work and lays down the maximum number of hours that can be worked. Both Japan and the EU have laws protecting the security of employment of older people.

- The terms and conditions of trade with customers and suppliers: these cover issues such as delivery dates, terms of payment, return policies for defective products, warranties and so on. Most countries have statutes relating to the sale of goods and services. Usually the law requires the terms of sale to be clear, consistent, and reasonable.

- The tools of competition: this relates to how firms compete with rivals and treat customers. Many developed economies have competition laws regulating business behaviour. In the USA and the EU, for example, the law is hostile to powerful firms exploiting their monopoly power by charging customers high prices or tying them in through the imposition of exclusive contracts which force them to buy all their requirements from the same supplier. EU and US law also disapproves of firms squeezing rivals through, for example, artificially low prices. Companies wishing to go in for takeovers can also be affected by the legal environment. In 2001, the EU Commission prohibited the merger of General Electric, the giant US conglomerate and Honeywell, the American producer of electronic systems. Both the USA and EU also prohibit cartels where firms come to an agreement to avoid competition by agreeing a common price or by sharing the market out geographically.

  The law may also protect firms from competition from the grey market. The grey market refers to trade in goods through distribution channels that have not been authorized by the manufacturer. This often occurs when the price of the product varies from country to country. The good is bought in the country where it is cheap and sold at below market price in the country where price is high (wordiQ.com). It is sometimes called parallel importing. The practice is particularly prevalent in cigarettes, pharmaceuticals, cars, music and films, satellite television, and in electronic goods such as cameras and games consoles. The grey market can also arise when a good is in short supply in one area but plentiful in another. When Sony first introduced its PlayStation Portable in Japan, it quickly found the console being imported into Europe. The law requires that grey importers have to get the manufacturer's permission where the good is brought in from outside the EU. Sony pursued this through the British courts, stating that no permission had been given and claiming that its trademark was being infringed (*The Guardian*, 23 June 2005).

- Ownership of assets: legal systems usually confer and protect rights of ownership and possession of company assets, both physical like buildings and machinery and intellectual assets. For example, the law will often protect intellectual property by giving the holder exclusive rights to exploit the asset for a certain period of time. Protection may also be accorded to holders of copyright covering creative and artistic works including books, films, music, paintings, photographs, and software, on trade marks which are signs distinguishing the products or services of firms, and on product designs. Trade secrets may also be protected by the law.

- Financial reporting: many countries lay down rules and regulations regarding the reporting of the financial state of the company and its performance. There are also moves afoot to establish international reporting standards. Around 100 countries require, are moving towards, or allow the use of the International Financial Reporting Standards (IFRS) which establishes a framework for the preparation and presentation of financial statements so that financial information provided by companies is transparent and comparable. This harmonization of reporting standards has become more important for companies as they increasingly look overseas not only for market and investment opportunities but also to raise finance. Harmonized reporting allows firms more easily to evaluate potential distributors and candidates for joint ventures and takeovers. While the EU and many other countries around the world now subscribe to international financial reporting standards the US stands alone with its own generally accepted accounting principles (GAAP) (the International Accounting Standards Board is responsible for establishing the IFRS, see www.iasb.org).

In 2002, after several major accounting scandals including those at Enron and Worldcom, the USA passed the Sarbanes-Oxley Act. This required firms to provide more financial information and to introduce rigorous internal procedures to ensure the accuracy of that information.

The purpose of these legal requirements is usually the protection of life or health, the protection of the environment, the prevention of deceptive practices, or to ensure the quality of products, the preservation of competition, and the promotion of technological advance.

Learning Task

The bank, UBS, analysed the impact of introducing the IFRS on 27 blue chip companies including Vodafone and Telecom Italia. It showed that, under the IFRS, reported profits could vary by an average of 12% with some companies showing increases and others declines. It also found that the IFRS pushed up debt on the balance sheet by an average of 28% (*Financial Times*, 17 October 2005).

1. Advance reasons why firms might be unhappy about their government adopting the IFRS framework.

2. Go to the web site set up by the consultants Deloitte at www.iasplus.com. This shows the countries that have signed up to the IFRS. Look at the position of China and discuss the implications of this for foreign firms looking for takeover opportunities there.

Systems and Sources of Law

Contrary to a widespread misapprehension, laws are not simply the product of decisions made by governments and parliaments. There are four major legal systems in the world which are drawn, in large degree, from different sources. They comprise civil law, common law, customary law, and religious law. Civil law and common law systems are predominant in the world and, for that reason, are of most importance to business.

The particular systems operating in countries or regions are the result of the interaction of many historical forces, socio-cultural, political, economic, and technological. One particularly important influence in many countries is the historical legacy of empire. Thus, countries in Africa who were part of the French empire are likely to have a law based on the French system while former British colonies tend to have systems based on English law. Furthermore, the boundaries between the different systems can break down as the systems evolve over time. Globalization contributes to this blurring of the boundaries because one country's legal system can end up incorporating elements from others. Thus, the system in Japan has been heavily influenced by the German legal code and has also been subject to English and American influences. Similarly, the Chinese system reflects, to a degree, Soviet and Continental legal principles.

Business can find that the various legal systems create very different legal environments within which to operate. Laws, regulations, procedures, and outcomes may vary enormously from one system to another.

Civil Law Systems

Most legal systems in the world have their basis in civil law (see Figure 8.1), the primary source of which is legislation. Civil law is a body of laws and legal concepts which have their basis in the legal codes of the Roman Empire. Civil law systems give precedence to written law, sometimes called codified law. Judges apply and interpret the law which is drawn from legal codes and statutes—statutes are written laws passed by legislative bodies such as national or regional parliaments.

The legal systems in Continental Europe and in Central and South America are largely codified and set out in legislation. In the USA, Louisiana is the sole State having a legal

Figure 8.1 Legal Systems Across the World

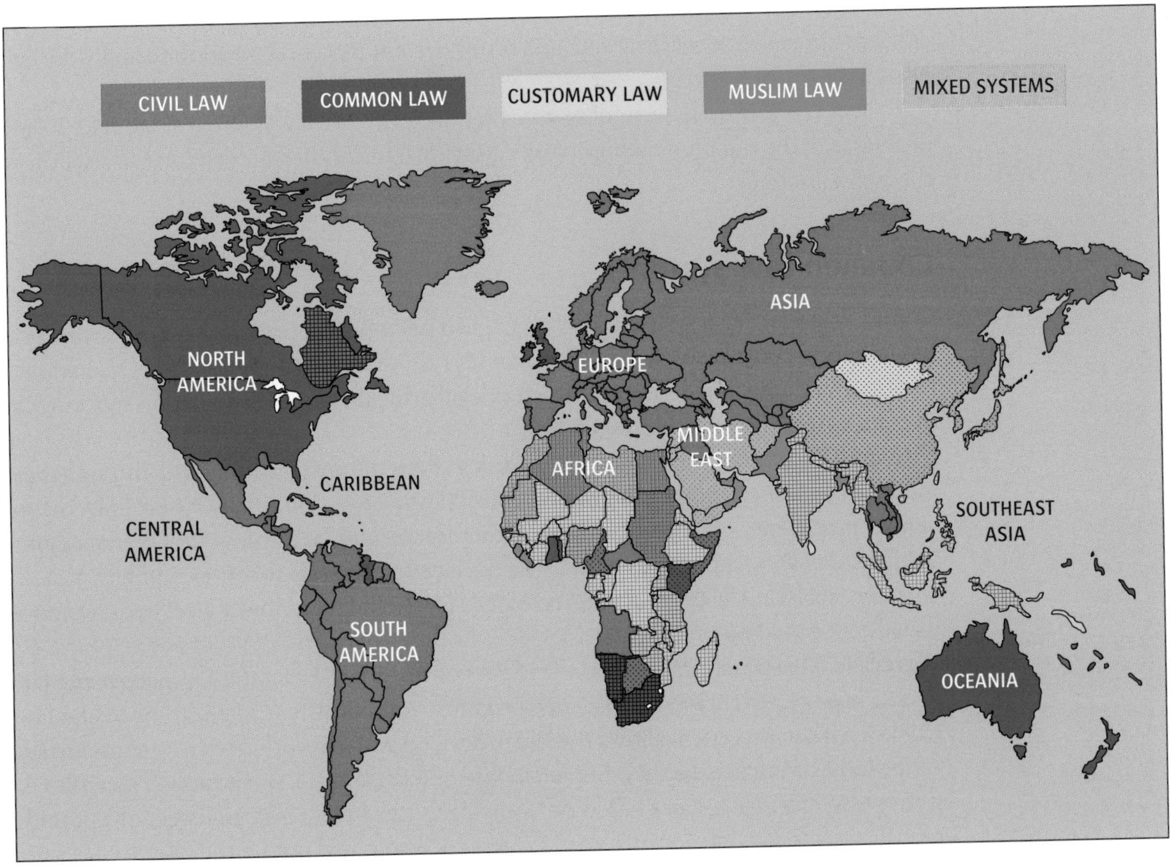

Source: University of Ottawa. Available at www.droitcivil.uottawa.ca

structure based on civil law with Quebec being in a similar position in Canada. Scottish law is heavily influenced by Roman law but has not gone in for the extensive codification so prevalent on the Continent. Other countries, for example in Scandinavia, while not so influenced by Roman law, have systems akin to civil law because of their heavy dependence on the laws written into statutes.

The procedure in civil law systems is inquisitorial where judges collect evidence and question witnesses to discover the truth. Rather than orally presenting their case, each side must provide written statements of it to the judge. A consequence of this emphasis on the written word is that lawyers act as advisors rather than as oral advocates of their client's case to the judge. Judges then decide, on the basis of the evidence, whether the case should go to trial but trials are relatively rare. Should a trial occur, panels of judges or lay assessors review the written evidence gathered by the judge and come to a decision. Juries are used in some criminal trials. In civil systems, court decisions applying the law may influence subsequent decisions but do not become binding.

One advantage to business of civil law systems is that because the law is codified in written form, it is easier to find and to articulate clearly (Duhaime Law at www. duhaime.org). On the other hand, the emphasis on written evidence means that there must be effective document storage and retrieval systems to handle all the paperwork generated by the system if the law is to be properly applied. While this may be the case in Continental Europe, many poorer countries say in Africa or Latin America do not have efficient bureaucratic systems and, as a result, are not in a good position to apply the law effectively.

To avoid confusion it is useful to note that the term civil law is also used to refer to law dealing with the rights and duties of one individual to another, for instance, in relation to the law of contract.

Common Law Systems

Common law is a legal system based on English law which accords greater importance to judgments in court cases than to written codes and statutes. Common law is also known as case law or judge-made law inasmuch as legal principles are determined by judgements in court cases (Mayson *et al.* 2005, p 26).

Courts, by interpreting and applying the law, determine its meaning and, through their judgements, fill in gaps in the legislative code (Mayson *et al.* 2005, p 26). Court judgements can set precedents which are binding on themselves and on lower courts when judging similar cases—in other words it becomes the law for everyone to follow. Binding precedents are usually made by courts at the higher levels. Judges in lower level courts cannot usually issue binding precedents.

Precedent has a very important role in the common law. From the perspective of business it has the advantage of ensuring certainty and consistent application of the law. Unlike civil law, precedent allows the law to develop and to respond to changes in society. At the same time it may be very difficult to find or to state as it is spread across many cases. It may also give rise to laws based on court decisions in extreme, unusual, or unevenly argued cases—to put it another way, a case may be decided not on the relative merits of the evidence but because a lawyer has made an effective presentation of the case in court.

Common law systems are found in countries that have had close ties with Britain such as the USA, Canada, India, and Australia. In some of these countries the common law system may sit alongside codes and statutes but it remains the fundamental basis of the legal system.

Learning Task

Look at the map in Figure 8.2 below indicating the legal systems in place in Europe.

- Which is the dominant legal system in Europe?
- What are the main characteristics of the dominant system?
- What legal issues might be encountered by a Hungarian firm wishing to do business in Scotland (both of which form part of the EU)?

Figure 8.2 Legal Systems Across Europe

Source: University of Ottawa. Available at www.droitcivil.uottawa.ca

Where there is a clash between legislative statutes and common law, statutes take precedence. So statutes generally have the power to change the established common law, but the common law cannot overrule or change statues (www.leeds.ac.uk/law).

Common law, in contrast to civil law systems, is adversarial in nature. Thus, both sides are in competition to persuade judge and jury of the legitimacy of their case. In proceedings, lawyers act as the principal advocate of their client's case and witnesses are called to give oral testimony. Oral argument plays a more important in common law. In court cases the judge plays the role of impartial arbiter.

Customary Law Systems

There is no single agreed definition of customary law. It can be seen as a body of rules, values, and traditions based on knowledge gained from life experiences or on religious or philosophical principles. It establishes standards or procedures to be followed when dealing with social relationships such as marriage, adultery, and divorce but can also play a part in the ownership and use of land and issues around fishing rights. Customary law, like common law, is often not written into statutes and can be fluid and evolutionary. While hardly any countries operate under a legal system which are wholly customary there are a large number of countries where it plays an important role. This is true in a number of African countries in some of which it operates in combination with either civil or common law systems depending on whether the area was colonized by France or Britain. It also plays a part in the legal systems of China and India as well as islands in the South Pacific (see Care 2000).

Muslim Law Systems

Muslim law systems are codes of law mainly based on Sharia law which is derived from the religious principles contained in the Koran and in the teachings and example of Mohammed. In some Muslim countries the law is limited to regulating personal behaviour while, in others, its impact is much more wide-ranging. Examples of the latter include countries such as Iran, Saudi Arabia, Sudan, and Libya, and parts of Nigeria. This regulates all aspects of life, both public and private. The law forbids consumption of alcohol and pork as well as gambling, usury that is lending money and charging the borrower interest, especially at an exorbitant or illegally high rate, fraud, slander, and the making of images (Britannica Concise Encyclopaedia).

Mini Case Sharia Law and the Financial Sector

This case shows how financial institutions have responded to clients who demand financial products that conform with Sharia law. The high price of oil has meant that investors in Muslim countries in the Middle East have billions of dollars available for investment and thus constitute a potentially lucrative market for the financial sector.

In 2006, Societe Generale, the French bank set up the first Sharia-compliant hedge funds in London. Hedge funds often sell shares short. Selling short means that you agree to sell a security that you do not own at, let us say, its current price, in anticipation of a fall in its price. Once the price falls you buy the share and then transfer it to your customer at a profit. Selling short is not compliant with Sharia law. Consequently the bank put in place systems to replicate the effects of selling shares

short without breaking Islamic law. The bank did this by offering investors sukuks, Sharia-compliant bonds.

Another example concerned the buy-out of the company that makes James Bond's favourite car, the Aston Martin. The finance associated with this had to be Sharia-compliant because the key financiers behind the deal were two Kuwaiti groups that only invested in accordance with Islamic principles. West LB, the German bank, was given the task of arranging £225 million of finance in a way that accorded with the Koran's opposition to interest and speculation. It was expected that the finance would be raised by the issue of sukuks.

Sources: *Financial Times*, 22 December 2006 and 17 March 2007

Important Aspects of the Law for Business

There is a wide range of laws applicable to business such as the law of contract, tort, criminal law, and international law. Contract law and the law of tort deal with disputes between business and the firms and individuals it deals with. Both give rise to actions by the concerned/aggrieved parties through the civil courts. Criminal liability on the other hand, involves a business committing a crime against the State. Cases are initiated by State bodies such as the Crown Prosecution Service in the UK or the Department of Justice in the USA and are heard in the criminal courts.

Contract Law

When firms do business they are constantly entering into contracts which can either be written or oral. Essentially contracts are struck when a firm buys or sells goods or services from a supplier or a customer, or takes on employees. The contract is a legally binding agreement between the parties concerned and may be formal, informal, written, or oral. The contract is likely to cover such elements as price, payment terms, contract duration, the consequences of breaching the contract, the process for resolving disputes between the parties and what will happen if there are unforeseen events such as wars or revolutions (see John Hagedoorn for a discussion of contract issues technology partnerships between firms). The contract obliges those involved to fulfil their side of the agreement. If they fail to do so then they are in breach of contract and may be pursued by the aggrieved party through the courts.

Mini Case Contract Law—The Diva and the Rock Star

The opera singer Dame Kiri Te Kanawa was taken to court in Australia for breach of contract because she had reneged on an agreement to perform with Australian rock singer, John Farnham. The legal action was taken by Leading Edge, the promoters, who claimed that they had been forced to cancel a series of lucrative concerts in 2005 when Te Kanawa broke her contract by withdrawing from the tour. Consequently they were suing the singer for US$1.6 million. The promoters argued that the opera singer had pulled out of the concerts after seeing Farnham's fans throw underwear at him on stage. Dame Kiri said she was embarrassed when she saw a DVD of a Farnham concert showing him collecting knickers as 'some sort of trophy'. She cancelled the tour despite assurances that no underwear would be thrown on stage when the pair appeared together.

The judge dismissed the case, finding that there was no binding contract at the time that Dame Kiri scrapped the plans for the tour. However her company, Mittane, was ordered to pay over US$100,000 costs to Leading Edge because it had not been truthful about her reasons for withdrawing from the tour.

Source: www.contactmusic.com; *The Express*, 2 February 2007; *The Guardian*, 22 March 2007; www.BostonHerald.com

Tort Law

Tort is an area of the law concerned with injuries to people or damage to their assets. The law obliges firms to ensure that their activities do not cause damage, intentional or accidental, to others and is in addition to any contractual arrangement that may exist. Business activities, therefore, that involve, for example, negligence leading to injury to a customer, selling defective goods or counterfeiting another company's product is a tort (The Stationery Office, *Business Law* available at www.bcentral.co.uk).

A very famous tort case was the McDonald's coffee case in the USA. A customer called Liebeck won millions of dollars of damages against McDonald's when she claimed that the company's negligence had caused her to get burned with coffee that was far too hot. A

Learning Task

A case of tort occurred in the UK when a drugs trial conducted in 2006 by a US company, Parexel, went wrong. Six men ended up fighting for their lives after suffering severe reactions on taking the drug. Their bodies swelled up to enormous proportions and one of the six ended up losing fingers and toes. TeGenero, the German company that had developed the drug, went out of business as a result of the botched drugs trial. Four of the victims started legal action against Parexel after it had failed to discuss the possibility of compensation.

1. What would you expect to be the basis of the victims' case under the law of the tort?

2. What was the effect of the case on the companies involved? (Check out the result of the legal action against Parexel.)

more recent tort case was brought by Alcatel-Lucent, a French-based multinational communications company employing around 80,000 people and operating in 130 countries. Alcatel took Microsoft to court claiming an infringement of two of its MP3 technology patents which allowed for digital encoding and compression of music which could then be sent over the internet. The US court found in favour of Alcatel and ordered the software giant to pay US$1.5 billion in damages (*Financial Times*, 23 February 2007).

Criminal Law

Criminal law applies across many business activities and has become increasingly important in areas such as financial reporting, the proper description and pricing of goods and services, and the safety of goods and services, particularly food. In the USA, after several business scandals involving the likes of Enron and WorldCom, both of whom were involved in fraudulent accounting (WorldCom artificially inflated its profits by billions of dollars), Congress introduced much criminal legislation. This tightened the rules in areas such as financial reporting, tax crimes, foreign currency violations, health and safety in the workplace, and crimes against the environment.

Siemens, the giant German multinational, came under the spotlight of the criminal law when State prosecutors in Germany carried out a criminal investigation. The case concerned an alleged €420 million **bribery** scandal at the telecommunications division of the company. Siemens conceded that something had gone awry and admitted that there were important weaknesses in its financial controls.

The case had an undesirable knock-on effect for Siemens' management because it raised questions among banks, financial analysts, and Siemens' big shareholders on whether Siemens was too big or too complicated to be managed properly and whether it would be better broken up into smaller units.

The bribery allegations reinforced their concerns because it followed Siemens' failures with its mobile phone, semiconductor and telecoms equipment, and personal computer operations. The bribery case also raised concerns in other German companies including MAN, Continental, and Linde about tightening their anti-corruption systems (*Financial Times*, 14 and 22 December 2006, 15 March 2007).

International Law

Usually when operating in foreign countries, business has to follow the law of the land. However, international law is playing an increasingly important role in the world of international business. As business has become more globalized, so has the law, developing in ways aimed at facilitating international trade and investment. Another development is that international contracts are increasingly being written in English (Jennings 2006, p 240).

International law can reduce the uncertainty, costs, and the disputes associated with international commerce when there are doubts about which country's laws apply. In such situations firms, unsure of their rights, could be less willing to go in for foreign trade and investment. There are a variety of organizations, conventions, codes, and treaties which play a role in international commerce. We now look at some of the most important.

Codes and Conventions

Some national laws have ended up being used by firms involved in international business. One example is the Uniform Commercial Code in the USA. It sets down standard rules governing the sale of goods, is in force in many US States, and has been adopted by other countries (www.ilpf.org).

Another element of international contract law is the United Nations Convention on Contracts for the International Sale of Goods (CISG) of 1980. It is very similar in content to the Uniform Commercial Code. It aims to make international trade as convenient and economical as trading across state borders in the USA. By 2006, 70 States, accounting for around two thirds of world trade had signed up to this convention. The CISG establishes a set of rules governing sales of goods between professional sellers and buyers who have their places of business in different countries. By adopting it, a country undertakes to treat the Convention's rules as part of its law. The Convention aims to reduce the uncertainty and the disagreements that arise when the sales law of one country differs from that of another (http://law.pace.edu).

Given that so many countries have signed up to it, the CISG might seem like a significant advance in the law relating to international trade. However, the reality is that many firms deliberately do not use the convention. In the EU, this is true of producers of oils, seeds, fats, and grain and of most large Dutch companies. This unwillingness to use the agreement appears due to some of the terms used in the convention being open to differing interpretations. Also it may be that firms are ignorant of various elements of the CISG and are not prepared to invest time and money to find out. Another deterrent factor is that the convention only covers some aspects of the relationship between the buyer and seller so that in other areas national laws apply. Finally, several countries such as the UK, Ireland, and Portugal are not party to the convention (Smits 2005).

An organization trying to facilitate the legal processes around international commerce is the International Institute for the Unification of Private Law (Unidroit) which lays down principles for international commercial contracts. It is an independent, intergovernmental organization whose purpose is to help modernize, harmonize, and coordinate commercial law between states. In 1964, a convention was signed relating to the Law on the International Sale of Goods. However, the agreement did not apply to the sale of all products. For example, it did not cover sales of financial products such as stocks and shares, or sales of electricity. In 2002, a law relating to franchises was agreed (see www.unidroit.org).

The World Bank carries out research on the problems associated with doing business in different countries. It researches legal issues around the setting up of a business and with the enforcement of contracts in different countries. It found that setting up a business in Australia took 2 days but 694 in Suriname. It also found very large variations between countries in terms of the efficiency of the judicial system in resolving a commercial dispute.

The charts below show two of the main indicators for enforcing contracts. They are:

- time in calendar days to resolve a dispute
- cost in court fees and attorney fees, where the use of attorneys is mandatory or common, expressed as a percentage of the value of the claim.

Figure 8.3 Number of Days to Resolve Dispute

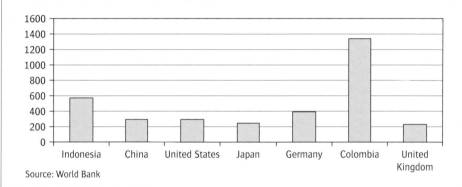

Source: World Bank

Figure 8.4 Cost as % of Claim

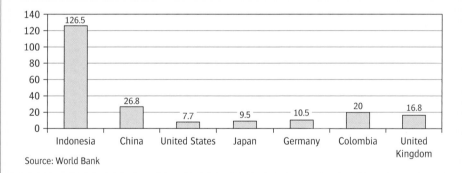

Source: World Bank

Examine the charts and answer the questions below.

1. In which country does it take most/least time to enforce a contract through the local courts?
2. Which countries are most/least expensive?

Now consult the table on enforcement of contracts on the World Bank web site at www.doingbusiness.org and find out:

- How much time it takes in Italy?
- How expensive it is in Mozambique?

What can be said about the difficulties of doing business in these countries?

International Arbitration

Sometimes disputes arise between firms based in one country and firms or governments of other countries. For example, there can be disagreement between the firms as to which national law should apply. That such disputes arise is hardly surprising given the rapid growth of international trade and investment. In such situations, international arbitration has become increasingly popular for businesses. There are a number of international agencies who will arbitrate between the warring parties. For example, firms can use commercial arbitration under the New York Convention set up in 1958 under the aegis of the United Nations (see United Nations Commission on International Trade Law at www.uncitral.org).

Another international body helping to resolve disputes between governments and foreign business around investment, is the International Centre for the Settlement of Investment Disputes (ICSID) which is based at the World Bank in Washington. It deals with cases such as that involving three Italian mining companies who filed a complaint against South Africa, saying that the Pretoria government's positive racial discrimination laws violated investment treaties with other countries. The companies complained that their granite mining operations had been expropriated because they were not conforming to South Africa's black economic empowerment policy and that this violated treaties that South Africa had signed with Italy and Luxembourg (*Financial Times*, 9 March 2007; for other cases and information about ICSID go to the web site at www.worldbank.org/icsid).

Mini Case Dispute at the World Trade Organization

This case traces the outcome of a dispute lodged by the tiny Caribbean country, Antigua and Barbuda against the USA at the WTO.

The dispute arose because, in 2006, the USA enforced the law which declared it illegal for American banks and credit card companies to process payments to online gambling businesses outside its borders (see Case Study at start of Chapter). However, banks could continue to process payments for gaming firms operating within the USA. Antigua argued that this was discriminatory, broke WTO rules, and was effectively stifling Antigua's thriving gaming industry.

The Organization ruled that the USA had broken WTO rules by discriminating against offshore gambling firms through not applying the same rules to American operators. It allowed Antigua to impose an annual US$21 million of trade sanctions against America. In response to the ruling, Washington subsequently announced its intention to remove internet gambling from its WTO treaty obligations.

The European online gambling sector which had also been shut out of the USA, hoped to use the Antiguan case as leverage to put pressure on the USA to re-open its market. It urged the EU to take the case to the WTO. However, the USA avoided further disputes on the issue being lodged with the WTO by conceding trade concessions in postal services and warehousing to the EU. This was good news for European firms involved in providing mail services and warehousing but bad news for gaming firms that still could not access their most lucrative market. Deals were also struck with other aggrieved parties, Canada, and Japan, as compensation for the USA breaching WTO rules.

The case shows the difficulties confronted by business in getting international law applied to powerful countries such as the USA when they break the rules.

Source: *Financial Times*, 22 December 2007

The World Trade Organization, where its rules have been broken, also arbitrates in disputes on matters of foreign trade, investment, and intellectual property rights. Firms can not take a complaint direct to the WTO for the disputes procedures can only be activated at the request of a member government. This is illustrated by the dispute between the USA and the EU over subsidies being given to Boeing and Airbus. Both sides, at the behest of the two companies, complained that the billions of dollars of subsidies were in breach of the WTO rules (for information on disputes at the WTO see www.wto.org).

When companies agree to insert an international arbitration clause into a contract it means that disputes between them are dealt with by an independent arbitrator rather than a court. This has a number of advantages over litigation through national courts. The first advantage is neutrality because arbitrators have to meet strict independence tests and can be drawn from countries other than those of the firms concerned. The second is confidentiality. Proceedings, unlike court cases, are normally private so that there is no public washing of dirty linen. Third, the procedures are flexible and lastly, awards made, for instance under the New York Convention can be widely enforced in almost all trading countries, unlike national court decisions. The disadvantages are that it can be more costly than court litigation, there is normally no right of appeal, it does not work so well when there are more than two companies involved and, finally, there is no possibility of a quick decision even when there is no justifiable defence.

International Law and IPRs

Globalization has put on an onus on firms to find ways of protecting intellectual property rights abroad. This has become particularly important in certain sectors such as film, music, and software where the growth of the internet and digitization makes copying much easier. Such protection is relatively well developed in the rich economies of North America and Europe but much less so in poorer countries such as China and India—a further deterrent in pursuing cases in China is the corruption of the judiciary, and in India, the time it takes for the wheels of justice to turn. It is therefore hardly surprising that companies prefer to pursue infringements of their IPRs in countries with well developed systems of protection where cases are dealt with in a timely fashion and where the judiciary are not tainted by corruption. Thus, 3M, the US technology multinational chose to file an IPR lawsuit with a federal court in Minnesota and the US International Trade Commission against other producers of laptops including Sony, Matsushita, and Hitachi of Japan and Lenovo of China. 3M complained that the laptop makers had infringed the technology it used in its lithium-ion batteries (Techworld available at www.techworld.com).

As pointed out in the section on protecting technology in Chapter Six, the costs of taking out protection can vary significantly from one country to another as can the time taken to get protection the level of protection given and the ease with which firms can pursue violators of their property rights.

Intellectual property laws can vary from country to country—even in the EU there is still no single system of granting patents. Usually an application in one country for protection of a firm's IPRs only results in the granting of protection in that country. In the

Learning Task

There have been a variety of alternative explanations put forward to explain the differences in degrees and level of protection accorded to IPRs by countries. One explanation suggests that differences have their roots in legal traditions. It is argued that two of the major traditions, the British Common law and the French Civil law, differ in terms of the priority they attach to protecting the rights of private investors as against those of the State. Historically British Common law gave priority to the protection of private property owners against the crown while the French Civil law was more concerned to support and consolidate the power of the State. This led French Civil law to focus on the rights of the State and less on the rights of the individual investors when compared to British Common law. These different tradition spread as France and Britain expanded their empires. The theory predicts that the legal tradition will be a major determinant of property rights protection (Ayyagari 2006).

Some results of Ayyagari's research are shown in Table 8.1 opposite. Examine it and the map (Figure 8.1) and consider to what extent the predictions of the theory are accurate.

Scores go from 1 to 5 with higher numbers indicating better government enforcement of the law protecting IPRs.

Table 8.1 Protection of IPRs

Country	Score
Australia	5
Zimbabwe	2
Mauritius	4
France	4
UK	5

Source: Ayyagari, Demirguc-Kunt and Maksimovic 2006

past, firms seeking protection in other countries had to make separate applications in each which could be very costly in terms of money and time.

However, the situation is changing. Two systems now exist that reduce the need for separate national applications. The Patent Cooperation Treaty allows firms to file a single application indicating in which countries it is seeking protection. The European Patent Convention allows for an application to be filed at the European Patents Office in Munich. The Office can grant separate national patents for specified countries. There have also been some moves towards harmonization of laws as a result of international treaties including the Agreement on Trade-Related Aspects of Intellectual Property Rights (TRIPS) agreed through the WTO. It aims to establish minimum levels of protection that each government has to give to the intellectual property of other WTO members. Member governments have to ensure that their intellectual property rights systems do not discriminate against foreigners, that they can be enforced in law, and that the penalties for infringement are tough enough to deter further violations. The procedures must not be unnecessarily complicated, costly, or time-consuming (www.wto.org).

European Union

The European Union (EU) comprises 27 members all of whom are bound by the EU laws. The primary source of EU law is the Treaties such as the Treaty of Rome as modified by the Single European Act, the Treaties of Maastricht, Amsterdam, and Nice. The secondary source of EU law consists of directives which are binding on the member states but whose implementation is their responsibility, regulations which are binding and implemented consistently across the EU and finally, decisions which are made by European institutions like the Commission, the Council of Ministers and the European Parliament which deal with specific issues, countries, institutions, or individuals. European law develops through a combination of case law setting precedents and statutory law. In any clash with national law, EU law takes precedence.

Mini Case An EU Decision—Genetically Modified Foods

From the 1990s there have been fears in the EU about the effects of genetically modified (GM) foods on human and animal health and on the environment. GM foods are grown from seeds whose genes have been modified to increase the yield or quality of the crops of products such as wheat, rice, cotton, and potatoes. They were being promoted by big multinationals such as Monsanto from the USA and the German company Bayer who had been involved in developing the GM seeds.

In 2003 the EU Parliament and Council made a decision that GM food could only be sold in the EU subject to certain conditions. It had to be proved that: it did not adversely affect human or animal health or the environment; the consumer was not being misled about the fact that the food had been genetically modified; its nutritional value would not be less for humans or animals than the foods it was replacing.

The EU decision was bad news for GM companies cutting them off from a very lucrative market. The USA, Canada, and Brazil complained to the World Trade Organization that the EU was breaking WTO rules. The WTO found in favour of the complainants.

Source: www.istockphoto.com

Sources: See Council Directive 90/220/EEC of 23 April 1990 on the deliberate release into the environment of genetically modified organisms and Regulation (EC) No 1829/2003 of the European Parliament and of the Council of 22 September 2003 available at http://eur-lex.europa.eu; www.wto.org

Single Market Programme

An essential element of the EU project is the Single Market programme. The programme, by removing internal barriers such as frontier checks, different technical standards for goods and services, and obliging members to recognize academic or vocational quali-fications gained in another member state, tries to ensure that goods, services, capital, and people can move freely across borders. The Single Market requires that laws of the various member states do not favour domestic firms over those of other members in areas such as trade, investment, the establishment of businesses on their territory, or the movement of workers.

The EU has seen that different national contract laws can constitute a barrier to the movement of goods and services so it has passed several directives, at least twelve accord-ing to Smits, to deal with this. However, they do not replace national laws by laying down a general law of contract but only apply to certain types of contract and to specific areas of contract law such as that relating to the sale of tour packages and timeshares, on com-bating late payment in commercial transactions or in the distance marketing of financial services.

For example, the Consumer Sales Directive does not attempt to harmonize different national laws nor does it require firms to offer the same product guarantee throughout the EU. It does however require firms to provide specific information on product guarantees. The information has to be written in plain and intelligible language regarding the con-sumer's legal rights under the national legislation and has to make clear that these rights are unaffected by the product guarantee. The guarantee also needs to indicate the dura-tion and territorial scope of the guarantee and how to make a claim (Schulte-Nölke). The EU is trying to enable consumers to pursue EU-wide claims against firms providing faulty goods or services. As the Commissioner responsible for consumer affairs put it, 'I want a citizen in Birmingham to feel as comfortable shopping for a digital camera from a website in Berlin or Budapest as they would in their high street' (*Financial Times*, 14 March 2007). The Commission wants to encourage consumers to buy more abroad.

Smits points out that EU directives in the field of contract law allow member states to create more stringent rules in the area covered by the directive. In particular in the area of consumer protection, some member states tend to enact rules that are tougher than the directives prescribe. This means that business still has to deal with differences in national legislation among the member states which may make it less convenient and more costly to do business abroad.

The result is that there remain significant differences in contract law within the EU with each country in the EU having its own contract law. These can be classified in three main groups. First, England, Ireland, and Cyprus have common law systems which emphasize judge-made law. The second type is the civil law system which holds sway in France, Belgium, Luxemburg, Spain, Portugal, Italy, Malta, Germany, Austria, Greece, and the Netherlands. The civil law is in place in nearly all of the former Communist countries of Eastern Europe that entered the EU in 2004 such as Poland, the Czech Republic, Slovakia, Hungary, Estonia, Lithuania, Latvia, and Slovenia (see Smits who sees the new entrants as somewhat distinct from the other members operating civil law systems). Finally, the Scandinavian countries of Denmark, Sweden, and Finland form the third group which have a number of common statutes relating to contract.

Competition Law

Business operating in the EU is also subject to the competition laws which are important in helping to maintain a barrier-free single market. These laws which are policed by the Commission cover four main areas.

Firstly, cartels that prevent or distort competition in the EU are strictly forbidden by Article 81 of the Treaty. Cartels are often popular with firms because it allows them to avoid competition by agreeing to set the same price for their products or by sharing the market out between them (see Table 8.2). Firms are tempted to set up price-fixing cartels by the significant hike they can make in their prices. It has been calculated that international cartels overcharge their customers by an extra 30–33% on average (*Financial Times*, 9 May 2006). In 2006, seven chemical companies including Solvay of Belgium, Total of France, Finland's Kemira, the Dutch group Akzo Nobel, FMC of Spain, and Italy's Snia, were fined €388 million for price-fixing and market sharing (the Commission has the power to fine companies up to a maximum of 10% of their annual turnover). The industry had been the subject of several cartel investigations and some of the companies were repeat offenders (*Financial Times*, 4 May 2006).

Second, Article 82 prohibits firms with a strong market position from abusing their dominant position by, for instance exploiting customers through high prices or squeezing their rivals through artificially low prices. Following a complaint from a rival, United Parcel Services, the Commission found that Deutsche Post, the German postal company, had illegally used profits from its letter handling service in which it had a monopoly to cross-subsidize its business parcel service. As a result the parcel division could charge artificially low prices. It was fined €24 million for abusing its dominant position (*Financial Times*, 21 March 2001).

Table 8.2 Ten Highest Cartel Fines by Company

Year	Company	Product	Fine €
++2007++	ThyssenKrupp	elevators and escalators	479.669.850
2001	F. Hoffmann-La Roche AG	vitamins	462.000.000
2007	Siemens AG	gas insulated switchgear	396.562.500
2006	Eni SpA	synthetic rubber	272.250.000
2002	Lafarge SA	plasterboard	249.600.000
2001	BASF AG	vitamins	236.845.000
2006	Arkema SA	methacrylates	219.131.250
2001	Arjo Wiggins Appleton Plc	carbonless paper	184.270.000
2006	Solvay SA/NV	hydrogen peroxide	167.062.000
2006	Shell	synthetic rubber	160.875.000

Source: http://ec.europa.eu

The third area of the law covers mergers. Under the EC Merger Regulation, the Commission has the power to regulate big mergers. Firms have to notify the Commission of proposed mergers. The Commission can wave the merger through as it did with the takeover of Scottish Power by the Spanish firm Iberdrola or it can approve the merger subject to certain conditions. When Nestlé wanted to take over Perrier it had to agree to sell off some of its brands before the Commission would give its approval. Similar conditions were imposed in both pharmaceutical mergers between Sanofi and Synthélabo and Pfizer and Pharmacia. Finally, permission can be refused where the acquisition would reduce competition in the market place. Thus, the merger between Tetra Laval the dominant producer of packaging for carton drinks, and Sidel, a market leader in the production of machines used for making PET plastic bottles was turned down (see http://ec.europa.eu and www.freshfields.com).

Finally, Article 87 of the Treaty frowns on assistance given by governments to firms that distort or threaten competition and impedes the smooth functioning of the single market programme. It wants to avoid governments giving aid to domestic firms to the detriment of their foreign rivals. The German region of Saxony decided to give Volkswagen a grant of around 800 million German marks for investing there. Rivals like Ford complained that this was unfair and the Commission, seeing the aid as violating competition law, responded by blocking the full aid package reducing the figure by some 240 million marks (Thielemann 1998). In 2005, Olympic, the struggling Greek airline, was forced to repay up to €540 million euros in illegal State aid to the Greek Government. The Commission ruled that the payouts gave the airline an advantage not available to competitors (www.bbc.co.uk).

The Internet

There has been a massive growth of e-commerce. However, no single code of law applies to the internet alone. And Hedley sees the laws that apply as 'a bewildering mix of the specific, the general and the metaphorical' (2006 p 1). Some legal commentators see Internet law as incomprehensible (see the section on crime in Chapter Twelve for more discussion of cybercrime).

Legislation, either national or international, makes very few specific references to the Internet but many areas of law can be applied to it, for example legislation on communications in the areas of trade, defamation, and pornography. Contract law is also problematic since the extent to which it applies to the Internet is a matter of debate. For example, traditionally contracts require a signature to be legally valid but there is, as yet, no agreed definition on what constitutes a legally valid electronic signature. And while it may be widely accepted that certain activities on the Net breach criminal law, there can be great obstacles to enforcing it. For instance, the victim of someone hacking into their computer systems may be based in one country, say the USA and the perpetrator thousands of miles away in another, China.

Moreover, there is no obvious means for any one government to control the Net. Individual States find it difficult to control the activities of Internet users when the activity is taking place outside their territory and Hedley questions their ability even when the activity occurs within their national frontiers. He goes on to argue that effective legal control can only be exercised at the international level. To that end, an International Convention on Cybercrime came into effect in 2004. By 2006, 39 European countries had signed up to it and 15 had put it into effect. Other signatories included the USA where it came into force in 2006, Canada, Japan, and South Africa (Council of Europe). The Convention required countries to include a range of internet-related activities in their domestic laws, for example relating to computer hacking, child pornography, computer-related fraud, and infringements of copyright (Council of Europe).

Up to now, Internet Service Providers (ISPs) like AOL, MSN, and Tiscali have borne the main burden of regulation and control. They have been obliged by national police and intelligence services to spy on customers and to provide data such as telephone conversations, e-mail records, and web pages viewed to the authorities.

● CHAPTER SUMMARY

As we have seen the law constitutes a very important element of the environment within which firms must operate. Every aspect of a business operation can be affected by the law from its inception to its demise. The law can have a major influence on what firms produce, the production processes used, the prices they charge, where they sell, and how they go about advertising and promoting their goods and services. The strategies and policies that firms pursue to boost revenues, cut costs, and increase profits are shaped by the legal environments within which they operate. However, the law should not be seen solely as a constraint on business activities. It acts as a protection to firms and offers opportunities as we saw with the issue of Sharia-compliant sukuk bonds.

Companies wishing to get involved in international trade and investment find very different legal environments across the world. The principles on which the systems are based, and the procedures under which they operate, can vary widely depending on the prevailing legal system. Business can find that what is acceptable in common or civil law systems may not be permissible in countries where the system of Sharia law prevails. Even where countries have a similar legal tradition, firms may encounter very different experiences in each. For example, Germany, Italy, and Colombia all have civil law systems but the time taken to enforce a contract through the local courts varies enormously.

Some of the problems of dealing with different national legal frameworks is being eased by the development of international laws and arbitration procedures under the auspices of institutions such as the WTO and the EU.

The law relating to the Internet is seriously underdeveloped at both national and international level. There is no code of generally accepted internationally agreed laws to which business can have recourse and the mixture of laws which do seem to apply are complex. As a result, firms involved in e-commerce face much risk and uncertainty when wishing to have recourse to the law or when they themselves are being pursued through the courts.

Business operating internationally whether through trade or investment has to be aware of the national and international systems of law. It needs to monitor how the law is changing and must be prepared to deal effectively with the constraints and opportunities generated by the legal environment.

● REVIEW QUESTIONS

1. Why is the legal environment important for business?

2. Explain why knowledge of different legal systems would be useful for firms involved in international trade and investment.

3. Discuss the reasons for the increasing business interest in supplying Sharia-compliant products. What are the issues that need to be addressed by firms wishing to provide such products?

4. Explain why firms involved in international trade might use the Uniform Commercial Code.

5. In 2005, an EU regulation (Regulation (EC) No 261/2004) came into force requiring airlines to compensate passengers for flight delays and cancellations by providing accommodation, refreshments, means of communication, or financial reimbursement and to inform passengers of their rights to these.

    What are the implications of the regulation for airlines?

    Go to Europa, the official EU web site, to find out how the industry has responded to the regulation. See the Report at http://ec.europa.eu

6. Imagine that you are working in the market research department of a firm based in the UK. The firm wishes to set up an operation in Argentina. Your boss asks you to find out:

    - which system of law prevails there;

    - which other countries have been the main influence on the Argentinian legal system;

    - the processes the firm would confront had it to go to court.

7. In 2007, Tate & Lyle, the UK based sugar refiner and corn miller accused 3 Chinese manufacturers and 18 USA and Chinese distributors of violating patents on Splenda its artificial sweetener. Its USA subsidiary filed the complaint with the US International Trade Commission.

    - Why would the company choose to pursue the case in the USA?

    - Find out the result of the case and the reasoning behind the Commission decision.

8. What specific legal issues would a Western firm encounter in wishing to set up a joint venture in China? The following web site will help you answer this question: www.lawinfochina.com

9. In 2005, the European Commission started an investigation into the pricing of Apple Computer's music downloading service, iTunes. The Commission was trying to discover whether a price difference of 20% for downloading music between the UK and other member states was a breach of Article 82.

    What was the result of the investigation? Do you think that Apple was happy with the decision?

Case Study Tobacco and the Law

The first 50 years of the 20th century were a golden era for tobacco firms. By 1950, Americans were smoking 350 billion cigarettes a year. Since the early 1950s, when medical studies showed a link between smoking and lung cancer, the tobacco industry has been under attack. By 1953 the six leading US companies had agreed that a collective response was required. They embarked on a lavish public-relations campaign denying any causal link between smoking and cancer. This worked ➔

Source: www.istockphoto.com

→ well until 1964, when a devastating report from the US surgeon-general in effect ended medical uncertainty about the harmfulness of smoking.

In the late 1990s it was estimated that tobacco was killing more people in the USA than the combined total of those who died from AIDS, car accidents, alcohol, murder, suicide, illegal drugs, and fire. The deaths of more than 400,000 Americans each year, 160,000 of them from lung cancer made a strong case for the prohibition of tobacco, and particularly of cigarettes. In the 1990s, the industry faced a barrage of cases brought by several States in the USA, aiming to reclaim the cost of treating sick smokers. The States in 1998 accepted a settle-ment of US$246 billion over 25 years. Shortly afterwards tobacco firms put up the price of cigarettes by 45 cents. Almost 10 years later the industry was hauled up again before the US courts. Philip Morris, RJ Reynolds, Brown & Williamson, British American Tobacco, and Lorillard Tobacco were found guilty of conspiring to deceive the public about the dangers of smoking.

The judge found that the industry had, for decades, publicly denied, distorted, and minimized the hazards of smoking despite recognizing that smoking caused death and disease.

Legal restrictions have been imposed on advertising and sales promotion and companies have been forced to put health warnings on cigarette packets. In addition, laws banning smok-ing have become increasingly common with several US States imposing tough rules on smoking, including banning smoking in offices and public places. Significant steps have also been taken to promote smoke-free environments in the EU. In the early 1990s a number of directives laid down restrictions on smoking at work. The EU also called on Member States to provide protection from exposure to tobacco smoke in indoor workplaces, enclosed public places, and public transport. Comprehensive bans on smoking in all enclosed public places and all workplaces, including bars and restaurants, were intro-duced in Ireland, Northern Ireland, Scotland, England, and Wales. Legislation is also in place in Italy, Malta, Sweden, →

France, Finland, Lithuania, Belgium, Cyprus, Estonia, the Netherlands, Slovenia, and Spain. At international level, 141 countries ratified the WHO Framework Convention of Tobacco Control (WHO FCTC) which recognizes the unequivocal link between smoking and death and disease. The Convention obliges its signatories to tackle exposure to tobacco smoke in indoor workplaces, public transport, and indoor public places.

In the face of the legal assault and with their traditional markets in decline, the industry responded by moving into the growing smokeless tobacco products market in the USA and by attempting to grab more of the enormous and growing international cigarette market—particularly in Asia. For example, Philip Morris International which produces famous brands such as Marlboro Light, has moved to capture more of the huge cigarette markets in developing countries such as China which accounts for 35% of the world consumption of cigarettes, and markets including India and Vietnam.

Sources: EU Commission, 'Towards a Europe free from tobacco smoke: policy options at EU level'. Green Paper, (2007) 27 Final; www.bbc.co.uk, 17 August 2006; *The Economist*, 15 March 2007; *Financial Times*, 2 February 2007

Questions

1. Why has the legal environment become threatening for the tobacco industry in the last 50 years?

2. What are the threats posed to the tobacco industry by its legal environment?

3. How has the industry responded to those threats?

4. Why are tobacco firms increasingly looking to poor countries?

5. To what extent have tobacco firms been successful in weathering legal attacks? To answer this question, have a look at the BAT (British American Tobacco) and the Altria web sites (Philip Morris is a subsidiary of Altria).

Online Resource Centre
www.oxfordtextbooks.co.uk/orc/hamilton_webster/

Visit the supporting online resource centre for additional material which will help you with your assignments, essays and research, or you may find these extra resources helpful when revising for exams.

● FURTHER READING

For sources of EU Law see Europa, the official web site of the EU and the Cornell University site at http://library.lawschool.cornell.edu

The book by Day and Griffin covers the main legal aspects of overseas sales. It includes an examination of the developments in e-commerce.

● Day, D. M. and Griffin, B. (2003) *The Law of International Trade*, 3rd edn. Oxford: Oxford University Press

The book by Glenn gives a global view of the traditions of various legal systems, for example Islamic and Jewish. It examines national laws in the wider context of legal traditions.

● Glenn, H. P. (2007) *Legal Traditions of the World: Sustainable Diversity in Law*, 3rd edn. Oxford: Oxford University Press

The following reference is a standard text on international commercial law. It examines the legal framework and its application to commercial cases.

- Goode, R. (2007) *Transnational Commercial Law: Text, Cases and Materials*. Oxford: Oxford University Press

The book by Matsushita takes a comprehensive look at the history of the World Trade Organization, the law under which it operates, and its policies and practices.

- Matsushita, M., Schoenbaum, T. J. and Mavroidis, P. C. (2006) *The World Trade Organization: Law, Practice, and Policy*, 2nd edn. Oxford: Oxford University Press

● REFERENCES

Abbott, K., Pendlebury, N. and Wardman K. (2007) *Business Law*, 8th edn. London: Continuum

Ayyagari, M., Demirguc-Kunt, A. and Maksimovic, V. (2006) 'What Determines Protection of Property Rights? An Analysis of Direct and Indirect Effects'. Robert H. Smith School Research Paper No RHS 06-032

Britannica Concise Encyclopaedia. Available at www.britannica.com

Care, J. C. (2000) 'The Status of Customary Law in Fiji Islands after the Constitutional Amendment Act 1997'. *Journal of South Pacific Law*, Vol 4

Council of Europe. Convention on Cybercrime. Available at http://conventions.coe.int/Treaty

Dixon, M. (2007) *Textbook on International Law*, 6th edn. Oxford: Oxford University Press

El-Gamal, M. A. (2006) *Islamic Finance Law, Economics, and Practice*. Cambridge: Cambridge University Press

Hagedoorn, J. and Hesen, G. (2007) 'Contract Law and the Governance of Inter-Firm Technology Partnerships—An Analysis of Different Modes of Partnering and Their Contractual Implications'. *Journal of Management Studies*, 44(3)

Hedley, S. (2006) *The Law of Electronic Commerce and the Internet in the UK and Ireland*. London: Cavendish Publishing

Jennings, M. M. (2006) *Business: Its Legal, Ethical, and Global Environment*, 7th edn. Ohio: Thomson West

Len, S. A. and Hooley, R. J. A. (2003) *Commercial Law: Text, Cases and Materials*. Oxford: Oxford University Press

Lexadin. Available at http://www.lexadin.nl—this site contains lots of articles covering various areas of the law, e.g. commercial law, doing business in France/Belgium, etc

Mayson, S., French, D. and Ryan, C. (2005) *Mayson, French and Ryan on Company Law*, 22nd edn. Oxford: Oxford University Press

METRO: Institute for Transnational Legal Research. Available at http://www.unimaas.nl

Raisch, M. J. 'Religious Legal Systems: A Brief Guide to Research and Its Role in Comparative Law'. Available at www.nyulawglobal.org

Schulte-Nölke, H. (ed) (2006) 'EC Consumer Law Compendium—Comparative Analysis. December.' Available at http://ec.europa.eu

Smits, J. M. (2005) 'Diversity of Contract Law and the European Internal Market'. Maastricht Faculty of Law Working Paper 2005/9. Available at www.unimaas.nl

World Legal Information Institute. Available at www.worldlii.org

CHAPTER NINE

The Financial Framework

LEARNING OUTCOMES

This chapter will enable you to:

- Explain what money is and its importance for business

- Assess the significance of inflation, interest rates, and exchange rates for the business environment

- Analyse the role and importance of international financial institutions and markets

- Explain the restructuring and the increasing integration of the international financial system

- Explain the characteristics of financial crises

- Assess the challenges faced by financial regulators

Case Study The City of London—A Hub of International Finance

This case study illustrates the growth and importance of London as a centre for international finance.

By the early 1980s, the financial markets in London, often referred to as the City, had become international in their orientation. As a result, London had far more foreign banks than any other financial centre and held the biggest share of the foreign-exchange market. But although the banking sector had opened up to the world, there remained a glaring exception in the City, the stock exchange. The exchange had a set of rules regulating competition and protecting the incumbent firms from takeover.

In 1986, far-reaching reforms were introduced, the so-called 'Big Bang'. The reforms swept away the cosy rules protecting the firms operating in the market. This deregulation allowed member firms to be taken over by outsiders, abolished both the system of fixed commissions on share deals paid by investors, and got rid of the strict separation of brokers who were only allowed to act for investors, and jobbers who were wholesalers in securities.

The effects of the reforms were remarkable. The decision to admit outside capital into the stock exchange led to the entry of dozens of domestic and foreign banks increasing the intensity of competition and putting profit margins under pressure. By 2006, there were 260 foreign banks operating in the City, and more than 300 foreign firms listed on the London Stock Exchange. The influx of foreign operators meant that, by the turn of the century, most of the big UK-based firms operating on the London markets had been taken over by foreign firms. Consequently, London is often referred to as the Wimbledon of the finance world. In other words, it is an ideal arena for star foreign players to come and do their stuff with British competitors making little impact in the competition. Shortly after the Big Bang, London became one the world's first financial centres to replace face-to-face trading of shares with trading taking place via computers and telephones.

Annual turnover in UK equities rose from £161 billion in 1986 to £2.5 trillion in 2005, a 15-fold increase. London became the largest market in the world for over-the-counter derivatives trading, and daily foreign exchange turnover increased 24-fold to £639 billion in the 20 years after the reforms. It also became a major centre for trading in international shares with 43% of the global market and the world's leading market for international insurance.

Sources: Reuters, 2006. 'Twenty years of post-Big Bang boom feted'. 25 October; www.Timesonline.co.uk 21 October 2006. 'The day that spelt doom for the long City lunch'; *The Economist*, 19 October 2006; City of London, Key facts about the City of London and the 'Square Mile' www.cityoflondon.gov.uk

Source: London Stock Exchange press office

Introduction

In this chapter we are going to look at the international financial environment, that part of the international economy concerned with money, interest rates, exchange rates, and financial assets such as deposits, company shares, bonds, derivatives, and foreign currencies. We examine the major private financial institutions and the markets where they operate and the extraordinarily fast rate at which these institutions and markets have grown both at home and abroad. We also look at the operation of organizations such as the Bank for International Settlements, the International Monetary Fund, the World Bank, the European Central Bank, and the European Bank for Reconstruction and Development and their implications for the financial environment.

We go on to examine the characteristics of financial crises that shake the international monetary system at regular intervals. Finally, we consider how the financial system is regulated and the effectiveness of regulation in maintaining stability in the international financial system.

Money

Money is an essential element of the international financial environment, playing as it does, a number of vitally important roles for business:

- A medium of exchange—money allows businesses to receive payment from customers both at home and abroad and to pay their suppliers. It reduces the time and effort needed to carry on trade because, without money, firms would have to exchange what they produce for the goods and services they need. This is called barter and such a system would be very time-consuming and costly say, for a firm producing computer chips to find a supplier who has the goods and services it requires and is prepared to exchange them for the chips that the firm has on offer.

- A common measure of value—money enables firms to place a value on the goods and services that they buy and sell. In a barter system there is no common unit with which to measure and compare the value of goods and services. Money gets round these problems by enabling business to express in money terms, the value of revenues, costs, and profits and this, in turn, enables it to evaluate its performance.

- Divisibility—money can be broken down into different units of value, cents and dollars or pence and pounds, facilitating the process of exchange. The availability of small units of money means that firms and their customers are not compelled to buy or sell goods and services in large quantities.

- A store of wealth-money gives business the ability to store wealth. Businesses can build up reserves of money now which can then be used later to buy goods and services or to invest.

The Importance of Confidence

Underpinning the idea of money is an agreement to accept something that, in itself, may have no fundamental use to us, or, as the Cree Indian prophecy puts it:

Only after the last tree has been cut down.
Only after the last river has been poisoned.
Only after the last fish has been caught.
Only then will you find that money cannot be eaten.

Normally, we have confidence that it can be exchanged in the market for something that does have use, goods and services. Were that confidence to melt away, the whole financial and economic system would be under threat. In such a situation, neither individuals nor businesses would be prepared to accept money in exchange for goods and services and the system of monetary exchange would collapse with drastic consequences for the economy in general, and business in particular.

Money takes various forms moving from the more to the less liquid. Liquidity refers to how quickly and cheaply an asset can be converted into cash. Thus paper money or cash is the most liquid asset because it can be exchanged very easily for goods and services. Current bank accounts are another example of high liquidity insofar as the money in them is quickly and easily accessible and also because the money in them can be easily transferred by cheques or electronic means. Less liquid are savings accounts and deposits which need notice before money can be withdrawn. Even less liquid are a variety of financial assets such as stocks and bonds which are less easily turned into cash.

The Money Supply

Governments are interested in the quantity of different forms of money available within their economies because either they or their central banks take on the responsibility of controlling the money supply and interest rates because they see that as a way of controlling inflation. To that end they try to measure the money supply and how it is changing over time. The supply is classified into categories. The USA has two categories, the EU three, while India has four. The categories are usually designated as follows, M0, M1, M2, and M3. Each category includes all the financial assets covered by the previous ones and, as we go up the scale from M0 to M3, the assets included are less and less liquid.

Inflation, Interest Rates, and Exchange Rates

We are now going to look at three phenomena in the financial environment that can be important for business, inflation, interest rates, and exchange rates.

Inflation

Inflation can be defined as an increase in the overall price level of goods and services in an economy over a particular period of time. It is usually measured by collecting price information on a representative sample of goods and services and using the information to calculate a Price Index that shows the change in the general price level. Businesses operating in countries with relatively high rates of inflation can find their international competitiveness undermined as the rising costs of goods and services feed higher costs of production. And it may be that this process is exacerbated when workers respond to rising prices by demanding higher wages. On the other hand this could open up selling opportunities for firms operating out of low inflation economies. They are likely to find it easier to compete with firms operating in countries suffering from high inflation.

The rate of inflation in rich countries started to pick up after 2004 with the vigorous growth in the global economy. The rapid growth, particularly in countries like China, led to increases in demand for commodities such as oil and other raw materials which pushed up their prices. Up to then low import prices had helped to hold down rich country inflation rates. The Federal Reserve estimated that falling import prices had reduced US inflation by between 0.5 and 1 percentage point a year from the mid 1990s. Rising inflation was viewed with concern in most countries with the major exception of Japan where economic growth had been stalled for many years. The rise in inflation above zero was seen as finally signalling the end of that country's 15 years of stagnation.

Interest Rates

All the world's leading central banks, concerned about rising inflation, increased their interest rates. An interest rate is the price paid for the temporary use of someone else's funds. Interest is a cost to borrowers but income to lenders. When interest rates rise in a country then this increases the cost of borrowing to business. Business could, given the removal of barriers to the movement of capital, shop around in other countries for cheaper rates. A hike in interest rates may also depress demand for goods and services as consumers find it more expensive to borrow to buy consumer durables such as cars, computers, plasma TVs, and so forth. On the other hand rising interest rates could benefit financial institutions who lend money because they can charge more for their loans.

Exchange Rates

An exchange rate is the price of one currency as expressed in another or, to put it another way, the rate at which one currency is exchanged for another. Movements in exchange rates can be an important influence on the business environment—good news for some, bad for others. A rise in the exchange rate can make imports cheaper which is good news for those firms buying a lot of goods and services from abroad. On the other hand it is likely to be bad news for exporters as it could make them less competitive in foreign markets. The French car firms, Peugeot and Renault calculated that a 1% rise in the euro against other currencies would reduce their profits by €70 million and €33 million respectively (*Financial Times*, 25 January 2003). Similarly, for businesses producing abroad it could reduce the value of their foreign sales and assets when translated back into their domestic currency.

The Bretton Woods Agreement, agreed in 1944, obliged the signatory countries to adopt a monetary policy that maintained the exchange rate of their currencies at a fixed value, plus or minus one per cent, in terms of gold. The US dollar became the pre-eminent world currency reflecting the American dominance of the global economy. This was, reinforced by its commitment to convert dollars into gold which increased the willingness of people outside America to accept payment in dollars and to hold dollar assets. The system prevailed for a good 25 years but came under increasing strain in the 1960s. As a result, the fixed exchange rate system collapsed in 1971 following the USA's suspension of convertibility from dollars to gold. The old system gave way to more flexible exchange rates where currencies were freer to move with market forces of supply and demand.

Learning Task

It was reported in 2005 that Peugeot Citroen and Toyota, the French and Japanese carmakers had saved €200 million (US$265 million), or 13%, of the cost of their new jointly-owned €1.5 billion factory in the Czech Republic because the strong euro slashed the cost of imports of machinery, such as robots and welders made in Japan. Japanese car exporters had also benefited when importing cars into Europe because their sales had surged due to fall of around 16% in the yen against the euro. Japanese firms claimed that they had not taken advantage of the weak yen to cut prices in the Eurozone but to boost profits (*Financial Times*, 1 March 2005).

1. Explain how the strength of the euro helped the Peugeot and Toyota joint venture in Czechoslovakia.

2. How might the weakness of the yen have helped Japanese sales in the Eurozone market?

3. The Japanese car makers claim not to have reduced prices but their sales still increased. In the light of their claim, how could you explain the surge in sales?

Countries may adopt a fixed exchange rate policy where they peg the value of their currency against another. Mexico, whose major trading partner is the USA, pegged the peso against the US dollar. Such a policy gives a degree of stability to Mexican importers and exporters. China also adopted a similar policy. However, it acceded to pressure to revalue the rate from the US authorities who were worried about the burgeoning trade deficit with China. As can be seen in the diagram below, China allowed the spot rate—the current exchange rate that the renminbi could be bought at 'now'—to rise against the dollar. In June 2005 US$1 bought just less than 8.29 renminbi. A year later, US$1 only bought around 8 renminbi (see Figure 9.1).

Countries may also choose to have floating exchange rates where the rate is determined solely by the supply and demand for the currency on the foreign exchange markets. Here the currency value would be determined by the requirement to finance imports and exports, the movement of capital across borders, the country's interest rates relative to others, and the demands of speculators. In this situation the rate could be very volatile and this could create problems for firms that are heavily involved in international trade and

Figure 9.1 Spot Exchange Rate of Renminbi/US Dollar

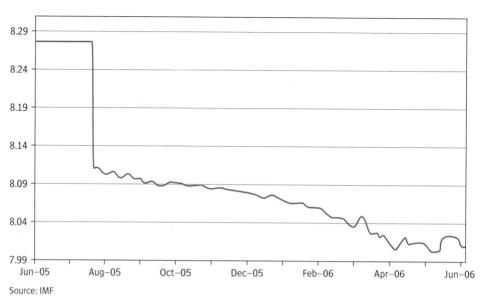

Source: IMF

investment. They could face wild fluctuations in import prices and in the value of export earnings and foreign assets.

Or it may be that the authorities decide that they are prepared to see the value of the currency fluctuate within prescribed bands against another currency. When the currency looks as if it is going to break through the bands, the authorities intervene to buy the domestic currency when it is sinking too low or to sell it when it is threatening to rise too high in value. This gives business less certainty than the fixed rate regime but more certainty than a floating regime.

Financial Institutions—Who are they and What do they do?

The functioning of the international economy and the production and the trading and investment activities of the organizations and individuals within it, is dependent on the effective operation of a variety of financial institutions, both public and private. We first of all look at several international financial institutions and their functions and then we examine an array of other organizations in the financial sector.

International Financial Institutions

There are several international financial institutions whose main aim is to facilitate the effective operation of the international payments mechanism and to ensure stability in the international financial system.

The Bank for International Settlements (BIS) was established in 1930. Its 55 members are sovereign countries represented at the BIS by their central banks. The BIS fosters international monetary and financial cooperation and serves as an international central bank for national central banks such as the Federal Reserve, the European Central Bank, and the Bank of China. It acts as a forum to promote discussion and policy analysis among central banks and in the international financial community.

The BIS deals with the central banks on a daily basis and, by buying and selling foreign currencies and gold, helps them manage their foreign currency and gold reserves. It also advises the central banks and other international institutions on how to prevent financial fraud. On average, over the last few years, some 6% of global foreign exchange reserves have been deposited by central banks with the BIS and in 2006, its total currency deposits amounted to around US$273 billion. In times of financial crisis, the BIS offers short-term credits to central banks and may also coordinate emergency short-term lending to countries.

In 1944 the International Monetary Fund (IMF) was established. The key function of the IMF was to preserve international financial stability, in other words, to avoid financial crises that could threaten the international financial system. Up to the early 1970s that meant sustaining the system of fixed currency exchange rates set up by the Bretton Woods Agreement. Member countries contributed funds to a pool from which they could borrow on a temporary basis when running balance of payments deficits. Applicants for loans may face IMF demands for changes in government policy such as cutting public expenditures on social programmes, reducing subsidies on basic necessities, increasing taxes, eliminating import tariffs, and the privatization of publicly owned assets (Leonard 2006).

The move in the 1970s away from fixed exchange rates seemed to remove one of the main reasons for the IMF's existence. However, its services were still required. In 1976, the British Government was forced by a steep fall in the value of sterling to approach the Fund. The IMF demanded massive public spending cuts in return for urgently needed loans (see Burk 1992). The IMF was called on again in the mid 1990s when the stability of the international financial system came under threat due to a wave of financial crises in large developing countries, Mexico, South East Asia (see end Case Study), Russia, Brazil, Turkey, and Argentina. In the cases of Brazil, Russia, and Argentina, the IMF intervened massively in the currency markets by pumping in millions of dollars to support their exchange rates.

The IMF has increased its initial membership from 44 countries to 185. It has some very ambitious aims: to promote global monetary cooperation, secure financial stability, facilitate international trade, promote high employment and sustainable economic growth, and reduce poverty. The IMF differs from the BIS insofar as it can provide temporary financial assistance to members to enable them to correct international payment imbalances. The idea is that such assistance will discourage countries from trying to rectify their balance of payments deficits by resorting to policies that could have disruptive effects on the international trading and financial systems such as competitive currency devaluations, exchange controls, or resorting to trade protection.

In 1969, the IMF created the Special Drawing Right (SDR) an artificial currency whose value is calculated on a weighted basis of the world's major trading currencies the euro,

Japanese yen, the pound sterling, and the US dollar. The SDR was created to ease world liquidity problems thereby facilitating the expansion of world trade and enabling countries to support the system of fixed exchange rates. At the start the SDR total of 9.3 billion was used to supplement the foreign exchange reserves of its members and was used solely as a central bank reserve asset. Later, with the collapse of the fixed exchange rate system, and with currency markets becoming more volatile, the need for SDRs fell but it did start to be used in commercial transactions by those wishing to protect themselves against depreciation in the US dollar. By the 1990s 21.4 billion SDRs had been created by the IMF.

In total the IMF has some $340 billion available for all intervention—which is minuscule compared with the size of international capital markets (IMF Annual Report 2007). While the IMF can make an impact on individual countries, it is difficult to envisage the IMF making a significant difference were there to be a full-blown financial crisis of global dimensions such as that starting in autumn 2007.

Learning Task

Go to the IMF web site and find out:

- the value of an SDR in terms of US dollars, the Euro, and sterling
- the allocation of SDR by country
- the current total allocation of SDRs in US dollars.

Now look at the Cofer statistics of foreign exchange reserves on the IMF web site. What are the major components of the reserves? Does the total SDR allocation make a significant addition to world liquidity?

The World Bank, like the IMF, was established in 1944 and currently has 185 member countries. It is an international organization set up to reduce global poverty and to improve standards of living. It provides low cost loans and interest-free credit to developing countries for education, health, and for the development of infrastructure projects in water supply, transport, and communications. World Bank projects can be a source of lucrative contracts for businesses such as water, energy, and telecommunications utilities as well as construction companies.

A particular area of interest to the Bank is how political institutions in poorer countries make decisions and how institutional resources are used to manage society's problems and affairs—the technical term for this area is governance. The Bank is interested in improving governance and, to that end, has encouraged governments to stamp out corruption. Its main focus nowadays is on achieving the Millennium Development Goals of eliminating of poverty and implementing sustainable development (see Chapter Eleven for further discussion of the Goals). It has a budget of some US$25 billion (Annual Report 2007). Like the IMF, the Bank may have the capacity to bring about change in individual countries but its budget does not equip it to have a major impact on the billions of people who continue to live in poverty.

The World Bank, along with the IMF, has come in for criticism. The critics claim that neither institution works in the best interest of poor countries but on behalf of the rich economies. They provide assistance to debt-ridden or near-bankrupt developing countries that are powerless to resist their demands for the introduction of reforms that remove barriers to business in advanced economies wishing to export goods or services to those poor countries, import raw materials from them, or to invest there. In addition, poor countries are pressurized to prioritize repayment of debt to foreign banks and investors. This hits the poor in those countries as jobs are cut, health and education budgets reduced, price supports removed, and food and natural resources exported abroad (see Stiglitz 2002; Chossudovsky 1998; *The Ecologist*, September 2000).

The European Central Bank (ECB) is the central bank for countries that are members of the Eurozone. Its main job is the control of inflation. It uses the tools of monetary policy, in other words the money supply and interest rates to achieve price stability. Its decisions on monetary policy can have important effects on business. A decision by the ECB to raise interest rates would push up business costs by increasing the costs of borrowing and could reduce demand by making customers reluctant to borrow money to buy goods and services. The ECB conducts foreign exchange operations on behalf of member states, manages their foreign reserves, and promotes the smooth operation of payments systems within the zone. It carries out the tasks typically associated with national central banks.

Private Financial Institutions

There are a whole range of other financial institutions carrying out a range of functions invaluable for business. Banks, insurance companies, pension funds, investment trusts, unit trusts, all act as intermediaries between those who wish to borrow money and those who wish to lend. Retail banks take deposits from private individuals, firms, and other bodies. Insurance companies, pension funds, and unit trusts collect longer-term savings which they then invest in a variety of stocks and shares. By not being dependent on the shares of a single company, they offer savers the possibility of spreading risk. Investment banks (also called merchant banks) provide a range of financial services to business. They give advice in areas such as mergers and acquisitions, the disposal of businesses, and arranging issues of new shares.

Venture capital companies are another source of funding for business. These firms gather funds from private and public pension funds, charitable foundations, business and wealthy individuals and use them to finance smaller, sometimes start-up, companies. They usually do this in return for a share in the ownership of the company.

Functions of Financial Institutions

We now look in more detail at some of the important functions performed by financial institutions for business.

Mini Case Microfinance and Developing Countries

While credit is usually easily obtainable in rich countries, business and populations in developing countries have great difficulty in accessing finance from mainstream financial institutions because they are regarded as high risk.

To remedy this difficulty, the concept of microfinance has been developed. This provides loans often of US$100 or less in poor countries with a particular emphasis on rural areas. It is seen as an effective way of assisting local business. It creates employment, and reduces poverty. In 2008, up to 25,000 microfinance institutions were serving around 70 million clients in over 100 countries in Asia, Africa, and Latin America. Grameen bank was a pioneer in the field.

Borrowers are trusted to pay back the loan so they are not required to provide any security (collateral). Neither do they need to pay high rates of interest, nor do they come under legal and other pressures to pay back loans.

Photograph: Brett Matthews

Sources: Sengupta and Aubuchon 2008; and for a critical assessment of microfinance see, Beck and Ogden 2007

Mobilizing Savings and Providing Credit

The mobilization and pooling of savings is one of the most obvious and important functions of the financial sector. Savings facilities such as bank accounts, enable businesses and households to store their money in a secure place. In countries, where secure facilities for savings are lacking, or where there is a lack of confidence in the stability of the financial sector, for example in some developing economies, people often opt to save in physical assets such as gold or jewellery, or store their savings at home. In such situations business can find it difficult to raise finance and may have to rely on internally generated profits. By offering such facilities, the financial sector pools savings and channels them to businesses to be used productively in the economy. Interest paid on savings may increase the amount saved, giving a boost to the funds available for businesses to invest.

Financial intermediaries, by pooling the savings of firms and individuals and lending them on to business, can make it easier and cheaper for business to export and import and to finance investment for expansion or for the introduction of new technology. Thus the sector can help firms service new foreign markets and sources of supply and can also make it easier for firms to improve competitiveness by increasing productivity or by introducing new products.

Payment Facilities

Financial intermediaries facilitate the exchange of goods and services both in terms of domestic and cross-border transactions by providing mechanisms to make and receive payments. To be effective, payments systems need to be readily available for both domestic and foreign buyers and sellers through bank branches or electronically and they also need to be affordable, fast, and safe from fraud.

Good payments mechanisms free up firms to concentrate on what they do best, make goods and services, and this ability to specialize makes it easier for them to innovate and to increase productivity. Anything that reduces transactions costs and better facilitates the exchange of goods and services—whether that be faster payments systems, more bank branches, or improved remittance services—will help to promote business growth.

Normally payments systems are more highly developed in the advanced economies than in poorer countries but systems can vary from one rich country to another. The existence of multiple payments systems can raise problems of inter-operability, that is the ability of the various systems to accept payments from others. Inter-operability may be made more difficult when systems are using incompatible hardware or software systems. While this may not be such an important issue for big multinational companies whose subsidiaries are trading with each other and where payments systems are internal to the company, it does have major implications for firms dependent on making or receiving cross-border payments from third parties.

There are various systems which operate internationally and facilitate cross-border payment:

- SWIFT, the Society for Worldwide Interbank Financial Telecommunication, was established in 1973 by 239 banks, including central banks, from 15 countries. It was set up to increase the automation of financial transaction processes. By the end of 2002, more than 7,400 financial institutions from 198 countries were connected. Its services are used by banks and other financial institutions such as securities brokers and dealers, investment management institutions, and money brokers. The average daily value of payments on SWIFT has been estimated to be in excess of €6 trillion. SWIFT is the most widely used payment services provider worldwide.

- Continuous Linked settlement (LS) was set up in 2002. By 2006 it had 56 of the world's largest banks and more than 700 other institutions using the system to settle 240,000 foreign exchange payments a day. It was dealing in the 15 currencies representing almost all global trade in foreign exchange and with an average daily value exceeding US$2.5 trillion.

- Visa International and MasterCard are other international organizations offering a range of cashless payment services. Visa is an association owned by 21,000 financial institutions worldwide. Membership is limited to deposit-taking financial institutions and to bank-owned organizations operating in the bank card sector, such as Carte Bleue in France and Servizi Interbancari in Italy. MasterCard has approximately 25,000 members, and it and Visa each have around 1 billion cards circulating worldwide.

- PayPal and Alibaba are two online payments companies who offer secure methods of payment for goods and services on the web on sites such as eBay. They are not registered as banks and therefore need the support of existing financial institutions to offer their services. PayPal claims to be operating in multiple currencies in more than 100 countries and with millions of account holders.

Learning Task

Examine the statistics in Table 9.1.

1. Calculate the share of the USA, Latin America, and the Caribbean in the number of cards and the value of transactions.

2. Come up with some explanations for the differences between the USA and Latin America.

Table 9.1 Key Visa statistics (as of 30 September 2002)

	Worldwide total	Asia-Pacific	Canada	CEMEA	European Union	Latin America & Caribb	United States
Transaction data for the 9 months ending on 30 September 2002							
Purchase transactions Value (USD billions)	1,522.8	220.3	61.9	14.1	446.3	41.5	738.7
Cash transactions Value (USD billions)	862.6	173.2	7.1	72.1	245.8	132.8	231.8
Total transactions Number of transactions (millions)	33,352	3,434	961	1,077	10,833	2,906	14,141
Change vs same period one year ago (as a %)	14.6	26.3	4.6	38.6	14.2	14.7	11.6
Value of transactions (USD billions)	2,385.4	393.4	69.0	86.1	692.1	174.2	970.5
Status data as at 30 September 2002							
Customer base							
Number of accounts (millions)	811.3	157.1	19.2	37.5	180.7	118.6	298.2
Number of cards (millions)	960.2	177.3	26.5	41.6	198.5	131.2	385.0

Note: Includes all card programmes (Classic, Premium, Commercial/Business, Electron, Credit and Debit Programmes). Excludes Interlink.
Source: *Visa International Quarterly Statistical Report.*

Electronic payments systems have become more widely available and this has enabled firms to move their business-to-business (B2B) and business-to-consumer (B2C) activities on to the web. Electronic payments across the European Union are now fast and cheap, and are generally more efficient than payments within the USA. In Japan, cash is used extensively compared with other industrial countries. However, Japanese businesses and consumers do also use direct debits, credit transfers, credit cards, debit cards, and bills and cheques. Payments made using these have been increasing, partly reflecting the development of a variety of access channels such as ATMs, the internet, and mobile phones.

Cheques which, for a long time, were one of the most important means of payment have generally been in decline in rich countries being replaced by debit and credit cards and telephone and on-line banking. This trend has been accelerated by the spread of Automated Teller Machines (ATMs). They have removed the need to write cheques to get access to cash or to make payments to others. While cheques continue to be used in the UK and France, Sweden has totally abandoned them as a means of payment.

By contrast, in a less developed economy such as Russia the population continue to prefer payment in cash. This is the major payment means used for retail payments for goods and services. Cash is also used for paying salaries, pensions, welfare allowances, and grants. However, the use of ATMs is growing very rapidly as is the use of 'plastic' as a means of payment with Visa and MasterCard the main players. Compared to richer countries the Russian payments system is underdeveloped.

Reconciling Liquidity and Long-Term Finance Needs

Business investment projects often require a medium to long-term commitment of capital whereas many savers prefer to have ready access to their savings. In other words, they like their savings to be 'liquid'. Banks and other financial intermediaries can offer finance to business for medium and long-term investment because they combine the savings of many households and businesses. Experience shows that savers do not usually all want to withdraw their money at the same time. As a result, financial institutions need only keep a proportion of their assets in a liquid form to meet the demands of those savers wishing to withdraw money whilst, at the same time, being able to provide medium to long-term capital for business investment.

Spreading the Risk

Savers are usually averse to risk and generally reluctant to invest all their money in a single project. They much prefer to spread the risk by investing in a range of projects. Financial intermediaries such as banks, stock exchanges, and hedge funds facilitate the spreading of risk by aggregating savings and then spreading them among both low and high risk investment projects. This enables business to get finance for high risk projects such as those involving ground-breaking technology.

Market Restructuring and Diversification

Financial institutions have similar objectives to other private sector commercial organizations: at the most basic level they wish to survive, but they also aim to make profits and grow. Profits are made from the commissions, charges, and interest rates levied on the financial services offered, both domestically and increasingly abroad. They also benefit from arbitrage which involves taking advantage of price differences between markets when a financial product can be bought cheap in, say, Tokyo and sold for a higher price in Amsterdam.

Domestic Consolidation and International Expansion

In pursuit of their objectives, financial institutions have been getting bigger at home through mergers and acquisitions and also through organic growth—in other words increasing their own output and sales. This has led to market restructuring in the major economies. In 1995, 20 banks in the UK accounted for 75% of sector turnover while 10 years

Table 9.2 Increasing Concentration in the Banking Industry (Number of banks covering 75%)

	1995	1998	2001	2004
United Kingdom	20[2]	24	17	16
United States	20[3]	20	13	11
Japan	24	19	17	11
Singapore	25	23	18	11
Germany	10	9	5	4
Switzerland	5	7	6	5
Hong Kong SAR	13–22[4]	26	14	11

[1] For 2004, upper bound subject to revision. [2] 68%. [3] 70%. [4] Depending on the market.
Source: BIS

later the number had dropped to 16. Similar trends were taking place in the USA (20 banks down to 11) and Japan (24 to 11) (BIS; see Table 9.2). In 2006, the 10 biggest US banks controlled about 50% of the country's banking assets, up from 29% a decade previously.

Fifty years ago, banks and other financial institutions tended to confine their operations to their domestic markets. Increasingly, with the passage of time, they have expanded their operations abroad. The big German bank, Deutsche Bank offers a wide range of financial services to private and business clients in 76 countries (www.db.com).

US banks, such as Citigroup, the world's largest financial institution, and European banks, like Royal Bank of Scotland (RBS), have also gone in for mergers, both at home and abroad, to get round the problem of slow-growing domestic markets. Both have made moves into China. RBS paid almost £2bn for a 10% stake in the Bank of China while Citigroup was prepared to pay over US$3 billion for a controlling stake in the Guangdong Development Bank (*Financial Times*, 19 August 2005 and 15 November 2006).

The strategies pursued by financial institutions have led to a restructuring of the sector and have resulted in the creation of large financial conglomerates selling a range of products in a variety of countries.

The fall of communism in 1989 provided opportunities for banks to pursue their internationalization strategies. Foreign banks moved in to Central Europe and now control 80% of the top local banks. Poland is a good illustration of this trend. In 1993, there were only 10 foreign banks operating there. By 2005, 50 of the 61 banks were foreign-owned. In 2006, two of Sweden's biggest banks, Swedbank and SEB were earning more than 20% of their profits in the former Soviet states of Estonia, Latvia, and Lithuania (*Financial Times*, 3 November 2006; *The Economist* 18 May 2006; EBRD).

Product Diversification

Financial institutions have also grown by expanding their product range. Traditionally banks borrowed and lent money but did not sell insurance or trade in shares. Building

societies made long term loans on the security of private houses but did not provide banking services such as current accounts. In their quest for profits and growth, they have
diversified and consequently have become less specialized. Big retail banks, for example,
have increasingly seen their future as financial supermarkets selling a range of financial
products and services. As a result the various institutions now compete with each other
over a wider product range.

Product Innovation

The financial sector has been very inventive in devising new financial products. A major
development has been the growth of the hedge fund. Hedging implies action to reduce
risk. While hedge funds do attempt to reduce risk they also trade in a range of financial
assets from equities to bonds to commodities and strive to take advantage of arbitrage
opportunities. So, for example, if a currency or commodity is selling for one price in
London and a higher price in New York then hedge funds will buy in London and sell in
New York. Hedge funds often use complex mathematical models to make predictions
of future price movements of financial assets to determine their trading strategies. Their
aim is to produce good performance regardless of the underlying trends in the financial
markets. In 2006, global investment in hedge funds totalled US$361 billion (BIS).

Derivatives, Swaps, and Options

In financial markets, stock prices, bond prices, currency rates, interest rates, and dividends go up and down, creating risk. Derivatives are financial products used to control
risk. Swaps are derivatives which firms can use to cover themselves against adverse movements in interest rates, inflation, exchange rates, and the possibility of borrowers defaulting on their loans. Thus, pension funds can use inflation swaps to protect the value of their
assets against increases in inflation while lenders, concerned about defaulting loans, can
use credit default swaps. These work like this: two banks, one of whom has lent to General
Motors and one to VW, can diversify their risk by agreeing to swap part of their liabilities.
Both would then be less exposed to a default by their original borrower. This ability to
spread risks may make financial institutions more willing to lend consequently making
it easier for non-financial firms to borrow. The market in credit derivative products grew
to such an extent that in 2006 US$26,000 billion was outstanding. Much of the trade in
derivative products does not take place through financial markets but between individual institutions. Such trade is called over-the-counter (OTC) trading. According to the
BIS, the value of OTC trading in derivatives amounted to US$516,407 billion in June 2007.
Interest rate derivatives accounted for over two thirds of the total with foreign exchange
contracts trailing with less then 10%.

Another product is the option to buy or sell a specific amount of a given derivative at a
specified price over a certain period of time. The buyer pays an amount of money for the
option and the potential loss is limited to the price paid. When an option is not exercised,
the money spent to purchase the option is lost. So a firm could take out an option to
borrow money at a specific rate of interest of say 8% over a certain time, for example six
months. If the interest rate rises above 8%, the firm can exercise its option. If the interest
rate falls below 8%, then the firm borrows at the lower rate and loses the price it paid for

the option. The market for interest rate derivatives in Europe grew about sixteen-fold from a very low base in 1992 to 2005.

Motives for Market Restructuring and Diversification

Economies of scale—financial organizations hope to gain scale economies in the purchasing of supplies and savings from getting rid of duplication (a merged bank does not need more than one HQ building, one marketing department, and so on). This proclivity to merge has continued despite research literature showing that economies of scale can be exhausted by the time a bank reaches a relatively modest size. A study of European banks in the 1990s, published by the European Investment Bank, put the figure for savings banks as low as €600 million (US$760 million) in assets. More recent studies suggest far higher thresholds, up to US$25 billion (*The Economist*, 18 May 2006).

Economies of scope—the idea here is that the extra costs of selling additional products alongside the old ones are small compared to the increase in revenues. So a bank can diversify into credit cards or insurance and apply its traditional skills of selling loans to the marketing of these products. The logic is that selling extra financial products through established branch networks to existing customers, offers a low cost, high productivity method of distribution.

Market Share—when a bank takes over a competitor this increases its market share, reduces competition and may, because the takeover makes it bigger, reduce the vulnerability to takeover.

Other reasons for pursuing these strategies:

- To finance the increase in international trade and investment which grew at unprecedented rates in the period after the Second World War.
- Economic expansion in developing nations in South East Asia has led to an increased demand for financial services. It has been suggested by some commentators that China alone may account for over 25% of new global demand for financial services in the five years up to 2010 (*The Economist*, 18 May 2006).
- To avoid regulation by the monetary authorities. Financial institutions have been very clever in developing business outside regulated areas where there are profits to be made. Austrian banks, for example, faced lighter regulation than their German counterparts regarding the amount of information they had to provide on their borrowers. The Austrians attracted German clients by advertising their lax rules leading to complaints of unfair competition by German banks (*The Economist*, 19 May 2005).
- The large increase in the price of oil in the 1970s led to oil-producing countries having very big trade surpluses. International syndicates of banks were formed to channel the enormous sums of money from those countries to borrowers in other nations.
- Opportunities offered by the progressive deregulation of financial markets which has been occurring since the early 1970s. Deregulation involves the removal or reduction of certain governmental controls on financial institutions allowing them to move into other product areas and also into other countries.

Learning Task

1. Add up the assets held by the top 10 banks in 1985, 1995, and 2004. Calculate and comment on the percentage increase between 1985 and 1995 and then between 1995 and 2004.

2. The nationality of the top 10 banks has changed over time.

   Draw up a table putting the years in the first column and the countries, Japan, USA, UK, Switzerland, France, Germany, and China on the top row.

   Now count how many banks have their base in each country and monitor how that has changed over time. How would you explain the number of Japanese banks in the table?

3. Go to the HSBC web site to find out:

   • the number of countries in which it operates;

   • how many offices it has;

   • the range of financial products it offers.

4. The Royal Bank of Scotland took over Natwest in 1999/2000. Have a look at the press around the time of the takeover. To what extent does the Royal's justification of the takeover accord with those given in the text?

Table 9.3 World's Top Ten Banks by Assets US$ billion

	2004		1995		1985
UBS	1,533	Deutsche Bank	503	Citicorp	167
Citigroup	1,484	Sanwa Bank	501	Dai-Ichi Kangyo Bank	158
Mizuho Financial Group	1,296	Sumitomo Bank	500	Fuji Bank	142
HSBC Holdings	1,277	Dai-Ichi Kangyo Bank	499	Sumitomo Bank	135
Crédit Agricole	1,243	Fuji Bank	487	Mitsubishi Bank	133
BNP Paribas	1,234	Sakura Bank	478	Banque Nationale de Paris	123
JPMorgan Chase	1,157	Mitsubishi Bank	475	Sanwa Bank	123
Deutsche Bank	1,144	Norinchukin Bank	430	Crédit Agricole	123
Royal Bank of Scotland	1,119	Crédit Agricole	386	BankAmerica	115
Bank of America	1,110	ICBC†	374	Crédit Lyonnais	111

* Mitsubishi-UFJ Financial Group was formed in October 2005 with assets of $1.71trn. †Industrial & Commercial Bank of China
Source: *The Economist*, 19 May 2005

The product and geographical diversification strategies followed by the financial sector have increased the international integration of financial institutions and markets. This has been facilitated by the falling cost and the cross-border diffusion of information and communications technologies. Institutions can move funds around the world to markets in different time zones easily, cheaply, and quickly. New technology has, according to

The Economist, helped financial institutions, 'by-pass international frontiers and create a global whirligig of money and securities' (*The Economist*, 3 October 1992).

Financial Markets

Financial institutions usually operate through markets. Markets are mechanisms for bringing together borrowers and lenders. For example, capital markets, such as the bond and stock markets, bring together organizations, both public and private, wishing to borrow and lend long-term funds in exchange for shares and bonds. The issue of new bonds and shares to raise money takes place in the primary market. Stock exchanges also enable shareholders to buy and sell existing shares in the secondary market. Non-financial organizations also purchase bonds or shares in the secondary market. Money markets, on the other hand, enable organizations to borrow and lend short-term for anything up to, or just over, a year trading in such instruments as derivatives and certificate of deposits (CDs). Companies with surplus cash that is not needed for a short period of time can earn a return on that cash by lending it into the money market.

Other financial markets include the foreign exchange market which facilitates trading between those who wish to trade in currencies such as importers and exporters and speculators. A variety of institutions trade in foreign currencies, non-financial companies wishing to buy goods and services abroad, central banks trying to influence the exchange rate, commercial banks trading on their own account, financial institutions wishing to buy foreign securities and bonds, hedge funds, governments financing their military bases abroad and so on. In fact, importers and exporters account for only a very small proportion of this trading as foreign currencies have increasingly been seen as assets in their own right. The amount of foreign exchange traded on a daily basis is enormous. BIS figures show that turnover increased from almost US$2 trillion in 2004 to US$3.2 trillion in 2007, the major currency traded being the US dollar. BIS suggested that this massive growth in foreign currency turnover was due, in part, to trends in exchange rates and interest rate differentials (Figure 9.2). Investors could borrow in low interest rate currencies, such as the US dollar, and move the money into a higher interest rate currency with an appreciating exchange rate such as the Australian dollar.

International banking activity has grown very rapidly since the 1960s when banks in London were permitted to accept foreign currency deposits. These banks were able to attract US dollar deposits, or eurodollars, because they faced a lighter system of regulation than banks in the USA. The political climate created by the hostility of the Cold War between the West and Communism at the time also helped this process along. The then Soviet Union, along with oil-exporting States who received payment for their oil in dollars, were looking for a safe refuge outside the USA for their hard currency earnings. They deposited a significant amount of US dollars in banks in London (McGuire and Tarashev 2006). The eurodollar market became so large that it was described as a 'vast, integrated global money and capital system, almost totally outside all government regulation, that can send billions of "stateless" currencies hurtling around the world 24 hours a day' (Martin 1994).

Figure 9.2 Global Foreign Exchange Turnover US$ billions*

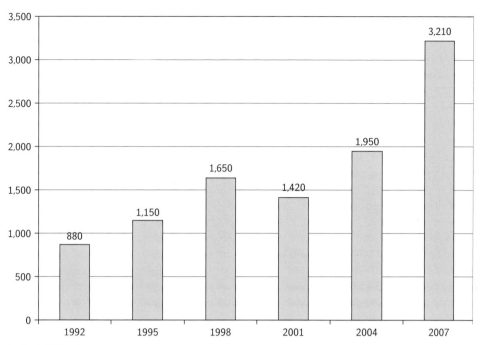

* at April 2007 exchange rates
Source: BIS 2007

Mini Case Business and Exchange Rates

In the second half of 2006 the dollar weakened against currencies such as sterling and the euro. By December, sterling had risen 13.6% against the dollar. This made it much more difficult for UK and other European companies to export to the USA because of the effect of the weak dollar on their competitiveness. About 22% of UK company earnings came from the USA and a further 10% from regions in South America and Asia having currencies tied to the dollar. Those companies with large dollar revenues, and therefore more vulnerability to the dollar's fall, included the big pharmaceutical companies, media groups like Pearson and Reed Elsevier, and financial firms such as Amvescap and Man Group. The USA was Britain's most valuable tourism market with US tourists accounting for a fifth of the £14.25 billion of spending by visitors. So prospects for the tourism sector looked gloomy. The industry expected a 10% depreciation of the dollar to lead to a 14% drop in earnings from US visitors. A further effect of the dollar fall for non-US companies was that their dollar earnings would be reduced in value when translated into their home currencies.

But it was not all bad news for British and European firms. One upside was that because most energy and commodity inputs were priced in dollars, the rise in sterling also had beneficial effects on UK and European company costs. The dollar's weakness was also good news for companies selling US holidays, with some Tour Operators reporting a 30% rise in bookings for 2007.

Source: *Financial Times*, 1 and 2 December 2006

Photograph: Elaine Tuffery

The Major Markets

Modern communications and information technology allow financial institutions to operate from virtually anywhere nowadays, yet the financial sector prefers to cluster in certain locations. London and New York are the two leading global financial centres and appear to act as a magnet for finance companies. London is preeminent in international bond trading and leads the way in OTC derivatives, marine insurance, and trading in foreign equities. It is also the most popular place for foreign banks to locate, with 264 foreign banks operating there in 2005, compared to 228 in New York (www.mondaq.com). Tokyo, Chicago, Frankfurt, Singapore, and Hong Kong are other important centres.

Financial Crises

There is no generally accepted theory to explain the causes of financial crises but one thing is sure, they are a recurring phenomenon. They involve bouts of speculation when

Table 9.4 Share of Financial Services Markets by Country 2006 %

	Britain	United States	Japan	France	Germany	Others
Cross-border bank lending	20	9	8	9	10	44
Foreign equities turnover	40	34	nil	nil	3	23
Foreign-exchange turnover	32	18	8	3	5	34
Over-the-counter derivatives turnover	43	24	3	10	3	17
Marine insurance net premium income	20	11	12	6	8	43
International bonds (secondary market)	70	na	na	na	na	na
Hedge-fund assets	21	66	2	1	nil	10

Source: www.mondaq.com

assets are bought, in the hope that the price will rise, or sold, in the expectation of a fall in price. If the price rises, those who purchased the asset can sell and make a profit. If the price falls, sellers can profit by buying the asset back at a lower price. The objects of speculation can be financial assets such as shares, bonds, or currencies, or physical assets such as land, property, or works of art. Crises occur when the speculation destabilizes the market causing prices to rise or fall dramatically.

Galbraith (1990) and Stiglitz (2002) examine how destabilizing speculative episodes, so-called bubbles, develop. When an asset is increasing in price it attracts new buyers who assume that prices will continue to rise. This boosts demand for the asset and its price goes up. With prices soaring, investors charge in to take advantage of the easy profits to be made. Speculative euphoria develops as market participants come to believe that the upward movement in prices will go on indefinitely. As the value of the asset rises, investors are able to use it as security to borrow money from the banks to buy more of the asset. However, inevitably, there comes a turning point, the causes of which are much debated, where some participants decide to withdraw from the market. The resulting fall in price sparks off panic in the market with investors rushing to off-load their assets leading to a market collapse. Stiglitz (2002) makes the point that the excessive optimism or euphoria generated by bubbles is often followed by periods of excessive pessimism. Financial crises are contagious domestically and internationally. For example, a banking crisis can make borrowing more difficult and costly for firms and consumers. This could cause them to reduce their demand for goods and services leading to spare capacity, bankruptcies, and increasing unemployment. In an increasingly interconnected world, a financial crisis in one country can very quickly spread to others as happened during the South East Asian crisis of the late 1990s and the credit crunch of 2007.

In summary, financial crises are characterized by:

- bouts of speculative activity, market euphoria, and rapidly rising prices;
- a turning point which leads to panic selling, excessive pessimism, and plummeting prices;
- contagion of domestic and foreign economies.

The account offered above gives a useful guide in understanding the financial crisis that started in Thailand in 1997 and then spread to other Asian countries (see Case Study at end of the Chapter). Thailand experienced a property and stock market bubble in the 1990s fuelled by huge amounts of speculative money flowing into the country from abroad. Land and property prices soared. Property developers, trying to cash in, rushed to put up new buildings. Banks lent more, reassured by the fact that the value of the property (the collateral) on which the loan was secured was rising.

The bubble burst when foreign and domestic investors started to withdraw funds from Thailand. As a consequence, the Thai currency, the baht, collapsed falling overnight by 25%. Thais who had borrowed abroad, and who had to pay back their loans in foreign currencies, found their interest payments soaring. Encouraged by the IMF, the Thai Government raised interest rates to attract foreign capital to help support the exchange rate. This made it even more difficult for domestic borrowers to pay back loans. Large numbers of highly indebted companies went bankrupt and unemployment soared. The crisis spread to Indonesia and South Korea, and, to a lesser extent, Hong Kong, Malaysia, and Laos. Stiglitz (2002) concludes that, 'these bubbles always burst and when they do, the economy crashes' (p 101).

The credit crunch of 2007/08 has similar characteristics to other financial crises. As in Thailand there was much speculative activity in the US property market. House prices were rising and financial institutions were happy to lend to borrowers with poor credit

Mini Case   Northern Rock—A Credit Crunch Casualty

Northern Rock, one of the biggest mortgage lenders in the UK, financed most its lending by borrowing from other financial institutions and relatively little from individual savers. In the summer of 2007, liquidity in credit markets started to dry up due to the sub-prime mortgage crisis in the USA. As a result,

Photograph: Alex Gunningham

Northern Rock found it increasingly difficult to raise money by selling its securitized or bundled mortgages to other financial institutions, or borrow on the money markets. Faced by its inability to raise money, it was forced to go cap in hand to the Bank of England. When this became public, worried depositors flocked to Northern Rock bank branches to withdraw their savings, in other words there was a 'run on the bank'. The value of Northern Rock shares plummeted. The Bank of England bailed out Northern Rock to the tune of £25 billion and the Government guaranteed the deposits of all the company's savers. After unsuccessfully trying to sell Northern Rock to a private buyer, the British Government took the company into public ownership. It was predicted that 3,000 Northern Rock employees would lose their jobs. The case raised questions about the failure of the regulatory system to address the issue of bank liquidity and about the lack of coordination between the three responsible bodies, the Bank of England, the Financial Services Authority, and the Treasury.

Sources: *The Observer*, 16 September 2007; www.Telegraph.co.uk 23 January 2008: www.Ft.com 17 and 20 February 2008

histories. But lenders did not keep these sub-prime mortgages on their books. On the strength of the future income streams from the loans, they borrowed more money by issuing bonds which they sold to other financial institutions in the USA and abroad. This process is called securitization. However, the bonds were based not simply on the high-risk mortgages but were bundled up with other financial products of varying risk.

Like any other security, the bonds were used as collateral by their buyers to raise loans. However, when US interest rates rose and house prices fell, many borrowers defaulted. The value of the securities plunged and market euphoria evaporated as hedge funds and banks faced up to huge losses. Because mortgages had been sold in combination with other products, no one could be quite sure about the distribution of risk. As a result, a crisis of liquidity arose as banks became unwilling to lend to each other because they were unable to assess which banks were carrying most risk. The crisis spread very rapidly across markets and continents. Hedge funds went bankrupt, banks wrote off huge amounts of assets and central banks had to pump in billions of dollars of liquidity to prevent the credit system from seizing up completely. Banks were taken into public ownership in the USA, UK, the Netherlands, France, Iceland and Portugal. The Icelandic economy went into meltdown with its government forced to go cup in hand to the IMF (see case study at end of Chapter Four).

Financial Regulation

Regulation plays an important role at both a domestic and an international level. It is a big element in the financial sector's external environment because of the effect it can have on their sales turnover, costs, and profits.

Effective regulation is also important for non-financial firms. Businesses and individuals dealing with financial institutions have an interest in those institutions being effectively regulated and supervised. Regulation can avoid hiccups in payments systems, protect customers against financial fraud, ensure financial institutions are prudent in weighing up risks and that they have enough cash and other liquid assets on hand so that they do not go bankrupt when things go wrong. The Bank of England has estimated that a full-blown banking crisis costs the country concerned an average of 16% of GDP. Many countries have experienced such crises, including Sweden, Turkey, the Czech Republic, Argentina, South Korea, Indonesia, Russia, and Japan (*The Economist*, 19 May 2005).

So regulation is necessary, not simply to protect the interest of customers, but also to ensure the stability of the whole financial system. Evidence also shows that effective regulation can have a positive effect on a country's economic income and output, which could be good news for business seeking expanding markets (Levine, Loayza and Beck 2000; OECD 2006).

Different Systems of Regulation

Regulatory systems can vary quite considerably from one country to another. The authorities face a number of dilemmas regarding regulation. Tight regulation could

Mini Case The Need for Regulation

Long Term Capital Management (LTCM), a New York hedge fund, had been spectacularly successful from 1994 to early 1998 generating annual returns of around 40%. By early 1998 LTCM had built up capital of US$4.8 billion, had a borrowing facility of US$200 billion and held derivatives with a notional value of US$1250 billion. Investors included both big private financial institutions from around the world and the central banks of Italy and Japan. US law allowed LTCM to operate without any regulatory supervision.

LTCM used financial theory and powerful mathematical models to identify US, European, and Japanese government bonds whose interest rates were higher or lower than their normal historical patterns. LCTM made the crucial assumption that the interest rates would revert to normal. In other words, it was betting that history would repeat itself as far as interest rates patterns were concerned.

In August of 1998, the Russian Government defaulted on its debt, financial markets were destabilized and the historical regularities that LTCM depended upon failed to hold. It lost US$4.6 billion in four months. Although it had no regulatory control of LTCM, the Federal Reserve stepped in to sponsor a bail-out of LTCM by its creditor banks. The Federal Reserve intervened to prevent the LTCM failure from precipitating a financial crisis. The creditor banks were prepared to help in the rescue, not only because they were worried about the security of their loans, but also because they could have lost even more were the LTCM difficulties to cause an international financial crisis. LTCM did survive this crisis but went into liquidation in 2000.

Source: *Le Monde Diplomatique*, November 1998; www.sjsu.edu

reduce the attractiveness of their financial centres, while too little regulation could frighten customers away.

At one extreme is a State-owned banking system in which banks are an arm of government and are never allowed to go bust; at the other is a lightly regulated system of private banks without an explicit safety-net in which bank failures are common. Either extreme faces certain dangers. Banking systems, where no bank can be allowed to fail, and depositors face no risk of loss, may breed management and depositor recklessness. At the other extreme, systems which rely only on market discipline run the risk of unnecessary bank and possibly, systemic failure and great loss to depositors.

In many countries, the State has a major presence in the financial sector. State intervention plays an important role in both the developing and the developed world, taking various forms of intervention from explicit intervention in the banking system in China and Germany to implicit government-sponsored enterprises in the USA. Intervention is particularly prevalent in banking, where public sector banks still account for an estimated 40% of total banking sector assets. A large swathe of the German, French, and Austrian banks is publicly owned while the banking system is in private hands in many countries, including Canada, Japan, New Zealand, the UK, and the USA, at least they were up to the financial meltdown in 2008. Up to 1991 Indian banks were nationalized, and used as a source of finance for public sector spending and investment by big companies. Liberalization has since taken place only very slowly but India, like Italy, continues to restrict foreign ownership. State intervention can also extend to insurance schemes and pension funds, but generally these are subject to less systematic regulation than the banks (*The Economist*, 19 October 2006; IMF Survey, Vol 33, No 10, 31 May 2004).

In the Eurozone, the European Central Bank carries out a supervisory function in cooperation with the national central banks and regulatory bodies. The UK has a tradition of 'light-touch' regulation and the regulatory and supervisory structure is much simpler, the functions being shared between the Financial Services Authority (FSA) and the Bank of England. Some developing countries do have regulators but, as in the case of India, often seem to find it difficult to strike an appropriate balance between regulating the sector effectively and providing a good enabling environment for financial sector development.

New Products and Internationalization—The Regulatory Challenge

Financial markets are being transformed by a remarkable wave of cross-border growth and innovation in the form of new products such as derivatives. National regulatory systems find it difficult on their own to keep pace with these developments. To address these challenges and to promote financial stability, more cooperation and coordination among supervisors is needed.

Some progress has been made on international supervisory cooperation and on the harmonization of regulatory standards. The Basel Committee on Banking Supervision comprising regulators from the major industrialized countries, sets minimum standards for the supervisory responsibilities and powers of home and host countries. The Basel Accord of 1988 set a minimum of 8% ratio of capital to assets, with banks expected to observe this ratio by the end of 1992.

The subsequent Basel II Framework accord came out in 2004 and is slowly being implemented worldwide. The implementation process varies from one country to another however. Basel II was, in part, a response to the grave financial crisis in East Asia in the second half of the 1990s. Basel II replaced the capital rules of 1988 and aimed to strengthen the stability of the international financial system. It tried to ensure that banks and other financial institutions had sufficient capital to meet their commitments and to encourage them to improve their approach to risk management. The capital requirements have been made more flexible, and are more closely aligned to the risks associated with different areas of business. It was hoped that the new framework would remedy the failings of the 1988 capital adequacy rules that were being frequently circumvented by clever financial innovators. Basel II also recommended that financial institutions operate transparently with regard to disclosure of information with respect to financial status and to the internal risk management procedures (Basel Committee 1998).

Actual implementation of the Accord was expected by 2008 in many of the over 100 countries currently using the Basel I accord. However, by the end of 2006, US regulators had still not agreed on their approach to the framework. The Financial Stability Institute, part of the BIS, found in a 2006 survey of 115 countries not in membership of the Basel Committee that 95 were planning to implement Basel II (www.bis.org/).

Despite the increased cross-border cooperation and coordination among regulators and the Basel II framework, fears remain about the ability of the international financial system to sustain shocks, such as a stockmarket crash, a foreign-exchange crisis, or the failure of one or more of the big financial conglomerates. The framework depends on financial institutions assessing their own levels of risk and this, according to some commentators, is similar to having no regulation at all (Ward 2002). Observers, such as Eatwell (*The Observer*, 9 June 2002) see the increased transparency of information as a possible destabilizing influence on the financial system. His view is that, formerly, there was a diversity of information which called forth different reactions so that behaviour of one institution might be offset by that of another and the result would be to stabilize the market. Now transparency means that the same information will be available at the same time to all market participants. They are likely to react in the same way thereby pushing the market even further in a certain direction or as Eatwell puts it they will, 'act as a herd, charging toward the cliff edge together' (*The Observer*, 9 June 2002). If true this could deepen the troughs and heighten the peaks of the cycle in economic growth.

The tendency of financial institutions towards conglomeracy and the increasing cross-border integration of the sector could mean that a shock in one part of the sector, or of the

Learning Task

The Japanese financial system is regulated by the Financial Services Agency (FSA). The Securities and Exchange Surveillance Commission (SESC) is the watchdog responsible for ensuring that the securities markets operate in a fair, equitable, transparent manner. It can recommend that the FSA impose fines on firms who break the rules.

In 2006, an SESC investigation found that Daiwa Securities, Japan's second largest securities firm, had breached insider trading rules. Insider trading refers to the buying or selling of a security based on information that is not available to the general public. In many countries such trading is illegal.

Now examine Table 9.5 below and answer the questions.

1. Why do you think that insider trading has been made illegal in many countries?

2. Look at the table of complaints filed by the SESC. Does insider trading seem to be a growing problem in Japan compared to other misdemeanours?

3. Why might firms be concerned about the spreading of false information or rumours about them on the stock exchange?

Table 9.5 Number of Complaints filed by the SESC

Category	SESC Year 1992–1999	SESC Year 2000	SESC Year 2001	SESC Year 2002	SESC Year 2003	SESC Year 2004	Total
Total	31	5	7	10	10	11	74
Submission of securities reports containing false information, etc.	6	1	3	3	2	2	17
Spreading of rumours, etc.	4	1	0	2	0	1	8
Market manipulation	3	1	1	0	2	2	9
Insider trading	11	2	3	5	6	6	33
Compensation for losses	7	0	0	0	0	0	7

Source: www.fsa.go.jp

world, could very quickly spread and turn into a big threat to the system as a whole, as was the case with the credit crunch of 2007. Furthermore, regulatory systems in some countries remain very loose (see OECD 2006). There is also a danger that some regulators have been captured by the financial institutions they are supposed to regulate. This is reflected in their willingness to take on trust what the financial institutions tell them rather than subjecting them to intensive scrutiny. Furthermore, any number of areas lack any real regulation to speak of—the British Virgin Islands and the Cayman Islands being two examples. But it is not just small obscure islands that are involved. The big international financial markets, London, New York, and Tokyo all have a thriving offshore business operating safely away from the eyes of the regulator (www.bbc.co.uk). A final issue is that regulation is not applied uniformly across the range of financial products, for some financial products are tightly regulated whilst others face hardly any regulation at all.

CHAPTER SUMMARY

In this chapter we have examined the importance of the financial environment for business, whether that be in the provision of money and credit, the operation of systems of payment, or providing protection against risk by the financial sector or the impact of monetary phenomena such as inflation, interest rates, or exchange rates. We have also seen how the big financial institutions and the increasingly integrated financial markets of London, New York, and Tokyo are vital for the effective functioning of business and the economies in which it operates.

In the advanced economies business has relatively easy access to finance through a variety of financial institutions offering a wide range of financial products. As we have seen, access to finance in developing countries is much more difficult making it harder for businesses to start up and grow.

The financial sector has grown rapidly in terms of output and employment and has become highly internationalized. The industry has come to be dominated by a small number of very large and diversified companies operating across the globe. These big financial institutions have become very powerful actors on the world stage.

Because of their size, the extent of their diversification and internationalization, and their ability to invent new financial products, they continue to pose great challenges to the regulatory authorities. The regulation of the financial sector is fragmented within and between different countries and can vary considerably from one State to another. Financial crises occur regularly in the system, affecting not only the country where they started but moving at terrifying speed across continents and markets. This combination means the stability of the international finance system cannot be taken for granted.

REVIEW QUESTIONS

1. Discuss why money is important for business.
2. Why is it vital for business to have confidence in the international payments system?
3. Explain the increasing internationalization of the banking system. What factors have made it easier for banks to internationalize their operations?

4. Why do financial institutions like to cluster in places like London given the obvious disadvantages of traffic congestion, overcrowded and unreliable public transport, and high office prices by international standards? (A useful source of information is the Global Financial Centres Index produced by the City of London and available on its web site.)

5. The BIS and the IMF have become increasingly concerned about a bubble developing in housing markets around the world. In its 2006 Annual Report, the BIS stated that lending on property represented a rapidly growing component of banks' business and profits outpacing that of corporate or consumer lending in many countries.

   Look at the graph below. How have house prices changed on the Continent? Which countries have been most/least affected by the housing bubble?

Figure 9.3 Real House Prices 1992–2005

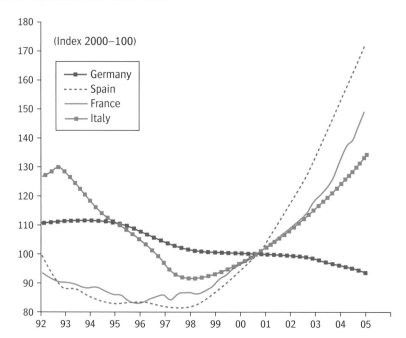

Source: BIS 2006

In the April 2008 issue of its World Economic Outlook, the IMF showed that there had been a major fall in house prices. Despite these falls, the IMF claimed that houses were still over-priced in several countries.

Now go to the IMF web site to find out where houses were most over-priced.

Analyse the implications for financial institutions in these countries were house prices to fall significantly.

6. In the chapter it was stated that one of the motives for the restructuring of the banking sector had been to cut costs. Do the figures in Table 9.6 below indicate that the banks have been successful in reducing costs? Which banks seem to have been particularly effective at cutting costs?

Table 9.6 Operating Costs of Major Banks (as a percentage of total average assets)

	2003	2004	2005
United States (12)	3.77	3.75	3.32
Canada (5)	3.26	2.93	3.00
Japan[2] (15)	2.14	1.59	1.42
Australia (4)	2.39	2.18	2.08
United Kingdom[3] (9)	2.62	2.25	1.80
Switzerland[3,4] (5)	2.78	2.46	2.39
Sweden[3] (4)	1.63	1.40	1.05
Austria[3] (3)	2.58	2.41	2.09
Germany[3,4] (9)	1.58	1.48	1.25
France[3,4] (7)	2.07	1.80	1.36
Italy[3] (6)	2.99	2.65	1.99
Netherlands[3,4] (4)	2.12	1.56	1.35
Spain[3,4] (5)	3.17	2.49	2.17

[1] The figures in parentheses indicate the number of banks included. [2] For 2005, annualized ratios based on bank reports for the first half-year. [3] 2005 figures are based on IFRS. [4] Preliminary data for 2005.
Source: BIS 2006

7. Now examine Table 9.7 below and compare it with the table in the previous question. Do the most profitable banks have the lowest costs? Give some explanations for your answer.

Table 9.7 Profitability of Major Banks[1] (as a percentage of total average assets)

	Pre-tax profits		
	2003	2004	2005
United States (12)	2.20	1.81	2.06
Canada (5)	1.08	1.23	1.01
Japan[2] (15)	0.11	0.26	0.84
Australia (4)	1.63	1.48	1.76
United Kingdom[3] (9)	1.24	1.16	0.99
Switzerland[3,4] (5)	0.42	0.67	0.67
Sweden[3] (4)	0.87	1.04	0.91
Austria[3] (3)	0.61	0.78	0.85
Germany[3,4] (9)	0.04	0.17	0.41
France[3,4] (7)	0.68	0.80	0.70
Italy[3] (6)	0.80	0.87	1.07
Netherlands[3,4] (4)	0.69	0.51	0.60
Spain[3,4] (5)	1.61	1.37	1.46

[1] The figures in parentheses indicate the number of banks included. [2] For 2005, annualized ratios based on bank reports for the first half-year. [3] 2005 figures are based on IFRS. [4] Preliminary data for 2005.
Source: BIS 2006

8. China has become a major attraction to Western financial institutions, as can be seen from the table.

   a) Discuss the economic reasons for Western financial institutions taking a stake in Chinese banks.

   b) Why do you think the stakes, with the exception of the Citigroup consortium, are generally small?

Table 9.8 Stakes in Chinese Banks

Purchaser	Target	Date	Stake %
Citigroup-led consortium	Guandong Development Bank	Nov 2006	85
BBVA	Citic Bank	Nov 2006	5
BBVA	Citic International	Nov 2006	15
Allianz	Industrial & Commercial Bank	Jan 2006	2.3
American Express	Industrial & Commercial Bank	Jan 2006	0.5
Bank of America	China Construction Bank	Jun 2005	8.5
Goldman Sachs	Industrial & Commercial Bank	Jan 2006	5.8
HSBC	Bank of Communications	Aug 2004	19.9
Merrill Lynch	Bank of China	Aug 2005	0.7
RBS	Bank of China	Aug 2005	4.3
UBS	Bank of China	Sep 2005	1.3

Source: *Financial Times*, 10 November 2006; 23 November 2006

Case Study The East Asian Financial Crisis

This case shows the costs of financial instability can be significant both from the point of view of business and of society more generally. The typical financial crisis claims around 9% of GDP, and the worst crises, can reduce income and output by more than a fifth. The case study below looks at the crisis in South East Asia in the second half of the 1990s.

Origins of the Crisis

The crisis erupted in 1997 and occurred against the backdrop of several decades of outstanding economic performance in Asia. In the early 90s, countries such as Thailand, Malaysia, South Korea, and Indonesia had experienced annual growth rates of GDP of more than 7%. As a consequence, they became known as the Tiger economies. There were significant inflows of capital from investors in rich countries, attracted to the area by high rates of return. Investors were further attracted by the fact that

some of these countries had pegged their currencies against the US dollar, thereby reducing the risk of loss through a depreciation of the currency.

The crisis was caused by a combination of macroeconomic problems, such as unsustainable balance of payments deficits, and overvalued and relatively fixed exchange rates. Other factors were inadequate supervision of the financial sector by the authorities, and weak financial institutions making poor lending decisions that permitted investment of inflows of capital in low quality projects such as speculative property development, also contributed to the crisis.

The crisis started with a series of attacks by speculators on the Thai currency, the baht. As the value of the baht fell, it spread rapidly to other economies in the region that seemed vulnerable to an erosion of competitiveness after the devaluation of the baht—or were perceived by investors to have similar financial or macroeconomic problems. As the contagion ➔

→ spread to Korea, the world's eleventh largest economy, the possibility of a default on its international debts raised a potential threat to the international monetary system. These events led to a financial panic with foreign creditors, concerned that Asian countries would be unable to meet their debts, trying frantically to withdraw their money.

The crisis threatened these countries' financial systems, caused large contractions in their GDP—in 1998 the Indonesian and Thai economies contracted by around 14% and 9% respectively. The Thai and South Korean exchange rates slumped by more than 20%. The crisis also caused much human suffering. It has been estimated the Asian crisis increased the incidence of poverty in the region by 22 million people. In South Korea alone, the total number of poor rose from six million in 1997 to more than ten million in 1998 and there was a significant increase in crime, divorce, drug addiction, and suicide. In addition to its severe effects in Asia, the crisis put pressure on emerging markets outside the region and shook up international financial markets.

Fearful of the threat to the stability of the international financial system, the International Monetary Fund, in cooperation with the World Bank and Asian Development Bank, stepped in to arrange support packages for Thailand, Indonesia, and South Korea, and extended a credit to the Philippines to support its exchange rate and other economic policies. The support package for Thailand was US$17.2 billion, for Indonesia about US$40 billion, and for South Korea US$57 billion. By 2000 the crisis appeared to have subsided, with the East Asian economies starting once again to expand.

Sources: CRS Report The 1997–98 Asian Financial Crisis. Available at www.fas.org; IMF; Eichengreen 1998

Questions

1. What were the major causes of the East Asian financial crisis?

2. Discuss the economic impact of the crisis in East Asian countries.

3. What possible connection could there be between the economic impact and the social effects of the crisis?

4. Why was the financial crisis of great concern to rich countries?

5. What was the response of the international community?

6. Did the response appear to be effective?

Online Resource Centre

www.oxfordtextbooks.co.uk/orc/hamilton_webster/

Visit the supporting online resource centre for additional material which will help you with your assignments, essays and research, or you may find these extra resources helpful when revising for exams.

● FURTHER READING

For more on the international monetary system see:

● World Economic Forum (2007) *The International Monetary System, the IMF and the G20: A Great Transformation in the Making?*. London: Palgrave Macmillan

For an analysis of financial crises refer to:

● Caprio, G., Hanson, J. A. and Litan, R. E. (eds) (2005) *Financial Crises: Lessons from the Past, Preparation for the Future*. Washington DC: The Brookings Institution

For a critical examination of policies pursued by the IMF and the World Bank:

● Stiglitz, J. E. (2002) *Globalization and its Discontents*. London: Penguin

● REFERENCES

Basel Committee (1998) Enhancing Bank Transparency. September

BIS (2006) 76th Annual Report. 26 June

BIS (2007) BIS Quarterly Review, December

BIS, CPSS (2003) Red Book

Beck, S. and Ogden, T. (2007) 'Beware of Bad Microcredit'. *Harvard Business Review*, Vol 85, Issue 9, September

Burk, K. (1992) *Good-bye Great Britain: 1976 IMF Crisis*. Yale: Yale University Press

Chossudovsky, M. (1998) *The Globalisation of Poverty: Impacts of the IMF and World Bank Reforms*. Zed Books: London

DFID (2004) 'The Importance of Financial Sector Development for Growth and Poverty Reduction'. Policy Division Working paper. Available at www.dfid.gov.uk

Eichengreen, B. (1998) *Globalizing Capital: A History of the International Monetary System*, 2nd edn. Chichester: Princeton University Press

Galbraith, J. K. (1990) *A Short History of Financial Euphoria*. London: Pelican

Johnson, H. J. (2000) *Global Financial Institutions and Markets*. Oxford: Blackwell

Leonard, T. M. (2006) *Encyclopaedia of the Developing World*. London: Taylor & Francis

Levine, R., Loayza, N. and Beck, T. (2000) 'Financial Intermediation and Growth: Causality and Causes'. *Journal of Monetary Economics*, Vol 46, Issue 1, August

Martin, R. (1994) 'Stateless Monies, Global Financial Integration and National Economic Autonomy: the End of Geography' in Stuart Corbridge *et al.* (eds) (1994) *Money, Power and Space*. Oxford: Blackwell

McGuire, P. and Tarashev, N. (2006) Tracking international bank flows. BIS Quarterly Review, December

OECD (2006) Regulation of Financial Systems and Economic Growth, Working Paper 34

Porter, T. (2005) *Globalization and Finance*. Cambridge: Polity

Sengupta, R. and Aubuchon, C. P. (2008) 'The Microfinance Revolution: An Overview'. Federal Reserve Bank of St. Louis Review. 90(1), January/February

Stiglitz, J. E. (2002) *Globalization and its Discontents*. London: Penguin

Ward, J. R. (2002) 'The supervisory approach: a critique'. CERF Working Paper No 2, June. Available at www.cerf.cam.ac.uk

CHAPTER TEN

The Ecological Environment

Dorron Otter

LEARNING OUTCOMES

This chapter will enable you to:

- **Explain the ecological impacts of business activity**

- **Describe the range of global initiatives designed to address ecological problems**

- **Engage in the debates as to the role of business in causing, preventing, and helping to cure ecological damage**

- **Analyse the problems posed by global climate change**

- **Evaluate the range of policy responses to global climate change**

Case Study The Gaia Hypothesis

James Lovelock published 'The Gaia Hypothesis' in 1972. Lovelock is an independent scientist with a background in both chemistry and medicine and is best described as a geo-physiologist or 'planetary physician'.

Source: www.istockphoto.com

For Lovelock the bio-sphere, or the relatively thin layer of land and water between the molten interior of the Earth and the exterior upper atmosphere supports all life. The Earth can be seen as a single system which is self-regulating. This system ensures that interactions and feedbacks between all the physical, chemical, biological and human components of the Earth make life on the planet possible. To this Lovelock ascribed the name 'Gaia' (after a Greek Goddess) as a metaphor for the Earth as a living system. However, Gaia is now under threat as a result of a rise in the levels of carbon dioxide in the atmosphere. It is these levels that control the temperature of the Earth (Lovelock 1979). In the past 'Gaia' has been able to ensure that life on Earth was not only possible but was also comfortable, however, Lovelock now argues that there is clear scientific evidence that we are approaching 'the tipping point' at which levels of carbon dioxide (CO_2) will not only lead to rises in global warming and the severe consequences for human life that these will entail but also that once this tipping point is reached the feedback mechanisms that have led to rises in these temperatures will lead to even faster increases.

In his most recent exposition of his ideas 'The Revenge of Gaia' Lovelock writes: 'We are now approaching one of these tipping points and our future is like that of the passengers on a small pleasure boat sailing quietly above the Niagara falls, not knowing that the engines are about to fail' (Lovelock 2007).

Introduction

The relationship between business and the ecological environment has become enormously important especially because of the widely acknowledged impact of climate change.

This chapter will examine the nature of this relationship and the debates as to the responsibility of business both in terms of its contribution to global ecological problems and the possible responses to dealing with these challenges.

Put simply: Is business activity the source of the problem or to what extent will business responses help us to solve the global ecological problems of the 21st century?

The Ecological Problem

It is simple to outline the basic ecological problem. We need to extract the resources that we need for production from the ecological environment. If we exploit the sources of these materials without replacing what we have taken then we face a long term problem of resource depletion. Not all resources can be replaced especially the fossil fuels on which so much of the world's energy supplies currently depend. It is also clear that the nature of much of our productive processes results in pollution or other forms of ecological damage. Nature itself can provide ways of neutralizing these harmful by-products in the form of 'sinks' such as the oceans and plants that can absorb the pollutants. As we will see the debate provoked by attempts to quantify the 'state of the world' in terms of the rate of resource depletion and its effects on food supplies, water availability, and energy is hotly contested. This is the concept of the 'carrying capacity' of the planet.

The Economic Approach to Explaining the Ecological Problem

Economic analysis has been very influential in explaining why there is a conflict between our rational desire to increase our standard of living and our ability to increase our quality of life.

While free markets in theory bring about consumer satisfaction and profits for producers, there are dangers of market failure. In relation to the external ecological environment it may well be the case that while markets ensure that private benefits accrue to consumers and producers, there may well be social costs that are incurred. Social costs or negative externalities occur as the result of the production or consumption of goods and services but for which no individual or organization pays. They will therefore need to be identified and mechanisms devised to either reduce or eradicate them or at least allow them to be paid for.

The analysis of ecological problems as the negative externalities of market failure has become commonly accepted, but what is contested is where the responsibility for such externalities should fall, and the range of policy measures we should adopt to address these.

Mini Case Study The Cost of Driving

The simplest case of illustrating the external environmental problems of business activity is that of motor transport. Driving any form of motor vehicle produces a vast amount of pollutants damaging in many ways to the environment not least of which is the production of greenhouse gases. Drivers and their passengers or the customers for whom they are driving, derive enormous benefit from this activity and of course pay a lot for the activity. The cost of motoring is high. There are the initial costs of the vehicle itself and the substantial running costs including the high cost of the (fossil) fuels needed to power the vehicles, construct the roads, and the other support infrastructure required.

Of course these private costs are not the only costs. There is the substantial external environmental cost of driving. It is argued therefore that it is only fair that motorists sitting inside the relative comfort of their vehicles should pay for the external costs that they are imposing on society. This process of 'internalizing the externality' otherwise known as the 'polluter pays principle' is a key feature of the economic approach to tackling ecological problems. If we as individual motorists combine to collectively damage the environment then we should be expected to pay for this.

Perspectives on the Role of Business

Business activity is essentially the conversion of the resources of nature into goods and services to satisfy the needs, wants, and desires of human beings.

Human beings are constantly striving to both make the best of the limited resources that we have, as well as constantly trying to discover untapped resources, or improve the efficiency of how we use these limited resources. If it is the case that human beings constantly want to improve their standard of living we will need economic growth to increase the amount and range of goods and services available. But what happens if in the pursuit of such economic growth we are both exhausting the finite resources at our disposal as well as generating negative externalities in the form of pollution and other types of environmental damage?

Business plays a pivotal role in this generation of economic growth but also therefore in the creation of environmental problems. As producers they are the direct generators of a large proportion of negative externalities. Industries such as steel, cement, oil, power generation, chemicals, and transport are heavy polluters in a range of ways. There are competing perspectives about the nature of the external environment that will be most conducive to allowing businesses to contribute to this shared goal of boosting economic growth.

Views from the Right

For free market exponents it is the ability of private businesses to operate in markets free from government regulation that will drive economic progress.

As well as the natural resources that exist on 'Planet Earth' we have our own labour power and ingenuity. This ingenuity can take the form of invention or innovation which allow us to boost productivity and so increase the output of goods and services for any given input of resources. Technological progress is a major ingredient for economic prosperity as is entrepreneurial activity.

While the indirect cost of growth might be environmental damage there is a trade off to be made between this and growth in living standards. Indeed business itself can play a vital role in developing 'environmentally friendly' technologies—given the right incentives. Where this isn't realistic then the negative costs can be measured and businesses can be charged for the environmental damage according to the 'polluter pays principle'.

Views from the Left

There are however, many objections to this version of the secret for economic success.

Critics of business see them as being primarily interested in maximizing profits no matter what the environmental cost. If cutting costs and maximizing profit means treating the environment as a free 'sink' for pollution etc, then businesses will resist pressure to change their practices.

Businesses themselves have a vested interest in encouraging consumers to buy more and more and so are indirectly responsible for the rampant consumer societies that have been created. While it could be argued that businesses are simply responding to the wishes of consumers and therefore it is 'consumerism' that is to blame, it is the business in pursuit of profit that has every interest in fuelling consumer demand. Isn't the institution of marketing itself an indication that businesses thirst after increasing sales?

A major source of disquiet is the belief that the distribution of income and wealth that results from free markets is highly unequal. In this view of the world, the immediate problem facing the world is not that there is not enough to go around, but that the fruits of economic growth are enjoyed by the richer members of society whilst the poor lose out. The biggest global problem is the gap between the living standards of the 'Global North' as opposed to the 'Global South' and that those consumers in the former are responsible for far more global environmental damage than those in the latter.

Governments also need to ensure that businesses do not develop positions of monopoly power but all too often they struggle to enforce environmental control over the power of 'Big Business'.

Green Views

There have always been voices raised to challenge the view that economic growth represented human progress. Even at the beginning of the industrial revolution in Europe a range of people from poets to social activists and politicians were anxious about the costs of economic growth. These criticisms were often centred on what they saw as the destruction of the natural environment, as industrialization grew so rapidly, and also the effect on traditional ways of life as capitalist production techniques took hold. The dramatic success of the industrial revolution clearly had a severe impact on a range of environmental factors such as public health, pollution, and sanitation and it was clear that there was an urgent need for governments, both local and national, to clean up the mess that was often a by-product of economic growth.

In the 20th century it became accepted that business activity needed to be regulated in order to protect the natural environment, and that the government would have to take direct control over a range of environmental areas to deal with these externalities. We can trace the development of the modern 'green' movement to the latter half of the 20th century. 'The Silent Spring' by Rachel Carson, published in 1962, is often cited as being hugely important in the development of this new movement. A biologist, Carson became very concerned about the increasing use of pesticides in agriculture and their effects on human beings through links with cancers, and on wildlife—hence the emotive title of the book, looking into a future where bird song was not heard. Her books and articles had a huge influence on the grass roots environmental movement in the USA and resulted in the formation of the Environmental Protection Agency and the eventual ban of the pesticide, DDT (Dichloro-Diphenyl-Trichloroethane), in the USA. It also attracted a large volume of criticism from the chemical industry (Carson 1962). This theme of environmental claim and business counter-claim will be seen again in this chapter.

In 1968 Garrett Hardin sought to provide a clear critique of what he saw as an essential problem for the future of humanity. His essay, 'The Tragedy of the Commons' published in the journal *Science*, argued that when human beings have access to commonly owned

Learning Task

The following extracts refer to the proposal to build a new third runway at Heathrow Airport. Read these and consider the questions that follow

> 'Heathrow is the UK's only hub airport and one of Britain's most important economic assets. But today Heathrow is full, operating at 99% of permitted runway capacity and vulnerable to foreign competition. Without further growth, Heathrow will not be able to meet the demands of business and leisure travellers and the health of the UK economy will suffer' (www.heathrowairport.com).

It is not necessary

78% of businesses in London oppose it (London Chamber of Commerce Report 2006). There is no hard evidence to show that the UK economy will suffer if Heathrow doesn't expand.

It will contribute to climate change

Aviation already accounts for 13% of UK global warming emissions and is the fastest-growing contributor to climate change.

It will destroy communities

Thousands of people will be forced out of many communities, as expansion plans will require the demolition of schools, pubs, shops and at least 750 homes.

It will destroy people's quality of life

At least 150,000 people will be under the flight path to the new runway, most of them experiencing aircraft noise for the first time. And the prospect for people living under the existing flight paths is frightening: a plane every 90 seconds virtually throughout the day (www.stopheathrowexpansion.com).

1. What is the economic case for airport expansion in the case of Heathrow?
2. What is the case against such airport expansion?
3. Is the growth in air travel an example of success or is it a type of 'tragedy of the commons'?

resources which they do not have to pay for then we will each as an individual seek to get as much as we can from this shared resource but collectively the result of this action will be that we will all soon exhaust the resource and so all lose out (Hardin 1968).

The Limits to Growth focused on the key areas of population: food production, industrialization, pollution, and consumption of non-renewable resources (Meadows 1972).

Pestel provided an abstract of the report which concludes:

1. If the present growth trends in world population, industrialization, pollution, food production, and resource depletion continue unchanged, the limits to growth on this planet will be reached sometime within the next one hundred years. The most

probable result will be a rather sudden and uncontrollable decline in both population and industrial capacity.

2. It is possible to alter these growth trends and to establish a condition of ecological
and economic stability that is sustainable far into the future. The state of global equi-
librium could be designed so that the basic material needs of each person on earth
are satisfied and each person has an equal opportunity to realize his individual
human potential (Pestel 1972).

Other influential books include *The Costs of Economic Growth* (Mishan 1969) and *Small is
Beautiful* (Schumacher 1973). The former was one of the first economics books to outline
the costs of economic growth and the methods of cost-benefit analysis that are needed
when judging economic decisions and the latter's focus is clear in its subtitle: *Economics as
if People Mattered*.

Global Cooperation—Establishing Effective Environmental Regimes

Perhaps one of the most significant changes in the debates about the impact of business
on the ecological environment has been the growing recognition of the global nature of
environmental problems. While it is at the micro-level that individual acts of consumption and production can cause ecological damage it is the global aspects of the problem
that are now clearly under focus.

What is the point of one country or area having stringent environmental safeguards if
others do not, since ecological systems overlap? In other words environmental problems
are often 'trans-boundary'. Not only would such policies alone not be sufficient but they
would put businesses in such countries at a severe competitive disadvantage. In the field
of International Relations this is a recurrent theme, namely, how can international cooperation be achieved in a world of 'anarchy' or, in other words, one in which there is no
overall global authority to which all countries must obey.

There are a number of global commons issues that require international cooperation
if they are to be addressed. The following are examples that have been the focus of
attempts to develop a global response:

- Desertification
- Deforestation
- Loss of Bio-diversity
- Whaling
- Protection of fisheries and the marine environment
- Acid Rain
- Protection of the Ozone Layer
- Climate Change

For effective action to be undertaken it is important to devise a system of international
cooperation and this is referred to in international relations literature as a 'regime'. To

establish such regimes multilateral treaties are required and these may either be regulated through a committee of organization or through what is referred to as the convention/protocol process or a combination of both. The International Convention for the Regulation of Whaling makes annual schedules of catch regulations and the Convention on International Trade in Endangered Species of Wild Fauna and Flora regulates which species are to be controlled. In such regimes States do have the right to 'opt out'.

In the Convention/protocol process, initially States come together and agree an initial 'framework convention' to identify the problems and ways of dealing with these but which initially may not contain specific obligations. Once agreement is made for the convention this is then followed by a series of meetings at which 'protocols' are negotiated which then do require member states to sign up to specific actions. The Montreal Protocol (1987) was the first global agreement to phase out those chemicals held responsible for ozone depletion. The Kyoto Framework Convention (1997) was the first step in developing a regime to tackle climate change.

The pressures on the ecological environment are seen to be a global tragedy of the commons as a range of problems from global climate change, de-forestation, and decline of

Mini Case Ozone Depletion

Ozone in the upper atmosphere is important as it acts as a barrier to prevent ultraviolet radiation getting through to the earth. If there is a depletion of the ozone layer then this can lead to

Source: www.istockphoto.com

increases in skin cancers, immune disorders for humans, and other species as well as crop damage. In the 1970s it became clear that the release of CFCs into the atmosphere was indeed causing depletion of the ozone layer. CFCs were primarily used for refrigeration and air-conditioning and were also commonly found in aerosols and fire extinguishers.

What has been remarkable is the speed with which action was taken to curb the use of CFCs and other ozone depleting substances. Initially the industries involved in the manufacture of CFCs, such as DuPont, were resistant to changing their behaviour, arguing that it was not feasible to develop substitutes for CFCs. However, a combination of consumer pressure and US Government determination to take a lead in regulating against their use, once the scientific evidence became clear, was vital. At the global level the signing of the Montreal Protocol in 1987 established a very effective international regime for cooperation to phase out CFCs. Since customers would now be obliged to use substitutes to CFC producing goods even if these were more expensive and once it became clear that the market for these was now a global one there was a real incentive for the chemical companies such as DuPont and others to spend the required research and development funds in developing substitutes.

bio-diversity are all seen as being global in nature and therefore any individual responses to these challenges must be taken in the context of global cooperation and action. In 1972 the Stockholm conference was held to explore the causes of 'acid rain' and its effects on lakes and forests in Northern Europe and this led to the formation of the United Nations Environment Programme. The notion that pollution does not respect national borders was given direct expression when the radio-activity from the Chernobyl nuclear explosion in 1984 covered most of Western Europe and in the recognition of the effect of chloro-fluoro carbons (CFC) gasses on the ozone layer.

In *1987 Our Common Future*, a report from the United Nations World Commission on the Environment and Development (WCED) was published. This sought to build on the work of the Stockholm conference which also looked at environmental concerns more widely. The publication of *Our Common Future* and the work of the WCED led to the 1992 Conference at Rio de Janeiro and the adoption of Agenda 21, the Rio Declaration, and to the establishment of the Commission of Sustainable Development. As the focus of this book is on the international business environment it is these global dimensions of the ecological crisis that this chapter addresses.

The fact that States have the right to exert their own sovereignty over their own resources makes the process of environmental regime creation a complex and at times very slow process with conflicts between the interests of States and of course differences in their respective power and influence.

As well as the problems of establishing such global cooperation there are also specific problems that relate to the nature of environmental issues.

Risk and Uncertainty

The main obstacle when examining environmental problems is that often these problems are not immediately obvious.

Environmental policy requires people and organizations to change their behaviour in relation to resource use so that we recognize that the ecological environment is not a free good and that we are made fully aware of the social costs of environmental damage. For us as individuals, it is clear that across many parts of the world there has been an increase in environmental awareness and in areas such as re-cycling this has changed behaviour. However, a major barrier to effecting more widespread environmental improvements lies in our lack of knowledge of exactly what our ecological impact is and indeed the measures we should take to minimize this.

Environmental policies involve a 'trade-off' in that there is a conflict between short term production and the immediate gratification of consumption and longer term well-being. While people may well be more aware of the costs of motoring and air travel the predicted rises in the uses of these modes of transport shows that people are not prepared to alter their behaviour voluntarily.

For both consumers and producers the costs of adapting to ecological change may appear to be simply too great and the task for environmental policy lies both in how to deal with this resistance and in persuading us all that in fact the long term benefits of preventing ecological damage are greater than the costs of taking action now to minimize it.

The Role of Science

In order for these risks to be quantified, we do need careful research and analysis and this entails further problems. Such scientific surveys are often very complex and contradictory and most people lack the understanding to unravel the findings. Faced with this lack of understanding it is easy for people to simply ignore the debates and carry on as usual.

The Sceptical Environmentalists

There are a large number of environmental sceptics who question the supposed risky nature of many business activities. Often these sceptics arise from within the business community. Research shows that businesses can often expend large sums of money and time in funding groups to provide evidence that downplays the social costs of their activity and emphasizes the positive role of their activity. However, it is fair to say that not all such denials can be attributed to covert or overt political lobbying. Bjorn Lomborg in his book *The Skeptical Environmentalist*, argues that both the risks of global warming are overestimated and also that even where such risks can be proven, it is important for us

Mini Case The Business of Climate Denial

One of the clearest examples of business vested interests operating against the well being of society has been the historical actions of the tobacco companies. By denying the link between cigarette smoking and ill-health, suppressing the research that proved that link and through the PR campaigns that sought to prevent action against smoking, the long road to effective action against smoking was a protracted one.

For environmental activists there is clear evidence that many businesses are using similar tactics to protect their own commercial interests at the expense of the planet by their actions to promote their views concerning the denial of climate change and its effects. Big business is certainly keenly interested in the issue of climate change that we will explore later in the chapter. They lobby hard with strong business representation at both the signing of the Kyoto Protocol meeting in 1997 and at the Bali meetings in 2007 which sought to further strengthen the framework laid down at Kyoto.

Melanie Jarman highlights the role of one of the strongest industry sponsored lobby groups. The Global Climate Coalition was supported by a range of US oil and manufacturing companies and the PR company Burson-Marsteller (Jarman 2007).

This group funded scientists who denied either the existence of climate change or sought to deny that it was caused by anthropogenic activity. While this group was formally wound up in 2001 it is argued by many that similar work still goes on through the actions of many big companies. Foremost amongst these is ExxonMobil the US oil company known in the UK as Esso.

In 2006 the *Guardian* reported that the Royal Society had written a letter to Exxon-Mobil urging it to stop funding climate denial through organizations such as the International Policy Network in London and the George C Marshall Institute in the USA (Adam 2006). ExxonMobil for its part denies that this is what it is doing and instead adopts a cautious approach which accepts that the climate is warming and CO_2 emissions are rising and that fossil fuels are one source of these emissions (see www.exxonmobil.com).

George Monbiot, an environmental writer and campaigner writes more fully about the activities of such groups and he describes this as 'The Denial Industry'. He reveals the efforts that have gone into persuading people and policy makers through industry funding that global warming is either not a reality or even if it is that it is not serious or primarily an anthropocentric effect (Monbiot 2007, Ch 2).

Learning Task

1. How aware are you about the science behind the debate about global warming?

2. What changes have you made, if any, to minimize your own 'ecological footprint'?

3. Have a go at measuring your own ecological footprint (see, for example, www.footprint.wwf.org.uk). What reaction do you have to such a footprint exercise?

not to prevent the present generations from reaping the fruits of economic growth for the uncertain prediction that unspecified groups in the future might suffer as a result of environmental damage (Lomborg 2001).

The Contemporary Ecological Debate

In the 21st century it is clear that ecological concerns have now entered the mainstream of debates about the impact of business activity on its external environment. At the forefront of these has been the publication of the Stern Review commissioned by the British Government in 2006 which has tried to compare the costs of taking no action to combat climate change with the costs of taking action now, and the 4th impact assessment report of the Intergovernmental Panel for Climate Change (IPCC) which brought together scientific opinion across the world about the likely impacts of climate change.

The film *An Inconvenient Truth* presented by the former Vice President of the USA, and then presidential candidate in the 1998 election, Al Gore, has been a best seller and as a result of its impact and the work of the IPCC secured them a shared Nobel Peace prize. That this was the recipient of the Nobel Peace prize spoke volumes for the way in which people have come to accept the challenge of global warming. It is argued that the main impact of this will be on the poor countries in the 'Global South' and that depletion of resources and population movements will in turn increase the prospect of conflict over resources. The research, conducted on behalf of organizations as diverse as the Pentagon in the USA and the European Commission, agrees that there is an increased likelihood of political upheavals (Traynor 2008).

In 2007 the economist Jeffrey Sachs was chosen to deliver the BBC's annual Reith Lectures and he chose to highlight the problem of global warming. For Sachs we are living in the 'age of the anthropocene' a notion developed by the atmospheric chemist Paul Crutzen who won a Nobel Prize for his work on the hole in the ozone layer. For Crutzen our current age is marked by the undoubted impact that human beings have had on the ecological environment. The title of Sachs' first lecture was 'Bursting at the Seams':

> for the first time in history the physical systems of the planet, chemical fluxes, the climate, habitats, bio-diversity, evolutionary processes, are to an incredible and unrecognized extent under human forcings that now dominate a large measure of the most human central ecological, chemical and biophysical processes on the planet (Sachs 2007).

Mini Case Plan A or Plan B?

Marks and Spencer is a business with a reputation as being one of the foremost in terms of both recognizing and seeking to minimize its ecological impacts across its range of operations.

Launched in 2007, its Plan A maps out a five year programme with clear targets. The following is an extract from the web site that monitors the progress of this plan:

> Plan A is our five-year, 100-point 'eco' plan to tackle some of the biggest challenges facing our business and our world. It will see us working with our customers and our suppliers to combat climate change, reduce waste, safeguard natural resources, trade ethically and build a healthier nation.
>
> We're doing this because it's what you want us to do. It's also the right thing to do. We're calling it Plan A because we believe it's now the only way to do business.
>
> There is no Plan B.

(www.marksandspencer.com)

Marks and Spencer aim to support this plan with what they call the five pillars of: Climate Change, Waste, Sustainable Raw Materials, Health, and being a Fair Partner.

Each pillar has its own goal, and the aim is that by 2012 Marks and Spencer will:

- Become carbon neutral
- Send no waste to landfill
- Extend sustainable sourcing
- Help improve the lives of people in our supply chain
- Help customers and employees live a healthier life-style

For many environmental activists there is a feeling that businesses at best pay lip service to the changes that are needed if they were to become genuinely 'green'. Indeed there does exist amongst many such activists the view that, where ➔

Source: www.mandslibrary.co.uk

→ commitments to be green are made, they are done in a cynical attempt to gain market advantage and (as such) it is not a 'greening' of business but an attempt to 'greenwash' their brand images.

Even where such cynicism does not exist environmentalists such as Lester Brown argue that in order for real change to occur it is not businesses alone that can effect such change. Since 1974, when he founded the Worldwatch Institute, Brown has been an influential figure in the world environment movement and the research from this institute has done much to bring to people's attention the range of environmental problems. In 2001 Brown established the Earth Policy Institute to act as a more direct campaigning organization (also) which translates research into policy proposals. For Brown there has to be an alternative to what he terms 'Plan A' (not related to the Plan A of M and S) or the belief that despite this range of problems there is no alternative than to follow the 'Business as Usual' model (Brown 2008) (see www.worldwatch.org or www.earth-policy.org).

The latest version of this is Plan B 3.0, and in this Brown both charts what he sees as the fundamental challenges facing us, as well as the policies that need to be developed to combat these. We will explore some of these policies later in the chapter.

The central question that needs to be posed is the extent to which the response of businesses is such as to fully address the ecological challenges.

Learning Task

- In what ways do businesses potentially have a negative impact on the ecological environment?
- To what extent do you think that strategies such as Marks and Spencer's Plan A are an adequate response by business to the ecological challenge?
- In what sense do ecological problems represent a 'global tragedy of the commons'?

The Notion of Sustainable Development

At the heart of the debate about the nature of the ecological environment lies the concept of sustainable development. The commonly accepted definition of this was outlined in the Brundtland Report (1987): 'Sustainable Development is development that meets the needs of the present without compromising the ability of future generations to meet their own needs'.

This statement is the one that is most commonly quoted and clearly shows the commitment that is made here to ensuring intra-generational equity. However, what is often left out is the full version which goes on to say:

> it contains within it two key concepts: the concept of 'needs', in particular the essential needs of the world's poor, to which overriding priority should be given; and the idea of limitations imposed by the state of technology and social organization on the environment's ability to meet present and future needs (WCED 1987, 43).

This second statement directly argues that growth is needed if it is to help the poor and that as important is 'inter-generational' equity or the need to ensure that people living today are able to benefit from growth.

While this has become the widely accepted definition of sustainability there is still wide disagreement as to the implications of this statement.

How exactly do we define the 'needs of the present'? President George W Bush made it clear that he would not take any environmental action if it was against the 'economic interests' of the USA. In the UK, the then Director General of the Confederation of Business Industry, Digby Jones, criticized the government for 'risking the sacrifice of UK jobs on the altar of green credentials' (Jarman 2007).

Radical critics argue that development is as much about enabling the benefits of growth to be more widely shared today as it is about re-thinking our attitudes to growth. The environmental sceptics too are able to claim that our priority has to be about ensuring that growth does indeed meet the needs of the present without being alarmist about possible future environmental effects. Indeed the world of the future may well bring technological developments that mean we can tackle or prevent these future problems without compromising today's levels of growth. The following is illustrative of such a view:

> those who are so urgent about not inflicting poverty on the future have to explain why they do not attach even higher priority to reducing poverty today (Solow in Rao 2000, p 86).

The 1992 Earth Summit was pivotal in that it formulated Agenda 21, a comprehensive programme to be adopted globally, nationally, and locally to promote sustainable development in the 21st century. The Rio declaration outlined 27 key principles concerning the actions that States should take in order to safeguard the environment and these were adopted by the 178 countries that took part in the Earth Summit.

The Rio Declaration was a firm environmental call to action and was supplemented by the proposals embedded into Agenda 21 and re-affirmed at the 2002 Johannesburg summit (see www.un.org for the full text of this) and together they lay down a comprehensive programme for environmental policy at the global level.

Agents for Change—The Global Responsibility of Citizens, Business, and Governments

If development and growth are to be sustainable then it is clear that there will need to be changes in the ways in which we use resources. A major source of pressure for such change has been the activity of a range of environmental non-governmental organizations which have sought to bring pressure on us as consumers, on business, and on the framework of governance that needs to be developed both at the national and international level.

At the heart of 'green thinking' is the belief that we need to move away from an anthropocentric view of the world which sees human beings as the driving force of nature and the sole beneficiaries of the resources that are there to be exploited to an eco-centric view of the world that recognizes our interdependence on nature. Whilst there is an enormous range of opinion within the green movement there is this common agreement that our lives would be improved by not abusing nature but by recognizing that we need to alter the prevailing economic model of growth which simply seeks to boost Gross National Product with no accounting for the environmental costs of such growth.

In relation to business this has led to calls for businesses to acknowledge their wider social responsibilities and these wider issues are best encapsulated in the term 'Global Responsibility'.

At the global level, the development of the UN global compact is an attempt to provide an enabling framework in which businesses can address issues concerning human rights, labour standards, the environment, and measures to combat corruption (see Chapter Eleven).

The Globally Responsible Leadership Initiative (GRLI) is a network of Business Schools and Businesses which seeks to support the UN Global Compact in recognition of the fact that if change is to occur then there will need to be a change in business approaches and the values that underpin these. It defines Globally Responsible Leadership as being:

> the global exercise of ethical, values-based leadership in the pursuit of economic and societal progress and sustainable development. It is based on a fundamental understanding of the interconnectedness of the world and recognition of the need for economic and societal and environmental advancement. It also requires the vision and courage to place decision making and management practice in a global context (www.efmd.org).

The GRLI has sought to define what it sees as these new values and these are centred around a commitment to:

- Fairness
- Freedom
- Honesty
- Humanity
- Responsibility and solidarity
- Sustainable development
- Tolerance
- Transparency

(see www.grli.org).

For many critics this is simply asking too much of businesses and shows the gap between rhetoric and reality.

In 2007 Ipsos Mori, in a poll surveying attitudes to public awareness of environmental issues, found that 80% of all people surveyed felt that it was very/fairly important for businesses to show environmental responsibility and that they would consider a company's environmental record when shopping. The same poll found that 70% of people do not feel that businesses pay enough attention to their environmental responsibilities (Armstrong 2007a). There is a strange consensus between both critics of business and its defenders. For critics, business will always put its own interests first. For defenders this is simply as it should be.

In relation to the three principles that relate to the environment the UN Global Compact is keen to impress on businesses that there need not be a conflict between preserving the environment and business success. The underlying philosophy is that there is a clear business case for adopting these principles.

This could be best seen in terms of a continuum in that if businesses do not take action now to reduce their environmental impact their profits will suffer in the future. This short term action to prevent longer term costs is referred to as mitigation. Whilst this involves short term costs it is seen as a long term investment in that it will help reduce the costs of ecological damage in the long run. At the same time since it is argued some changes as a result of ecological damage are already upon us businesses will need to play their part in adapting to these changes. If they do not do so now it is likely that much greater adaptation changes will be needed in the future.

Principle 7 emphasizes the importance of the approach that needs to be adopted by business in order to operationalize the precautionary principle. Box 1 below outlines the UN Global Compact's views as to the nature of such an approach.

Box 1 A Business Approach to the Concept of Precaution

The key element of a precautionary approach, from a business perspective, is the idea of prevention rather than cure. In other words, it is more cost-effective to take early action to ensure that irreversible environmental damage does not occur. Companies should consider the following:

1. While it is true that preventing environmental damage entails both opportunity—and implementation —costs, remediating environmental harm after it has occurred can cost much more, e.g. for treatment costs, or in terms of company image.

2. Investing in production methods that are not sustainable, i.e. that deplete resources and degrade the environment, has a lower, long-term return than investing in sustainable operations. In turn, improving environmental performance means less financial risk, an important consideration for insurers.

3. Research and development related to more environmentally friendly products can have significant long-term benefits.

Source: www.unglobalcompact.org

It is acknowledged that a major obstacle for businesses to overcome is the existence of uncertainty and to deal with this a range of methods are suggested:

- environmental risk assessment;
- life cycle assessment to explore the possibility of more environmentally friendly methods of production;
- environmental impact assessment;
- strategic environmental assessment. This would ensure that environmental considerations are placed at the heart of business strategy.

In Principle 8 the UN Global Compact is clear that there is a compelling case for 'environmentally responsible business practice'. It refers to Chapter 30 of Agenda 21 which outlined what environmental responsibility for business meant. Here it is defined as:

> responsible and ethical management of products and processes from the point of view of health, safety and environmental aspects. Towards this end, business and industry should increase self-regulation, guided by appropriate codes, charters and initiatives integrated into all elements of business planning and decision making, and fostering openness and dialogue with employees and the public. (www.unglobalcompact.org/AboutTheGC/TheTenPrinciples/principle8.html)

For the UN there is a clear and compelling 'business case' for environmental action and the arguments can be summarized as follows in Box 2:

Box 2 Towards Environmentally Responsible Business Practice

Business gains its legitimacy through meeting the needs of society, and increasingly society is expressing a clear need for more environmentally sustainable practices. One way for business to demonstrate its commitment to greater environmental responsibility is by changing its modus operandi from the so-called 'traditional methods' to more responsible approaches to addressing environmental issues.

Source: www.unglobalcompact.org/AboutTheGC/TheTenPrinciples/principle8.html

---

- Cleaner production and eco-efficiency leads to improved resource productivity and lower costs.
- New economic instruments (taxes, charges, trade permits) and tougher environmental regulations will reward those companies who seek to improve eco-efficiency.
- Insurance companies prefer to cover a cleaner, lower risk company and banks are more willing to lend to a company whose operations will not burden the bank with environmental lawsuits or large clean-up bills.
- Being seen to be green helps a company's brand image and employees tend to prefer to work for an environmentally responsible company.
- Environmental pollution threatens human health.
- Customers are demanding cleaner products.

Finally Principle 9 asserts the important role that business can play in both developing and adopting the technologies that will enable the environment to be safeguarded.

The impact of business on the ecological environment is explicitly recognized in the environmental regulations with which businesses have to comply. In the UK you can explore the range of such legislation by visiting www.Envirowise.gov.uk. At the global level as a result of the 1992 Rio declaration the international standard, ISO 14001, was developed to provide a framework for the development of an environmental management system and the supporting audit programme (see www.iso-14001.org.uk) for the details of how businesses can seek accreditation for this.

Businesses are now urged to genuinely show their commitment to change through moving away from simply reporting their financial bottom line. It is argued that they should also report on their 'social' and 'environmental' impacts and this has in turn produced a variety of systems to account for the environment. In 1994, John Elkington developed the concept of 'triple bottom line accounting' as a way of highlighting the responsibility of businesses in relation to social and environmental performance as well as financial performance and this is commonly referred to as the trio of 'People, Planet and Profit' (Elkington 1994).

However, there is no commonly agreed set of procedures for doing this and instead there is a hotchpotch of approaches developed by some businesses eager to publicize their social credentials. Whilst many leading businesses have been undertaking a range of environmental initiatives, there remains an unwillingness to be subject to government regulation to enforce compliance. The desire to be green still sits uneasily with the temptation to trumpet it to secure competitive advantage.

Examples of business groups who are at the forefront of pushing for change are organizations such as the World Business Council for Sustainable Development (see www.wbcsd.org) or in the UK Business in the Community (see www.bitc.org.uk) which has developed its own environmental index for auditing purposes.

Learning Task

Look at cases which are profiled as examples of responsible business practice in relation to the ecological environment (see for example www.bitc.org.uk).

What are the problems that businesses face in addressing environmentally responsible business practice, and how convincing do you think the case for this is?

Businesses are subject to a range of environmental policies and measures have been developed to ensure that the polluter pays. These range from green taxes such as congestion charges on motorists, to allowing businesses pollution permits, where in the short term there is no avoidance of the pollution caused in production. If there is no reasonable alternative to the side effects of a particular activity then we need compensation agreements to help mitigate these. If there is market failure then policies need to be devised to correct these.

The rise in air travel is the fastest rising contribution to the emission of GHGs. One proposal to counteract this is that there should be widespread provision of carbon offsets. Whenever a flight is purchased a sum of money is paid and used to develop projects which absorb the carbon emitted, or through the development of new forms of non-fossil fuel burning technologies.

There are many reservations that are advanced about such market based solutions.

Mini Case Carbon Offsetting

In 2007 Virgin Atlantic introduced a Carbon Offset Scheme together with a Swiss charity company called 'myclimate' which is involved in researching into ways of tackling climate change and promoting clean energy projects in the developing world.

Examples of such projects are one in India for a power plant that runs on farming waste to produce electricity for local communities and a hydropower plant in Indonesia.

Virgin Atlantic was aware there had been criticisms of such offset schemes and was keen to show that this scheme had the support of a range of Non-Governmental Organizations. It claimed that it was able to calculate the amount of carbon for each of its flights using the services of an independent carbon verification company.

Source: www.virginatlantic.com/offset

Source: Myclimate

Business as Usual

One of the biggest fears for those concerned about the environmental impact of businesses is that, even where they recognize potential problems, all too often businesses fail to recognize the extent to which they may need to change their behaviour. This is referred to as maintaining 'Business as usual'.

Indeed, as we have seen, critics of business go further and argue that businesses will actively seek to resist pressure to change in order to preserve their profits.

The levying of environmental charges may encourage the false belief that the problem is solved even though the environmentally damaging behaviour still continues. This has been described By Robert Goodin as the 'selling of environmental indulgences' (Goodin 2007). For Goodin the only long term alternative to polluting activities is to prevent that pollution occurring.

Equity Implications

To what extent is it 'fair' to charge green taxes if richer members of society or more prosperous businesses can afford to pay while poorer people and businesses are unfairly penalized? On a global level, there is an inherent inequity in resource use, and a potential one in the solutions being designed to deal with environmental problems. The developed world got rich by being able to industrialize in a world where the environment was effectively ignored. Now that policies are being implemented to deal with these it would not be fair if the developing world was being asked to adhere to the same levels of environmental protection. It is argued that the richer countries can afford to pay for the cost of the environmental harm they have mostly caused, and developing countries should not be asked to adopt environmental regulations at their early stage in the development process.

Learning Task

1. What are the negative externalities involved with the expansion of air travel?
2. Would you be prepared to pay 'green taxes' every time you purchased an air ticket?
3. Find out about how the 'carbon offset' market might work. How effective do you think such markets might be?

Global Climate Change

It is clear that the most pressing ecological problem of our age is that of global climate change.

The Intergovernmental Panel on Climate Change was established in 1989 by the World Meteorological Office and the United Nations Environment Programme to provide an objective source of information about climate change. In its 4th Assessment Report published in November 2007 it is clear that global climate change is occurring, that 'anthropogenic' activity is a contributing factor and that there is a need to reduce the GHGs that are the cause of global warming. This report is important as it can be seen as ending the debate about the precise role of human beings in increasing the threats posed by climate change (IPCC).

Aubrey Meyer is a campaigner who founded the Global Commons Institute. Meyer illustrates the problem of global warming by using a 'bath-tap' analogy. The dominant green house gas from anthropogenic sources is carbon dioxide (CO_2) and business is responsible for around 40% of these emissions. Just as a bath will fill if the tap is left running, so the atmosphere fills up as emissions flow from sources such as the burning of fossil fuels for energy use. If there is no outflow from the bath over time the constant flow will mean that the stock of water will rise. If there is a plug hole with no plug then this stock need not rise so fast as some of the water is drained away. In relation to our CO_2 emissions this means that if we have 'sinks' to absorb the carbon such as forests or the oceans then not all the carbon will be added to the total stock. If, for example, the flow of water is twice the rate at which it drains away then the net increase in the stock of water will be 50% of the flow.

Meyer reports that in recent years this has indeed been the case with the 50% of carbon emissions being retained in the atmosphere and the remaining 50% being re-absorbed. It has been on that basis that future projections of the rise in global temperatures have been made. Ice core sampling allows CO_2 atmospheric concentration to be measured for half a million years. This has fluctuated in the band of 180 to 280 parts per million by volume (ppmv) and there is a very close correlation with these fluctuations and the changes in global temperature.

During the last 200 years there has been a rise in CO_2 concentration from 280 ppmv to 380 ppmv and this has led to 1° rise in average global temperature. Up until recently the annual increase of atmospheric CO_2 has been 1.5 ppmv. Since each additional ppmv adds 2.13 billion tonnes (gigatonnes expressed as GTC) of carbon to the atmosphere this means that the stock of carbon in weight terms has been 3.3 GTC. In total the annual emissions of carbon however have been around 6.5 GTC as the sinks have absorbed around 50% of all emissions. As of 2007 the rate of concentration was at 430 ppmv.

However, in the period 2003–05 the rate of atmospheric increase rose to nearer 3 ppmv meaning that we were approaching the point at which 100% of emissions were retained in the atmosphere. This 'aggravated accumulation' will mean that the level of the bathwater will rise more quickly and is in serious danger of overflowing. Emissions are increasing and the sinks' ability to absorb these are decreasing as the oceans warm and acidification occurs and forests are burned to increase land availability.

For Meyer the implication is clear and that is that we need urgent cuts in emissions ppmv and that the current targets of the UK Government to stabilize emissions at 550 ppmv are simply too high and will result in runaway climate change (Meyer 2007). This echoes James Lovelock's views outlined earlier.

The 4th Assessment Report re-affirmed the five areas of concern that had been high-lighted in the 3rd Assessment Report. These areas of concern are as follows:

Risks to Unique and Threatened Systems

If global temperatures were to exceed 1980–1999 levels by 1.5 to 2.5°C then in the words of the summary report there is medium confidence that 20–30% of plant and animal species are likely to be at increased risk of extinction. It warns also of increases risk of coral reef damage and increased vulnerability of indigenous peoples in the Arctic and small island communities.

Risk of Extreme Weather Events

The report has 'higher confidence' in the projected increases in droughts, heatwaves, and floods as well as their adverse consequences.

Distribution of Impacts and Vulnerabilities

The most vulnerable people will be people in the weakest economic position especially the poor and the elderly in both developing and developed countries alike. It is estimated that 32,000 people died in Western Europe as a result of the heatwave in 2005.

Aggregate Impacts

The report attempts to counter an often expressed view that while global warming may well cause problems for some it will also equally bring benefits to others. It is easy to see how people living in cold northern climates might welcome warmer conditions! However, if global warming were to increase the report argues that the net costs will increase over time whilst any possible benefits will decrease.

Risk of Large Scale Singularities

There is high confidence that the melting of the Greenland and Antarctic ice sheets will give a greater rise to sea levels then current models predict, but that will be a centuries long process.

In terms of the future the IPCC emphasize that adaptation and mitigation measures are unlikely to stop all climate change effects but (that combined) they can significantly reduce the risks. Conversely delays in reducing emissions will significantly constrain the opportunities to lower stabilization levels and increase the risk of severe climate change impacts.

Technology, both that which is presently available and that which is likely to become commercially available, is seen as offering a realistic hope that stabilization levels can be achieved.

Published in 2007 and before the final reporting of the 4th Assessment Report, the UK Government asked the respected economist Nicholas Stern to look at the economics of climate change. For Stern, 'The scientific evidence is now overwhelming: climate change presents very serious global risks, and it demands an urgent global response' (Stern Review, p i).

The Review is clear that there is a need to take an international perspective:

> Climate change is global in causes and consequences, and international collective action will be critical in driving an effective, efficient and equitable response on the scale required. This response will require deeper international co-operation in many areas—most notably in creating price signals and markets for carbon, spurring technology research, development and deployment, and promoting adaptation, particularly for developing countries.
>
> Climate change presents a unique challenge for economics; it is the greatest and widest ranging market failure ever seen (p i).

Stern is clear that the costs of climate change in terms of Gross National Product and quality of life will be much greater than the costs of taking action to mitigate against these now. It is also clear that these costs significantly rise the later we start on this process. According to Stern, even if the rate of the annual flow of emissions was not to rise (which is highly unlikely), the concentration of carbon will reach 550 ppmv by 2050. But if business as usual continues this level will be reached much earlier and means that there is a very high chance that the rise in global temperatures will exceed 2°C and indeed there is some evidence that they may rise even as high as 5–6°C in the next century which would 'take us into territory unknown to human experience and involve radical changes in the world around us' (Stern Review p ix).

If this were to be the case over the next two centuries there could be a reduction in global GNP in the range of 5–20%. This is a high range of uncertainty but this is inevitable given the difficulty of estimating such costs in general and so far into the future.

In order to stabilize the climate Stern reinforces the essential principle that annual emissions need to be brought down to below the level that enables the Earth to absorb additional carbon through its natural sinks. Stern estimates this as being below 5 GTC. Since current annual emissions are around 40 GTC this would mean an 80% reduction in carbon in the long run compared to current levels.

Reducing carbon emissions is not going to be an easy task. At present levels are continuing to rise, so adding to the stock of carbon and the longer this goes on the greater the difficulty in reducing this. Stern is optimistic that it will be possible to stabilize the climate at 550ppmv by allowing annual emissions to peak in the next 10 to 20 years and then gradually cutting emissions by 1–3% each year until 2050. However, since it is the richer developed countries that are currently the main producers of carbon this will require these countries to make severe cuts in their carbon.

In the Climate Change Bill, which was due to be ratified in 2008, the UK Government target is for a reduction in carbon emissions of 60% compared to 1990 levels. For critics such as Meyer and the environmental campaigner George Monbiot, and cuts of at least 80% are needed.

The Stern Review highlights four main policy areas that need to be addressed if we are to be able to mitigate against the worst effects of climate change and adapt to those that will occur.

- Reducing demand for emissions intensive goods and services.
- Increase resource efficiency.
- Action on non-energy emissions such as avoiding deforestation.
- Switching to low carbon technologies for power, heat and transport.

Stern is keen to emphasize that while this may be seen to be a threat to business as usual behaviour, in practice these changes may well provide opportunities for businesses in terms of opportunities to create markets for low-carbon energy products, the reduction in costs brought about developing new low energy systems, and the decreases in ill-health and mortality that are a direct effect of poor environmental conditions.

The move to decrease carbon emissions and other GHGs has resulted in calls for the development of carbon pricing to reflect the social costs of carbon. This could be achieved through the creation of markets in emissions trading based on the 'cap and trade' principle. Under the Kyoto Protocol caps are placed on emissions for each country and then in turn individual companies are allocated their share of the overall cap. Businesses which reduce their emissions below this target could sell their quotas to other businesses that may exceed their targets. In this way the polluters are paying a charge for polluting whilst those that cut pollution are rewarded. The most developed scheme is the European Emissions Trading System which is now in its second phase (which is due to run out in 2012).

Another aspect of the Kyoto Protocol is the Clean Development Mechanism which allows high carbon emitters in the developing world to 'offset' their emissions by funding emissions reduction projects in the developing world.

Whilst these markets are in their infancy and were hindered by setting allowances in excess of what was needed thus leading to a collapse in the price of carbon, lessons have been learned and carbon markets are seen as being fundamental to reducing carbon emissions. For many businesses this is seen as the best way of ensuring reductions in GHGs. In 2005 at a climate change roundtable held during the G8 meetings in the UK, a number of leading multinational companies issued a statement advocating the need for global action and the use of carbon trading (WEF).

Will businesses be able to undertake this challenge of cutting carbon emissions voluntarily or will increasingly stringent legislation require them to do so?

● CHAPTER SUMMARY

The nature of many environmental problems is that they are trans-boundary, and if we are to avoid potential tragedies of the (global) commons then there needs to be concerted action at the global level, which is then translated into national and local environmental action.

It is clear businesses have a big role to play. As converters of resources into products attention has to be focused on their roles as sustainable businesses not just in relation to the 'bottom' line of profit but also in relation to their impact on people and profit. The Rio Declaration and Agenda 21 established a comprehensive set of ambitious principles for States to promote in relation to environmental policy. The UN Global Compact then translated these principles into the principles for responsible business behaviour.

It is evident there are obstacles to environmental policies. Businesses have to balance the risks of incurring the costs of environmental compliance with the risks of not doing anything. Here there is a clear role for science and economics to specify these risks. For businesses with the short term goal of maximizing shareholder value it is all too easy to maintain 'business as usual' but the increasing recognition of the range of global environmental problems means that this is not a realistic possibility. Across the spectrum of business there are many examples of how individual businesses are seeking to address these concerns but, especially, in relation to climate change it is argued that the response has not been enough. It is clear that unless businesses rise to the challenge there will be calls for tougher environmental regulation. It is also equally clear that in order to make these changes businesses do need help and advice from outside of the company, and there is a need to then embed global responsibility into the overall business strategy.

● REVIEW QUESTIONS

1. What is the meaning of the term 'the tragedy of the commons' and how does this relate to ecological damage?

2. Explain how it is argued that market based measures such as the 'polluter pays principle' address ecological problems.

3. Why do 'green' thinkers and activists argue that such market based measures are not adequate to tackle the ecological problem?

4. What are the range of measures that businesses themselves can make in response to ecological problems?

5. How can governments ensure businesses adhere to their ecological responsibilities?

Case Study Role of Business in Combating Climate Change

We referred to the business of climate denial in an earlier case study. Balanced against this though is the undoubted change in the recognition of many businesses about the existence of global climate change and its effects. In April 2008 a joint statement of the G8 Tokyo Business Summit which represented the Business Associations of the eight largest industrial nations showed the commitment to dealing with climate change.

> Climate change is one of the most serious challenges facing the world today. Climate change is global in both its causes and impacts, and requires cooperative action to reduce greenhouse gas (GHG) emissions on a global basis (www.wbcsd.org).

Many leading businesses now regularly highlight their commitment to reducing their contribution to carbon emissions. However, there is no compulsion on businesses to do so. If they do there is now an internationally recognized GHG Protocol which has been jointly developed by the World Resources Institute and the World Business Council for Sustainable Development (see www.wri.org).

To what extent is current action sufficient to achieve the cuts required?

In the statement above the tension between commitment and action is clear. While there is the commitment to reducing GHGs this is balanced by the belief that technology will in future allow alternative fuels to be used and that businesses should not be subjected to regulation that will eat into profits so hindering what they see as their efforts to invest in the technologies needed for the future. There is a professed optimism

that technology will also come to the rescue in the form of the development of artificial carbon sequestration methods such as 'carbon capture'. These may involve the development of alternative fuels such as hydrogen or ways of 'scrubbing' out the carbon content of emissions in power stations etc. There is also the hope that it will be possible to inject carbon safely into the oceans. However, such technologies remain highly tentative.

There have been clear attempts by businesses in Europe to prevent the EU from tightening the caps on carbon and clear protests that the costs of mitigation are simply too high at the moment.

For David Ballard even where businesses show the most commitment to reducing their GHGs they are 'missing the point' and essentially it is still business as usual (Ballard 2007).

The Carbon Disclosure Project is an organization that operates on behalf of shareholders to elicit information on the impact of climate change on shareholder value and commercial operations. Its reports can be found at www.cdproject.net.

In 2008 1,300 corporations supplied carbon emissions figures to the CDP and in the CDP5 survey which looked at the top 500 companies in the FT index there was evidence that the gap between awareness and action about both the need for mitigation and adaptation was narrowing.

In a survey using this data, but concentrating on the FTSE100 companies, the *Guardian* and Forum for the Future further broke down this data (Armstrong 2007b)—68 firms were willing to reveal their carbon emissions. There are problems with the data however in that there are two different methods of ➔

→ reporting used: the internationally accepted GHG Protocol Initiative and an earlier one developed by the Department for Environment and Rural Affairs. Another problem is only the direct production and indirect purchased energy use emissions are included with all the other indirect emissions along the supply chain (such as transport, waste disposal, and the extraction of resources) being excluded.

Using an estimated carbon price of £35 per tonne the *Guardian* estimated the cost of trading all this carbon for the 100 companies would be more than £16 billion and that would represent an average loss of profits of 9%. However, the real social cost of this carbon is estimated by the treasury as being £70 per tonne and rising by £1 for every year that no action is taken. That would be over £48 billion if all 100 companies' emissions were included.

It is clear businesses are reluctant to be exposed to compulsory regulation which will both require them to report and cut carbon emissions. As reported in the The Green List above, six of the largest 10 companies in the world are oil companies which, between them, account for 91% of the total emissions of the top FTSE100, and yet for some companies emissions are rising whilst even for those with a commitment to cut emissions it is simply too little.

Many commentators now feel that the Stern Review has seriously underestimated the costs and speed of climate change. Similarly, many feel that the business response to the challenge is too small. Forum for the Future, a UK environmental organization, profiles what it calls Leader Businesses to show that changes in business behaviour are occurring but in a report profiling such businesses it concludes:

> Are today's leading practices bold enough to overcome current global sustainability challenges? Do they demonstrate a true understanding of the changes that are required to our social and economic systems? We suspect not.
>
> Given the scale and complexity of the global sustainability challenge, there is a worrying lack of urgency from government and many business leaders. While there is definite evidence of progress from the leader businesses we feature in this report, the current rate of change is not commensurate with the challenges that we face. We do not believe that single-digit carbon reduction targets, or the use of language such as 'where possible', are adequate responses to current global challenges. We need to see an immediate injection of urgency, reflected in faster, braver and bolder action. On climate change we need a reduction in CO_2 by 90% against 1990 levels by 2050, with year-on-year targets along the way. Nothing less will do.

Questions

1. What are the main challenges climate change presents for business?

2. What are the main obstacles that lie in the way of achieving the changes in business practices that may be required?

3. What policies are needed to encourage businesses to be able to address the potential problems of climate change?

4. How optimistic are you that action can be taken to combat the effects of climate change?

Online Resource Centre

www.oxfordtextbooks.co.uk/orc/hamilton_webster/

Visit the supporting online resource centre for additional material which will help you with your assignments, essays and research, or you may find these extra resources helpful when revising for exams.

● FURTHER READING

● Porritt, J. (2007) *Capitalism as if the World Matters*. London: Earthscan

Jonathon Porritt is Co-Founder and Programme Director of Forum for the Future. In this book he outlines how he feels changes can be made to ensure that the capitalist system delivers sustainable development.

- Stern, N. (2007) *The Economics of Climate Change—The Stern Review*. Cambridge: Cambridge University Press

This book identifies the causes of global climate change and proposes policies to combat it.

- Worldwatch Institute (2007) *State of the World—Ideas and Opportunities for Sustainable Economies*. London: Earthscan

Published annually this book has a wealth of up to date data concerning the state of the planet and both reviews and evaluates policy responses.

- Judge, E. (2007) 'Business and Sustainable Development' in Wetherly, P. and Otter, D., *The Business Environment—Themes and Issues*. Oxford: Oxford University Press

This chapter provides a good introduction to the issues surrounding the relationship between business and sustainable development.

REFERENCES

Adam, G. (2006) 'Royal Society tells Exxon—Stop reporting Climate Change Denial'. *The Guardian*, 20 September. Available at www.guardian.co.uk

Armstrong, M. (2007a) 'Care to Comment, The Green List'. *The Guardian*, 5 November. Available at www.guardian.co.uk

Armstrong, M. (2007b) 'Counting Carbon, The Green List'. *The Guardian*, 5 November. Available at www.guardian.co.uk

Ballard, D. (2007) 'Mostly Missing the Point: Business Responses to Climate Change' in *Surviving Climate Change—The Struggle to Avert Climate Catastrophe*. D. Cromwell and M. Levene (eds). London: Pluto Press

Brown, L. (2008) *Plan 3.0—Mobilizing to Save Civilization*. Earth Policy Institute: Washington

Carson, R. (1962) *The Silent Spring*. Boston: Houghton Mifflin

Elkington, J. (1994) 'Towards the Sustainable Corporation—Win-Win-Win Business Strategies for Sustainable Development'. *California Management Review* 36 (2)

Forum for the Future (2008) 'Leader business 2.0—hallmarks of sustainable performance'. Available at www.forumforthefuture.org.uk

Goodin, R. (2007) 'Selling Environmental Indulgences' in Dryzek, J. S. and Schlosberg, D. *Debating the Earth—The Environmental Politics Reader*, Oxford: Oxford University Press

Hardin, G. (1968) 'The Tragedy of the Commons'. *Science*, 162, 13 December, American Association for the Advancement of Science

IPCC (2007) Fourth Assessment Report—Synthesis Report. Available at www.ipcc.ch

Jarman, M. (2007) 'First they blocked, Now do they Bluff? Corporations Respond to Climate Change' in *Surviving Climate Change—The Struggle to Avert Climate Catastrophe*, D. Cromwell and M. Levene (eds). London: Pluto Press

Lomborg, B. (2001) *The Skeptical Environmentalist*. Cambridge: Cambridge University Press

Lovelock, J. (1979) *A New Look at Life on Earth*. Oxford: Oxford University Press

Lovelock, J. (2007) *The Revenge of Gaia*. London: Penguin

Meadows, D. H. *et al.* (1972) *The Limits to Growth*. New York: Universe Books

Meyer, A. (2007) 'The Case for Contraction and Convergence' in *Surviving Climate Change—The Struggle to Avert Climate Catastrophe*, D. Cromwell and M. Levene (eds). London: Pluto Press

Mishan, E. (1969) *The Costs of Economic Growth*. London: Penguin

Monbiot, G. (2007) *Heat—How to Stop the Planet Burning*. London: Penguin

Pestel, E. (1972) 'An Abstract of A Report to the Club of Rome', Meadows *et al*. Available at www.clubofrome.org

Rao, P. K. (2000) *Sustainable Development—Economics and Policy*. Oxford: Blackwell

Sachs, J. (2007) 'Bursting at the Seams', Reith Lectures, BBC. Available at www.bbc.co.uk

Schumacher, E. F. (1973) *Small is Beautiful—Economics as if People Mattered*. New York: Harper and Row

Stern, N. (2007) The Stern Review, Executive Summary—the Economics of Climate Change, HM Treasury. Available at www.hm-treasury.gov.uk

Traynor, I. (2008) 'EU told to prepare for flood of climate change migrants'. *The Guardian*, 10 March

WCED (1988) *Our Common Future*. Oxford: Oxford University Press (commonly known as Brundtland Report)

WEF (2005) Statement of G8 Climate Change Roundtable. Available at www.weforum.org

CHAPTER ELEVEN

Corporate Social Responsibility

LEARNING OUTCOMES

This chapter will enable you to:

- Define corporate social responsibility

- Assess the free market case against corporate social responsibility

- Explain the business and normative cases for Corporate Social Responsibility

- Identify corporate social responsibility issues in the global economy

- Propose ways in which business can respond to global inequalities

In Chapter One we defined globalization as a process in which barriers (physical, political, economic, cultural) separating different regions of the world are reduced or removed, thereby stimulating greater exchange and linkages between nations.

We also said that business operates in a world where globalization is going on at an accelerating rate and that as globalization progresses, it confronts business with important new challenges. Some of these challenges relate to the way business is done. This case relates to one of those challenges, the use of 'child labour'.

Case Study   Child Labour

It is November, 2007 and Gap's crisis disaster team is in action to reassure a sceptical public that it does not condone children working in the factories that provide the clothing it sells in its many stores. Western consumers might want the cheap clothing it provides but they don't like the thought of that clothing being made in the sweatshops of the world and especially when there are children as young as 10 years old working in these sweatshops.

Gap has been discovered using child labour at a sub-contracted textile facility in New Delhi, India. The clothes being made were, ironically, for Gap Kids. Estimates of the number of child labourers in India vary from the 13 million quoted by the Indian Government to the 60 million estimate of some activist groups. The International Labour Office put the number at about 44 million.   →

Source: Tom Pietrasik/Save the Children

→ Child labour is not totally banned in India although the Government is progressively moving to that. The employment of children under 14 years of age in households, roadside restaurants, and hotels only became illegal in 2007. In a country of extreme poverty there are mixed signals from Government. Commenting on this revelation of child labour a Government Minister accused activists of over-hyping the extent of child labour and claimed that the resulting bad publicity could be an attempt by rich countries to limit exports from poor countries such as India and that this was a type of non-tariff barrier. Simply closing down these factories is not always the right answer as this could lead to more poverty or worse.

Certainly many of the children who end up in the sweatshops are from extremely poor rural areas of extreme poverty. Families with 7 or 8 children will sell one or more children for the equivalent of £7. They are then sold on and can end up working as slaves in the city sweatshops. There they work for 16 hours a day for no wages, in filthy conditions, and subject to threats and beatings.

This is not the first time Gap has hit the headlines for working conditions found in its supplier factories. In 2002 workers and union leaders from Africa and Central America confronted shareholders at the annual general meeting with evidence of violence and intimidation and sweatshop conditions in factories supplying Gap clothing.

In 2003 the Gap and other companies faced a lawsuit by workers in Saipan alleging unpaid overtime, unsafe working conditions, and forced abortion policies. A US$20 million settlement was made but without any admission of liability.

In 2004 Gap undertook its own internal investigation and found that many of the 30,000 factories in 50 different countries supplying Gap clothing failed to comply with minimum labour conditions, including under age employment. In 2003 Gap revoked contracts with 136 factories because of serious and persistent violations.

The company produced its first social responsibility report in 2004 and has endeavoured to promote itself as an ethical leader in promoting socially responsible manufacturing. It has drawn up a strict code of practice for factories and has 90 inspectors travelling the world to monitor the factories it uses to supply Gap clothing. As a result of this process it stopped working with 23 factories in 2006.

The fact that another example of child labour has emerged will do little to quieten the critics of Gap and Western clothing retailers in general. They claim that codes of conduct are just window dressing and that the demand for cheap clothing in Western retail outlets will continue to spawn the sweatshops of India employing child slave labour.

Sources: *Observer*, 28 October 2007; *PR Week*, 5 November 2007; *Financial Times*, 29 October 2007

Introduction

Multinational corporations are often accused of a number of abuses related to their business activities. Many have appeared in the press accused of, inter alia, bribery and corruption, abusing human rights, sanction busting, dumping, undermining governments, exploiting uneducated consumers, forced labour, low wages, poor health and safety standards, exploiting natural resources and, as in the above case study, using child labour. One of the many problems for business operating internationally is that standards and 'the way of doing things' differ from country to country. That is not to say this is a justification for the type of abuses listed above, but it does bring into question the fundamental question of the role of business in society, and to what extent business has any responsibility for the problems of society. This chapter explores the concept of corporate social responsibility, discusses some examples related to the concept, and looks at the implications for business.

Corporate social responsibility (CSR) can be defined as the notion that corporations have an obligation to society to take into account not just their economic impact but also their social and environmental impact. Or, according to Motorola:

> Corporate responsibility means harnessing the power of our global business to benefit people. It also means doing the right thing in all aspects of our business, including how we treat the environment, our employees, our customers, our partners and our communities.

We use the term corporate social responsibility throughout this chapter but it appears that business is not very keen on this term. *The Economist* reported (17 January 2008) that Marks and Spencer refers to its CSR activities as 'Plan A', because there is no 'Plan B'. In other words this is how we do business and we do not need to give it any special label. Others have dropped the 'social'—which some object to as too narrow, or 'outside our remit', or as a label imposed from outside. Other labels used are 'triple-bottom-line reporting' (i.e. economic, social, and environmental), 'sustainable development', and the most recent 'corporate citizenship'. Although there are different interpretations of these different terms they are all essentially about the obligation to society in its widest sense.

Debates About CSR

CSR is not new, but whether or not business has any social responsibility has been the subject of endless debate.

For some there is only one social responsibility of business and that is, in the words of Milton Friedman (1970) 'to use its resources and engage in activities designed to increase its profits so long as it stays within the rules of the game, which is to say, engages in open and free competition without deception or fraud'. This reflects the view that a free market society is made up of a number of groups each with a specialist role within society. The role of business is economic, and the people who run businesses are expert in that field. Their role is to combine resources to produce some product or service for sale at a profit. They compete with other firms by keeping costs as low as possible and supplying consumers with the goods and services they want, at the lowest possible price. Those who are effective at doing this survive and make a profit. Those who fail go out of business. It is the drive to supply consumers with the goods and services they want, while making as much profit as possible by driving costs down and selling as much as possible, which makes a dynamic and efficient economy. If there are social and environmental problems then this shouldn't be a business problem because it would divert them from the role for which they are best equipped—and the result would be a less efficient economy. These problems are best left to be solved by governments, who are experts in those fields.

In this debate, and particularly in the field of international business, we are talking about a particular form of business organization and that is the 'corporation'. To become a corporation a business has to go through a legal process which creates a body which has a separate legal existence from its owners and from those who work in or manage it. Gap Inc., BP, and Motorola exist quite separately from the people who work in or manage the organization, and from those who own a share in the assets of the business, the share-holders. Shareholders change as shares are bought and sold through various stock exchanges. Managers and other workers change, but the corporation continues in exis-tence. It is said to have perpetual succession.

In Friedman's view the corporation should act no differently from the single owner business. Managers are employed as the agents of the principals (the owners) and should work in their interest and that, in his view, is to make as much profit as possible. In that way both dividends and share value would increase. They are not experts in social welfare or dealing with environmental problems, so how would they know what would be the most effective use of resources to deal with these problems. Nor, unlike politicians, have they been elected so the use of funds for some purpose other than profit maximization would not only be wasteful, it would be undemocratic, particularly as managers as a group do not tend to be representative of the population at large—usually being more conservative than the general population.

Friedman's criticisms of CSR were not that business did not have a social role, but that its role and its obligation to society was to supply goods and services at the lowest price possible. His view was founded in a fundamental belief in the virtues of a free market economy in which each player contributed, without knowing it, to the greater good of society.

A further criticism by Friedman was the notion of a corporation, a legal creation, assuming moral responsibilities. In his words, 'What does it mean to say that "business" has responsibilities? Only people can have responsibilities. A corporation is an artificial person and in this sense may have artificial responsibilities, but business as a whole can-not be said to have responsibilities, even in this vague sense' (Friedman 1970). There is no argument that the corporation exists as a separate legal entity with legal rights and duties. It is capable of owning and disposing assets, employing people, entering into contracts, incurring and being owed debts, inflicting and suffering damage, suing and being sued. If it (the corporation) is held responsible for these actions why then can it not be morally responsible for its actions? As Goodpaster and Mathews (1982) point out 'if a group can act like a person in some ways, then we can expect it to behave like a person in other ways'. We have no problem referring to a company's business strategy or its marketing plan. We would not think or refer to these examples as an individual's strategy or plan. This is because corporations have complex internal decision-making structures which arrive at decisions in line with corporate goals (French 1979). The outcome is rarely attributable to any one person, but is usually the result of a series of discussions between directors, man-agers, and staff. In other words the corporation acts just like an individual. Examples from legal cases support the difficulty in identifying individuals responsible for corporate deci-sions. In *P & O European Ferries (Dover) Ltd* (1991) 93 Cr App R 72 Mr Justice Turner ruled that a company may be properly indicted for manslaughter. That case however, ended in the acquittal of the defendant company because the Crown could not show that a 'controlling mind' had been grossly negligent. The 'controlling mind' of a company is somebody who can be shown to be in control of the operations of a company, and not responsible to another person. In large companies the 'controlling mind' has proved difficult to identify, but the smaller the company the more likely it can be identified. In the 'Lyme Bay' disaster several school children, who were canoeing across Lyme Bay, died because of the poor safety standards of the company. In this case it was possible to identify the Managing Director, Peter Kite, as the 'controlling mind' and he was successfully prosecuted for corporate manslaughter.

Another argument supporting the case for assigning moral responsibility to a company is the existence, not just of a decision-making structure but also, of a set of beliefs and values which guide individual decision-making. This is commonly known as the 'culture' of the organization. Nowadays this is more often than not enshrined in a written statement, such as the one below for the HSBC group. Note that its values include 'the exercise of corporate social responsibility'.

HSBC operates according to certain key business values:

- the highest personal standards of integrity at all levels;
- commitment to truth and fair dealing;
- hands-on management at all levels;
- commitment to quality and competence;
- a minimum of bureaucracy;
- fast decisions and implementation;
- putting the team's interests ahead of the individual's;
- the appropriate delegation of authority with accountability;
- fair and objective employer;
- a diverse team underpinned by a meritocratic approach to recruitment/selection/promotion;
- a commitment to complying with the spirit and letter of all laws and regulations wherever we conduct our business; the exercise of corporate social responsibility through detailed assessments of lending proposals and investments, the promotion of good environmental practice and sustainable development, and commitment to the welfare and development of each local community (www.hsbc.com).

Learning Task

Give examples where HSBC's values, and particularly CSR, might conflict with the quest for profit maximization.

The Social Role of Business

Some find this view of the modern corporation at odds with reality. They particularly dispute the view that modern capitalism is at all like the classical capitalism of economics textbooks where firms have no economic or political power because they are subject to market forces. As we saw in Chapter Three most modern markets are oligopolistic in nature with a few very large and powerful firms dominating many markets. We also saw in Chapter One that these players are active politically using their power to influence policy in their favour, for example, in removing barriers to trade and investment. The idea that the modern corporation is a passive player in the economy is far from the truth. They are powerful players in the world economy whose actions will have an impact both economically and socially so the modern argument about CSR is not whether corporations should engage in CSR but how they do and why they do. In terms of how, as we shall see, there is no universal agreement about what constitutes good CSR.

The view of the corporation as a private body with an agent(s) acting for a principal(s) is peculiar to the UK and North America. In Europe and Japan corporations are viewed much more as public bodies with objectives including obligations to a wider set of groups, investors, employees, suppliers, and customers. There is no difficulty in these countries regarding corporations as social institutions with a strong public interest agenda. In these companies managers are charged with pursuing the interests of all stakeholders whereas in the UK and North America the maximization of shareholder value is the goal. In the UK the Companies Act 1985 extended the duties of directors to act not just in the interest of its members (shareholders) but also employees. This has been extended in the Companies Act 2006 which includes the following section:

172 Duty to promote the success of the company

(1) A director of a company must act in the way he considers, in good faith, would be most likely to promote the success of the company for the benefit of its members as a whole, and in doing so have regard (amongst other matters) to –

 (a) the likely consequences of any decision in the long term,

 (b) the interests of the company's employees,

 (c) the need to foster the company's business relationships with suppliers, customers and others,

 (d) the impact of the company's operations on the community and the environment,

 (e) the desirability of the company maintaining a reputation for high standards of business conduct, and

 (f) the need to act fairly as between members of the company.

Note that this is to 'promote the success of the company'. Rather than driving a new agenda, this is legislation catching up with reality as most large corporations have already realized that to be successful, or at least not to court disaster, then they must, as a minimum, take into account all of their stakeholders. In the words of the UK Government 'It enshrines in statute the concept of Enlightened Shareholder Value which recognizes that directors will be more likely to achieve long term sustainable success for the benefit of their shareholders if their companies pay appropriate regard to wider matters such as the environment and their employees'.

Why Do Firms Engage in CSR?

In terms of why firms engage in CSR there are two cases. The first is the 'business case' which argues that firms should engage in CSR because it is in their interest to do so, in other words it is 'enlightened self interest' that could help them grow, increase profits, and maintain market share. The second arises from a desire to 'do good', the normative case, which says what firms ought to do. It may also be the case that firms engage in CSR for both of these reasons.

The Business Case

According to the UK Government 'CSR is essentially about companies moving beyond a base of legal compliance to integrating socially responsible behaviour into their core values, in recognition of the sound business benefits in doing so' (www.csr.gov.uk).

For the UK Government the reason for business to undertake CSR is because it makes good business sense—although it would be difficult to sell to business in any other way. In many cases business has come to accept CSR, not because of the positive benefits it might bring but because they have awakened to the risks of ignoring it. Scandals such as those at ENRON and Worldcom undermined public trust in big business. Shell's failure to consult with, or to take into account the reaction of Greenpeace to their proposed sinking of a North Sea oil platform led to international protests and a damaged reputation. Nike, Gap, Big Pharma, Yahoo! and many others have suffered damage to their reputations from well publicized CSR failures. Reputation management is a critical component of corporate success and one of the reasons that, according to Porter and Kramer (2006) 'of the 250 largest multinational corporations, 64% published CSR reports in 2005'. The authors go on to say that much of this was about demonstrating the company's social sensitivity rather than a coherent framework for CSR activities. Very often this activity is lodged in the Public Relations departments of these companies and is a defensive reaction focused on avoiding the disasters that have struck others.

From the corporation's point of view there is good reason for this as modern consumers are better and more instantly informed than ever. An oil spill in Alaska, a chemical explosion in India, violation of tribal rights in Nigeria, an explosion at an oil refinery in Texas, the revelation of child labour in a garment factory all make headline news in the Western media. Consumers want to know where the products they consume come from, under what conditions they were produced and, more recently, what size the carbon footprint is. Body Shop built its marketing strategy around being aware of these concerns and responding to them.

Non-governmental organizations (NGOs) such as Greenpeace, Friends of the Earth, Christian Aid, Oxfam, WWF, and Amnesty International are also watching. There are literally hundreds of thousands, if not millions, of these organizations operating across the world, many of them exceedingly well resourced (see Crane and Matten 2006; Chapter Ten). Greenpeace operates across 41 different countries and has 2.8 million supporters actively financing its activities, as well as receiving money from charitable foundations. Oxfam in 2006/07 raised £290.7 million to finance its activities.

Another reason that many large corporations have increased the size of their CSR departments is to deal with NGOs. NGOs of course differ in their view of business. Some, such as the Business Council for Sustainable Business, have a membership made up of some of the world's leading companies. The council has as part of its vision 'to support the business license to operate' by being a 'leading business advocate on sustainable development' (www.wbcsd.org). So not all NGOS are critical of business, but many are, and some, such as Oxfam, have a quite different view of the world and a different set of priorities—especially in the international arena. Sensible companies try to build relationships with relevant NGOs either through dialogue or in some cases through partnership. The World Food programme, managed by the UN, has a number of corporate partners including TNT, the Boston Consulting Group, and International Paper (US). TNT is a global mail, express, and logistics company and supports WWF by organizing airlift services in emergencies such as the Asian tsunami in 2004. It also has an active volunteering programme with staff seconded to WWF around the world (http://group.tnt.com/wfp; www.wfp.org).

Leading companies have now moved from the defensive stances of early CSR efforts to explore new ways of engaging with a range of external stakeholders. A stakeholder is any individual, group, or organization that is affected by or can affect the activities of a business. They therefore have an interest in the decisions of the business and equally, it is argued, the determination of strategy should take into account the actions and wishes of stakeholders. This would be true whatever the motivations of the firm but in arguing that firms have an obligation to society other than their economic role then the recognition of who and what is affected is fundamental to the realization of that obligation. Stakeholder analysis, or mapping, aims to identify a firm's stakeholders likely to be affected by the activities and outcomes of a firm's decisions and to assess how those stakeholders are likely to be affected.

Post, Preston and Sachs (2002) put forward a new approach to managing what they called the 'Extended Enterprise' (Figure 11.1). This stressed the role of recognizing stakeholder relationships in managing wealth creation. It recognized that a network of relationships existed which were not just a matter of contracts but which also needed to be managed through building relationships. Essential to realizing the benefits of CSR is the need to recognize and manage stakeholders in ways, according to Porter and Kramer 'most appropriate to each firm's strategy'. Too often, they say, companies have felt pressured into CSR activities so that approaches are 'fragmented and so disconnected from business and strategy as to obscure many of the greatest opportunities for companies to benefit society'. They go on to say:

> If, instead, corporations were to analyze their prospects for social responsibility using the same frameworks that guide their core business choices, they would discover that CSR can be much more than a cost, a constraint, or a charitable deed—it can be a source of opportunity, innovation, and competitive advantage (Porter and Kramer 2006).

Sustainability Ltd in their report, 'Buried Treasure, Uncovering the case for corporate sustainability' (available at www.sustainability.co.uk) identify 10 benefits which make up

Figure 11.1 The Stakeholder View of the Corporation

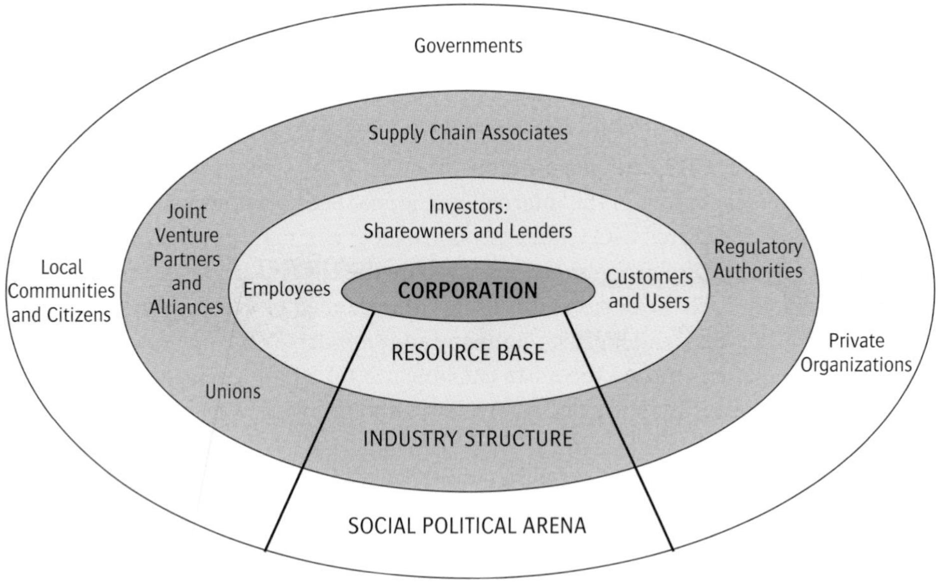

Source: Post, Preston and Sachs 2002

Mini Case Unilever in Africa

Unilever is the leading seller of soap across Asia and Africa, supporting many projects in Asia, investing in health infrastructure and facilities, and above all emphasizing the importance of hand washing with soap. It has now turned its attention to Africa, although it has been involved there for more than 100 years—when Lever Brothers first began exporting Sunlight soap to South Africa.

It has now formed a partnership with UNICEF, USAid, the London School of Hygiene and Tropical Medicine, the Belinda and Bill Gates Foundation, and several NGOs. They are joining in a campaign in Uganda, Kenya, Tanzania, Senegal, and Benin, to encourage hand washing—and the use of Lifebuoy soap. The campaign has a strong public interest motive as, according to the World Health Organization, in Uganda alone, 140 out of 1,000 children will die before the age of five, 17% from diarrhoea and 21% from pneumonia.

Unilever brings its marketing skills to the campaign with sophisticated ways of shaping behaviour, and stands to gain by sharing the cost of marketing and being seen to be in partnership with well known and trusted organizations such as UNICEF. They are hoping that their Lifebuoy soap will be linked so closely with hygiene and health that people will be prepared to pay more for it than the basic soap already available.

Therein lies a problem for some as they see poor people who already have ordinary soap being manipulated by big business to buy more expensive branded soap. On the other hand Unilever are quite open about their intentions. They have not claimed to be corporate 'do-gooders', they want to make washing hands a habit because it enables them to sell more bars of soap. According to Myrian Sidibe, who heads the campaign for Unilever 'It's the fact that we make money which makes our involvement sustainable ... people know we're not going to leave next year when the chairman's wife finds a new charity'.

Sources: *Financial Times*, 15 November 2007; International Water and Sanitation Centre (www.irc.nl)

Source: www.istockphoto.com

the business case. The first four of these are financial performance measures, while the remaining six are the financial drivers of that performance:

- Shareholder value—seen by many as the best way to measure performance especially over the long term. CSR activities were found at worst to be neutral and in some instances added considerable value.

- Revenue—there was strong evidence of a positive impact on revenues.

- Operational efficiency—more efficient environmental processes can lead to operational efficiency as can reducing waste. Better motivated staff (see below) can also help companies reduce their operating costs.

- Access to capital—CSR activity has limited impact on availability to capital as investors have traditionally looked only at the financial indicators of performance but as companies improve their CSR strategies and financial performance improves as a result of this then greater access to capital should follow. There is now an increasing number of investment funds which screen out companies that do not meet certain CSR performance criteria, e.g. anything to do with the arms trade. This is commonly known as socially responsible investing (SRI).

- Customer attraction—many surveys show that customers are concerned about the environmental impact of the products they consume, about who made them and under what conditions they were made. Some are prepared to pay a premium price for goods which they consider meet high CSR standards.

- Brand value and reputation—is strongly influenced by CSR activities. The market value of a company is largely dependent upon its reputation and the value of its brands. According to Interbrand (www.interbrand.com) in 2007 Coca Cola was the most valuable brand in the world at US$65 billion, with Microsoft second at US$59 billion. Ford and Gap, for which consumers had negative perceptions in 2007, lost 19% and 15% respectively from the value of their brands.

- Human and intellectual capital—just as prospective employees are put off from what are seen as bad employers then those seen as leaders in the field of CSR will more easily attract and retain staff. Moreover they are likely to have a more highly motivated workforce.

- Risk profile—i.e. the extent to which a company is at risk of losing reputation. In our opening case study Gap was found to be using, through one of its suppliers, child labour but it was swift to respond because it had the policies and infrastructure in place to do so. It was also a member of the Business Leaders Initiative on Human Rights, a group of companies wanting to find ways of applying human rights in global business.

- Innovation—the incentive to design and deliver new products, services, or processes can come from the drive to undertake CSR activities. Water is vital to Coca Cola so they are involved in a number of projects (see www.thecoca-colacompany.com) one of which is plant performance—in which they have been able to improve water use efficiency by more than 19% since 2002.

- Licence to operate—this is the level of acceptance by customers, local communities, NGOs, and other stakeholders of the company's right to operate. A poor reputation can lead to constant criticism from activist groups and a loss of reputation. Conversely those with a good reputation can often more easily recover when things go wrong. Monsanto is the world's leading producer of genetically modified seed and also adopts fairly aggressive marketing methods. It does not seem to be particularly concerned about its 'licence to operate' and as a result tends to be more targeted by activists than do similar companies.

Learning Task

Access the report from Sustainability Ltd to help you explain the ways in which each of the drivers of performance could lead to improved financial performance.

The Moral Case for Corporate Social Responsibility

The moral case for CSR is that it is the right thing to do, not because it yields greater financial return, but as a good corporate citizen with the same social and environmental obligations of any other citizen, i.e. you and me.

The first stage in this argument attributes the status of 'personhood' to the corporation so that they could be considered 'moral agents' and be held accountable for their actions. See the argument above (Goodpaster and Mathews 1982, French 1979) which likens the corporation to an individual.

The second strand of the argument emphasizes the social nature of the corporation, i.e. that it is a creation of society and should therefore serve the needs of society. Writers (Donaldson 1982, Anshen 1983) draw on social contract theory (the view that individuals' moral and/or political obligations are dependent upon an agreement between them to form society) to support these arguments. Anshen argues that the agreement is one which changes as society evolves. In the 1950s when living conditions were much worse in the West than they are now society's expectation of business (and so their obligation to society) was to produce the goods required by society. Indeed it is as well to remember that, from society's point of view, the basic purpose of business is to be the efficient provider of goods and services. Environmental damage, poor working conditions, and inequalities were seen as a fair price to pay for the improving standard of living. As Western societies grew richer the trade off between material well-being and the quality of life changed, and the expectations of business to provide safe places to work, not to damage the environment, to respect human rights etc. have become the expectation confronting business.

Stakeholder theory is an offshoot of this theory which says that business corporations are part of the wider society in which they develop relationships with groups or constituencies (to include the natural environment). They are part of a social system and dependent on each other, as opposed to the Friedman view which sees them as separate entities operating at arm's length.

Other writers, such as De George (2005), reinforce this view of corporations as social institutions by emphasizing that they are indeed creations of society. They are legal creations permitted by the State. They have to go though a process of application to receive their 'charter of incorporation' which brings them into existence and as such society can then expect these institutions to act for society as a whole. It is the corporation's 'licence to operate' which can of course be withdrawn if those expectations are not met. This also underpins the 'corporate citizen' view of the corporations in which the corporation is regarded as an institutional citizen with rights and obligations just like any other citizen.

Other arguments put forward include the following:

- Large corporations have enormous power and are endowed with substantial resources which they should use responsibly for the good of society. If we were to list countries in order of their GDP then Wal-Mart, the biggest company by revenue, would be 21st on the list. ExxonMobil would be 22nd, relegating Austria to 23rd with Royal Dutch Shell standing at 24th (see Table 11.1).

Table 11.1 The Size of Companies

Country	GDP 2006 $US Mill	Company	Revenue $US Mill
Poland	337,000	Wal-Mart	351,139
Austria	309,300	Exxon Mobil	347,254
Saudi Arabia	286,200	Royal Dutch Shell	318,845
Indonesia	264,400	BP	274,316
Norway	261,700	General Motors	207,349
Denmark	256,300	Toyota Motor	204,746
South Africa	200,500	Chevron	200,567
Portugal	176,600	DaimlerChrysler	190,191
Venezuela	147,900	Conoco Phillips	172,451
Malaysia	131,800	Total	168,357
Pakistan	124,000	General Electric	168,307
Czech Republic	118,900	Ford Motor	160,126
Colombia	105,500	ING Group	158,274
Chile	111,800	Citigroup	146,777
Hungary	113,100	AXA	139,738

Source: *Fortune Magazine*, 23 July 2007, Available at http://money.cnn.com; CIA World Factbook (2007)

- Business decisions will have social and environmental consequences so corporations must take responsibility for those decisions.
- Business has been instrumental in causing many of today's problems, such as global warming and resource depletion, and therefore has a responsibility to solve these problems and avoid creating further problems.

As we have seen CSR is definitely on the corporate agenda, but whether business sees this as a duty to society, in the sense implied here, is open to great doubt. The evidence presented earlier paints a picture of business reluctantly taking up CSR as a defensive reaction to protect reputation possibly leading to recognition that CSR activities may well improve business performance. Many commentators would argue that the argument is a distraction. In the words of David Grayson (Doughty Chair of Corporate Responsibility, Cranfield School of Management):

> In my experience, business leaders committed to Corporate Responsibility do it for a mixture of 'it just makes business sense and it's the right thing to do.' In practice, those percentages may vary for the same business leader depending on the topic; and certainly will vary even within a business and between businesses. I think we should stop searching for the Holy Grail of precise motivation. We would be much more sensibly employed on improving the practice of management so that whatever the particular motivation, the performance can be commercially viable (Sense and Sustainability: Inaugural lecture 2007).

Learning Task

Access the business principles document of Royal Dutch Shell Plc by searching on their website at: www.shell.com

Having read the above how would you classify Shell's commitment to corporate social responsibility? Using this document design a stakeholder map for the Shell company.

Global CSR

Is global CSR any different from domestic CSR? Not in principle but the implementation is far more complex. Take the argument above that modern CSR reflects the changed expectations of society and that the trade off between growth and the negative impacts of that growth is no longer acceptable. China could justifiably argue that they are at that stage in their growth where the cost of their improved living standards, in terms of damage to the environment, is acceptable. They are of course growing in entirely different conditions—in which global warming is a threat to everybody—but what does this mean for the global corporations operating in China? Should they be able to operate under the less stringent environmental legislation that exists in that country or should they be working to the same standards that they work to in their home economy? Is there is an obligation on the West to share new technologies with developing countries as much of the growth of companies in the West took place in an era of less stringent environmental controls?

Countries differ not just in their environmental legislation but also in the institutions that govern the countries which in some cases, e.g. China, are not very effective. They also differ in their customs and their culture (see Chapter Five). Setting up operations overseas because it is cheaper might be very attractive, but why is it cheaper? Wages are lower, working hours longer, health and safety regulations are lax and not policed very well. Is this acceptable? Child labour is illegal but quite common. Would you tolerate this if these were your factories or if it was happening in your supplier's factories? If the answer is no and an undercover investigator discovers this and reports it to the Western media, how would you react? Would you instantly close down the factory? What effect would this have on the children working there? These are the types of issues facing global companies in their everyday operations and it isn't that there is one domestic set of circumstances, and one overseas set of circumstances, every country will have some differences. Shell, for example, is a global group of companies working in more than 130 countries and territories and employing 108,000 people worldwide.

Whose Standards?

Global companies have the problem of doing business in many countries in which the 'ways of doing things' differ. They therefore have the difficult task of deciding which standards to adopt. Should they take a principled stand and adopt a universal set of principles wherever they operate or take a different approach in each country and operate according to the appropriate standards of that country? The first approach appears morally attractive in that we have a tendency to assume that our own standards are the 'right' or 'best' standards and we therefore tend to judge others by those standards but this can result in an ethnocentric (believing that the customs and traditions of your own nationality are better than those of others) morality which opens multinational companies to the charge of cultural imperialism. It would satisfy those critics who accuse MNCs of exploiting cultural differences for their own benefit but it may offend those host cultures whose accepted practices may be very different or it may well be impossible to operate without adopting host country practices. For example, Yahoo! and Google operate search engines in China which are self-censoring in order to satisfy Beijing. This offends many in the West who are used to freedom of expression but Google argues that it would be more damaging to pull out of China altogether.

Learning Task

Consider the claim put forward by Google that it would be more damaging to pull out of China altogether. Why would it be more damaging? Draw up a map of stakeholders and assess the impact of withdrawal on each of them. Do you think Google is right to stay in China? You might want to access the web site of the pressure group Reporters without Borders (www.rsf.org).

The other extreme is termed cultural relativism and, put simply, says 'when in Rome do as the Romans do'. This approach recognizes that countries and cultures are different and that MNCs in operating in different countries should recognize and accommodate those differences. This is often used as a reason by MNCs to adopt practices which enhance their profits but would be questionable in their home country.

These extreme ethical approaches are useful to business decision makers to the extent that they do serve to highlight the problems. Donaldson (1989) has suggested that there are some universal principles that companies and nations could agree to work towards. This entails respect for and promotion of some minimal rights:

- Freedom of physical movement
- Ownership of property
- Freedom from torture
- Fair trial
- Freedom from discrimination

- Physical security
- Speech and association
- Minimal education
- Political participation
- Subsistence

One might argue about which rights should be included, and this may appear as a peculiarly Western set of rights, but this approach to prescribing minimum standards is the approach that has been developed albeit in a fragmented fashion. Many companies have responded to the CSR debate by developing their own codes of conduct for their global operations and many international organizations have developed principles which seek to guide companies to best practice in CSR. The United Nations (UN) Global Compact is one such initiative. The Global Compact was launched on 26 July 2000, when several dozen business leaders came together at UN headquarters to join an international intiative that would bring companies together with UN agencies, labour, and civil society to advance universal social and environmental principles. There were originally nine principles in the areas of human rights, labour, the environment and a tenth concerning anti-corruption was added in 2004. Today the Global Compact is the world's largest CSR initiative with around 6,000 participants (of which over 4,000 are businesses) in 120 countries.

The Ten Principles

The principles are derived from:

- The Universal Declaration of Human Rights
- The International Labour Organization's Declaration on Fundamental Principles and Rights at Work
- The Rio Declaration on Environment and Development
- The United Nations Convention Against Corruption

The Global Compact (www.unglobalcompact.org) asks companies to 'embrace, support and enact, within their sphere of influence, a set of core values in the areas of human rights, labour standards, the environment, and anti-corruption'.

(See Chapter Ten for a more detailed analysis of the global compact Principles 7, 8, and 9.)

Learning Task

Chapter Ten outlines the business case for adhering to Principles 7, 8, and 9. Access the UN's web site on the Global Compact and make the business case for adhering to the other principles of the global compact. Do you think that this is asking too much of business?

Table 11.2 UN Global Compact Principles

Human Rights	Principle 1: Businesses should support and respect the protection of internationally proclaimed human rights; and
	Principle 2: make sure that they are not complicit in human rights abuses.
Labour Standards	Principle 3: Businesses should uphold the freedom of association and the effective recognition of the right to collective bargaining;
	Principle 4: the elimination of all forms of forced and compulsory labour;
	Principle 5: the effective abolition of child labour;
	Principle 6: the elimination of discrimination in respect of employment and occupation.
Environment	Principle 7: Businesses should support a precautionary approach to environmental challenges;
	Principle 8: undertake initiatives to promote greater environmental responsibility;
	Principle 9: encourage the development and diffusion of environmentally friendly technologies.
Anti-Corruption	Principle 10: Businesses should work against corruption in all its forms, including extortion and bribery.

Source: www.unglobalcompact.org

Four of the major weaknesses of these codes are:

1. Not many of the world's MNCs are members. Four thousand sounds like a lot but is actually only a small proportion of the world's tens of thousands of MNCs. However, many of those who have joined are important in terms of size and reputation.
2. The codes are voluntary and the UN cannot afford to be too selective about who joins the initiative.
3. It is difficult to monitor the impact the Compact is making.
4. No effective sanctions for breaches of the code.

Companies that join are simply required to work towards implementation of the principles. They do have to report annually on their activities through what the compact refers to as 'Communication on Progress'. This entails a statement of continuing support, a description of practical actions, and a measurement of outcomes. In measuring outcomes participants are encouraged to use the Global Reporting Initiative (GRI). The GRI is an attempt to produce standard sustainability reporting guidelines and make it as routine for companies as financial reporting. The GRI produces a standard format for companies to report on their economic, environmental, and social performance. Over 1,000 organizations, ranging from companies, public bodies, NGOs, and industry groups, use the guidelines which makes it the most common framework in use.

The picture then is of a complex global system in which the ability of the State to look after the public interest, even in relatively developed economies, is diminished. Global companies operate in many States which are weak and often corrupt. There are major

Figure 11.2 Per cent of respondents that agree completely that their company should do the following activities versus what their company actually does

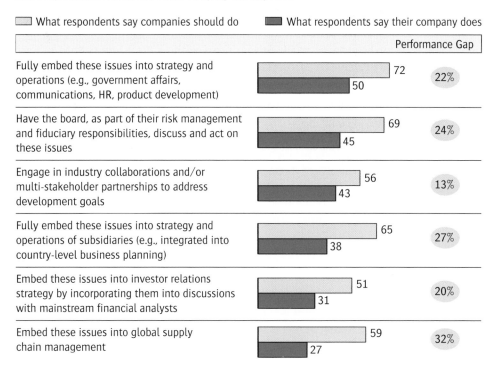

| | What respondents say companies should do | | What respondents say their company does |

		Performance Gap
Fully embed these issues into strategy and operations (e.g., government affairs, communications, HR, product development)	72 / 50	22%
Have the board, as part of their risk management and fiduciary responsibilities, discuss and act on these issues	69 / 45	24%
Engage in industry collaborations and/or multi-stakeholder partnerships to address development goals	56 / 43	13%
Fully embed these issues into strategy and operations of subsidiaries (e.g., integrated into country-level business planning)	65 / 38	27%
Embed these issues into investor relations strategy by incorporating them into discussions with mainstream financial analysts	51 / 31	20%
Embed these issues into global supply chain management	59 / 27	32%

world issues such as climate change, poverty, health issues, human rights, corruption, and ecosystem problems which are also beyond the powers of national governments and internationally there is a lack of effective governance. There are also a growing number of very active NGOs, often campaigning on a single issue, who are demanding action from companies. In turn the health of companies will in the long term depend on the health of the global economic, social and political, and environmental systems. The case for CSR rests on a recognition by companies of this scenario and that they are in a unique position to address these issues. Many have responded, perhaps for defensive reasons, by engaging with their stakeholders and developing codes of conduct for their global activities. International organizations have also added to the drive for CSR by developing their own codes or sets of principles to which they encourage companies to adhere. How much of this is rhetoric or reality is difficult to say but a survey of business executives in the USA found that although a majority believed in embedding CSR activities into operations a considerable gap existed when asked if they believed the activities were embedded (see Figure 11.2).

Having examined the case for CSR we now turn to examine in more detail some of the specific issues facing global companies.

Corruption

Corruption is a major issue for international business. Corruption occurs when organizations or individuals profit improperly through their position. According to the World

Bank, 'It involves behaviour on the part of officials in the public and private sectors, in which they improperly and unlawfully enrich themselves and/or those close to them, or induce others to do so, by misusing the position in which they are placed'. It occurs in both the public and the private sectors, for example, when private businesses want public contracts or licences or when private firms wish to do business with others. Bribery is only one example of corruption. It can also include extortion, that is where threats and violence are used to get someone to act or not act in a certain way, favouritism, nepotism, embezzlement, fraud, and illegal monetary contributions to political parties (SIDA, see www.sida.se). In some cultures corruption is accepted as the norm and many commentators, and sometimes the law, make a distinction between bribes and so called 'facilitation payments' which are everyday small payments made to officials to 'ease the wheels of business'. International pressure groups such as Transparency International make no such distinction.

What's Wrong with Bribery and Corruption?

According to Sue Hawley (2000) Western businesses pay massive amounts of money to gain contracts or concessions they would not otherwise have won. She estimates that something in the order of US$80 billion a year is paid and that this is about the amount that the UN believes would be needed to eradicate world poverty. The cost of these bribes falls mainly on the poor, whether it is through the diversion of aid money into corrupt officials pockets, or the hiking of prices when the cost of a bribe is passed on in raised prices to consumers.

- Bribery and corruption undermine the proper workings of a market economy which can seriously reduce GDP in the poorest countries. It distorts price and cost considerations so that resources are not necessarily used in the most efficient way. Decisions are based on 'who pays the biggest bribes' rather than price, quality, service, and innovation. This raises prices for everyone which has the greatest impact on the poor.

- Resources are often diverted away from public service projects such as schools and hospitals towards more high profile projects such as dams and power stations where there is more scope for improper payments. This again impacts most on the poor who are denied vital public services.

- Corruption is ethically wrong. It is an abuse of power which undermines the integrity of all concerned.

- Corruption undermines the democratic process and the rule of law. Just as business has to earn its licence to operate so does Government. Politicians, Government officers and institutions all lose their legitimacy in a climate of corruption. Again the poor are likely to be the biggest losers in such a situation.

- The environment is also likely to suffer in such a regime through the lack of environmental legislation or its non-enforcement as corrupt officials fill their pockets in return for turning a blind eye.

- For business there are several risks:

- ○ The risk that accusations of corruption, whether proved or not, can lead to loss of reputation.

- ○ A legal risk. Bribery and corruption is generally illegal wherever it occurs but even if not, because of international pressure (the UN convention against corruption), it is becoming increasingly illegal at home to engage in these practices elsewhere.

- ○ In paying bribes there is no certainty you get what you want and no recourse to any retribution or compensation if you don't.

- ○ If you are known as a bribe payer then repeat demands are likely to be made.

- ○ It adds substantially to the cost of doing business.

- ○ If you cheat so will your competitors. It makes doing business much more difficult.

- ○ Employees and other stakeholders will lose trust in the business.

Each year Transparency International produces the Corruption Perception index. This index ranks 180 countries according to the level of corruption perceived to exist among public officials and politicians. A score of zero indicates highly corrupt and a score of 10 highly clean.

On the map (Figure 11.3), the darker the colour the higher the perceived incidence of corruption which is lower in North America, Western Europe, and Australasia and high in Central and South America, Africa, Asia, and Eastern Europe.

Figure 11.3 Corruption Perception Index 2007

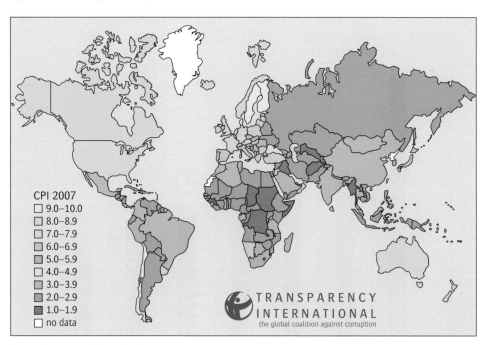

CPI 2007
□ 9.0–10.0
□ 8.0–8.9
□ 7.0–7.9
□ 6.0–6.9
□ 5.0–5.9
□ 4.0–4.9
□ 3.0–3.9
□ 2.0–2.9
■ 1.0–1.9
□ no data

TRANSPARENCY INTERNATIONAL
the global coalition against corruption

Source: Transparency International

Learning Task

Access the web site of Transparency International at (www.transparency.org) and access the Corruption Perception Index on which the map above is based.

1. Explain what the Corruption Perception Index measures.
2. Look up Table 2.1 in Chapter Two. For each of the countries plot on a graph their rank and CPI score against their GDP. What conclusions can you draw from your graph?

In an international survey of corruption by law firm Simmons and Simmons and Control Risks (2006) more than 4 out of 10 firms claimed that bribery by a competitor had caused them to lose business. The problem was particularly acute in Hong Kong where more than three quarters of companies said that they had lost business in the previous five years (Figure 11.4). Even in the USA where the Foreign Corrupt Practices Act has been in force since 1977, and where the Sarbanes-Oxley Act has imposed stringent requirements on business regarding corporate governance, 44% of companies said that they had lost business due to corruption.

The sectors most affected were construction, oil, gas, and mining. A respondent from Hong Kong commented that bribery was 'just part of business' (p 6). More than one third of the respondents claimed that they had been put off from investing in countries because of their reputation for corruption. The nationality of the firms who were deterred from

Figure 11.4 Companies believing that they had failed to win a contract or gain new business because a competitor had paid a bribe over the last 5 years / 12 months

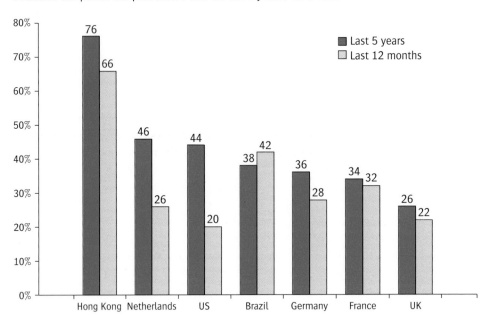

Source: Simmons and Simmons and Control Risks 2006

Mini Case Corruption in Costa Rica

Costa Rica is a small, relatively poor country in Central America. Reports of corruption in the health service started to emerge in 2001. Corruption took several forms and operated at different levels in the service. Investigators found that excessively high prices had been paid for the purchase of medicines and equipment, private training courses, and medical research; the construction of hospitals; and management services.

In 2004, the chief executive of the health service, members of the board of directors, several health service managers, and the former president of the country Rafael Angel Calderón were charged with corruption. It was alleged that they had pocketed US$39 million of a Finnish government loan intended for the modernization of hospitals. The modernization contract was won by a Finnish consortium, Instrumentarium Corporation Medko Medical (ICMM). ICMM paid a commission of US$8.8 million (20% of the value of the loan) to Corporación Fischel, the consortium's Costa Rican representative. This commission ended up in the foreign bank accounts of health service directors and senior government officials. Journalists discovered that the head of the health service was living in a house worth US$750,000, which had been paid for by Corporación Fischel.

Corruption appears to be endemic in the health service for the ICMM case is not the first. Little action was taken by the authorities against those responsible. This may be due to the close links between senior officials in the health service and political parties.

Source: Transparency International

investing could be seen as a reflection of their domestic attitude to corruption. Most deterred were British, US, and Dutch firms. Least deterred were companies from Hong Kong and Brazil.

Attempts to control corruption vary markedly from one country to another. According to the World Bank developed countries put more effort into control measures whereas developing countries and eastern European States are particularly prone to ignore corruption or to restrict the powers of independent agencies which are required to be set up under the UN convention (*Financial Times*, 15 December 2006).

Child Labour

In the world today over 300 million children aged between 5 and 17 are economically active (so called 'child work') with over 200 million involved in child labour and more than 120 million doing work that is damaging to their mental, physical, and emotional development. They do it because their survival, and that of their families, depends on it.

Trying to arrive at a clear picture of child work is a difficult task. We are all familiar with the horror pictures of child mine workers, soldiers, and prostitutes but most child work takes place within the family in agriculture and domestic work and in societies where this is often seen as culturally acceptable. The ILO divides child work into three different categories, economically active, child labour, and children in hazardous work. Economically active is a very wide category which refers to any form of productive work, paid or unpaid.

Child labour is work that is done by a child under the specified age for work which either deprives them of schooling, causes them to leave school early, or requires a combination of schooling and long hours of work. In 2004 there were 166 million children between the ages of 5 and 14 involved in child labour.

The worst forms of child labour are those which expose children to hazardous conditions and are those which most of the international community has agreed to try to end. In 2004 of the 166 million child labourers between the ages of 5 and 14 years of age 74 million fell into this category.

Not all work done by children is considered harmful, and therefore in policy terms it is not just a case of eliminating all child work. Work that does not damage health or interfere with schooling may be considered positive in contributing to personal development by developing skills and experience and preparing children for adult life, so called 'child work'. The International Labour Organization (ILO) has two conventions relating to child labour. Convention 138 allows 'child work' but aims at the abolition of child labour and stipulates that the minimum age for entry into the workforce should not be less than the minimum age for finishing school. Convention 182 calls for elimination of the worst forms of child labour for all under 18s. This includes slavery, forced recruitment for use in armed conflict, prostitution, any illicit activity, and work which is likely to harm the health, safety, and morals of children. These conventions lay down the basic principles to be implemented by ratifying countries and are tools for governments to use, in consultation with employers and workers, to draft legislation to conform with internationally acceptable standards. Nearly 87% of ILO members covering 77% of the world's children have ratified convention 182 and 79%, covering less than 63% have ratified convention 138. This still leaves a large number of children in countries which have made no commitment to either convention

Child labour is not simply a problem of the developing world, although most takes place there. The ILO estimated that in 2004 some 2.5 million children between the ages of 5 and 14 were economically active in the developed world. The Asian Pacific region has the highest number of child workers with 122 million, representing nearly 19% of the age group. This had fallen from 2000 but not by much. The greatest reduction had taken place in the Caribbean—from 17.4 million to 5.7 million. In Sub-Saharan Africa the numbers increased, but not as fast as the population so there was a slight decline in the activity ratio, although this remains the highest ratio at just over 1 in 4 children in this age group being economically active.

Why do Children Work?

Reasons for child work can be divided into push and pull, or supply and demand, factors. On the supply side or what pushes children into work:

- Poverty—poverty remains the most important factor which pushes children into work.
- Lack of educational opportunities—poor educational facilities or expensive facilities can exacerbate the problem.
- Family breakdown—divorce, death, illness can leave the family unit short of income. This has become a major problem in Africa because of the HIV/AIDS epidemic.
- Cultural practices—in many countries it is the practice for young children to help the family by looking after younger brothers and sisters or helping out on the land, by collecting firewood, or tending chickens for example.

Mini Case Cocoa Production in West Africa

The Global Chocolate market is worth more than US$5 billion per year. Most of that chocolate starts life in West Africa where 75% of the world's cocoa production is grown. The Ivory Coast is the largest producer with 40% of world production. Here some 650,000 small family run farms of less than 4 hectares grow cocoa as a cash crop alongside crops grown for food. Farms are often remote and as mechanization is not appropriate production is labour intensive.

The global supply chain is quite complex with many intermediaries before the chocolate reaches the final consumer. Cocoa growers generally sell to a middleman for cash once or twice a year and have to take whatever price they can get. The middleman sells on to processors or exporters. Prices are ultimately determined on the London Cocoa Terminal Market and the New York Cocoa Exchange but like many cash crops the farmer receives only a fraction of the world price.

There is therefore great pressure on the farmer to keep costs down and one way of achieving this is to employ child labour which is widespread. Most of the children are under 14, kept from schooling, work 12 hour days, using machetes to clear fields, applying pesticides and splitting the harvested cocoa pods to extract the beans. All of this falls into the ILO convention 182 of 'the worst form of child labour'.

In 2000 a British TV documentary was broadcast claiming that many children were working as slaves in the Ivory Coast. Because the demand for child labour outstrips the supply children were purchased from the neighbouring States of Burkino Faso, Mali, and Togo. Impoverished parents would receive between £70 and £100 for each child, depending on the age. These children, some as young as 6, were forced to endure the harsh working conditions, long hours, and many also faced physical abuse by their masters.

An IITA report in 2002 found that 284,000 children were working on West Africa's cocoa farms and that 2,500 may have been trafficked. The Ivorian Government blamed the international cocoa industry for keeping prices low. They in turn denied any knowledge or responsibility for the conditions on the farms as there were so many intermediaries in the supply chain. However an industry protocol was signed on 19 September 2001 which acknowledged that there were problems of forced child labour in West Africa and made a commitment to eliminate the problem. The protocol also established the International Cocoa Initiative made up of chocolate companies, confectionery trade associations, NGOs, and trade unions to work with governments to end the worst forms of child labour. The initial deadline was 2005 which was missed and extended to 2008 but a BBC programme in April 2007 uncovered evidence of continued widespread abuse, with children being kept out of schools and forced to work on farms without pay. US congress has given the industry until July 2008 to prove they are serious about ending child labour or they will face legislation.

Source: www.istockphoto.com

Sources: www.bbc.co.uk Anti-Slavery International, 'the Cocoa industry in West Africa: A history of exploitation'; Schrage and Ewing; IITA: Child Labour in the Cocoa Sector of West Africa, 2002

On the demand side or what pulls children into work:

- Cheap labour—employers tend to pay children less than their adult counterparts. Some, especially domestic workers, work unpaid.
- Obedience—even where children are paid the same rate as adults employers often prefer to employ children as they are much easier to control.
- Skills—the so-called 'nimble fingers' argument especially in industries such as carpet weaving. Probably a mythical argument but one which is used to justify the employment of children.
- Inadequate laws—or poorly understood and policed laws enable employers to continue employing children.
- Poor infrastructure—establishing the age of children in some countries can be difficult.

What's Wrong with Child Labour?

- Child labour is a denial of fundamental human rights. The United Nations has adopted the Convention on the Rights of the Child. Article 32 says that children should not be engaged in work which is hazardous, interferes with education, or is harmful to health.
- It steals their childhood from them.
- It prevents their education.
- Children are exploited by paying low wages or no wages at all.
- Children often work in poor conditions which can cause long-term health problems.
- It perpetuates poverty because lack of education limits earning potential.
- It can mean lower wages for everybody as they swell the labour supply and are usually paid lower wages than adults.
- Often replaces adult labour because they are cheaper to employ and easier to control.
- It is a long term cost to society as children are not allowed to fulfil their potential as productive human beings.

Millennium Development Goals

In 2000 the 189 members of the United Nations adopted the Millennium Development Goals. Eight goals with associated targets were established for the alleviation of world poverty and general development goals. These goals had been developed at a number of conferences that had taken place in the 1990s so although they were announced in 2000 the baseline for assessing progress towards them is 1990; the target date for achieving most of these is 2015. The goals and targets are:

Table 11.3 Millennium Development Goals

GOAL	TARGET
1 Eradicate extreme poverty and hunger	1 Halve, between 1990 and 2015, the proportion of people whose income is less the US$1 a day
	2 Halve, between 1990 and 2015, the proportion of people who suffer from hunger
2 Achieve universal primary education	3 Ensure that, by 2015, children everywhere, boys and girls alike, will be able to complete a full course of primary schooling
3 Promote gender equality and empower women	4 Eliminate gender disparity in primary and secondary education, preferably by 2005, and to all levels of education no later than 2015
4 Reduce child mortality rate	5 Reduce by two-thirds, between 1990 and 2015, the under-five mortality rate
5 Improve maternal health	6 Reduce by three-quarters, between 1990 and 2015, the maternal mortality ratio
6 Combat HIV/AIDS and other diseases	7 Have halted by 2015 and begun to reverse the spread of HIV/AIDS
	8 Have halted by 2015 and begun to reverse the incidence of malaria and other major diseases
7 Ensure environmental sustainability	9 Integrate the principles of sustainable development into country policies and programmes and reverse the loss of environmental resources
	10 Halve, by 2015, the proportion of people without sustainable access to safe drinking water and basic sanitation
	11 By 2020, to have achieved a significant improvement in the lives of at least 100 million slum dwellers
8 Develop a global partnership for development	12 Develop further an open, rule based, predictable, non-discriminatory trading and financial system
	13 Address the special needs of the least developed countries
	14 Address the special needs of landlocked countries and small island developing states
	15 Deal comprehensively with the debt problems of developing countries through national and international measures in order to make debt sustainable in the long term
	16 In cooperation with developing countries, develop and implement strategies for decent and productive work for youth
	17 In cooperation with pharmaceutical companies, provide access to affordable essential drugs in developing countries
	18 In cooperation with the private sector, make available the benefits of new technologies, especially information and communications

Source: The Millennium Development Goals Report Statistical Annex 2006 http://undp.org

The goals are not without their critics. See, for example, Clemens and Moss (2005) who argue that:

> Many poor countries, especially those in Africa, will miss the MDGs by a large margin. But neither African inaction nor a lack of aid will necessarily be the reason. Instead responsibility for near-certain failure lies with the overly-ambitious goals themselves and unrealistic expectation placed on aid.

How close is the world to reaching these targets? According to Gordon Brown (Prime Minister of the UK) in a speech to the United Nations in New York (31 July 2007) 'we are a million miles away from success'. According to him at current rates of progress the goal of reducing infant mortality rates by two-thirds would not be met until 2050, and of providing primary education for every child not until 2100.

The World Bank uses as its extreme poverty line an income of about US$1 a person per day, hence the target is framed in this way. Using this measure poverty has fallen in all regions since 1990 except in Sub-Saharan Africa where nearly 300 million people still live on less the US$1 per day, up from 240 million in 1990. The proportion for the world fell from 29% to 18% but the number fell by only 260 million because of population growth. Much of this fall was accounted for by the increased living standards in China. There are still about 1 billion people living on less than US$1 dollar a day. Sub-Saharan Africa stands out as the poorest area. The poverty rate rose from 42.3 % in 1981 to 47.7% in the mid 1990s. It has since fallen, but is still above 40% with some 298 million people living on less than US$1 per day. This represents about one third of the world's poor.

For the world as a whole the first target of halving the proportion of people living on less than US$1 a day in developing countries should be met but this depends on achieving a fairly rapid, by historical standards, average economic growth rate in developing countries of 3.6% per year. How this affects each area is dependent on the rate of economic growth in that area. Projections are that over 700 million people will be earning less than US$1 per day in 2015, and because of projected low growth rates in Sub-Saharan Africa the number of poor will actually increase to 345 million, nearly half of the world's poor.

In most areas of the developing world life expectancy has increased and varies from (in 2005) 63 years to 72 years. In Sub-Saharan Africa in 2005 it stood at 47 years, down from 49 years in 1990. This is because of an increase in the infant mortality rate, which at 163 per 1,000 is, by some way, the highest of the developing regions, and a high mortality rate in adults caused by HIV/AIDS.

UNICEF reported in December 2007 that the world is behind schedule for meeting almost all of the goals. Experts are, however, agreed that these goals are still achievable by 2015 but that this will require a stronger commitment from all involved. For much of the 20th century alleviation of the world's problems was largely seen as the task of governments and achieved by aid donations or through government sponsored organizations such as UNICEF. These organizations have dealt with the domestic governments of those countries in need, often themselves part of the problem. In the 1990s, following the 'fall of communism', the world changed as the 'Washington Consensus' (10 policy instruments Washington saw as necessary for economic success) encouraged States to step back and privatize and liberalize their economies. The private sector was encouraged to take on more responsibility and public-private partnerships have flourished both domestically and internationally. As a result companies have become much more involved in the activities of these countries and have a stake in their future success.

Kofi Annan (former United Nations Secretary General) has, in various speeches, pointed out that in a global society we are all responsible for each other's security and welfare and has called on business leaders to help achieve the MDGs. Making his final speech as Secretary General in December 2006 he said:

... it also applies to the increasingly integrated global market economy we live in today.

It is not realistic to think that some people can go on deriving great benefits from globalization while billions of their fellow human beings are left in abject poverty, or even thrown into it.

We have to give our fellow citizens, not only within each nation but in the global community, at least a chance to share in our prosperity.

Nelson and Prescott (2003), in an article for the United Nations Development Programme, point out why it is increasingly in the interests of business for the MDGs to succeed. They point out three business benefits:

- Investing in a sound business environment—a healthy and competent workforce, prosperous consumers, productive companies, and a well governed economy.

- Managing direct costs and risks—environmental degradation, climate change, HIV/AIDS, and poor health education systems can add to the cost and risks of doing business.

- Harnessing new business opportunities—innovative companies are finding that the MDGs are not just a matter of responsibility but that they provide long-term business opportunities.

Mini Case European Cooperative for Rural Development

The European Cooperative for Rural Development (EUCORD) is a Brussels based not-for-profit organization which was registered in 2003. Eucord specializes in bringing together public and private sector partners to undertake rural development projects. It works with local NGOs to implement these projects and takes responsibility for the overall management of the project and especially the financial reporting and accountability.

Eucord currently has four key projects on the go:

- the West African Potato Value Chain Development Project in Guinea and Senegal to enhance the income of potato farmers, mostly women;

- the Smallholder Initiative in Mali, Senegal, and Burkino Faso raising the income of farmers by using improved technologies;

- the Nigerian CropLife Training Programme trains young men in crop spraying techniques;

- the West African Sorghum Supply Chain project in Ghana and Sierra Leone.

The aim of this last project is the development of a reliable supply of sorghum. This five year scheme has received US$2.8 million in funds from the Common Fund for Commodities (a branch of the United Nations) and two private sector drinks companies, Diageo of the UK and Heineken of the Netherlands. Both companies brewed beer in many African countries but used traditional ingredients and imported barley produced elsewhere because conditions for growing barley are not ideal in Africa. Although they brewed beer with sorghum in Nigeria they did not in Ghana and Sierra Leone because they could not be sure of the reliability and quality of the supplies from local producers. But such has been the success of the project that when strong global demand led to rocketing prices for barley they were able to switch to using sorghum as their main ingredient. They are both now looking to brew beer from sorghum in as many African countries as possible. What has started as a socially responsible project in the end turned out to be a sustainable business enterprise.

Sources: www.eucord.org; *Financial Times*, 10 January 2008

Social Entrepreneurship

As in the above case solving social and environmental problems can be seen as opportunities for business development. In their book *The Power of Unreasonable People: How Social Entrepreneurs Create Markets and Change the World*, John Elkington and Pamela Hartigan argue that our future depends on what they refer to as 'social entrepreneurs'. Social entrepreneurs are people who look to establish social enterprises to deliver goods and services not yet met by existing market arrangements. The term entrepreneur is not new and these people are no different from the entrepreneurs of old in one sense, but the difference is that they are looking for solutions to some of the world's pressing problems. Profits are generated but the aim is to benefit those who are the worst off and grow the business. These are not the major multinational companies but, in the main, small and medium enterprises who are challenging the accepted ways of doing things. A good example is the UK's Belu Water, a bottled water company that donates all of it profits to global clean water projects. This company has changed the practices of the bottled drinks industry by using carbon-neutral packaging. It uses a compostable bottle made from corn and is challenging others to use similar packaging. With its profits it has installed hand pumps and wells for 20,000 people in India and Mali. Elkington and Hartigan (2008) urge conventional businesses to learn from the ways in which these new entrepreneurs work.

Similarly Bill Gates, founder of Microsoft, has made a case for leading businesses to 'do right by doing good' in what he calls 'creative capitalism'. In this he urged firms to turn their attention to solve the world's big problems, and particularly the world's inequalities. It is possible to make profits in these markets but where they couldn't he hoped recognition would be an incentive. Recognizing that this may not do the trick he also called on governments to favour those companies adopting 'creative capitalism' and pointed out the business benefits discussed earlier in this chapter, such as attracting increasingly values-driven young workers.

One aspect of company help to the world's poor has come from an increase in international volunteering. According to Hills and Mahmud (2007) 10 years ago there hardly was any international corporate volunteering but now 40% of major American corporations send volunteers around the world to work on development projects.

One example they give is of Pfizer (one of the world's leading pharmaceutical companies) which developed the Global Health Fellow program in 2002 to send skilled employees to provide technical assistance to partners for 3–6 months in Africa, Latin America, or Asia. One hundred and twenty-eight fellows had been deployed in 31 countries by September 2007. This provides much improved healthcare to these countries, increases the skill level of local staff, and improves the morale and leadership skills of Pfizer employees. It also helps Pfizer's image and subsequent relationships with global health providers to be seen actively providing solutions on a voluntary basis.

● CHAPTER SUMMARY

In this chapter we defined corporate social responsibility as the economic, social, and environmental obligations firms have to society. Some have a view that the only obligation that business owes to society is to maximize profit but many point out that this is not necessarily at odds with profit maximization as there is a strong business argument for pursuing CSR. Others argue that companies have a moral duty to pursue a wider set of objectives.

Firms operating in the international business environment face a more complex set of circumstances than those operating only in their own domestic economy not just because of the different economic and legal context but because of very different cultural norms. Firms must be wary of what might be seen as cultural imperialism. The United Nations has established the Global Compact which seeks to guide companies to best practice in CSR.

Two areas were highlighted to be of particular concern, child labour and corruption, both still common in much of the world. The Global Compact has standards to guide companies in both of these areas. The United Nations announced in 2000 the Millennium Development Goals, a set of targets for the alleviation of poverty and other development goals. They recognize the interdependence between growth, poverty reduction, and sustainable development. Some progress has been made but this has been far from uniform across the world or the goals. Their achievement will only be possible if business with government makes it their business in what Bill Gates calls 'creative capitalism'. Social entrepreneurs will also contribute to these major world challenges.

● REVIEW QUESTIONS

1. Explain what commentators mean when they claim that there is only one responsibility of business and that is to make as much money as possible for their owners.

2. Outline the benefits that might accrue to business by being socially responsible.

3. Social responsibility is just good PR. Discuss.

4. Explain, using examples, what is meant by cultural relativism.

5. Do western firms have any responsibility for the way in which their overseas suppliers operate?

6. You are working for a large multinational drinks company wanting to set up a bottling plant overseas. In order to obtain planning permission you need to make a facilitation payment (bribe) to a local politician but your company has a strict no bribes policy. The building of the plant will be subcontracted to a domestic construction company and one way round this would be to inflate the payment to this company so that they could make the facilitation payment. What would you do? Justify your decision.

7. Explain what is meant by child labour. What might the consequences be for a major western firm caught employing young children in overseas factories?

8. Define what is meant by **social entrepreneurship**. Explain, giving examples, how social entrepreneurs might contribute to the achievement of the Millennium Development Goals.

Case Study Saudi Arabia, Corruption, and BAE

Saudi Arabia has a population of around 28 million with a GDP per head in 2006 of US$13,600. It is rich in oil and natural gas and holds approximately 25% of the world's proven oil reserves. It is a monarchical State where power lies in the hands of the royal family, the Sauds. The royal family is widely perceived both domestically and abroad as being corrupt, the corruption being facilitated by the lack of transparency in government finances. No breakdown is given of revenues and expenditures and there is no independent audit of public finances. The royal family is perceived as misappropriating government funds, property rights, and contracts and as riding roughshod over civil and criminal justice procedure. The extensive Saud family is seen to profit from the award of arms contracts, oil revenues, and the profits from State-financed corporations. Transparency International ranks Saudi Arabia 70 out of 163 countries in its league table of corruption.

BAE, the UK defence equipment supplier faced allegations that it corruptly won orders for aircraft and military equipment orders in the al-Yamamah deal from Saudi Arabia. The allegations of illegal payments by BAE dated back to the 1980s and the £43bn for the supply of Tornado jets. BAE was accused of making payments worth £2 billion over a number of years to Prince Bandar, a leading member of the Saudi royal family. His attitude to corruption was encapsulated in a television interview when he said that it was human nature. BAE refuted the allegations claiming that it was committed to meeting the highest ethical standards and that it did not tolerate unethical behaviour.

An investigation was launched by the UK Serious Fraud Office but was forced to drop the investigation by the UK Government. BAE had lobbied the Government on the grounds that the Saudis would take their business elsewhere were the probe to continue. The then Prime Minister, Tony Blair, justified the decision to halt the probe, arguing that continuing the inquiry could threaten the flow of Middle East intelligence provided by the Saudis on Islamic terrorists.

The decision to drop the probe into BAE caused others to react. The US Department of Justice started an investigation under the Foreign Corrupt Practices Act because BAE had used the US banking system to transfer money to accounts controlled by Prince Bandar. It asked Britain to hand over all evidence of secret payments made to the Saudi Royal family to secure arms contracts. The OECD, a grouping of 30 big economies interested in fighting corruption, asked the UK authorities to explain why the Serious Fraud Office had stopped its investigation. A number of financial institutions also expressed concerned about the impact on the City of London as an international centre of finance. They wanted the rule of law to be enforced independently of any political considerations.

Sources: *Financial Times*, 15 and 22 December 2006, 4 January, 16 June 2007; Carnegie Endowment for International Peace (www.carnegieendowment.org); CIA Factbook; www.bbc.co.uk; *The Guardian*, 13 September 2003 and 16 July 2007; Transparency International (www.transparency.org)

Questions

1. What are the implications for companies wishing to do business in Saudi Arabia? Specifically, might US and UK companies feel the need to respond in different ways?

2. Was the decision to halt the investigation a good one for BAE? To answer this question look at the immediate impact on BAE's share price (the decision was made in the middle of December 2006).

Now consider whether it was such a good decision for the company in the longer run.

3. Discuss the arguments for and against the decision of the UK authorities to drop the investigation into BAE.

4. Advance reasons for the concerns expressed by:

  • financial institutions in London

  • the OECD.

5. Why do you think Saudi Arabia is dogged by corruption?

6. Go to the Transparency International web site www.transparency.org and find out the extent of corruption in the Middle East. Are there any Middle Eastern countries where companies wishing to avoid corruption could do business?

Online Resource Centre
www.oxfordtextbooks.co.uk/orc/hamilton_webster/

Visit the supporting online resource centre for additional material which will help you with your assignments, essays and research, or you may find these extra resources helpful when revising for exams.

FURTHER READING

For a textbook exploring ethics and the CSR agenda within the context of globalization read:

● Crane, A. and Matten, D. (2006) *Business ethics – a European Perspective: Managing Corporate Citizenship and Sustainability in the Age of Globalisation*, 2nd edn. Oxford: Oxford University Press

For a book advocating a strategic approach to CSR taking into account global stakeholders see:

● Werther, B. and Chandler, D. (2006) *Strategic Corporate Social Responsibility.* Sage Publications

To read more about Social Entrepreneurship see:

● Elkington, J. and Hartigan, P. (2008) *The Power of Unreasonable People: How Social Entrepreneurs Create Markets and Change the World.* Harvard Business Press

REFERENCES

Anshen, M. (1970) 'Changing the Social Contract: A Roll for Business'. Reprinted in Beauchamp, T. and Bowie, N. (eds). *Ethical Theory and Business*, 2nd edn. Englewood Cliffs, NJ: Prentice Hall

Anti-Slavery International (2004) 'The Cocoa Industry in West Africa: A history of exploitation'

Clemens, M. and Moss, T. (2005) 'What's Wrong with the Millennium Development Goals'. Centre for Global Development

De George, R. (2005) *Business Ethics*, 6th edn. Englewood Cliffs, NJ: Prentice Hall

Donaldson, T. (1982) *Corporations and Morality.* Englewood Cliffs, NJ: Prentice Hall

Donaldson, T. (1989) *The ethics of international business.* New York: Oxford University Press

French, P. (1979) 'The Corporation as a Moral Person'. *American Philosophical Quarterly.* Reprinted in Donaldson and Werhane (eds) (1983) *Ethical issues in Business.* Englewood Cliffs, NJ: Prentice Hall

Friedman, M. (1970) 'The Social Responsibility of Business Is to Increase its Profits'. Reprinted in Donaldson and Werhane (eds) (1983) *Ethical issues in Business.* Englewood Cliffs, NJ: Prentice Hall

Goodpaster, K. and Mathews, J. (1982) 'Can a Corporation have a Conscience?'. *Harvard Business Review.* Reprinted in T. L. Beauchamp and N. E. Bowie (1983) *Ethical Theory and Business*, 2nd edn. Englewood Cliffs, NJ: Prentice-Hall

Grayson, D. (2007) Sense and Sustainability. Inaugural lecture. Available at www.som.cranfield.ac.uk

Hawley, S. (2000) Exporting Corruption Privatisation, Multinationals and Bribery, Corner House Briefing 19

Hills, G. and Mahmud, A. (2007) Volunteering for Impact. Best Practices in International Corporate Volunteering. Available at www.brookings.edu

Nelson, J. and Prescott, D. (2003) Business and the Millennium Development Goals, A Framework for

Action. UNDP and the International Business Leaders Forum

Porter, M. E. and Kramer M. R. (2006) 'Strategy and Society: the link between competitive advantage and corporate social responsibility'. *Harvard Business Review*, 84(12)

Post, J. E., Preston, L. E. and Sachs, S. (2002) Managing the Extended Enterprise: The New Stakeholder View, California Management Review

Schrage, E. J. and Ewing, A. P. (2005) 'The Cocoa Industry and Child Labour'. *The Journal of Corporate Citizenship*

Simmons and Simmons and Control Risks (2006) International business attitudes to corruption—survey 2006. Available at www.crg.com

UNICEF (2007) Children and the Millennium Development Goals: Progress towards a World Fit for Children

CHAPTER TWELVE

Global Trends—Challenges of the Future

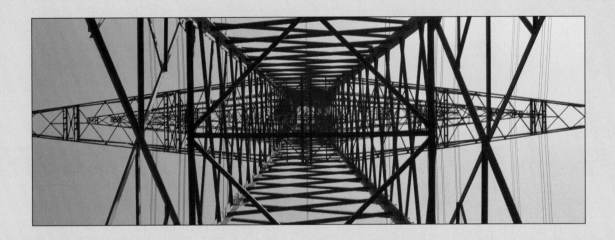

LEARNING OUTCOMES

This chapter will enable you to:

- **Identify trends in the growth of the global economy**

- **Summarize future changes in demography and migration**

- **Illustrate possible environmental scenarios**

- **Explain the impact of globalization on the future of crime**

We started this book with a chapter on globalization because we consider this to be the dominant trend in the international business environment. We described globalization as the creation of linkages between nations by the removal of barriers (physical, political, economic, cultural) separating different regions of the world. In the chapters that followed we examined in some detail those linkages so that we can better make sense of the complex international business environment. In this final chapter we want to look to the future and identify some of the major trends and issues in the global business environment and assess some of the implications for business. This is not an attempt to predict the future but a recognition that companies need to be aware of potential changes in the business environment, so they are prepared for the opportunities and threats at an early stage, and develop strategies to deal with them. This is not just an issue for those companies operating internationally, but for all firms as the effects of changes in the global business environment can impact every business.

Who would have predicted recent developments in the Chinese and Indian economies where rapid growth has not only created new markets, but also displaced jobs in advanced economies, not just in manufacturing, but also, with the growth of the internet, in non-tradable white collar jobs? According to the World Bank (2007a) global integration will continue with the ratio of exports to GDP growing from 25% in 2005 to 34% in 2030. International migration, financial integration, foreign direct investment, foreign travel and education, and improvements in mass communication have all contributed to globalization and world growth in the past and are likely to continue to do so in the future. Of course these forecasts can only be based on what has gone before, and although this can be a good guide to the future they can be very wide of the mark. The World Bank report points out that predictions made in 1900 would, based on the previous 30 years' growth in the 'G5' (France, Japan, Germany, UK, and USA), have been wide of the mark because the geo-political context changed dramatically. World War I was followed by 'the great depression' and then World War II which meant that actual GDP was way below predicted GDP.

Spyros Makridakis (1989) argues that the pace of change in the **information revolution** has proceeded at about four times the pace of change in the industrial revolution. Or put another way, the revolutionary changes in the organization of production which took place between 1760 and 1960 can today be achieved in just 50 years, less than most life times. Makridakis compares the making of a watch 200 years ago when the 250 parts would have been made individually and put together by a team of five and taken one month. Today a digital watch is made automatically using specially designed microchips in less than 1 minute. How could anybody have possibly foreseen this in the eighteenth century based on their existing knowledge of manufacturing processes? Thus, the scale of change which could take place in just 50 years is potentially huge. This is why, as noted in Chapter Four, some organizations construct several possible futures (or scenarios) so as to be prepared for any eventuality.

The trends we will look at in this chapter are the growth of the global economy, demography and migration, environmental degradation, technology, and crime.

The Global Economy

We can be fairly certain that by 2030 there will be another 1.5 billion people on the planet, that nearly all that population growth will take place in developing countries, and the populations of today's developed countries will be much older, as will China's. We also know these population changes, along with other factors will determine the future growth of the world economy—but what that growth will be is much less certain. The World Bank (2007a) estimates that the world economy will grow at an annual rate of 3% up to 2030 which will result in a more than doubling of world output (at constant market exchange rates and prices) from US$35 trillion to US$72 trillion. Growth will be higher in developing countries (4.2%) than high income countries (2.5%) with developing countries' share of total output increasing from one fifth to a third and their share of global purchasing power increasing to more than one half. There will be a modest convergence of per capita incomes but developing country incomes will still be only one-quarter of those of rich countries at US$11,000 in 2030. The number living below the poverty line of US$1 per day will halve to 550 million people despite there being an additional 1.5 billion people.

Goldman Sachs (2003), as outlined in the case study at the end of Chapter Two, looked further ahead to 2050 and others such as PricewaterhouseCoopers (2006) have followed suit. In their report Goldman Sachs paint a picture of a very different world economy by 2050 with growth in the developing economies and especially Brazil, China, India, and Russia making them a much greater force. In 2050, China and India are predicted to be the world's biggest and third biggest economies sandwiching the USA in second place.

For China and India this would be a return to their positions in the 19th century when they were the world's two biggest economies. In the 19th century together they accounted for around 30% of world GDP (Maddison 2003). Their populations were large then, as now, so per capita incomes were lower than Western Europe. In fact China remained the largest economy until 1890 when the lead was lost to Western Europe and the USA following the industrial revolution which originated in the mid-18th century in Britain. This transformed Western society from an agricultural economy with small scale cottage industries to an industrialized economy with large scale mass production carried out in factories in towns. There was massive migration from the countryside to the cities as a result of this.

The driver for all of this was the application of steam power not just in factories but also to transport which allowed the movement of relatively low value goods across large distances over both land and water. The benefits of this transformation were confined to the industrialized nations of the time largely because they held the advantage in technological progress but also because many of the countries of Africa, Asia, and Latin America were the colonies of the Western powers supplying primary products with worsening terms of trade to the industrialized nations. In the case of Africa they also supplied young men and women as free labour to the plantations of America.

In the 19th century until 1870 the UK was the dominant power producing 30% of total world industrial output but this position was changing as the USA and other Western European powers developed. By 1913, the USA was producing 36% of world industrial output and the UK only 14% (Dicken 2004). This pattern continued until World War II when the world divided into three different spheres.

The first sphere was the Western world led by the USA and organized along capitalist lines. It set up world institutions such as the World Bank, the IMF, and the GATT in order to aid recovery of the war torn Western European economies and to establish a 'world system' to combat the power of the soviet bloc. The 1950s also saw the emergence of Japan as a new competitor for the developed western world so that the bi-polar world of trade in manufactures became a tri-polar world dominated by the triad discussed in Chapter One.

The second sphere to emerge after World War II was the Eastern communist bloc led by Russia. Russia had become a communist State after the 1917 revolution, but it was after World War II that communism took hold in other countries. Some Eastern and Central European countries were invaded by Russia and others, Cuba and China, experienced revolutions. The Soviet Union was a centrally planned economy and this system was imposed on the satellite States of Eastern and Central Europe so that trade and investment between the two spheres was minimal. China became the People's Republic of China in 1949 and for the next 30 years had little to do with the world economy following a policy of self reliance. The Soviet bloc ushered in some political and economic reforms in the 1980s in a move towards becoming a democratic market economy and this was a prelude to popular revolutions which swept across Eastern Europe following the withdrawal of Soviet Union support for the communist regimes. In 1991, the Baltic States declared themselves independent and by the end of that year the whole soviet sphere unravelled with the Soviet Union itself ceasing to exist. China had started its move towards becoming a market economy in 1979, but unlike the Soviet bloc, communism still prevails there. The opening up of the Chinese economy was discussed in the case preceding Chapter Two.

The world is now less divided along political lines but there is still an enormous gap between those who have and those who have not. In East Asia a number of newly industrialized economies have emerged (initially South Korea, Taiwan, Singapore, and Hong Kong and later, Malaysia, Thailand, and Indonesia) to become global players, but for much of the rest of the world poverty remains a major problem and narrowing this gap will be a major challenge. We have already noted the growth prospects for the BRIC economies and to these PriceWaterhouseCoopers (2006) added Mexico, Indonesia, and Turkey to form what they called the E7. They also identified 13 other emerging economies including Vietnam, Nigeria, Philippines, Egypt, and Bangladesh with strong growth prospects (above 7% per annum) to 2050 and therefore of major interest to business as markets and investment opportunities. They estimate that by 2050 the E7 emerging economies will be 50% bigger than the current G7 economies of USA, Japan, Germany, UK, France, Italy, and Canada (see Figure 12.1 and Table 12.1).

It is estimated that by 2050 China's economy will be some 30% bigger than the US economy and India's about 12% smaller. Brazil, Russia, Indonesia, and Mexico will all be bigger than any of the European economies, with Turkey not far behind. These economies will provide opportunities for outsourcing manufacturing activities, opening new offices, mergers, acquisitions, and alliances but of major significance will be the emergence of a

Figure 12.1 Relative size of the G7 and E7 economies

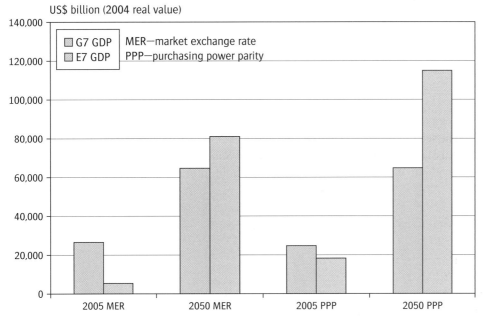

US$ billion (2004 real value)

Source: PricewaterhouseCoopers 2006

global middle class. In 2050 Russia, Mexico, Brazil, Turkey, China, Indonesia, and India will still have per capita incomes less than the USA, Japan, and Western Europe but they will be very much greater than today (see Table 12.1). The World Bank foresees an extra 800 million people in developing countries joining the middle classes by 2030, bringing the total to 1.2 billion, 15% of the world population; 361 million of these people will be in China. This will mean hundreds of millions of new consumers in developing countries with spending patterns similar to current residents of high-income countries, providing enormous opportunities to international business in the form of new markets. The Bank includes in its definition of the middle class all those with incomes of US$4,000 or more at 2006 prices.

We now turn to other issues which are threats to growth and at the same time consequences of growth. As we have seen, one of the downsides of globalization is that issues which could once be contained within national boundaries can now easily become global. Security threats, infectious disease, environmental degradation, and international crime can all spill over to other States. These threats often come from those areas of the planet which are the most impoverished, and with weak and often corrupt governments.

Rising incomes have brought a degree of political and social stability to some parts of Asia but those areas where development is not taking place, Afghanistan, rural Pakistan, and Burma, are potentially the most unstable. But even countries whose economies are growing very fast, such as China and India, could face social unrest were the jobs and income generated by economic growth to be very unevenly distributed amongst the

Table 12.1 Projected relative size of economies and relative per capita income levels

Country (indices with US = 100)	GDP at market exchange rates in US$ terms		GDP in PPP terms		GDP per capita in PPP terms (000s of constant 2006$)	
	2007	2050	2007	2050	2007	2050
US	100	100	100	100	44.4	93.3
Japan	32	19	28	19	29.3	70.5
China	23	129	51	129	5.2	34.5
Germany	22	14	20	14	32.4	72.1
UK	18	14	15	14	33.6	77.5
France	17	14	15	14	37.0	78.3
Italy	14	10	13	10	32.1	70.0
Canada	10	9	10	9	39.2	83.3
Spain	9	9	10	9	30.1	72.4
Brazil	8	26	15	26	10.4	39.0
Russia	8	17	17	17	16.2	60.5
India	7	88	22	88	2.5	19.9
Korea	7	8	9	8	25.0	72.3
Mexico	7	17	10	17	12.6	48.0
Australia	6	6	5	6	35.9	79.2
Turkey	3	10	5	10	8.7	36.3
Indonesia	3	17	7	17	4.1	20.9

Source: PricewaterhouseCoopers 2008

population. Poverty, inequality and high levels of unemployment in these countries could lead to social conflicts, civil unrest, and economic disruption that could spill over into neighbouring States and become more widespread.

Average incomes are set to rise in much of the developing world but income inequality between and within countries will rise with 2/3 of developing countries seeing greater internal income inequality. An estimated 1.9 billion people will still be living on less than US$2 per day in 2030 (World Bank 2007a). As technology is more easily diffused across the world and the skill levels required of labour increases, those who remain without skills will see their relative income fall. Those who are excluded from education, often girls, will suffer. Sub-Saharan Africa seems likely to see its share of the world's poor increase. These areas all pose potential threats to world security which is why poverty reduction is likely to be an item on the agenda of multinational businesses as well as governments and inter-national organizations.

Another potential threat is how rich countries react to the emergence of these large emerging economies. China and India are growing export markets and a source of cheap imports reducing industry costs and boosting the real value of incomes in rich countries as prices fall. They also pose a real competitive threat to the developed economies in many markets and as the educational levels and skills of Indian and Chinese workers improve they will ultimately move into the high-tech markets and financial services markets which the developed countries currently dominate. Both countries have enormous labour forces which will become more mobile so the pressures that have seen wage cuts and job losses in developed country workforces in manufacturing will only increase in the years to come and move into other sectors as well. If the rich countries counter this trend with protectionist policies then world growth is likely to be slower than predicted.

Demography and Migration

Future Population Growth

According to the UN (2007a), world population will increase by nearly 40% to around 9 billion between 2007 and 2050 (Table 12.2). However, as can be seen in Table 12.2, this is the medium calculation based on a continuing decline in fertility. World population could be as high as 10.8 billion or as low as 7.8 billion if the assumption on fertility is wrong. The UN (2007a) says that the world is being transformed from a situation of high death and birth rates to one of low mortality and low fertility.

Table 12.2 Population of the world, major development groups and major areas, 2007 and 2050

Major area	2007	Population in 2050 (millions)		
		Low	Medium	High
World	6,671	7,792	9,191	10,756
More developed regions	1,223	1,065	1,245	1,451
Less developed regions	5,448	6,727	7,946	9,306
Least developed countries	804	1,496	1,742	2,002
Other less developed countries	4,644	5,231	6,204	7,304
Africa	965	1,718	1,998	2,302
Asia	4,030	4,444	5,266	6,189
Europe	731	566	664	777
Latin America and the Caribbean	572	641	769	914
Northern America	339	382	445	517
Oceania	34	42	49	56

Source: UN 2007a

Population will rise most rapidly in developing economies in Africa and Latin America, but grow relatively slowly in Asia and in more developed regions like North America. Falls will occur in most European countries with the exception of the UK and Norway which will show moderate growth.

Ageing Population

Much of the population growth is due to people living longer rather than an increase in the birth rate and life expectancy is predicted to rise further. The American Life Extension Institute believes that average life expectancy in the US will reach 100 by 2029. The result of an ageing population is that by 2050, all developed countries are expected to have an average age higher than 40 years, with Japan having the oldest population in the world with an average age of 55. Populations in Asia, Latin America, and the Caribbean are expected to age more quickly than the populations of developed countries because of a very rapid decline in the birth rate. In contrast, populations in most countries in Africa will still be relatively young by 2050 (UN 2007a).

This ageing of the population will affect all the major economies bar India which will experience an increase in the share of those aged 15–59. In comparison, the USA, UK, Australia, Turkey, Indonesia, Mexico, and Brazil will all suffer a reduction of at least 5% in this age group with China being particularly affected by a fall of 15% in this age cohort (Figure 12.2; Global Futures and Foresight).

Figure 12.2 Working-age population growth, 2005–30

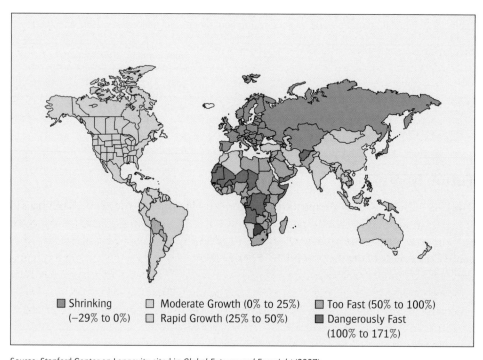

Source: Stanford Center on Longevity cited in *Global Futures and Foresight* (2007)

These trends have a variety of implications for business. As can be seen from the map, the population of working age will either shrink or grow very modestly in the richer countries of Europe and North America. The most rapid growth of the work force will be seen in developing economies. In developed economies, shortages of labour could occur raising labour costs and forcing firms to reconsider their choice of technology and how they organize production. Business may respond by automating production to a greater degree, taking on older workers, spending more on staff training and development to increase productivity, attracting workers from elsewhere, or by transferring production to countries with adequate supplies of labour.

Ageing populations also mean that business needs to revise its marketing strategy to target the older consumer. An ageing population affects the pattern of demand for goods and services. In developed economies, older people generally receive a higher proportion of income and control more of the wealth such as housing, at least up to the point when they retire. In the USA, those aged over 50 control 75% of the country's wealth whilst, in 2004, people born in the 1950s and 60s in the UK held four fifths of the wealth and were by far the most important buyers of expensive cars and ocean cruises (Global Futures and Foresight). This means that the elderly will account for a significant and increasing proportion of consumer spending, as has been happening in Australia. They also spend more than younger people on savings and investment products. This will expand markets for firms in the financial sector.

On the other hand, when people retire they tend to save less or even live off accumulated assets and savings earned during their working years. The World Bank (2007a) expects savings rates to rise while the baby boomers born in the 1950s and 60s continue to form part of the work force. However, as older people enter retirement savings will drop. The World Bank expects this trend to affect savings not only in the richer countries of the West but also Russia, China and somewhat later, Latin America and South Asia. In contrast, countries in the Middle East, North Africa, and Sub-Saharan Africa have relatively young populations and should experience increases in the labour force and in their savings. The Bank foresees a substantial drop in overall world savings by 2030. Another issue around ageing identified by the Bank, is that older people are likely to be reluctant to put their savings into risky investments. This could make it more difficult for firms involved in the more risky areas of business to raise finance.

Future Migration

The United Nations (2007a) expects the net number of migrants to developed countries to total 103 million between 2005 and 2050, or about 2.2 million annually. This is expected to more or less offset the net natural population decrease in developed countries, in other words, the excess of deaths over births. For developing countries, this emigration represents only a small proportion of the increase in their populations between 2005 and 2050.

Table 12.3 identifies the major receiving and sending countries up to 2050. The main receivers are the countries of North America and Western Europe, the main senders countries in Asia and Latin America.

According to the World Bank (2007a), the factors propelling international migration will persist. The significant gap in wages and living standards between less developed and

Table 12.3 Net migration (annual average (m) 2005–2050)

Receiving Countries		Sending Countries	
US	1.1	China	0.33
Canada	0.2	Mexico	0.31
Germany	0.15	India	0.24
Italy	0.14	Philippines	0.18
UK	0.13	Pakistan	0.17
Spain	0.12	Indonesia	0.16

Source: UN 2007a

richer economies, although diminishing, will continue to be an important driver of migration. It is estimated that around a tenth of the population of developed countries' populations are foreign-born. The desire to reunite family and friends will also be an important driver in migration and this will be made easier if transport costs continue to fall. However, the strength of this driver could be weakened were transport costs to rise due to high oil prices such as the US$130 per barrel, seen in 2008 (see the discussion below on Resources).

A further reason for continued migration is the effect of the ageing population on the supply of labour in richer countries. Shortages of labour and high levels of job vacancies could attract foreign workers from abroad and could encourage employers to recruit from countries better endowed with labour resources.

Finally, bodies such as the UN Intergovernmental Panel on Climate Change (UN 2007b) expect migration to increase as a result of climate change with huge numbers of people forced to leave their homes due to drought, hunger, and flooding particularly of coastal areas. Those most at risk include countries in Asia like China and Bangladesh, the Middle East, and Sub-Saharan Africa.

The World Bank (2007b) estimated that global migrant remittances were in excess of US$318 billion in 2007, most of it transferring from rich countries to developing regions, particularly China, India, Mexico, and the Philippines. This total relates to money that goes through official channels. It has been estimated that adding in unofficial flows could double the actual figure. The World Bank (2007a) expects remittance flows to increase along with migration.

Urbanization

Urbanization refers to the increase in the proportion of a population living in urban areas. The UN (2007c) expects urbanization to continue rising in both developed and less developed regions. It predicts that, by 2050, urban dwellers will likely account for more

Figure 12.3 World urban and rural population

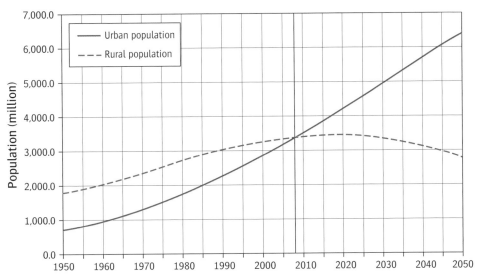

Source: UN 2007c

than four fifths of the population in the more developed regions and for two thirds in the less developed regions. Overall, the world urban population is expected to almost double from 3.3 billion in 2007 to 6.4 billion in 2050 which would mean that 70 out of every 100 people in the world would be living in towns and cities (Figure 12.3).

By 2050, the highest rates of urbanization, over 90%, will be found in Australia, New Zealand, and North America, while in Europe the rate is projected to be lower, at 84%. Among the less developed regions, Latin America and the Caribbean already have higher levels of urbanization than Europe. Asia and Africa remain mostly rural but are expected to urbanize more rapidly than the rest of the developing world. Nevertheless, by mid-century, they are forecast still to have lower proportions of their populations living in towns and cities than the more developed regions of Latin America and the Caribbean.

The world rural population is expected to increase up to 3.5 billion in 2019 but then to fall gradually to 2.8 billion in 2050 (UN 2007c).

One of the effects of increasing urbanization for business is that larger and larger numbers of consumers and workers are concentrated geographically. This could influence firms in terms of decisions regarding location of production, marketing, and distribution.

Resources

Predicted global growth of 3.5% over the next 30 or 40 years is good news in terms of reducing the number of those living in poverty and increasing living standards but it also means greater demand for resources, and thus more pollution and possibly greater climate change and water shortages.

In Chapter Two a mini case described China's visit to every resource rich country in Africa in their quest to secure resources. By 2006, China was consuming almost one third of the world's steel. Its demand for minerals such as steel, aluminium, nickel, zinc, and copper tripled in the previous decade. The demand for resources is likely to continue to grow especially as other emerging economies seek further industrialization and so are the prices of those resources. This commodity price inflation is a threat to long term economic growth because, in order to contain inflation, governments will have to dampen demand for goods and services which would effectively weaken economic growth.

The world oil price reached new heights rising by 80% in 2007. This was caused by a combination of rising demand and reduced production. According to the International Energy Agency there will be no problems of supply. It expects world consumption of oil to rise from 83 million barrels per day in 2004 to 97 million barrels per day in 2015 and 118 million barrels per day in 2030 and production to rise to meet this demand. On the other hand, the Energy Watch Group (www.energywatchgroup.org) claims that oil production peaked in 2006 and will decline by several per cent per year so global oil supply 'will be dramatically lower' in 2030. They claim this will require major structural changes to the economic system of the world, curbing our demand for oil, and requiring massive investment in renewable energy.

Environment

Angel Gurria, Secretary-General of the OECD, painted a grim picture when launching the OECD Environmental Outlook to 2030. The OECD's worst case scenario was that:

- Without new policies, global greenhouse gas emissions are projected to increase by over 50% by 2050. This could cause the global temperature to rise above pre industrial levels by a range of 1.7 to 2.4°C by 2050, and more than 4–6 degrees Celsius over the very long-term, leading to increased heatwaves, droughts, storms, and floods and resulting in severe damage to key infrastructure and crops.

- Without new policies, animal and plant species will continue to become extinct to 2030 due to pressures from expanding agriculture, urbanization, and climate change. Failure to stop biodiversity loss will result in further deterioration in essential ecosystems, as well as in the natural resource base for agro-business and pharmaceuticals industries, among others.

- Without new policies, over 3.9 billion people—that's 1 billion more people than today—will live in water stressed areas by 2030. Water scarcity will be exacerbated by pollution of water resources, agriculture being the largest user and polluter of water.

- Without new policies, the impact on human health of air and water pollution is expected to worsen. By 2030, we are likely to see four times as many premature deaths caused by ground-level ozone and over 3.1 million people dying early because they've breathed in fine particulates. And that doesn't include the health hazards resulting from exposure to chemicals in the environment and in products, where information available is still not sufficient to have a clear picture.

The message is that in order to prevent this worst case scenario then the OECD countries will have to work closely with the major emerging economies identified above and other developing economies.

Already we are seeing the effects of rapid economic and population growth on the prices of food and energy and the availability of water. In 2000 predictions were that 1/3 of the world population would be affected by water scarcity by 2025 but a Comprehensive Assessment undertaken by the International Water Management Institute found that this figure had already been surpassed in 2005.

2008 saw food riots across the globe because of rising prices. The price of wheat had risen by 130% in 12 months and the price of rice had doubled. For the first time in 30 years global food prices were on the agenda for the G8 summit in July 2008 such was the concern over the impact of the crisis. Riots took place in Haiti (killing four people), Bangladesh, Cameroon, Ivory Coast, Mauritania, Mozambique, Uzbekistan, Yemen, Bolivia, and Indonesia. In the Philippines the army had to supervise government distribution of rice. The cause is a combination of growing demand for food because of rapidly rising incomes in the emerging economies, and falling supply due to global warming, extreme weather, and increased biofuel production.

Western economies, and particularly the USA, have encouraged the production of biofuels to limit dependence on the import of expensive oil. The US Government gives farmers subsidies to grow corn to convert to ethanol which is then mixed with petrol to reduce prices at the pump. The effect of this is to reduce supplies of food as food crops are ripped up to be replaced by crops used for ethanol. Plans are for a massive increase in biofuel production in the US to 30 billion gallons per year by 2022.

Decreased rainfall in many areas also reduced crop yields but climate extremes have also had an impact. From 2003, droughts more than halved grain production in Australia, the world's second biggest exporter after the US. Floods in Malaysia and droughts in Indonesia hit production of palm oil which is now also being used as a substitute for diesel.

In order to sustain world economic growth, governments will have to consider and come to some agreement about trade in food, biofuel production, climate change, and improvements in agricultural productivity—which will need to double whilst at the same time using less water.

Technology

As regards technology, communications technology will leap ahead offering more capability at lower prices. Web 2, the latest evolution in the World Wide Web, will give business opportunities to develop more interactive platforms like eBay, Craigslist, Bebo, YouTube, Flickr, and Second Life. Nanotechnology, involving the manipulation of atomic and molecular particles, will facilitate the creation of new materials and more powerful computers and communications devices. It is also likely to lead to major advances in the treatment of disease with nanorobots being programmed to seek out and destroy viruses, bacteria, and cancer cells. Developments in biotechnology will, through use of human cell tissue, make it easier to treat disease such as HIV/AIDS, and resistant strains of tuberculosis and sexually transmitted disease, and to develop new plant and animal sources of food.

The Future of Crime

In 2005, the UN estimated world trade in drugs was worth US$320 billion, the value of trafficking in humans was US$32 billion, while trade in firearms was worth US$1 billion (UN 2007). According to Glenny (2008) it has been a 'vigorous springtime . . . for transnational organized crime'.

As globalization proceeds and national economies and societies become increasingly interlinked, more opportunities will open up for cross-border crime. The removal of barriers to the global movement of goods, services, capital, and people, along with continuing improvements in communications technology combine to make it easier for criminals to operate internationally. The growth in opportunities will make crime more attractive, and could lead to an increase in the number of criminals—especially in countries unable to satisfy the material aspirations of their populations, many of which are located in the developing world.

Criminals are entrepreneurial inasmuch as they rapidly recognize new opportunities and markets and are quick to exploit them. Where there are customers demanding prohibited goods and services—be that drugs, prostitution services, weapons, or illicit diamonds, criminals will be quick to supply them when profits can be made. Increasingly, criminal groups are mimicking legitimate business. They go in for joint ventures and strategic alliances, employ similar management and accountancy techniques and practices and exploit advanced information technology (Moynagh and Worsley 2008).

Growth of incomes in countries like China and India will offer criminals more opportunities to sell counterfeit goods such as designer clothes, pharmaceuticals, films, books, and music. Glenny describes massive Chinese factories, hidden in the mountains, producing huge numbers of counterfeit American and Japanese brands of cigarettes that are sold in Asia, the USA, and Europe.

Electronic Crime

Advances in communications technology have been a major facilitator of trans-national crime. While the UN claims that global trade in drugs is being contained, electronic crime has been growing exponentially.

Electronic crime takes various forms such as fraud, theft, blackmail, money laundering, and the rigging of gambling on online sites. It can be used to swamp a company's web site with external communications. The web site either fails completely or slows down to such an extent that service is denied to legitimate customers. It has been estimated that anything up to 3% of all traffic on the World Wide Web could be attacks aiming to bring about denials of service (Computer World UK, 1 April 2008). Such an attack in 2004 was responsible for the temporary collapse of the Google, Yahoo!, Microsoft, and Apple web sites (www.silicon.com). The perpetrators sometimes try to use these attacks to extort money from the victims.

As affluence increases in countries like India and China, the number of bank cards and credit cards will grow, offering more possibilities for credit card fraud. In China, according to the Tomorrow Project, there were half a million credit card users in 2006. It expects that figure to rise to around 600 million by the 2020s. The prospect of massive growth in cross-border fraud has serious implications for financial institutions, not only regarding the losses incurred but also in terms of the costs of extra safeguards they have to put in place to cut down fraud.

There is likely to be an increase more generally in computer related crime. Hackers have access to many cheap and easy to use toolkits of pre-packaged software allowing them to grab passwords and other sensitive information. Most toolkits have been devised by hackers in Russia and Brazil and can be bought online. Commentators talk of an emerging infrastructure of profit-driven crime syndicates dedicated to turning stolen passwords or credit card information into cash (*Financial Times*, 11 October 2006; IBM).

Control of Crime

How much confidence can legitimate businesses have in authorities' effectively controlling crime? Globalization has reduced the ability of countries to monitor and control cross-border flows of resources. Agencies like the police are confined to operating within their national territory which limits their ability to deal with criminal activity from another country. International bodies such as the WTO and the OECD do not have the clout to ensure rules are respected. Closer integration in bodies like the EU can make it easier for criminals to operate across borders and it can also facilitate the control of cross-border crime particularly if it leads to closer cooperation of national police forces and other agencies.

Paradoxically, crime occurs where there is too little regulation but also where there is too much as in the labour and agricultural sectors where illegal migration has kept down farm costs in the USA and Western Europe. Similarly, the fact that drugs in many countries are illegal can boost prices and make dealing in them attractive and profitable to criminal gangs.

Criminals will always look to weak States where the chances of being caught and punished are low. These include countries like Russia, Afghanistan, Pakistan, and Albania. It would be foolish of foreign companies to look to the Chinese authorities for support in the fight against crime, for, as Glenny reports, Western companies seeking help from China's Public Security Bureau have found it to be virtually useless and corrupt.

The new technologies that provide useful tools for criminals can also be used by the authorities and by business to prevent or deter crime. Companies, in future, will build up intelligence databases to record the incidence of crime and security breaches. This will allow them to conduct risk assessments and put prevention measures in place. They can also use information security software programs to combat cyber crime. These include encryption systems that encode data on a machine or during transmission making it accessible only to authorized users, firewalls that create a 'virtual' barrier guarding systems to guard against electronic intruders, and digital signatures that provide a computerized authentication of electronic documents (Association of British Insurers 2000).

Conclusion

There are always difficulties and uncertainties in trying to foresee the future. Bearing this in mind, what are the important future opportunities and challenges likely to be confronted by business?

Prospects for markets in developed economies are poor with their lower rates of economic growth and populations which are in decline and ageing. However, it does appear that the less developed countries will continue to grow more rapidly than advanced economies. Fast rising incomes and large and growing urban populations in countries like India and China signify that the markets in these countries will grow most rapidly and be a great attraction for business in terms of trade and investment. Opportunities will be enhanced if the authorities in these countries continue the process of liberalization, that is opening up their economies to foreign firms. This could be particularly important to companies in areas such as telecommunications and finance which, up to now in China and India have been difficult to enter.

Western firms, trying to exploit opportunities in less advanced economies like China and India, will have to meet the challenge of dealing with political and legal systems and social, cultural, and technological environments that are very different from their own. As we saw in the chapter on technology, foreign firms can encounter great difficulties in getting the Chinese legal system to protect their intellectual property rights. Hofstede's research, outlined in Chapter Five on the Sociocultural Framework, showed how firms have to adjust their managerial approaches to different cultural environments.

Despite wage increases, China and India still have vast pools of relatively low cost labour. This means these countries will continue to be sources of cheap manufactures and services. On the one hand, this offers opportunities for foreign firms to buy cheaply from these countries or to set up production there. On the other, firms can expect increasingly intense competition from these economies not only on traditional labour-intensive goods such as shoes, toys, and clothing but also in more technologically advanced products. China is already the third largest producer of IT hardware and India is a major centre from the development of computer software. Competition from China in world markets is likely to become even fiercer because the entry of foreign manufacturers into China has increased competitive pressures on domestic firms forcing them to become more efficient. As their economies become more prosperous, the tendency for firms in the less developed regions to go multinational, competing head-to-head with Western and Japanese multinationals, as Tata of India and Lenovo of China have done, is likely to increase.

The advances in communications technology will make it easier for criminals to commit cross-border cyber crime. To counter this, businesses will have to pay more attention to the risks this entails and devote more time and resources to establishing effective security for their IT systems.

The continued economic expansion in less developed countries will increase demand and competition for natural resources and put pressure on their prices. This could feed into production costs and in combination with fiercer global competition, squeeze profits.

Finally, the increasing recognition of changes in the natural environment could result in firms, particularly those regarded as causing pollution in industries such as cars, steel, and chemicals, facing up to much stricter regulation and a more punitive tax environment.

Online Resource Centre

www.oxfordtextbooks.co.uk/orc/hamilton_webster/

Visit the supporting online resource centre for additional material which will help you with your assignments, essays and research, or you may find these extra resources helpful when revising for exams.

● FURTHER READING

The World Bank looks at a range of growth scenarios from 2006 to 2030:

● World Bank (2007a), Global Economic Prospects 2006: Managing the Next Wave of Globalization

The book by Moynagh and Worsley has been produced by a group drawn from the business, government, and academic worlds in collaboration with the ESRC Centre for the Study of Globalization and Regionalization at the University of Warwick. It examines what will shape the world in the years ahead and the vital issues that need to be addressed.

● Moynagh, M. and Worsley, R. (2008). *Going Global: Key Questions for the 21st Century*. London: A&C Black

For an analysis of the factors underpinning China's increasing political, economic, and military power in the world see:

● Bergsten, C. F., Freeman, C., Lardy Nicholas R. and Mitchell, D. J. (2008) China's Rise: Challenges and Opportunities Institute for International Economics. Peterson Institute

The book on Shell shows how the company uses scenario planning to prepare for the future.

● Van der Veer, J. (2005) *Shell Global Scenarios to 2025: The Future Business Environment—Trends, Trade-offs and Choices*. Royal Dutch Shell Group

● REFERENCES

Association of British Insurers (2000) Future Crime Trends in the UK, General Insurance research Report No 7, June

Crude Oil The Supply Outlook: Report to the Energy Watch Group (2007) EWG-Series No 3/2007 www.energyatchgroup.org

Dicken, P. (2004) *Global Shift, Reshaping the Global Economic Map in the 21st Century*. Sage

Glenny, M. (2008), *McMafia: Crime Without Frontiers*. London: The Bodley Head

Global Futures and Foresight, The Future of Companies (2007) Briefing to the Senate Special Committee on Aging, Adele Hayutin, Director, Global Aging Project Stanford Center on Longevity, May 21

Goldman Sachs (2003): Global Economic paper No 99. Dreaming with Brics: The Path to 2050

'Hunger. Strikes, Riots. The Food crisis bites'. *The Observer*, 13 April 2008

Maddison, A. (2003) The World economy: Historical Statistics. Development Centre Studies OECD

Makridakis, S. (1989) *Long Range Planning*, Vol 22, Issue 2, April

OECD (2008) Environmental Outlook to 2030

PricewaterhouseCoopers (2006) The World in 2050: How big will the major emerging market economies get and how can the OECD compete

PricewaterhouseCoopers: Updated projections (2008)

United Nations (2007) World Drug Report 2007

UN (2007a) World Population Prospects. The 2006 Revision

UN (2007b) Intergovernmental Panel on Climate Change, Climate Change 2007, IPCC Fourth Assessment Report

UN (2007c) The World Urbanization Prospects: The 2007 revision

World Bank (2007a) Global Economic Prospects 2006: Managing the Next Wave of Globalization

World Bank (2007b) Remittance Trends 2006: Migration and Development Brief, 3 November

Glossary

Absolute cost barriers obstacles deterring entry of new firms because the capital costs of entering are huge or where the existing firms control a vital resource, e.g. oil reserves—the company Aramco controls 98% of Saudi Arabian oil reserves

Accountability the idea that organizations and people should take responsibility for their actions and their outcomes

Acquisition one firm takes over or merges with another; some authors use this term when the deal is contested

Advanced economy a country whose per capita income is by world standards high

Ageing population an increase in the average age of the population

Anthropocentric a view of the world that sees humans as being the most important species on earth

Applied research research specifically seeking knowledge that can be exploited commercially

Arbitration a process to resolve disputes that avoids using the courts

Authoritarian system one person or a group of people exercise power unrestrained by laws or opposition

Barriers to entry obstacles that prevents new firms from entering an industry and competing with existing firms on an equal basis

Basic research the pursuit of knowledge for the sake of it with no explicit aim to exploit the results commercially

Bio-diversity the variety of life forms which exist on Earth. There is clear evidence that ecological changes can lead to a reduction in this

Biofuels fuel made from renewable sources of energy such as plants

Biosphere the regions of the Earth, both above and below the Earth's crust that support life. This includes the atmosphere, air, and all water

Biotechnology the use of biological systems or living organisms to make or modify products or processes

Born Global refers to firms who get involved in international activities immediately after their birth

Bribery the offer of inducements in return for illegal favours

BRIC economy refers to Brazil, Russia, India, and China. Countries whose economies have been growing relatively rapidly in the first years of the 21st century and are seen as becoming major economic powers in the future

Brownfield investment where a firm expands by taking over existing production or service assets—most FDI is brownfield investment

Capital intensive where production of a good or service relies more heavily on capital, in the form of plant and equipment, than labour

Capital markets physical and electronic markets that bring together savers and investors, e.g. the stock market

Carbon neutral a production process or product that does not add to the carbon dioxide in the atmosphere

Cartel firms come together to agree on a common price or to divide the market between them

Cash crops crops grown to be sold in the market for money rather than for the consumption of the producer

Centrally planned economy major economic decisions, e.g. on production, prices, and investment are made directly by government rather than being left to market forces

Civil law system based on statutes and written codes

Clientelism politicians confer favours on members of the electorate in order to obtain votes—sometimes referred to as patronage

Collectivized where the means of production are owned by the people collectively or by the state on their behalf

Common law system accords more importance to court judgements than to written codes and statutes

Communist system usually a one-party system where the party controls the institutions of the state and owns and controls most of the production of goods and services

Comparative advantage the ability of a country to produce a good at lower cost, relative to other goods, compared to another country; even if a country is not the most efficient at producing the good, it can still benefit from specializing in producing and exporting that good

Competitive advantage strategies, skills, knowledge, or resources that allow firms to compete more effectively

Complementary product a product that is manufactured or used with another product, e.g. computers and computer software

Concentration ratio (CR) a way of measuring market concentration that takes the proportion of industry sales or output accounted for by the largest firms. A CR 5 shows the share of the 5 largest firms in the market

Contract a legally binding agreement between a buyer and a seller

Convention on Contracts for the International Sale of Goods (CISG) UN rules governing the sale of goods between professional buyers and sellers in different countries

Convertibility means that one currency can be legally exchanged for another

Copyright the holder has the exclusive right to publish and sell literary, musical, or artistic works

Corporate Social Responsibility (CSR) organizations take responsibility for the impact of their activities on society including customers, suppliers, employees, shareholders, communities as well as the environment.

Corporatist social model welfare system offering relatively generous benefits and where work is seen as very important—found in countries such as Germany and Japan

Corruption where people misuse their power to enrich themselves

Corruption Perception Index a ranking of countries by level of corruption carried out by Transparency International

Creative capitalism the notion that business needs to generate profits and to solve the world's problems, e.g. use market forces to better address global poverty

Creative destruction the process by which radical new products, processes, transportation systems, and markets transforms industry by destroying the old ways of doing things

Cross elasticity of demand a measure of the extent to which customers change their purchasing patterns when one firm changes its price

Cross-border merger when a firm based in one country merges with a firm based in another

Cultural imperialism the imposition of one country's culture on another country

Cultural relativism understanding other cultures and not judging them according to one's own cultural norms and values

Culture shared beliefs, values, customs, and behaviours prevalent in a society that are transmitted from generation to generation

Customary law body of rules, values, and traditions based on knowledge gained from life experiences or on religious or philosophical principles

Customs union a free trade area but with the addition that members agree to levy a common tariff on imports of goods from non-members

Cybercrime crime committed using computers and the internet

Deforestation the destruction of forests either as a result of logging for timber or as people seek to clear forests so that they can farm the land

Demography the study of population in its various aspects—size, age, gender, ethnic group, and so on

Derivative in financial markets an asset whose value derives from some other asset. Buying an equity derivative does not mean buying shares but involves taking out a contract linked to the level of share price. The contract can offer protection against adverse movements in the price of the share

Desertification the process by which once fertile areas of land become deserts. This is seen as a consequence of ecological damage

Devaluation a fall in the value of one currency against others

Developed Countries see Advanced economy

Developing Countries countries whose incomes are low by world standards

Directive (EU) laws that bind member states but are their responsibility to implement

Disposable income income remaining net of taxes and benefit payments available for spending or saving

Distribution of income the division of income among social groups in an economy or among countries

Diversified firm a business that operates in more than one industry or one market

Divestment where a firm disposes of part of the business

DTT Dichloro-Diphenyl-Trichloroethane, a pesticide that was widley used in agriculture in the 1950s

Dumping selling goods in a foreign market at below their costs of production or below the price in the domestic market

Eco-centric a view of the world that stresses that all species are important and that the health of the planet depends on our recognition of the mutual interdependence between all species

Economic growth the rate of change in GDP

Economic nationalism the state protects domestic business firms from foreign competition. They become richer and more powerful and this, in turn, increases the power of the state; same as mercantilism

Economies of scale reduction in unit costs associated with large scale production

Economies of scope cost savings resulting from increasing the number of different goods or services produced

Embezzlement refers to the stealing of money or other assets

Emerging economy an economy with low-to-middle per capita income; originally it referred to economies emerging from communism

Equity support regime government support for innovation by buying shares and taking a stake in the ownership

Ethnocentric a belief that the values of your own race or nation are better than others

Eurozone members of the EU having the euro as their currency

Excess capacity where demand is not sufficient to keep all resources in a firm or industry fully occupied

Exchange rates the price of one currency expressed in terms of another, e.g. £1 = $2

Executive branch implements laws, regulations, and policies and gives policy advice to government ministers

Export credits loans offered by countries, often at low cost, to buyers of exports

Export guarantees where exporters are guaranteed by governments that they will receive payment for their goods or services

Export processing zone (epz) an area where MNCs can invest, produce, and trade under favourable conditions such as being allowed to import and produce without paying tax

External factors components of the micro and macro environments of business

Extortion obtaining money or other benefits by the use of violence or the threat of violence

Factors of production inputs combined by organizations to produce goods and services: the main categories are land, labour, and capital

Favouritism where a person is favoured unfairly over others, e.g. in the award of contracts

Federal system there is a sharing of significant decision-making powers between central and regional governments

Feminine society one which values highly the quality of life and human relationships

Financial Markets these are mechanisms for bringing together buyers and sellers of financial assets—they can be located in one place or be dispersed

Fixed costs costs that do not vary with the level of output and are incurred whether output is produced or not

Fixed exchange rate when the exchange rate of a currency is fixed against others—in reality a completely fixed rate is difficult to achieve

Floating exchange rate when the exchange is allowed to float freely against other currencies

Foreign direct investment (FDI) the establishment, acquisition, or increase in production facilities in a foreign country.

Foreign indirect investment (FII) the purchase of financial assets in a foreign country.

Fraud deception by those aiming to make an illegal gain

Free trade goods and services are completely free to move across frontiers—i.e. there are no tariffs or non-tariff barriers

Free trade area member states agree to remove tariffs and quotas on goods from other members of the area. Members have the freedom to set the level of tariff imposed on imports of goods from non-members of the area

GATT an international organization set up to remove barriers, particularly tariffs and quotas, to international trade; was subsumed into the WTO

GHGs Green House Gases of which the most serious for climate change are carbon dioxide, methane, and nitrous oxide

Global Income the total value of world income generated by the production of goods and services

Global integration the interconnections between countries which increase with the reduction in barriers to the movement of goods, services, capital, and people

Global North this is not a geographically precise term but refers to those areas of the world which are regarded as being economically advanced or developed

Global South in comparison to the Global North this refers to all countries which are developing as opposed to being already developed countries

Global supply chain the sequence of steps that a good goes through to get from the producer of the raw materials to the final product

Globalization the creation of linkages or interconnections between nations. It is usually understood as a process in which barriers (physical, political, economic, cultural) separating different regions of the world are reduced or removed, thereby stimulating exchanges in goods, services, money, and people

Governance the structures and procedures countries and companies use to manage their affairs

Greenfield investment where a firm sets up completely new production or service facilities

Greenhouse gases gases in the atmosphere helping to bring about climate change: the most important are water vapour, carbon dioxide, methane, and ozone

Grey market goods sold at a lower price than that intended by the maker; the goods are often bought cheaply in one national market, exported and sold at a higher price in another

Gross Domestic Product the value of all goods and service produced within the geographical boundaries of a country

Guanxi the reciprocal exchange of favours and mutual obligations among participants in a social network in China

HDI (Human Development Indicators) used by the UN to measure human development: they include life expectancy, adult literacy rates, and GDP per capita

Hedge funds financial institutions selling financial products that allow clients to reduce financial risk or to speculate in equities, commodities, interest rates, and exchange rates; they also operate on their own account

Herfindahl-Hirschmann Index gives a measure of market concentration that includes all firms in the market. The more competitive the market the closer the value of the index is to zero. The value of the index for pure monopoly is 10,000

Horizontal merger where a firm takes over a competitor, i.e. the merging firms are operating at the same stage of production

ICSID agency based at the World Bank that resolves international commercial disputes between business

Impact analysis the process of identifying the impact on business of a change in its external environment

Income inelastic when the quantity demanded of a good or services changes proportionately less than national income, i.e. the value of income elasticity is less than one

Industrial revolution a transformation from an agricultural economy to an industrialized economy

with large scale mass production carried out in factories in towns

Industry comprises all those firms who are competing directly with each other

Infant mortality the death rate of children in the first year of life, expressed as the number of deaths per 1,000 live births

Inflation a rise in the general price level or an increase in the average of all prices of goods and services over a period of time

Information and Communications Technology technology that is relevant to communications, the internet, satellite communications, mobile telephony, digital television

Information revolution the increasing importance of information and the increasing ease with which information can be accessed

Innovation the commercial exploitation of new knowledge

Intellectual property rights (IPRs) legal protection of ideas and knowledge embodied in new goods, services, and production processes

Interest rate the price paid to borrow someone else's money, sometimes called the price of money

Internal factors the internal strengths and weaknesses of the organization

International arbitration companies in different countries who are in dispute can ask that their case be resolved under the New York Convention or by referring it to ICSID at the World Bank

International Comparison programme the world bank's programme which is developing ways of comparing relative standards of living

International Labour Organization a UN agency promoting social justice in the workplace

International Monetary Fund (IMF) an international agency promoting monetary cooperation and stability

Inter-operability the ability of systems such as IT systems to work together

ISIC the UN industrial classification system

Judicial branch institutions such as the police, courts, prison system, and armed forces responsible for enforcing the law

Labour intensive where production of a good or service relies more heavily on labour than on capital, i.e. plant and equipment

Lean manufacturing a process aimed at eliminating waste and reducing the time between receipt of a customer order and delivery

Legislative branch political institutions like parliaments with the power to make laws, regulations, and policies

Liberal democracy a system in which citizens have the right to elect their government and to individual freedom

Liberal social model a form of welfare system offering relatively low welfare benefits and distinguishing between those deserving welfare support and those who do not—found in North America and Australia

Liberalization the reduction of barriers to trade or of entry into a market

Licensing where a firm grants permission for another to use its assets, e.g. to produce its product, use its production processes, or its brand name

Life expectancy the average number of years that a person can expect to live from birth which varies significantly between countries

Liquidity the ease with which assets can be turned into cash

Lisbon strategy EU 10-year plan to improve competitiveness

Lobbying attempt to influence the decisions taken by others, e.g. state institutions

Macroenvironment comprises all the political, economic and financial, socio-cultural, technological, and ecological elements in the wider environment of business

Maquiladora a factory set up in Mexico close to the US border as a result of the establishment of NAFTA

Market comprises competing goods and services, the firms producing those goods/services, and the geographical area where the firms compete

Market concentration measures the distribution of market power by market share

Market deregulation the reduction of barriers of entry into a market

Market economy an economy where prices and output are determined by the decisions of consumers and private firms interacting through markets

Market growth the change over time in the demand for a good or service

Market ideology a set of beliefs asserting that all economic decisions are best left to private individuals and firms through the market; government intervention in the market is abhorred

Market size measured by the sales turnover of a good or service in a market: the relative size of the overall economy

Masculine society one where money, incomes, promotion, and status are highly valued

Mature market a market characterized by low growth

Mercantilism the idea that international trade should primarily serve to increase a country's financial wealth, especially of gold and foreign currency—in this view exports are good and imports bad

Merger occurs where two or more companies combine their assets into a single company; some authors use the term merger only when all parties are happy to conclude the deal

Microenvironment the components of the firm's immediate environment: rivals; customers; suppliers; potential competitors; and substitutes

Microfinance makes finance accessible to poor people in developing countries; seen as a way of relieving poverty

Migrant the UN defines migrants as people currently residing for more than a year in a country other than where they were born

Migration the movement of people across national borders from one country to another

Millennium Development Goals Eight Goals adopted by the United Nations concerning world poverty and general development

Monarchical refers to country where the monarch is the head of state

Monetary policy attempts by the authorities to influence monetary variables such as money supply, interest rates, exchange rates

Money an accepted medium of exchange for goods and services

Money laundering making illegally acquired money appear to come from a legitimate source

Money supply there are various definitions—all include the quantity of currency in circulation and then add various other financial assets such as bank current and deposit accounts

Monopolistic competition a market structure where there are many sellers producing differentiated products

Monopoly a market structure where there is only one seller

Multinational Corporations (MNCs) companies who own and control operations in more than one country

NACE the EU system of industrial classification

NAFTA a free trade area comprising the USA, Canada, and Mexico

NAICS the system of industrial classification used by members of NAFTA, the USA, Canada, and Mexico

Nanotechnology the science of the ultra-small

National income income generated by a country's production of goods and services—the same as GDP

Natural monopoly occurs where the market can be supplied more cheaply by a single firm rather than by a number of competitors, e.g. in the supply of water where it would not be economical to build more than one supply network

Negative externalities these are the costs of either the production or consumption of goods and services that are not borne by the direct producers or consumers but which affect society in general, e.g. exhaust fumes from vehicles pollutes the air that we all have to breathe

Neo-mercantilism government policies to encourage exports, discourage imports, control outflows of money with the aim of building up reserves of foreign exchange

Nepotism conferring favours on the members of one's family

New trade theory models of trade that incorporate market imperfections such as monopoly elements and product differentiation into their analysis

New York Convention a commercial body set up under the aegis of the UN to resolve international commercial disputes between companies

Non Governmental Organization (NGO) not for profit organizations who try to persuade government and business on a variety of issues such as human rights, the environment, and global poverty

Norms rules in a culture indicating what is acceptable and unacceptable in terms of peoples' behaviour

OECD international organization comprising 30 member countries, mostly advanced: tries to promote sustainable economic development, financial stability, and world trade

Offshoring transfer of jobs abroad

Oligopoly a market structure with few sellers where the decision of one seller can affect and provoke a response from the others

Open economy a completely open economy is one where there are no restrictions on foreign trade, investment, and migration

Opportunities occur where the external environment offers business the possibility of meeting or exceeding its targets

Opportunity cost the sacrifice made by choosing to follow one course of action: the opportunity cost to a country deciding to use resources to manufacture more of a product is the benefit it gives up by not using those resource to make another good

Option the right to buy or sell an asset at an agreed price

Organizational culture comprises the values and assumptions underpinning the operation of the business, for example regarding how authority is exercised and distributed in the firm and how employees are rewarded and controlled

Patent a patent gives the holder the exclusive right to exploit the invention commercially for a fixed period of time

Patronage see clientelism

Per capita per head

Perfect competition a market structure with many sellers, homogeneous products, free entry and exit, and where buyers and sellers have perfect knowledge of market conditions

PESTLE a model facilitating analysis of the macro-environment, the acronym standing for Political; Economic and Financial; Socio-cultural; Technological; Legal; Ecological

Piracy the unauthorized duplication of goods such as software or films protected by patent or copyright; robbery committed at sea usually through the illegal capture of a ship

Planned economy a system where the means of production are owned by the State on behalf of the people and where the State plans and controls the economy

Poverty occurs where people do not have enough resources to meet their needs in absolute terms and

relative to others; the World Bank uses income of $1/$2 a day to measure global poverty

Power difference the extent to which a society accepts hierarchical differences, e.g. inequality in the workplace

Precedent when the decision of a court binds others in subsequent cases when similar questions of law are addressed

Price leadership a situation where prices and price changes are determined by the dominant firm or a firm accepted by others as a price leader

Primary market a market where the first trading in new issues of stocks and shares occurs

Product differentiation where firms try to convince consumers that their products are different from those of their competitors through activities such as product design, branding, packaging, and advertising

Product life cycle stages of development through which a product typically moves: introduction; growth; maturity; decline

Productivity the amount of output per unit of resource input, e.g. productivity per worker; used as a measure of efficiency

Public procurement the purchase of goods and services by government departments, nationalized industries, and public utilities in telecommunications, gas, water

Purchasing power parity where the value of, e.g., GDP is adjusted to take account of the buying power of income in each economy. It takes account of the relative cost of living

Qualified Majority Voting (QMV) EU system where any proposal must receive three quarters of the votes to be approved

Quota limitation imposed by governments on the total amount of a good to be imported; the amount of money IMF member countries are required to subscribe to the Fund

Recession a significant decline in the rate of economic growth; technically it can be defined as a fall in GDP over two successive three month periods

Regional Trade Area (RTA) barriers to movement such as tariffs and quotas are abolished among the members

Regulation rules that take their authority from statutes

Regulation (EU) laws which must be applied consistently in all member states

Religious law based on religious principles, e.g. Sharia law or Muslim law is based on the religious principles contained in the Koran

Revenue the income firms generate from their production of goods and services

Risk analysis systematic attempt to assess the likelihood of the occurrence of certain events

Rules of origin laws and regulations determining the origin of a good—this can be an issue in free trade areas where the origin of the good determines whether a tariff is imposed

Sarbanes-Oxley Act a US law laying down tougher rules for publicly quoted companies regarding the reporting of financial information

Screening a technique to assess whether countries are attractive as a market or as a production location

Secondary market where stocks and shares are traded after their initial offering on the primary market

Secularism a doctrine opposing the influence of religion in politics, education, and social issues such as divorce and abortion

Security refers to a share, bond, or other tradable financial asset

Shadow economy goods and services are produced illegally—no tax is paid and laws and regulations ignored

Share option a right to acquire shares in the future at a fixed price; often given to founders or senior managers

Social Democratic social model welfare benefits are generous and available to all; the system is committed to maintaining high employment and low unemployment

Social Entrepreneurship where entrepreneurial/business approaches are used to deal with social problems, e.g. providing microfinance to help reduce rural poverty in developing countries

Soviet Bloc the Soviet Union and its allies in Eastern Europe such as Poland, East Germany, Hungary, and Romania; the bloc started to collapse in the late 1980s

Special Drawing Right (SDR) artificial currency created by the IMF to ease world liquidity problems

Specialization concentration on certain activities, e.g. the law of comparative advantage suggests that countries should specialize on producing those goods at which they are relatively most efficient/least inefficient

Spot price/rate the current price or rate

State a set of institutions having the legal power to make decisions in matters of government over a specific geographical area and over the population living there

Statute a law passed by a legislative body such as a national or regional parliament

Subsidies financial assistance from governments to business often to protect it from foreign competition

Sukuk a bond that is compliant with Sharia law

Supply chain the systems and agencies involved in getting a good from the raw material supplier to the final consumer

Sustainability the ability of productive activities to continue without harm to the ecological system

Sustainable development economic development that does not endanger the incomes, resources, and environment of future generations

Swap a means of hedging or reducing the risk of adverse price or rate changes

SWOT comprises four factors, Strengths, Weaknesses, Opportunities, and Threats arising from a structured analysis of their internal operations (SW) and their external environment (OT)

Tariff a tax levied by countries on imports or exports

Tax avoidance exploiting legal loopholes to avoid paying tax

Tax evasion illegally avoiding paying tax

Technological advance new knowledge or additions to the pool of knowledge

Technological diffusion the spreading of new technologies within and between economies

Technology the know-how or pool of ideas or knowledge available to society

Theocratic regime religious principles play a dominant role in government and those holding political power also lead the dominant religion

Threats occur when the external environment threatens the ability of business to meet its targets

Tied aid countries receiving financial aid are required to buy goods and services produced by firms in the donor country

Tort an area of law concerned with injuries to people or damage to their assets

Trade gap when imports of merchandise exceed exports of merchandise over a particular time period

Trade surplus when the value of goods exceeds the value of imported goods

Trans-boundary processes which occur across national frontiers. Pollution in one country can often cross over into other countries. Carbon emissions are a prime example of trans-boundary pollution

Transnational Corporation synonym for MNC—a company with operations in more than one country; also used to refer to MNCs who see themselves as a global company and thus not tied to any particular country

Triad comprises NAFTA, the EU, and Japan

Trillion one thousand billion, i.e. a trillion has nine zeros

UNCTAD a UN agency aimed at promoting trade and investment opportunities for developing countries and helping them integrate equitably into the world economy

Unidroit an organization trying to harmonize commercial law between countries

Uniform Commercial Code rules in force in many US states governing the sale of goods

Unitary system major decisions on policy, public expenditure, and tax rest with central government with regions having little power in these areas

Urbanization the increase in the proportion of a population living in towns and cities areas

Vertical merger a merger of firms at different stages of production of a product from raw materials to finished products to distribution. An example would be a steel manufacturer taking over a mining company producing iron ore

Vertically integrated firm a business operating at more than one stage of the production process of a good

World Bank international institution providing financial and technical help to developing countries

World Economic Forum (WEF) a think tank bringing together technical experts, and business and political leaders who try to find solutions to major global economic, political, and social problems. It holds an annual meeting in Davos, Switzerland

World System the global system whose countries and regions are interconnected through a network of trade, investment, and migration linkages

World Trade Organization (WTO) international organization aimed at liberalizing world trade and investment; the successor to GATT

Index